CLOSING THE OPPORTUNITY GAP

Closing the Opportunity Gap

WHAT AMERICA MUST DO TO GIVE EVERY
CHILD AN EVEN CHANCE

Edited by Prudence L. Carter and Kevin G. Welner

OXFORD
UNIVERSITY PRESS

OXFORD
UNIVERSITY PRESS

Oxford University Press is a department of the University of Oxford.
It furthers the University's objective of excellence in research, scholarship,
and education by publishing worldwide.

Oxford   New York
Auckland   Cape Town   Dar es Salaam   Hong Kong   Karachi
Kuala Lumpur   Madrid   Melbourne   Mexico City   Nairobi
New Delhi   Shanghai   Taipei   Toronto

With offices in
Argentina   Austria   Brazil   Chile   Czech Republic   France   Greece
Guatemala   Hungary   Italy   Japan   Poland   Portugal   Singapore
South Korea   Switzerland   Thailand   Turkey   Ukraine   Vietnam

Oxford is a registered trademark of Oxford University Press
in the UK and certain other countries.

Published in the United States of America by
Oxford University Press
198 Madison Avenue, New York, NY 10016

© Oxford University Press 2013

Closing the opportunity gap / edited by Prudence L.Carter & Kevin G. Welner.
p. cm.
Includes bibliographical references and index.
ISBN 978–0–19–998298–1 (hardcover : alk. paper) – ISBN 978–0–19–998299–8 (pbk. : alk. paper)
1. Educational equalization–United States.   I. Carter, Prudence L., editor of compilation.
II. Welner, Kevin Grant, 1963-editor of compilation.   III. Ladson-Billings, Gloria, 1947-
Lack of achievement or loss of opportunity?
LC213.2.C565 2013
379.2'60973--dc23   2012046978

ISBN 978–0–19–998298–1

9 8 7 6 5 4
Printed in the United States of America
on acid-free paper

To all the children who dare to dream even in the face of adversity and to the adults who work courageously to tackle that adversity

Contents

Acknowledgments

EDITED VOLUMES ARE a collective effort, and this one is no different. We are grateful for the support of many generous individuals and organizations. Major funding support came from the Ford Foundation, the National Education Policy Center (NEPC), and the Stanford Center for Opportunity Policy in Education (SCOPE). Jeannie Oakes at the Ford Foundation has been particularly and wonderfully supportive.

The initial seeds of ideas for this book were planted in 2007 at a special forum commemorating the 40th anniversary of the release of the Kerner Commission report at SCOPE, and then further developed over the subsequent years. We thank the NEPC and SCOPE staff, especially Alethea Andre, MarYam Hamedani, Janice Jackson, Barbara McKenna, and Terrance Turner for their organization and support of these meetings.

Invaluable editorial and research assistance was provided by Grey Osterud, Cristina Lash, Kathryn Wiley, Ryan Pfleger, Joshua Prudhomme, and Ken Libby.

Most importantly, we could not have generated this book without the willingness and generosity of our contributors. By reaching out to some of the nation's most accomplished scholars and researchers, we clearly benefited ourselves and the book's readers. But all are enormously busy people with many demands on their time, and we deeply thank them for setting aside their other important work to make room for this project.

Contributors

W. Steven Barnett, PhD, is Director of the National Institute for Early Education Research and Board of Governors Professor of Education at Rutgers—The State University of New Jersey. His work focuses on early childhood policy.

Clive Belfield is an Associate Professor of Economics at Queens College, City University of New York, and a Research Fellow at Center for Postsecondary Education and Employment at Teachers College Columbia University.

Barnett Berry is the founder and CEO of the Center for Teaching Quality. Over the last 30 years, Dr. Berry's research has covered a range of teaching issues affecting excellence and equity for all students, especially teacher labor markets, including preparation, incentives, working conditions, and more recently, leadership. His 2011 book TEACHING 2030, written with 12 accomplished teacher leaders, outlines a bold vision for the future of the profession that makes all others possible. His second book, TEACHERPRENEURS, will be published by Jossey-Bass in July 2013.

Prudence Carter is Professor of Education and (by courtesy) Sociology at Stanford University and co-director of the Stanford Center for Opportunity Policy in Education. Dr. Carter's primary research agenda focuses on cultural explanations of academic and mobility differences among various racial and ethnic groups. Her most recent book is *Stubborn Roots: Race, Culture, and Inequality in U.S. and South African Schools.*

Linda Darling-Hammond is Charles E. Ducommun Professor of Education at Stanford University and co-director of the Stanford Center for Opportunity Policy in Education. Her most recent book, recipient of the Grawemeyer Award, is *The Flat World and Education: How America's Commitment to Equity Will Determine Our Future.*

Patricia Gándara is Professor of Education and Co-Director of the Civil Rights Project/Proyecto Derechos Civiles at the University of California, Los Angeles.

Harvey Kantor is Professor of Education in the Department of Education, Culture, and Society at the University of Utah. His research focuses on the history of education and social policy.

Gloria Ladson-Billings is the Kellner Family Chair of Urban Education in the Departments of Curriculum & Instruction, Education Policy Studies, and Afro-American Studies at the University of Wisconsin-Madison.

Cynthia E. Lamy has developed the system of metrics used to estimate the benefits of social programs at the Robin Hood Foundation and is a senior fellow at NIEER. Her book, American Children in Chronic Poverty, has recently been published.

Henry M. Levin is the William Heard Kilpatrick Professor of Economics and Education, Teachers College, Columbia University, and the David Jacks Professor of Higher Education and Economics, Emeritus, Stanford University. He is a specialist in the Economics of Education.

Robert Lowe is a historian of education at Marquette University.

Michele S. Moses is Professor of Educational Foundations, Policy and Practice at the University of Colorado Boulder. She specializes in philosophy and education policy studies, with particular expertise in higher-education policy issues related to race, class, and gender, such as affirmative action and equal opportunity policies.

Gary Orfield is Professor of Education, Law, Political Science & Urban Planning and Co-Director of the Civil Rights Project/Proyecto Derechos Civiles at the University of California, Los Angeles.

John Rogers is an Associate Professor in UCLA's Graduate School of Education and Information Studies and the Director of UCLA's Institute for Democracy, Education and Access (IDEA). He studies the role of public engagement in equity-focused school reform and civic renewal.

Richard Rothstein is a research associate at the Economic Policy Institute, and senior fellow at the Chief Justice Earl Warren Institute on Law and Social Policy at the University of California (Berkeley) School of Law. His books include *Class and Schools* and *Grading Education*.

Janelle Scott is an Associate Professor at the University of California. Berkeley, in the Graduate School of Education and African American Studies Department. Her research explores the relationship between education, policy, and equality of opportunity, and centers on three related policy strands: the racial politics of public education, the politics of school choice, marketization, and privatization, and the role of advocacy in shaping public education.

Christopher H. Tienken is an assistant professor at Seton Hall University, Department of Education Leadership, Management and Policy. His research interests include curriculum and assessment policy. He is the editor of the Kappa Delta Pi Record and the AASA Journal of Scholarship and Practice.

Karolyn Tyson is Associate Professor of Sociology at the University of North Carolina at Chapel Hill. Her research focuses on understanding educational structures and processes that contribute to inequality.

Amy Stuart Wells is Professor of Sociology and Education at Teachers College, Columbia University, and Director of the Center for Understanding Race and Education (CURE). Her research focuses broadly on the relationship between race/ethnicity and educational opportunities across an array of public policies.

Kevin G. Welner is Professor of education policy in Educational Foundations, Policy and Practice program area at the University of Colorado Boulder, and he is the director of the National Education Policy Center. His work examines the use of research in policy making, the intersection between education rights litigation and educational opportunity scholarship, and the school change process associated with equity-focused reform.

Yong Zhao is Presidential Chair and Associate Dean at the College of Education, University of Oregon. He is also a professor at the Department of Educational Methodology, Policy, and Leadership. His current research focuses on the implications of globalization for education.

CLOSING THE OPPORTUNITY GAP

1

Achievement Gaps Arise from Opportunity Gaps

Kevin G. Welner and Prudence L. Carter

THE DAILY HEADLINES tell a sad and frustrating story. "Failing schools shut down." "Replacement schools failing." "Replacement schools shut down." With each passing year, the students in these schools fall further behind—behind students in other Western democracies and behind American students in more advantaged neighborhoods.

This problem has not been ignored, but neither has it been addressed sensibly and meaningfully. With great fanfare, it has been misdiagnosed and mishandled. Like a gardener trying to increase her fruits' growth merely by weighing them anew each day, we have measured and documented multiple test-score gaps, but we have never mounted a sustained effort to attend to the gaps in sustenance—in opportunities—that must be addressed before we can expect to see meaningful progress.

Educational disparities and intergenerational economic inequality are highly correlated with skin color, ethnicity, linguistic and social class status. To be sure, the march toward civil rights and access to opportunity has seen notable successes over the past fifty years. Yet many of these successes have only been superficial. They merely prompted a morphing of the nature and sources of inequity, rather than a meaningful change in life chances.[1] The longer that lower-status groups have been denied equal access to opportunities, the more inequality has compounded the adverse effects on these groups—in some cases, rendering it difficult to catch up in subsequent generations. A recent study from the Organisation for Economic Co-operation and Development shows the United States to have among the lowest levels of intergenerational social mobility—and one of the highest levels of influence of parental socioeconomic status on students' achievement and later earnings.[2] The "opportunity gap" that exists across racial and associated class lines is expansive, and it widens as income and wealth inequality continue to rise.

Yet it is the disparities in certain achievement indicators that have dominated policy discussions over the past two decades; relatively little attention has been paid to disparities in opportunity. Current discussions of the "achievement gap" highlight and emphasize significant differences in school results between groups based on measured outcomes such as test scores and graduation rates. The persistent test-score gaps in our schools include those between African Americans and Whites, between Latinos and Whites, between students in poverty and wealthier students, between children of parents with little formal education and with greater formal education, and between English learners and native English speakers. The results seen in our schools are shocking. For example, the average White 13-year-old reads at a higher level and performs better in math than the average Black or Latino 17-year-old.[3] Similar gaps exist for other important outcomes, such as rates of high school and college graduation.

The US national high school graduation rate stands at 78 percent for the class of 2010, the most recent year for which data are available.[4] This is the highest the rate has been since 1976. But for members of historically disadvantaged minority groups, the picture is not nearly as positive. While White and Asian American students had graduation rates at 93.5 and 83 percent, respectively, the rates for African American and Hispanic students landed at 66.1 and 71.4 percent, respectively.[5] The dropout rate for Hispanics and African Americans is more than double the national average. In the largest metropolitan areas, at least half of students who attend public high schools do not graduate.

Failure rates are also telling; one in five African American students will fail a grade in elementary or secondary school, compared to the overall rate of one in ten. Even the classes that students of color do take and pass are often diluted.[6] Similar patterns are found in college preparatory enrollment, where only a third or less of African American, Latino, and Native American students are enrolled in such classes, compared to half or more of Asian American and White students.

Further, many of our African American and Latino youth are embedded in the school-to-prison pipeline that continues to expand. African American youth constitute 45 percent of juvenile arrests, although they make up only 16 percent of the overall youth population.[7] Their criminalization begins early in school: K-12 Black students are twice as likely as their White peers to be suspended from school and three times as likely to be expelled.[8] First-time offender Black students are far more likely than first-time offender White students to be suspended, even given the same offense.[9] This crisis is particularly acute among males.

The "opportunity gap" frame, in contrast, shifts our attention from outcomes to inputs—to the deficiencies in the foundational components of societies, schools, and communities that produce significant differences in educational—and ultimately socioeconomic—outcomes. Thinking in terms of "achievement gaps" emphasizes the symptoms; thinking about unequal opportunity highlights the causes. Learning and life chances depend on key out-of-school factors such as health, housing, nutrition, safety, and enriching experiences, in addition to opportunities provided through formal elementary and secondary school preparation, as Richard Rothstein explains in chapter 5. While school quality is extremely important, these out-of-school learning and learning-related resources and opportunities for children who live and grow in the nation's many disadvantaged communities must improve significantly before we can realistically expect to see achievement gaps close.

Opportunity and achievement, though inextricably connected, are very different goals. For instance, while not every American will go to college, all American children should be given fair opportunities to be prepared for college. This equitable principle lies at the core of American schooling and can be traced back at least as far as Horace Mann's celebrated call in the mid-nineteenth century for schools to be the "great equalizer" and the "balance wheel of society."[10] We are far from that ideal. Vast opportunity gaps limit children's future prospects every day in schools in almost every community across America. Talent is being wasted, particularly among those living in poverty and in disadvantaged communities of color. Children in these communities are not reaching their full potential and are not "closing the gap" in achievement—precisely because they are not receiving equitable and meaningful opportunities to reach that potential. Recent policy has attempted to solve problems on the cheap, looking for magic beans and silver bullets instead of investing in the key community needs and classroom resources necessary to create engaging, supported learning and learners.

A narrow focus on the achievement gap predictably leads to policies grounded in high-stakes testing, which in turn leads to narrow thinking about groups of students, their teachers, and their schools. While these assessments attempt to determine where students are, they ignore how they may have gotten there and what alternative pathways might be available for future students. Schools, principals, and teachers are told that they have "no excuses" and that they will be held accountable for results. Similar pressure is exerted on students. This accountability, however, is rarely extended to those making these demands. Policy makers are not required to provide supports necessary for equitable learning opportunities, nor are they held accountable for the consequences of these tests, such as those described by Tienken and Zhao in chapter 8 of this volume.

The predictable litany of achievement gaps cannot be a surprise to anyone who recognizes and understands these opportunity gaps. Moreover, the obsessive focus on measuring achievement through pencil-and-bubble tests while ignoring opportunity has led to a mountain of unintended consequences, many of which are apparent in the fallout from the No Child Left Behind Act of 2001. Students, teachers, principals, and schools are sanctioned when they produce low test scores, with policy makers hoping that the threat of sanctions will drive efforts that are more steadfast and adroit. Flying under a "no excuses" banner, this reform movement took an important and admirable first step by calling on educators to maintain high expectations for all students. But it never took the next crucial step: holding policy makers accountable for ensuring the conditions and resources necessary to create and maintain a system of excellence that offers universal opportunity. As a result, disadvantaged students are now caught in a downward cycle, facing poverty-related obstacles outside school as well as a system that generates a constant churning of teachers, principals, and schools. Even if it is called "accountability," this turmoil should not be mistaken for progress; in fact, it often results in just the opposite.

In this book we operate on the assumption that denying children equitable educational opportunities is bad policy and is inconsistent with basic American values. The denied opportunities described in the following chapters place unnatural constraints on the healthy growth of disadvantaged children. Outcome gaps that would otherwise not be nearly as troubling become appalling when they are systematically imposed upon targeted groups within our society.

Importantly, discussions of both achievement and opportunity gaps sensibly begin with the premise that we as a nation must act to redress the serious inequities that exist between and within schools, as well as among the different people, groups, and communities across the country. Both discussions include an understanding that outcomes should be measured, analyzed, and addressed. But test-score and attainment differences will not disappear until policy is dedicated to changing the conditions that shape and impede achievement.

According to demographic forecasts, Blacks and Latinos combined will make up a majority of the US population by the middle of the twenty-first century.[11] Unless we close the opportunity gaps described throughout this book, significant numbers of youth from these backgrounds will not be adequately prepared for higher educational attainment and subsequent leadership roles in society. Today, a college diploma is what a high school diploma became in the mid-twentieth century: the foundational credential for access to opportunity. In an increasingly knowledge-based economy, young adults require specialized skills, especially those providing opportunities amid the persistent forces of globalization. In the United

States and other developed countries, the economy requires graduates with strong math, science, and literacy skills. But these skills are not evenly or fairly distributed across groups within the country. Many of the nation's selective colleges and universities find themselves competing intensely over the limited "supply" of college-ready Black and Latino high school graduates while the vast majority of these students are never adequately prepared.[12] This problem is compounded by the fact that many students of color who are accepted into college do not have the financial capacity to attend.[13] The current economic downturn and diminishing higher-education budgets further threaten access to postsecondary education. The college attendance rates of African Americans, Latinos, and Native Americans point to what should already be claiming our attention: the ongoing salience of racial, ethnic, and class inequalities in American society and education.

The reality is stark: many children of color are denied crucial resources and opportunities, substantially harming their likelihood of attaining educational and life success. Although some members of historically disadvantaged groups will defy the odds and thrive, the overall standing of these social groups will remain lower if the ecology of their lives—the system that maintains the components for overall healthy educational well-being—does not evolve more effectively. The achievement gap discussion of recent decades has obscured and even ignored these needs; the contributors to this volume do not.

Because students' learning experiences and outcomes are deeply affected by many factors that are outside schools' immediate control, schools must become part of a larger effort to address unequal opportunities if they are ever to become Mann's great equalizers. In a pluralistic and democratic society, schools must respond to students' actual needs, build on their unique strengths, be culturally responsive, and provide the opportunities necessary to give every student a fair chance at academic success.

Yet we as a society also need to understand that the fair and sensible provision of educational resources among schools (including funding and teacher quality), while absolutely necessary, is not sufficient to cast out inequality. Sometimes the presumed effects of resource-rich schools are countervailed by other social factors. Racial, ethnic, class, and gender dynamics that pervade the wider society permeate school walls with great ease. In chapter 12, for example, sociologist Karolyn Tyson calls our attention to the contradictions embedded in schools with more material resources. Students of different social groups may attend "good" schools together, but the segregation that often occurs within them belies claims of equal opportunity. In many schools, African American, Latino, and Native American students are rarely exposed to the upper-echelon college preparatory classes. Tyson powerfully documents the interplay between the structure of tracking and students' own behavior, showing how people tend to "know their lines" and cling to classes, spaces, activities, social networks, and neighborhoods where others like them are likely to be.

Together, the chapters that follow construct a composite picture of an imbalanced opportunity structure that inexorably leads to massive differences in children's overall educational trajectories. They describe how the well-being of children and their families has largely been ignored, as have basic schooling inequalities tied to racial segregation, poverty, and native language. In a fundamentally unequal and unfair system characterized by widespread poverty and segregation, opportunity gaps are exacerbated when children are assigned to schools with substantially fewer resources than those in nearby middle-class communities. If the nation has any hope of addressing larger societal inequalities through the public education system, the opportunities provided within the school walls will have to be extraordinarily enriched; instead, they are pitifully curtailed.

The relative lack of attention paid to measuring or addressing inequitable opportunities helps to explain why policy has failed to engage with the hard work of facing the challenges and providing the supports and resources that lead to improvements in student learning. While the nation's leaders have concentrated almost exclusively on an achievement gap policy whereby students, teachers, and schools are measured and sanctioned, they have left untouched the vast opportunity gap—a gap that is even more at odds with American ideals.

To explore these and other fundamental ideas, this book brings together experts from across the nation. They offer concise, research-based essays that together paint a powerful and shocking picture of denied opportunities. These experts describe sensible policy approaches that are grounded in evidence and can restore and enhance opportunities.

The book is divided into three main parts, each of which looks at a particular type of obstacle and how it can be overcome: obstacles we create for children, those we create for schools, and those we create for equality. It concludes with a look at the cumulative economic costs of the opportunity gap and a consideration of the importance of equitable schools to a healthy democracy. Gloria Ladson-Billings sets the stage for all three parts in chapter 2, where she introduces readers to the concept of the opportunity gap and the idea of an "education debt." She explains that the achievement disparities we see in the United States are a result of historical, economic, political, and moral decisions that we as a society have made over time.

Part I, "Overcoming the Obstacles We Create for Children," contains three chapters that place school learning within the larger set of children's experiences, opportunities, and challenges. In chapter 3, Harvey Kantor and Robert Lowe describe how the nation's approaches to poverty, race, and education have changed over the past half century, as relatively weak compensatory education policies have been asked to shoulder the burden created by economic and racial inequalities—problems that our society and our policy makers have overwhelmingly failed to address. Kantor and Lowe help us to understand how twentieth-century social policies meant to alleviate poverty have mutated into programs that pose formal education as a panacea. They write that US policy makers began to "educational-ize" big social problems.

Gary Orfield, in chapter 4, focuses on racial issues, explaining the intertwined character and baneful consequences of segregation in housing and schools. He describes how segregated neighborhoods are linked to segregated schools and produce unequal education. Then, in chapter 5, Richard Rothstein puts school-ing inequalities within the larger context of disadvantages linked to poverty. When the nation essentially abandoned the nascent anti-poverty policies of the mid-twentieth century, it effectively locked in vast learning disadvantages that it then asked schools to overcome.

The four chapters in Part II, "Overcoming the Obstacles We Create for Schools," describe how the demands we place on schools are often undermined by inequali-ties in resources and incentives. Linda Darling-Hammond, in chapter 6, explains the basic resource inequities that pervade the current system and describes how a more equitable distribution of resources can yield more equitable outcomes. Similarly, in chapter 7, Steven Barnett and Cynthia Lamy describe how access to high-quality early-childhood education is crucial for closing the opportunity gap.

No depiction of the educational system in today's America is complete without understanding the role of standards-based, high-stakes testing and accountability policies. Chapter 8, coauthored by Christopher Tienken and Yong Zhao, describes how current policies exacerbate the conditions that afflict vulnerable children and consequently widen the educational opportunity gap. Then, in chapter 9, Janelle Scott and Amy Stuart Wells delve into the problems and potential of school choice in either exacerbating or alleviating the opportunity gap. They contend that school choice policies within a test-focused educational system can advance the goal of greater educational equity if they are conceptualized and constructed in a man-ner that acknowledges the structural inequality within which public schools exist today, and if they include sensible and powerful provisions to counteract the effects of those inequalities.

The chapters in Part III, "Overcoming the Obstacles We Create for Equality," explain the ways in which the demands we place on educators and students are often undermined by school practices and norms. In chapter 10, Prudence Carter describes how cultural behaviors and practices both among youth and within schools matter to student engagement and achievement. Latent and explicit forms of cultural inequality within schools and in wider society, Carter explains, exacerbate opportunity gaps. Chapter 11 explores the tremendous consequences of the under-education of students with a first language other than English. Patricia Gándara explains how current language policies are squandering an asset—students who have the great potential to be bilingual and biliterate—and turning it into a deficit. Students arrive at schools with a variety of different skills and experiences, but as Karolyn Tyson explains in chapter 12, schools can respond to those differences in ways that build on strengths and ensure opportunities to learn or by stratifying expectations and opportunities. She makes evident that capable students of color in racially diverse schools are severely underrepresented in advanced classes, contributing substantially to the opportunity gap. Such tracking practices have repeatedly been shown to be detrimental, yet they persist in most American secondary schools.

In chapter 13, Barnett Berry considers five common myths about schools and teachers. He also points to policy options that would lead to high-quality schools and teachers for all students. Because teachers are the most important in-school resource, the current national failure to invest in improving our teaching force and to equitably distribute this resource is contributing to the opportunity gap. These policies need not continue.

The book concludes with two chapters that put the opportunity gap in a larger context. In chapter 14, economists Clive Belfield and Hank Levin explore the overall costs of the cumulative opportunity gap, estimating that the economic benefit of closing the opportunity gap by just one-third would result in $50 billion in fiscal savings and $200 billion in savings from a societal perspective (for example, by lowering rates of crime and incarceration). By point of comparison, they note, total taxpayer spending on K-12 education, including national, state, and local expenditures, is approximately $570 billion.

Finally, in chapter 15, Michele Moses and John Rogers place the importance of equitable schooling in the context of our nation's democratic ambitions and argue that democracy benefits from more racially integrated, robust, and equitable learning opportunities. They focus on the development of civic capacity and show how diverse classrooms can enhance students' preparation for democratic deliberation. They explain as well how the quality of our society is shaped by decisions about who goes to school together and how we distribute learning opportunities across different students and different schools. Chapters 14 and 15 explain how closing the opportunity gap is not simply a matter of equity and adhering to core American values; it also implicates our economic and democratic survival.

Taken as a whole, the chapters in this book lead to the inescapable conclusion that American educational policy—because it has generally ignored opportunity gaps—has been captivated by perilous sirens and now veers toward the rocks. They highlight the discrepancies that exist in our public schools, focusing not on the gap in achievement but rather on how policy decisions and broader circumstances conspire to create the opportunity gap that leads inexorably to stark differences in outcomes. The much-discussed achievement gap, then, can best be understood as a predictable result of systemic causes—a representation of the disparities in opportunities available to children of different racial, ethnic, socioeconomic, and cultural backgrounds. Where engaging, culturally relevant instruction is lacking, expectations minimal, and resources scarce, students from disadvantaged groups tend to be outperformed by their more privileged counterparts. These educational consequences are no surprise and can shine little light on either the ability of these students or our potential as a nation.

In contrast, by shifting the nation's attention toward the opportunities and resources students are offered, we can hold a productive discussion about how to meet our national goals. We do not mean to suggest that measuring outcomes is unimportant or should be halted. As researchers, we consider this information a key component in an evaluative feedback loop, helping policy makers understand which needs are being met and which are not, as well as which policies and practices are most successful. Opportunity gaps and achievement gaps are tightly linked in a logical chain: the impetus for our current fixation on testing is found in the academic disparities between students of different racial and class backgrounds, and those disparities are due to opportunity gaps. But measuring outcomes does not directly generate meaningful improvement, nor—as we have learned through our experiences with No Child Left Behind—does improvement arise merely by attaching demands and sanctions to those outcomes.

In the imbalanced education policy world of today, we are told that poor children—who are less likely to possess the family, neighborhood, and material resources that we know improve test scores and other measures of achievement—have no excuses for not performing as well as middle-class and affluent children. To visualize how unfair this system has become, imagine two children asked to race to the top of a stairway. One child is well-nourished, well-trained, and well-equipped; the other lacks all these basic resources. But, instead of designing a system around the needs of this second child, her stairway (akin to the minimal opportunities and resources available at her school) is steep and slippery. Meanwhile, the first child's stairway is replaced with an escalator. Holding these two children to the same standards may allow for a comforting "no excuses" sound bite, but it does nothing to help that second child achieve.

In truth, as Patricia Gándara illustrates in chapter 11, children with perceived disadvantages are *not* one-dimensional; they arrive at our schools with important assets that educators can build on. But the core reality remains: children who are growing up in poverty, children of color, and children whose native language is not English are deprived of many valuable supports, high-quality teachers, stable housing, safe schools and neighborhoods, up-to-date textbooks, health care, one-on-one tutors, expensive test-prep programs, and so much more. Students who excel on tests have often been exposed to vastly different economic and social realities beyond the classroom than those who do not. The sad irony is that in such an inequitable context, the ways we now define academic success may very well threaten the well-being of millions of school-aged children who President George W. Bush famously said were subjected to the "soft bigotry of low expectations." High expectations become a punitive false promise if combined with low resources, low opportunities, and low supports.

Do you know what it means to miss New Orleans,

And miss it each night and day?

I know I'm not wrong, the feeling's getting stronger,

The longer I stay away.[1]

2

Lack of Achievement or Loss of Opportunity?

Gloria Ladson-Billings

THE GRAVELY, RASPY voice of jazz great Louis Armstrong is unmistakable. Before August 29, 2005, "Do You Know What It Means to Miss New Orleans" was just another romantic song about a place. It was like Frank Sinatra singing "New York, New York," or Count Basie's band playing "April in Paris." We enjoyed the melodies and sang along, but the lyrics held no special significance for us. Now, after the horrific events surrounding Hurricane Katrina, many hear Armstrong's question in an entirely different way.

I remain fixated on the social consequences of Katrina. The category 5 storm burst through the levees and flooded close to 80 percent of the Big Easy. The near-total collapse of social services left thousands stranded in their homes and in hospitals, nursing homes, and inadequate shelters. Hardest hit were the old, the young, the poor, and the African American residents of the city's famed 9th Ward. The real tragedy was not the storm but the complete failure of local, state, and federal systems in its wake. The evacuation plan made no provisions for people without private transportation or the money to pay for temporary housing. The lack of communication among governmental agencies was appalling. The federal response was disgraceful. Six years later, reconstruction plans have faltered. Currently, many people are living in substandard housing, and far too many remain homeless. According to Reckdahl, 23 percent of New Orleanians are homeless, one of the highest percentages of any major city.[2]

What do these facts about Hurricane Katrina and New Orleans have to do with education? When the storm hit, I was attending a meeting in London, so I witnessed the disaster and subsequent suffering from an international vantage point. Watching and hearing about what was occurring was surreal. Londoners repeatedly asked me, "What is going on in your country?" Initially, I was dumbfounded. As the reality of the disaster began to sink in, I realized that Katrina and its aftermath are a metaphor for the situation in which many poor people of color find themselves. Later, when Londoners asked what was happening in *my* country, I responded, "Well, now they're wet!" I said this to point to the horrible conditions of housing, employment, health, and education that existed in New Orleans for poor people and people of color, especially African Americans, before Katrina. Katrina made those inequities visible and gave us a unique opportunity to address reform from the ground up.

Except for its catastrophic cause, the situation in New Orleans schools resembles what is happening in urban public schools everywhere. The denigration and derogation of African Americans is without parallel. The symbolic and cultural abasement that Americans of African descent endure is rooted in the material reality of living well below the national standard throughout the course of US history. We must think about the opportunity gap against this backdrop.

The "achievement gap" has become a shared preoccupation of Americans across the political spectrum. Disparities between White students and their Black and Latino counterparts show up on the National Assessment of Educational Progress and on state and local tests, as well as in rates of graduation, dropping out, suspension, expulsion, and assignment to special education. In the greater New Orleans area alone the statistics are startling:[3]

- High school dropouts from the class of 2007 alone will cost the nation nearly $329 billion in lost wages, taxes, and lifetime productivity.
- 91 percent of Black fourth graders in Louisiana do not read at grade level.
- School suspensions rates for Black students in Louisiana are twice those of their White counterparts.
- Today, 21 percent of all Louisiana Black males between the ages of 19 and 64 are currently either incarcerated or under probation of parole supervision.
- At the beginning of the twenty-first century, one out of every six Black Louisiana males had been incarcerated during his lifetime. If current trends continue one out of every three Black males born today can expect to spend time in prison during his lifetime.
- The typical inmate upon entry into the correctional system is a Black male in his thirties who is living in poverty, has not finished high school, and functions at a fifth-grade level; is uninsured, unemployed, and lacks job training and skills; is substance addicted; and has either a diagnosable

mental illness, a chronic or infectious disease or a combination of health conditions.

• Almost one-half (45%) of Louisiana's children have a parent under the supervision of the corrections system.

Ample empirical evidence demonstrates that Black and Latino students perform at levels significantly lower than White students. The question is whether what we are encountering is an achievement gap or something else.

For almost five years, I have been writing and speaking about what I call the "education debt." How we frame an issue is at least as significant as the argument we make about it.[4] Calling the persistent achievement disparities between Black and Latino students and White students a "gap" suggests that something inherent in Black and Latino students, their families, communities, cultures, schools, and teachers is responsible for the disparities. Today, teachers and their unions are the main villains in the achievement gap narrative. Although I agree that some aspects of each of these elements might contribute to the problem, I think it is shortsighted and incomplete to target them as the only causes. These achievement disparities are a result of historical, economic, political, and moral decisions that we as a society have made over time.

DEBT VERSUS DEFICIT

One of the ways to understand the debt metaphor is to draw an economic analogy. When the federal government budgets for more spending than anticipated revenues, we acknowledge that it is operating under a deficit. The accumulation of deficits over time creates the national debt. Deficits reflect current problems; debt reflects long-term financial problems. Deficits are this generation's issues; debt belongs to generations to come.

In the world of educational achievement, year-to-year testing represents the deficit. We "budget"—that is, plan—for a certain level of student performance, but students regularly perform at lower levels. The long-term failure to produce equitable conditions to address these deficits creates the education debt. The idea of an education debt is not simply metaphorical. Economists calculate the loss of productivity (see Belfield and Levin, chapter 14, this volume), the need for remediation, the drain on social services, and the increased costs of law enforcement and imprisonment that result as a lack of educational attainment.

Unfortunately, school districts, states, and the nation are obsessed with the year-to-year progress scores. Each spring, newspapers and news broadcasts alert the public to the slightest rise or fall in annual test scores. The public reacts to these statistics, even if it is not informed as to whether or not the changes are statistically significant. Are the scores up or down? Who is winning, and by how many points? How can we raise the scores of the "losers?" I contend that the only way to truly understand achievement disparities is to understand the larger context in which they developed. Next, I will briefly explore the historical, economic, sociopolitical, and moral antecedents of our current educational situation and address some of the ongoing research and practical efforts toward remedying it.

ONCE UPON A TIME

The history of education is the United States has been one of idealism and disappointment. David Tyack's classic history of American urban education, *The One Best System,* points out that the United States engaged in a bold experiment to educate all its citizens regardless of social class, rooted in Thomas Jefferson's dream of an educated citizenry capable of governing itself.[5] However, this provision did not initially extend to African Americans. During slavery it was illegal to teach enslaved persons to read. After emancipation, northern missionaries established schools under the auspices of the Freedmen's Bureau to teach basic literacy skills.[6] African Americans were instrumental in founding schools; the 100-plus historically Black colleges and universities across the country attest to their commitment to educating themselves and subsequent generations.

Once Reconstruction was ended, some former Confederate states established separate schools for Blacks that operated only during the agricultural growing season. During the planting and harvest seasons, children's labor was needed to help their families eke out a living. Even in cities such as Birmingham, Atlanta, and New Orleans, Black children attended segregated schools taught by Black teachers and received cast-off, outdated, school books and materials from the White system. This deliberate inequity helped to create the disparities that continue today. After the 1954 US Supreme Court decision in *Brown v. Board of Education*, the White establishment found ways to maintain segregation. Whites created private "academies," some supported with taxpayer monies, and refused to send their children to newly desegregated public schools. The Nixon administration made the dismantling or at least the rolling back of school desegregation one of its highest priorities. This "Southern strategy" led to Republican electoral victories and the re-creation of the "solid South," the bloc of "red states" below the Mason-Dixon line.

The North deserves no commendations for its policy toward the education of African Americans. In most states, segregated neighborhoods resulted in de facto segregation. Shortly after the *Brown* decision, the Eisenhower administration pushed through the Interstate Highway Act, which enabled middle-income White families to move to the suburbs, away from Blacks and poor Whites.[7] According to Schwartz, "No federal venture spent more funds in urban areas and returned fewer dividends to central cities than the national highway program";[8] and Linville asserted, "Official housing and highway policies ... have helped to produce more intensely concentrated and racially segregated landscapes of contemporary urban America."[9] Today, most Black and Latino public school students attend schools where Blacks and Latinos are in the majority. The schools that serve children of color remain substandard. Exclusion is also part of the historical experience of Latinos, Native Americans, and poor Whites, particularly those in rural areas.

FOLLOW THE MONEY

The nation's historic refusal to provide Black, Latino, Native American, and poor White students with access to quality education is linked to the financial disparity that exists between school districts. Since schools are funded largely by property taxes, communities with more highly valued property receive more tax revenue and can spend more money. Jonathan Kozol has documented the funding inequities that exist between urban schools serving a majority of Black and Latino students and suburban schools serving middle-class White students.[10] Even when in subsequent years urban schools lobbied for and received more money from state and federal governments and philanthropists, they were so far behind their suburban counterparts that the increased funding has failed to make up for the long-time disparity. Impoverished school districts can be hard-pressed to demonstrate improvement in conventional ways because their needs are so great.

Getting an overall picture of funding inequity is difficult because we often work with state-level data. Unfortunately, we regularly see within-state differences that are larger than between-state differences.

> Inequity among districts means that children in lower-funded districts do not have access to the same resources—modern buildings, technology, highly effective teachers, supplemental supports, etc.—than do their peers in districts with higher levels of funding. Furthermore, low-income children and English language learners need extra resources to overcome disadvantages due to socioeconomic status of lack of English language proficiency. In many cases, not only are these children not receiving equal resources but they are also not receiving the extra supports they need in order to succeed.[11]

The Education Trust reported that the highest-poverty districts in 25 states received less state and local per-pupil funding than the lowest-poverty districts. My contention that the economic disparities are compounded over time is born out by the school funding data. States like New Jersey devote a higher percentage (5%) of their total taxable resources to education than a state like Louisiana (2.9%), but within those states there are districts (e.g., Camden, New Orleans) that are even more disadvantaged.[12]

Under the No Child Left Behind Act, all students from grades 3 to 8 are required to take annual standardized tests. States determine which tests to use and what constitutes a passing score. Variations in standards mean that a student who earns a passing score in one state could be considered failing in another. In urban schools serving large numbers of Black and Latino students, preparing for the test has become an all-consuming activity (see Zhao and Tienken, chapter 8, this volume). Subjects such as art, music, and physical education get short shrift when schools focus solely on basic skills. Schools spend an inordinate amount of money on test preparation, purchase, scoring, and security. Devoting additional funding primarily to assessment does not reduce the education debt.

GIVE US THE BALLOT

The third aspect of the education debt is the political debt. African Americans were disfranchised in many southern states until the Voting Rights Act of 1965. Black voter participation then rose; however, many states prohibit people with a felony conviction from voting, which depresses the voting strength of African Americans. In the case of Latinos, lack of access to information in Spanish can inhibit participation.

For these groups, political participation on school boards makes the most difference. However, current education reform efforts emphasize mayoral control of local schools. The mayors of New York City, Chicago, Philadelphia, and the District of Columbia control their school districts, attesting that having the mayor run the school district does not guarantee success.

Hurricane Katrina swept away most of the public schools in New Orleans, creating an opportunity to reconstruct the entire system. Education reformers seized the opportunity by proposing charter schools and alternative certification programs for teachers. Today, there are three governing agencies for New Orleans schools: the Recovery School District (RSD), the Orleans Parish School Board (OPSB), and the Board of Elementary and Secondary Education (BESE). RSD and OPSB administer both traditional public schools and charter schools, while BESE administers two charter schools. KIPP (Knowledge is Personal Power), First Line, and the University of New Orleans operate some of the charter schools. New Orleans is also known for employing alternatively certified teachers. However, according to the Louisiana State Department of Education, these teachers rarely stay in the district. Retention among Teach for America (TFA) teachers in the state is .04 percent, while retention among traditionally prepared teachers is 40 percent. Decisions about New Orleans schools have been made with little or no input from the electorate. Lack of political power has been an ongoing pattern for Black, Latino, and poor communities and constitutes another aspect of the education debt.

DO UNTO OTHERS

The final component of the education debt is what I call the "moral debt." It cannot be quantified or measured, but it is real. There is something deeply un-American about not allowing entire groups of people to participate equitably in an educational system that allegedly provides an opportunity for social and economic advancement. The nation recognized this injustice when President John F. Kennedy proposed and President Lyndon B. Johnson instituted the policy known as affirmative action. Johnson argued that it was unfair to keep people shackled for centuries, unshackle them, and then expect them to compete against those who have never known such restrictions.

Johnson's decision was motivated by both politics and economics: African Americans were starting to vote in larger numbers and to constitute a larger segment of the Democratic Party, and the nation needed to increase the scientific and technical knowledge and skills of its citizens in order to compete globally. But the policy also had a moral dimension. How could a nation that called itself the champion of freedom and justice justify its failure to redress the legacy of centuries of exclusion and discrimination? Affirmative action had striking political and economic results. William G. Bowen and Derek Bok demonstrated that affirmative action policies in college and university admissions almost single-handedly created today's Black middle class.[13] Bowen and Bok also point out that African American and Latino professionals trained in that era were more likely to choose work and/or volunteer opportunities in low-income communities serving Blacks and Latinos.[14]

Although many people bemoan the loss of civility in public discourse and national debate,[15] the real problem is that our discussions about morality remain centered on the individual. We want people to take personal responsibility for their health care, welfare, and education, but we neglect our social obligations.

What do we owe citizens who have historically been excluded and discriminated against? In *The Debt*, Randall Robinson commented that "no nation can enslave a race of people for hundreds of years, set them free bedraggled and penniless, pit them, without assistance in a hostile environment, against privileged victimizers, and then reasonably expect the gap between the heirs of the two groups to narrow."[16]

When I raise this question with my students, I take them back to the predicament that Abraham Lincoln faced before allowing Blacks to enlist in the Union Army. At a crucial point in the Civil War, Lincoln recognized that without the 200,000 Black soldiers, "we would be compelled to abandon the war in 3 weeks." According to historian Ronald Takaki, "Black men in blue made the difference in determining that 'this government of the people, by the people, and for the people did not perish from the earth.'"[17] What moral debt do we owe their heirs?

WHAT CAN BE DONE TO FIX OUR SCHOOLS?

Most education researchers and academics are relatively skilled at analyzing problems. But the public is looking for solutions. Those offered by politicians and pundits rarely address the real problems or provide lasting, comprehensive solutions. The buzzwords that are bandied about offer little or no real palliative to problems that are rooted in deep-seated, structural inequalities. At best, such solutions are temporary; at worst, they are designed to destroy public education in the same way other public services have been destroyed. In the current debate, the alleged roots of our school problems are the teachers and their unions.

Davis Guggenheim's widely acclaimed film *Waiting for Superman* dramatizes a whole panoply of public school ailments.[18] Indeed, the problems come so fast and furious that the viewer may miss the film's many inconsistencies and outright contradictions. For example, the filmmaker at one point acknowledges the problems with the testing systems, but throughout the film we are told about how poorly students perform on the tests as if they were legitimate. Moreover, unions are depicted as destructive, intractable, and antireform. The film lauds the accomplishments of Finnish schools, but Guggenheim neglects to mention the fact that teachers in Finland are fully unionized and very well paid. He also overgeneralizes the effectiveness of charter schools. Guggenheim reports that just one out of five charter schools is rated as "highly effective," but he spends most of the film systemically celebrating charter schools. No one remembers that the first person to publicly propose charter schools was the late Albert Shanker, past president of New York's United Federation of Teachers and the American Federation of Teachers. Ironically, union advocates are the villains in the film.

Noneducators such as Guggenheim and other people who should know better often recite the litany of bad teachers, bad unions, and bad public schools and proclaim that charter schools and alternative certification are our salvation. Thomas Friedman's November 20, 2010, *New York Times* column, which responded to Secretary of Education Arne Duncan's November 4, 2010, speech, is a perfect example. Friedman makes the typical invidious comparisons between the United States and other nations. He points out countries that outperform the United States, but that, in contrast, select teachers from the top 10 percent of their college classes. Like Guggenheim, he fails to tell us that these are fully unionized systems that pay teachers well and that these non-US national systems of education are not dependent on local property taxes but on the national budget. Even more disturbing, Friedman totally ignores the overwhelming role that poverty and other systemic problems play in education outcomes. I include this section on the film to underscore the ways in which popular depictions of public schools may sway public opinion and perceptions about what should be done. The film became a perfect foil for what is taking place in a city like New Orleans. Despite the lack of success in post-Katrina schools, the image of the successful charter has taken hold in New Orleans and will likely continue to be the dominant reform available to the Parish's poor and working-class school children.

Another by-product of the "post" public school model is the denigration of public school teachers and their profession, in general. Microsoft founder and billionaire Bill Gates, like Arne Duncan, does not believe that there is any benefit in rewarding teachers for earning advanced degrees. We keep saying that we need to have smarter teachers and more highly educated citizens, but our public and business leaders suggest that we can do this on the cheap, that we can take a group of college graduates, run them through six to eight weeks of training sessions, place them in the schools with the greatest needs, and expect success. Thus, New Orleans has become a primary site of alternatively certified teachers, despite the low retention rate noted earlier. What if we try a different strategy? What if we take highly motivated, well-educated young people and place them in suburban schools where students have more parental and community support, and shift the highly experienced, conventionally prepared suburban teachers to urban classrooms filled with high-needs students? No one, from suburban communities to their teachers, would go along with this idea. Parents in suburban communities expect their conventionally prepared teachers to be high quality, and if they do not show themselves to be high quality, the teacher evaluation process works to dismiss those who do not meet the standards.

I want to be clear that I am not against charter schools. I think that former American Federation of Teachers leader, the late Albert Shanker, was correct in proposing charter schools as an innovative way to invigorate public schools. In a speech to the AFT QUEST Conference Shanker said, "It's dangerous to let a lot of ideas out of the bag, some of which may be bad. But there's something that's more dangerous, and that's not having any new ideas at all at a time when the world is closing in on you."[19] Moreover, I believe that while charter schools can be a part of the solution; they cannot be the *only* solution. Public schools should be allowed to experiment on a variety of fronts—hiring, curriculum, the length of the school day and year, reward systems, classroom and class-size configurations, and governance—as long as state and/or local academic standards are met. Charter schools, like traditional public schools, work for some students. The question is how do we ensure that our schools work for most students and that school failure is not so predictably linked to students' race, ethnicity, income, first language, and immigration status. When we can predict how well students will do in school by looking at their zip codes, we know we have a serious systemic problem.

Looking for quick and easy solutions is prototypically American. We believe that we can neglect a situation for decades (or even centuries) and then expect to correct it overnight. We are unwilling to create the conditions for those society calls "the least of these" that will equal those of the most privileged. The cynic in me sees current trends as a neoliberal plan to privatize education and destroy our public system through voucher plans. The right wing's frequent use of the term "government schools" makes a pejorative out of what we envisioned as a "common school" that would develop citizens for a democracy. But the optimist in me sees the opportunity to reinvest in the public good by reinvesting in public education.

When I initially began researching successful teachers of African American students,[20] I had to contend with two initial challenges. The first was, why focus on African Americans? I countered this challenge by asking, were they not a worthy group to consider? What might I find out about their success that would be harmful to any other group of students? If we could find ways to improve the education of the nation's poorest-performing group, would that not be relevant to students throughout the system?

My second challenge was finding such teachers. I began by gathering information from all over the nation, visiting schools and classrooms with strong reputations for teaching African American students effectively. The Harriet Tubman Elementary School in Newark, New Jersey, like the schools in New Orleans, was in a devastated area. Newark experienced not a natural disaster, but social upheaval;

race riots in the late 1960s left much of the African American community burned out and abandoned. White merchants and middle-class African Americans vacated the city, leaving the Black and Latino poor to fend for themselves.

When I visited Tubman Elementary School in Newark's Central Ward in the late 1980s, it was led by principal Noah Marshall. Its student body was approximately 90 percent African American and 10 percent Puerto Rican. All of its kindergarten students were reading. The children throughout the school were reading at or above grade level. Attendance at Tubman exceeds that of any other public school in the city. Its state test performance is among the best in New Jersey. Its excellence has been recognized with a National Blue Ribbon Award. When I visited, there was a preschool program for three- and four-year-olds and after-school programs for children with working parents. The school stayed open until 11:00 p.m. and provided activities and sleeping accommodations for children whose parents worked the third shift. Teachers, whose average tenure there was 14 years, often planned weekend activities for students. Every adult in the building—including the custodian, school secretary, and crossing guard—taught a class, providing cocurricular lessons in drumming, bowling, and cooking. The kindergarteners and first graders were beginning Suzuki violin. All students were exposed to computers, at a time when most urban schools lacked access to computers. There was a vibrant and active parent-teacher association. Principal Marshall made it his business to visit parents regularly to gain their trust and enlist them to participate in the life of the school. When asked what he did when parents didn't respond, he replied, "I just keep coming back until they do."[21]

I highlight Harriet Tubman because what the principal, teachers, students, parents, and community members do there flies in the face of many of the current approaches to school reform. The school does not focus on remediation. The curriculum is not stripped-down, test-oriented, and scripted. Students' intellects are engaged and challenged. There is no presumption that working-class and impoverished parents are not interested in having their children succeed in school. The children are not considered products of a "culture of poverty,"[22] and teachers have no problem holding them to high academic standards. In the past 20 years I have seen and studied scores of individual public school teachers who fit the Tubman Elementary model. Unfortunately, they tend to be isolated in schools that are bogged down by bureaucracy and content with mediocrity, where their excellence is neither valued nor rewarded. Our challenge is how to replicate this kind of excellence across entire systems.

The excellent teachers I have observed are willing to meld academic demands with compassion. They do not perseverate on the achievement gap but work to create an enriched, as opposed to remedial, educational environment. They understand that helping to prepare citizens is one of teaching's highest callings, and they do it without recognition and adequate reward. They are not waiting for Superman, Batman, or someone from the Billionaire Boys' Club to make quality education a reality. The least we as a society can do is provide the kind of public support that is necessary to make the work possible.

PART I

Overcoming the Obstacles We Create for Children

3

Educationalizing the Welfare State and Privatizing Education

THE EVOLUTION OF SOCIAL POLICY SINCE THE NEW DEAL

Harvey Kantor and Robert Lowe

BELIEF IN THE capacity of public education to redress unequal opportunity and eliminate poverty is one of the most distinctive features of American social policy. It is especially evident in No Child Left Behind (NCLB), which has invoked an equality-of-results test of public school performance that neglects conditions inside and outside the schools that contribute to inequality. But belief in the efficacy of education to protect against the risks and uncertainties of the free market is hardly a new development in federal policy. For a half century, ever since Lyndon Johnson prioritized education over the project of building on the New Deal to create a robust welfare state, educational reform has been the federal government's favored solution to problems of poverty, inequality, and economic insecurity.

This faith in the power of education historically has justified greater access to schooling for low-income children as well as the investment of additional resources in the schools that serve them. But the idea that inequality and poverty are susceptible to educational correction has also had several less desirable consequences. It has not only reduced pressure on the state for other social policies that might more directly ameliorate economic distress; because education's capacity to redistribute opportunity has been limited by the absence of social policies that directly address poverty and economic inequality, it has also fueled disillusionment with public education itself for its failure to solve problems that are beyond its reach. In the current social and political context, this disillusion has generated support for market-oriented and business-based forms of education and social provision that threaten to deepen inequality rather than reduce it.[1] In this chapter, we examine the intensification of policy making around these strategies of educational reform by situating it within the history of education and social policy from the New Deal to the era of No Child Left Behind.[2]

FROM THE NEW DEAL TO THE GREAT SOCIETY

We begin with the New Deal because it institutionalized for the first time in the nation's history the idea that the federal government was responsible for ensuring the economic security and welfare of its citizens.[3] Education, however, played only an incidental role in the federal government's efforts to address these problems. Although President Franklin Roosevelt had no interest in providing federal financial assistance for public education, his New Deal spawned several education-related programs to respond to the ravages of the Depression. Most notably, the Civil Works Administration, predecessor to the Works Progress Administration (WPA), built and repaired a significant number of school buildings and hired thousands of unemployed teachers; the National Youth Administration offered work-study programs to high school and college students; the Civilian Conservation Corps provided some schooling to the young men it hired to do conservation work; and, more innovatively, the Federal Art Project and Federal Theater Project promoted cultural education. None of these was intended primarily as an educational project, however. In keeping with the New Deal's emphasis on economic relief and recovery, their chief purposes were either to provide jobs and income to the unemployed or to reduce the competition for jobs by keeping young people out of the labor market. When World War II increased the demand for labor, political support for New Deal work relief programs evaporated, and Congress abolished all of them before the war ended.[4]

Although the New Deal did not institutionalize public job creation, other New Deal programs intended to provide a measure of economic security and protection against the uncertainties of the market had staying power. These included a minimum wage, unemployment insurance, retirement benefits, federal support for public assistance, and the right of workers to organize. For a moment in the late 1930s and early 1940s, it appeared that a social democratic agenda might extend these benefits to the point where the federal government's responsibility for its citizens' economic and social welfare would approach the provisions of the welfare states being erected in northern and western Europe. These postwar social democratic governments in Europe sought to reduce unemployment and economic

deprivation by institutionalizing labor and income policies to guarantee a minimum standard of living. By the 1960s, however, this robust view of economic and
social provision in America would be replaced by a focus on education. Instead of
dealing with problems of social disadvantage and economic insecurity by expanding this nascent welfare state, President Lyndon Johnson's Great Society would
seek to address these problems mainly through compensatory education and job
training policies. These policies aimed not to protect the least advantaged from the
inequities and uncertainties of the labor market, but rather to develop individuals'
human capital so that they might participate in it.[5]

This evolution in social policy was propelled by several factors: Johnson's personal belief in the power of education; the way policymakers had come to think
about the causes of poverty and economic disadvantage, especially their commitment to the idea of a culture of poverty; and strategic political attempts to distance the liberal agenda from anything resembling collectivism during the Cold
War.[6] But the broadest context for this change was set by two other postwar developments. One was the containment of organized labor's social democratic agenda
within collective bargaining agreements.[7] The other was the NAACP's decision to
prioritize school desegregation efforts in its attack on racial inequality.[8] Private
negotiations between workers and employers over wages and fringe benefits,
together with African American demands for school desegregation, reduced political pressure on the state for public job creation, income redistribution, and other
social benefits. Instead, social policy making was reoriented around educational
reform.[9]

The Great Society's focus on education certainly did not exclude other forms
of public social provision. It created Medicare and Medicaid and devoted some
resources to food stamps. In addition, the need to staff other social programs
expanded employment opportunities for African Americans, Latinos, and the
poor. For the most part, however, the Great Society did not expand on the steps
the New Deal had taken toward building a floor under incomes and providing
public jobs for the poor. Absent a broad-based constituency in favor of a more
expansive welfare state, it turned instead to less intrusive, more politically palatable proposals. These included tax cuts to stimulate economic growth, educational
initiatives, and job-training programs designed to help those on the margins
without antagonizing business by interfering directly in the labor market or without alienating White middle- and working-class voters by transferring income to
African Americans and the poor. Johnson continually referred to this strategy as
a "hand-up not a hand-out."[10]

Ironically, it was Richard Nixon who contemplated offering an expanded system of social benefits. For a time, he supported a strategy of direct payments to

individuals, such as increasing spending on food stamps, indexing Social Security payments to inflation, and creating a federal income guarantee for the aged, blind, and disabled poor (Supplemental Security Income, or SSI). At the same time Nixon supported income security, he simultaneously tried to limit the growth of federal spending on education and other Great Society programs such as the Job Corps and Community Action. In the end, however, Nixon was neither deeply committed to universalizing the federal government's responsibility for income security, nor was he successful in limiting the federal commitment to education. Criticized by liberals who thought he set benefit levels too low and by conservatives who were opposed to extending "welfare" to employed workers, he gave up on a proposal for a guaranteed annual income (the Family Assistance Plan) and, under pressure from "pro-family" conservatives, vetoed the Comprehensive Child Development Act, which would have provided federal funding for child care.[11] At the same time, a bipartisan coalition in Congress thwarted his effort to limit the federal commitment to education, which resulted in increased federal spending for the Great Society's education programs.[12]

Nixon's retreat did not preclude other efforts to institutionalize more expansive protections against economic risk. Jimmy Carter liberalized eligibility for food stamps and expanded the Comprehensive Employment and Training Act (CETA), first passed in 1973, which provided public service jobs to the unemployed. He also tried to put a guaranteed annual income measure (Program for Better Jobs and Income) back on the social policy agenda. But, committed to budgetary restraint, he only pushed halfheartedly for it; and by the end of his term, he had come to believe that combating inflation and reducing the federal budget deficit required a reduction in expenditures for CETA and other social welfare programs.[13] Instead, he sought to raise the visibility of education in the federal bureaucracy by advocating and winning congressional approval for a cabinet-level Department of Education.[14] As a result, Carter wound up reinforcing the central place education had come to occupy in the nation's system of social provision while setting in motion the antigovernment rhetoric, particularly the idea that excessive government spending on social welfare was the chief cause of the nation's economic problems, that has been the central theme in debates about social policy ever since Ronald Reagan's election.[15]

RACE AND THE POLITICS OF EDUCATION IN THE GREAT SOCIETY

Although the Great Society embraced a more restricted conception of the benefits the state can provide than did the New Deal, it was much more racially inclusive.

In its efforts to alleviate distress and provide for the needy, the New Deal had certainly included African Americans and Latinos. With some notable exceptions, however (such as the program to fund Black graduate students set up by Mary MacLeod Bethune in the National Youth Administration and the modest affirmative action program that Harold Ickes initiated within the short-lived Public Works Administration), New Deal agencies took no action to counter racial discrimination. Minimum wage and maximum hour legislation, old-age benefits, and unemployment insurance excluded agricultural and domestic workers, who were disproportionately African American and Latino; the right to bargain collectively did little for those African American and Latino workers whom unions excluded from membership and, through the closed shop, from factory jobs altogether; and the Federal Housing Administration discriminated against African American and Latino home buyers by restricting federal mortgage guarantees to white neighborhoods. In sum, while the New Deal did not exclude African Americans and Latinos, its programs, as well as the passage of the GI Bill in 1944, rested rather easily with white supremacy and played a major role in both intensifying residential segregation and creating the racial disparities in wealth that continue to shape educational inequality today.[16]

In contrast to the New Deal, the Great Society sought to address racial discrimination. Although this concern for racial equality embraced Latinos and Native Americans, the main catalyst for it was the need to address the demands of African Americans.[17] In responding to pressure from the civil rights movement, Congress passed the 1964 Civil Rights Act, the Voting Rights Act of 1965, and the 1968 Fair Housing Act. Together, these measures sought to "undo the racial legacy of the New Deal" and to integrate African Americans into the welfare state by outlawing segregation in public accommodations, affirming African American voting rights, prohibiting the distribution of federal funds to racially segregated institutions, and extending civil rights protections to the labor and housing markets.[18] This legislation also empowered the federal government to intervene in states and localities to guarantee these rights, though the strong enforcement provisions that African Americans and many White liberals desired were typically watered down before final passage, especially in employment and housing.

The centerpiece of Great Society education legislation, Title I of the 1965 Elementary and Secondary Education Act (ESEA), promised to help African Americans by providing much-needed financial aid to schools that served low-income students, particularly in the South and in big cities. Title I, however, was not responsive to Black demands, which in the early 1960s focused mainly on school desegregation. Title I, in fact, was quite compatible with the persistence of racially segregated institutions. For this reason, the NAACP, other civil rights groups, and a few White liberals denied that the program was a meaningful response to the problem of racial inequality in the schools.[19]

It is not clear whether this preference for compensation rather than desegregation was intentional. Certainly, Commissioner of Education Francis Keppel and his successor, Harold Howe, believed that the passage of Title I would provide southern school districts with an incentive to comply with Title VI of the Civil Rights Act, which prohibited the distribution of federal funds to segregated schools.[20] But that is not how things turned out. Although most observers credit the threat of fund deferrals for pushing southern school systems from intransigent defiance to token acceptance of school desegregation, linking the implementation of Title I to the enforcement of Title VI produced a backlash in Congress that threatened the very survival of Title I and other Great Society education programs.[21] Consequently, President Johnson pressured Health, Education and Welfare officials to weaken the program's ties to federal desegregation efforts as the price the administration had to pay to ensure its continuation.

This trade-off did not eliminate subsequent conflicts over the connection between Title I and desegregation. In the early 1970s, the reauthorization of Title I became entangled with Nixon's efforts to win congressional approval for legal restrictions on school busing. Because of opposition from liberals in Congress, the most restrictive features of anti-busing measures that sought to limit court action failed. But when Congress reauthorized Title I in 1974, it not only limited the federal government's power to enforce Title VI of the Civil Rights Act but also prohibited the use of federal funds for busing. By then, even many who once considered themselves advocates of civil rights, particularly northern liberals who represented urban districts and were under pressure from their White constituents to oppose court-ordered busing, had begun to think of Title I as a substitute for, rather than a complement to, federal desegregation efforts.[22]

RACE, THE LIMITS OF REDISTRIBUTION, AND
THE PERSISTENCE OF EDUCATIONAL REFORM

Although educational reform appealed to policy makers because it appeared to be a politically palatable alternative to more direct forms of intervention in the labor market and because it was less expensive than a more expansive system of publicly funded social provision, the Great Society's strategy of relying on the provision of additional educational resources to low-income and minority children turned out to face its own obstacles. Since Title I posed no threat to segregated institutions and built new networks of professional, political, and financial interests committed to its survival, it turned out to be remarkably resilient. But because of poor implementation, insufficient funding, and the way available funds were disbursed, it never operated as more than a "modest supplement to very unequally distributed state and local educational resources."[23] Consequently, it did much less to improve educational outcomes for low-income students than its proponents initially hoped it would.[24]

School desegregation was a more robust method of redistribution. In contrast to Title I, which did not disturb power relations between the races, it sought to root out racial inequality by providing African American students with access to the superior resources of the schools White students attended. In doing so, however, it threatened white exclusivity, inspired massive White resistance, and proceeded at a glacial pace until the Supreme Court acted in the late 1960s to strike down freedom-of-choice plans that had failed to produce more than token desegregation. The court subsequently legitimated the use of school busing and began to require remedies for racially segregated schools in the North and West as well as the South. Though these actions were compromised by the unequal burden of busing, school closures, and teacher layoffs imposed on African American students and communities, and by the persistence of discriminatory practices within desegregated schools, they marked a sharp departure from Jim Crow schooling; opened up access to greater educational resources for African American students, especially for African Americans in the rural South; and helped accelerate Black educational progress.[25]

But this more assertive stance was short-lived. As the Black Freedom Movement challenged the distinction between de jure and de facto segregation that had limited desegregation to the cities and protected suburban housing markets and school districts from court-ordered integration, the already tenuous political support for more affirmative policies evaporated, and further action was rejected by officials in all three branches of government. Anxious to cultivate political support among White, middle-class suburbanites opposed to metropolitan remedies, Nixon, Ford, Carter, and Reagan all reaffirmed the de jure/de facto distinction and opposed busing across school district lines. So did bipartisan majorities in both houses of Congress, and, most importantly, a majority of justices on the Supreme Court. Transformed by the appointment of four Nixon nominees, the Supreme Court moved in 1973 to protect the financial advantages of property-rich suburban districts (*San Antonio v. Rodriguez*), and a year later it began a long retreat from its insistence that districts in violation of *Brown v. Board of Education* take aggressive action to overcome segregation when it reversed a lower court that had challenged the "housing/education nexus" and mandated urban-suburban desegregation in Detroit (*Milliken v. Bradley*). Subsequent school desegregation plans focused on voluntary urban-suburban transfers and magnet programs designed to hold White students in city school systems or attract them from the suburbs. Because they left intact the fusion of residential segregation and suburban political autonomy, however, they did not do much to alter the racial composition of most urban or suburban schools.[26]

The accumulated experience of Title I and desegregation ultimately eroded the intellectual credibility of the former and the political credibility of the latter. Although both programs continued to have steadfast advocates both inside and outside Congress, by the early 1980s the logic that had motivated and sustained these policies had vanished, and few policy makers saw them as viable approaches to the redistribution of educational or economic opportunity.[27] By institutionalizing the idea that poverty and income insecurity were chiefly matters of education, however, the Great Society actually increased expectations about what education could accomplish. As a result, the federal commitment to education and its role in social policy remained firmly in place despite the backlash against the Great Society's own educational programs.[28]

While the Great Society's commitment to federal policy making in education had won widespread support, even among many conservatives, disillusionment with its educational initiatives precluded further expansion of compensatory or redistributionist strategies of reform. In the 1970s, Title VI of the 1964 Civil Rights Act provided the rationale for the extension of civil rights protections to English language learners and disabled children, and Title I of ESEA remained the programmatic foundation on which future federal education policies would be built. But by the 1980s, federal policy no longer embodied the idea that the government should intervene to alter the arrangements that resulted in the segregation of African American and Latino students in underperforming schools or to compensate them for their unequal access to educational resources. Federal policy focused instead on trying to improve their educational outcomes without disturbing the advantages of the wealthiest schools and their predominantly White, middle-class clientele.

FROM THE GREAT SOCIETY TO THE ENABLING STATE

Between 1970 and 2000 the programmatic legacy of the New Deal/Great Society welfare state and the ideological consensus that sustained it was challenged by the popularization of a different conception of the role of the state in social policy. In contrast to the New Deal, which sought to build a minimal floor under incomes, and the Great Society, which sought to extend opportunity through the expansion of social services such as education and job training, this new view of the state's role in social policy proposed to limit the federal government's responsibility for income security and to restructure the system of social provision by minimizing direct redistributive measures in favor of more market-oriented forms of social protection.[29]

Nothing in this transformation altered the trajectory set in motion during the 1960s that placed educational reform at the center of social policy making. To the contrary, as political support for more expansive forms of publicly provided social provision eroded, belief in what education might accomplish actually became stronger, and policy making around education intensified. In fact, despite the widespread disillusionment with Great Society liberalism that became evident in the early 1970s and accelerated over the next three decades, when we view the years since 1980 through the prism of educational policy, we see a reassertion of the preference to offer protection to citizens against the uncertainties of the market by reformulating the problems of poverty, inequality, and income insecurity in terms of economic growth and educational achievement.

Our argument here is partially at odds with current thinking about the history of education and the welfare state that views the emphasis on educational policy since 1980 as symbolic of a shift away from the "social insurance type welfare state" inherited from the New Deal toward what Neil Gilbert and Barbara Gilbert have called an "enabling state."[30] The decades since 1980, in fact, have more in common with the past than it appears at first glance once we recognize that the chief characteristic of the system of social provision that evolved in the 1960s was not so much its efforts to expand the social insurance and welfare policies inherited from the New Deal as its reliance on education as an alternative to more interventionist policies to reduce poverty and economic distress and promote job security, employment, and economic opportunity.

What has distinguished the last thirty years is not the reliance on "enabling" measures but the broader shift in the ideological context of social policy. Though the Great Society turned to education as an alternative to direct public expenditures on social provision or assertive interventions in the labor market, it did not seek to reduce the income supports put in place during the New Deal or to dismantle the system of employment-based benefits it inherited. Rather, the Great Society sought to incorporate the poor and people of color into this system by promoting economic growth and by equalizing the conditions of educational provision. By contrast, the dominant trend in social policy after 1980 has been to minimize dependence on the state by placing responsibility for coping with economic risk on individuals and families, while relying more heavily on education to promote self-reliance, individual responsibility, and labor market participation.

Thus we have been witnessing the apparent paradox of even more intensive federal intervention in education coupled with efforts to minimize federal responsibility for other forms of social and economic provision.[31]

This shift in policy can be attributed in part to the effects of globalization and deindustrialization, most importantly the post-1973 slowdown in industrial productivity and economic growth, which put pressure on the federal budget.[32] But the diminution of the federal commitment to forms of social provision other than education was hardly an inevitable response to the effects of economic change on the federal budget. What tipped the balance were changes in the ways different groups and classes viewed the government's relationship to the market and its role in social provision and their relative power to influence politics and governmental policy making.

Among these changes, much scholarly attention has focused on the escalating backlash from blue-collar workers and middle-income suburbanites who, worried about urban decline and rising tax rates, rebelled against social policies they believed catered to the needs of people of color and the poor at their expense.[33] More important, however, was the political mobilization of business leaders. Faced with declining profits and an increasingly competitive international economic environment, they turned their backs on the employment-based system of public/private provision they had helped to construct after World War II. Instead, they proposed to "infuse a capitalist ethos" into the politics of social provision and financed the creation of an unprecedented number of new business associations, think tanks, foundations, and lobbying organizations to develop an intellectual rationale for applying market-oriented principles to social policy and to elect political leaders who supported those principles.[34]

Social Security and Medicare, which served the elderly and benefited a broad working- and middle-class constituency, persisted despite these pressures. So did SSI which served those whom policy makers considered to be the "deserving poor." But absent an "effective political counterweight"[35] willing or able to challenge the logic of the market and the legitimacy of large corporations, the effect of this business mobilization and the proliferation of conservative and free-market think tanks it sponsored was to shift the terrain of debate in favor of the idea that public social provision could not ameliorate the problems it was intended to solve but in fact had made them worse by discouraging work, encouraging dependence on the state, and interfering with economic growth. The result was social policy that sought to reduce direct public provision in favor of programs, such as Temporary Assistance to Needy Families (TANF) and the Earned Income Tax Credit (EITC), which limited access to welfare and encouraged work and educational reforms that aimed to prepare children from poor families to participate more successfully in the labor market so that they could deal with economic risk through their own efforts.[36]

This reorientation did not go uncontested. Concerned about deteriorating wages and growing income inequality, in the 1980s a few liberal Democrats led by Representative George Miller, Senator Ted Kennedy, and members of the Congressional Black Caucus supported greater funding for education programs in association with policies for full employment, health care, housing, and a minimum standard of living.[37] However, after the failure of Carter's proposal for a guaranteed income in 1978 and the termination of CETA in 1982, neither Republicans nor Democrats sought to combine education policy with a thoroughgoing system of income support, family allowances, or public employment. They turned instead to an expansion of education policy as a way to minimize the demand for more robust public policies to alleviate economic insecurity. Republicans, with support from many moderate Democrats, pushed a combination of tax and deficit reduction policies that constrained the government's capacity to fund other forms of social provision.[38]

THE REINVENTION OF THE EDUCATIONAL STATE

Based on the conviction that the expansion of educational policy making would foster and help legitimate the reorientation of the welfare state around a new social contract, which its supporters referred to as "public support for private responsibility," this movement extended the federal government's preference—first evidenced in the 1960s—for providing economic security through education. But this movement rejected the idea that the federal government should intervene to address the effects of economic disadvantage and racial segregation. Hostile to redistributionist strategies of reform, it sought instead to remodel the education system in accordance with the same principles that were restructuring the rest of the welfare state. The result has been a reorientation of education policy around market-based and business-derived models of organization that heightened expectations for education but left intact inequities between schools with wealthier students and those with large numbers of low-income and students of color.

Led by a coalition of business and political elites,[39] this movement coalesced in the 1990s around two forms of state action, one based on public financing for privately provided educational services (e.g., vouchers and other forms of privatization) and the other based on a corporate model of organization that emphasized local responsibility in return for centralized regulation of specific, measured school outcomes. Different in orientation, these strategies nonetheless shared the assumption that school failure had less to do with class- and race-based inequities in the conditions of educational provision than with the lack of accountability for how schools used the resources they had to educate their students.[40]

Voucher experiments were instituted in some urban school systems, most notably Milwaukee and Cleveland, and a few states have adopted limited non-means-tested voucher plans and voucherlike tax credit policies.[41] No state or school district, however, has yet fully embraced the idea of publicly financing private schooling where accountability is determined by a school's capacity to attract and retain voucher-bearing students. But much of this market-oriented idea has now been incorporated into public systems across the country in the form of charter schools and charter-school networks, which frequently contract with private companies to run the schools. Today there are over 5,000 charter schools in 40 states serving over 1.5 million students (see Scott and Wells, chapter 9, this volume).[42] Because they technically remain public, charters have not satisfied the most ardent advocates of privatization and market-based reform. Yet by restructuring public systems around the principles of flexibility, competition, and choice, they have begun to transform long-standing conceptions of public responsibility in education, not only individualizing responsibility but also putting families in competition with one another for access to educational resources at the expense of more collective remedies intended to address the racial and economic arrangements on which public school systems have long been based.[43]

Still more influential among federal policymakers has been the idea of accountability-based reform, which culminated the year after George W. Bush's election with the passage of the No Child Left Behind Act (hereafter, "NCLB") in 2001.[44] The most significant federal initiative since the passage of ESEA in 1965, NCLB codified the rejection of compensatory and redistributionist strategies of educational reform. Although it took incremental steps to concentrate more money in high-poverty schools, its main goal was to use federal policy to reorient public education around the principles of business organization on the assumption that the chief problem facing American education had less to do with the inequitable distribution of resources than with the bureaucratic arrangements that protected underperforming schools from the consequences of failure. To remedy this required states to set minimum proficiency standards for all students and to implement a prescribed set of sanctions against schools that failed to meet them, including access to public school choice, the provision of private supplementary educational services, and state-mandated restructuring of local schools.[45]

A number of state and local school officials as well as advocates of states' rights in education opposed this strategy of reform.[46] But its emphasis on accountability received support from several other groups. It was attractive, for example, to many suburban Whites who favored expanding educational opportunities for the least advantaged while preserving their own access to good schools. Yet, because it effectively shifted the blame for educational failure from the child to the school, it was also popular with some civil rights organizations, Black and Latino parents, and liberal advocacy groups. These organizations and groups believed that accountability offered a more robust sense of opportunity than Title I, which had been framed in a language of cultural deprivation that blamed poor children for their own educational failures. It also appeared at first glance to have been responsive to the view held by many African American educators that, contrary to what James Coleman, Christopher Jencks, and other sociologists seemed to imply,[47] schools do indeed matter, especially for low-income children and children of color, and that, in the post–civil rights era, racially and economically segregated schools and school systems can be organized to foster high achievement and promote greater economic opportunity.[48]

Although NCLB appeared to many to have embraced a broader vision of equal opportunity than the policies that preceded it,[49] those hopes were soon dashed. While it rightly rejected the stigmatizing practices that had often accompanied the Great Society's compensatory programs and depressed the educational achievement of low-income children, NCLB, like Title I, more often functioned to reproduce educational inequality than reduce it. This time, however, the result was not due primarily to reformers' deficit assumptions about the intellectual capacities of African American, Latino, and low-income children. It was due rather to the fact that the application of NCLB's provisions to unequal schools typically wound up reinforcing class- and race-based differences in access to educational resources rather than increasing the resources available to those who lacked them.

Why and how this happened became apparent when researchers began studying the consequences of the NCLB's requirement that test scores be disaggregated by subgroup. This provision was included in NCLB at the insistence of liberals in Congress who believed that aggregated scores obscured differences in achievement between different groups of students. But because teachers and administrators in schools with large numbers of low-income students and students of color faced the historically insurmountable barrier of annually raising the test scores of multiple subgroups, including special education students, so that all of them attained the same level of proficiency, they sought to meet this goal by narrowing the curricula in their schools to focus on preparation for the requisite tests in reading and mathematics at the expense of other subjects.[50] At the same time, middle-class schools, which typically had fewer subgroups, made few changes in their regular practices but continued to offer a relatively enriched curriculum.[51] In this way, the disaggregation of test scores by subgroup, which was NCLB's most progressive feature, actually produced regressive results.

Theoretically, NCLB's provisions for choice, as well as the growth of charter schools, offered low-income students the opportunity to escape this predicament. But choice plans also encountered obstacles. Not only did the act's provisions for choice offer no incentives for high performing districts to accept students from lower-scoring urban schools, whom they feared would bring down their own school's test scores and thereby subject them to federal sanctions,[52] but the lack of availability of a sufficient number of good public and charter schools in urban districts continued to limit the opportunities for low-income families to partici-pate in the education marketplace.[53] As a result, more options typically did not translate into more opportunity.

EDUCATION, THE ENABLING STATE, AND THE OBAMA ADMINISTRATION

Barack Obama has tried to alter the balance between public and private respon-sibility in economic and social policy, but he has not tried to substitute public for private authority in the market or alter the structure of the compromised welfare state he inherited. Rather, faced with the worst economic crisis in over half a cen-tury, he proposed and passed an economic recovery bill that focused on federal support for state governments and spending for privately contracted construction projects to relieve unemployment and encourage economic stabilization, much as Roosevelt's Public Works Administration did in the early days of the New Deal.[54] Similarly, his plan to expand access to health care relies on federal subsidies to uni-versalize privately provided health insurance. That these measures have provoked so much opposition speaks more to how much the ideological reinvigoration of antistatism that began in the 1970s has intensified differences about what activi-ties the federal government should carry out than it does to any dramatic expan-sion Obama proposed to the welfare state.

Despite some efforts to modify the direction of social policy, nowhere has Obama proposed to reduce the nation's reliance on education as its chief bulwark against poverty and economic insecurity or to alter the direction of the education policy he inherited. He not only continues to tout education as "the best antipoverty program" and the key to individual and national well-being,[55] but he also remains committed to reconstructing public education in accordance with market-oriented principles of motivation and business-based models of organization. In fact, though some of his supporters had hoped that he would reject these principles and models in favor of less competitive, more collectively oriented approaches, his administration's main education initiatives—e.g., to make the receipt of Title I funds conditional on improvements in school performance, to accelerate the proliferation of charter schools, and to improve instruction by evaluating and paying teachers according to students' test scores—actually constitute an intensification of them. Consequently, his policies have reinforced the preference for educational solutions to the problem of social welfare at the same time that they have confined debates about educational policy to technical questions such as how to manage schools more efficiently, measure achievement more precisely, encourage teachers to work harder, and manipulate incentives to maximize choice. This narrowed discussion has largely ruled out more fundamental questions about race-based and economic disparities in educational opportunity.[56]

While the recent intensification of policy making around education has made school reform a national priority, it actually has diminished the ability of public schools to equalize educational opportunity. By substituting education for direct forms of social provision, it has limited the federal government's capacity to address the poverty that destabilizes children's lives and erodes school achievement. At the same time, by substituting accountability for redistribution, it has further reduced the fiscal and curricular capacity of urban schools to produce the superior outcomes seen in the schools affluent students attend and deepened the sense that these schools do not merit additional public investment. A serious effort to equalize economic opportunity requires both a robust welfare state and schools with the ample resources and rich subject matter the well-to-do enjoy, free of tracking and the low expectations African American and Latino students often face (see Tyson, chapter 12, this volume).

Despite how far social policy has strayed from these goals, signs of dissatisfaction are emerging. Not only have conservative efforts to eliminate the last vestiges of the welfare state generated widespread opposition, but also the shortcomings of NCLB have begun to raise questions about the desirability of the choice and accountability agenda in education policy. Chastened by experience, even some of the most ardent advocates of choice and accountability have recently changed their minds about this policy agenda.[57] Whether this dissent will alter the future trajectory of social and educational policy is impossible to predict. But more than at any time during the past two decades, it provides a glimmer of possibility that we can redirect social and educational policy to restore a commitment to broadening public social provision and establishing conditions both outside and inside the schools that will reduce disparities in opportunity and engage students in serious intellectual work.

4

Housing Segregation Produces Unequal Schools

CAUSES AND SOLUTIONS

Gary Orfield

EDUCATIONAL OPPORTUNITY IS directly and deeply connected with housing. Segregated neighborhoods linked to segregated schools produce unequal education. Where a family lives generally determines the quality of the schools its children attend. Since the housing market is heavily segregated by race as well as income, better schooling is most common in White neighborhoods. The gap in neighborhoods and the very different schooling opportunities that are attached to them are a central part of the opportunity gap. Students of color will soon form a majority of students in the public schools, but even middle-class African American and Latino children often must attend low-performing schools because of residential segregation. A recent study of metropolitan Boston found that Black families earning five times as much as low-income White families were living in neighborhoods with many poor people and that very few poor Whites faced such conditions.[1]

From the 1960s through the 1980s, school desegregation efforts opened middle-class, all-White schools to millions of students of color, particularly Black students in the South. Now, however, most of the gains of urban desegregation have been lost. Moreover, the segregation of Latino students has increased steadily since the 1960s. Since the Supreme Court supported the termination of court-ordered desegregation in 1991, school segregation has risen continually for both groups. Families with children are even more residentially segregated than other households.[2]

The vast majority of schools serving predominantly low-income children of color offer worse education than White and Asian students typically receive. Their students have lower test scores, much higher dropout rates, and weaker college preparation than those who attend schools with mostly White, more-affluent children. This disparity is not the fault of families of color, who strongly desire school success, but of the effects on families of poverty and segregated neighborhoods. When parents have less money, few home-educational resources, and low levels of education, children's educational possibilities are limited. Poor children are at greater risk of having developmental difficulties; chronic, untreated medical problems; and inadequate nutrition (see also Rothstein, chapter 5 in this volume). They often face family disruptions related to poverty and joblessness. They have fewer models of educational and economic success, and more experience with the negative and sometimes pathological effects of exclusion, failure, and illegal behavior. Minority families are much more likely to live in rental housing and to move more frequently than White families, disrupting the continuity of children's education. Their neighborhoods have been disproportionately hit by the foreclosure crisis, resulting in lost homes and forfeited assets. Children in impoverished neighborhoods have fewer economically mobile peer influences.

Schools compound these inequities because they are deeply affected by social inequalities. As described throughout this book, among the most important school features that influence student outcomes are teachers, student peer groups,[3] supports for students and teachers, and the curriculum and level of instruction. All schools tend to differ markedly with the racial composition and poverty level of the neighborhoods they serve. While test scores are strongly related to family resources and peer-group influence, low-performing minority schools are disproportionately branded as failures.[4] Generally, teachers are blamed for their schools' failure, and many view such evaluation policies as deeply unfair. Consequently, frustrated teachers tend to move away, leaving schools where they are unfairly blamed for schools where they are credited for the success of more-privileged students.[5]

Schools with high concentrations of students needing strong academic support are often staffed largely by inexperienced teachers who are not yet effective educators, and some do not want to be there. The combination of weaker teachers and less-prepared classmates exposes many children in disadvantaged schools to less-challenging instruction. High schools where an insufficient number of students are prepared for advanced and honors classes either do not offer them or dilute the curriculum to increase the pool of students eligible for enrollment in those classes. The cumulative effect is a profoundly unequal educational experience, even when there is no overt discrimination. Systemically unequal schooling helps perpetuate inequality.

The struggle for urban school desegregation sought to break the links between housing and educational inequality by providing children of color with access to better schools in other neighborhoods. It created clear educational gains and changed the future of many students.[6] But that effort has been largely abandoned as the Supreme Court changed the law. The illusion that the schools by themselves can produce equality while ignoring segregation was fostered by the Reagan administration's policy of insisting on high standards in extremely unequal schools, and simultaneously fighting in the courts to end desegregation.[7] These sentiments continue to dominate national education policy. Huge racial gaps in achievement-test scores remain. They declined from the 1960s to the late 1980s, but little, if any, progress has been made since.[8] Though overall graduation rates have improved significantly in the past decade after a third of a century of stagnation and the large white-black gap fell slightly, the Latino-white gap actually increased.[9] These inequalities reflect opportunity gaps as described throughout this book, often rooted in the bedrock issue of housing.

This chapter analyzes the political, legal, and demographic roots of neighborhood-based inequality and suggests ways in which the vicious cycle of resegregation and intergenerational inequality could be broken to enable more communities to experience lasting integration. A first step is for lawmakers, educational advocates, and the broader public to realize that, in many important ways, *housing policy is educational policy*, and neither works well without a clear goal of racial integration.

INEQUALITY ON THE MAP

If you draw a map of racially segregated residential areas in a metropolitan area, you get a good approximation of the pattern of educational inequalities in both opportunities and outcomes. School segregation resulting from housing patterns, which are themselves shaped by discrimination, is largely accepted as something natural, and a large majority of White Americans believes that nothing more need be done to remedy the situation.[10] Segregation is a reality that everyone adjusts to, whether by commuting two hours each day between work and an outer suburb where the schools serve few poor, racial and ethnic minority children or by desperately searching for a viable charter or private school in a central city. Ironically, the political power and control of institutions exercised by African Americans and Latinos is largely based on segregated constituencies, and neither their elected representatives nor White public officials makes integration a priority. No serious, sustained initiatives against housing segregation have been launched since the 1970s.

In contemporary policy discussions, residential segregation is seen as voluntary and relatively harmless. Yet the residential isolation of excluded groups tends to perpetuate itself, feeding both negative adaptation among the excluded and a sense of superiority among the privileged. Children growing up in communities without jobs, with few college-educated residents, weak schools, and relatively few stable two-parent families in communities exposed to crime and violence learn to function in their setting.[11] This toxic combination of minority isolation and racial bias deepens inequality. Segregated housing is not necessary to create inequality, but it makes it much easier to maintain, and its mechanisms are relatively invisible to the majority. It is built into many aspects of the housing market and shapes the ways families search for and find homes. Housing officials rarely collaborate on positive policies to prevent its spread and increase lasting integration.

Whites in the United States tend to interpret segregated areas as the products of individual choice.[12] At the same time, surveys show that both Blacks and Latinos strongly prefer diverse areas, although they do not want merely token integration.[13] For more than a decade, only about a quarter of all Americans have believed that discrimination is the basic cause of inequality for Blacks in the United States; about 60 percent agree that those "who can't get ahead in this country are mostly responsible for their own condition."[14] Yet inconsistencies in beliefs and actions abound. Large majorities of Whites often respond in polls by saying that minority children have equal education, but almost no White family with a choice sends its children to African American or Latino schools.[15]

The public supports policies asserting that segregated schools can be made equal through accountability or competition, even though ample evidence shows that those approaches do not address the basic problem.[16] Once institutionalized, segregation is a durable and expansive system that tends to be seen as normal.[17] A 2008 survey found that 96 percent of Americans believe that "equal treatment of different races and ethnicities" is important, and 85 percent say that the government should act against discrimination. But 55 percent believe that government is already doing enough.[18] The effects of segregation generate and reinforce stereotypes.[19] The combination of segregation and a widespread assumption that everyone has a fair chance means that the consequences of unequal opportunity are widely misinterpreted as personal failures or the failings of an entire social group. The dominant policy response has been to put increasing pressure on the schools and teachers serving communities of color, often with counterproductive results (see Zhao and Tienken, chapter 8 in this volume).

Although Black-White residential segregation has declined modestly since 2000, school segregation has become much worse.[20] Though segregation is spreading into suburbia, very little is being done to avoid repeating the processes of resegregation that proved harmful to many city neighborhoods. Local authorities in suburbs whose racial composition is changing usually ignore the issue or try to slow or isolate the change. In segregated White areas, many pretend that this change in neighborhood racial composition will not come. The process is only discussed in euphemisms in public and in stereotypes in private. Often officials working on housing policy do not even exchange data and discuss policies with school officials, who are profoundly affected by their actions or inactions.[21]

Segregation feeds stratification, inequality, and the denial of opportunity. Location is very heavily priced into housing costs everywhere because it involves prestige, convenience, social networks, future wealth, youth peer groups, contacts that may lead to jobs, safety and comfort in daily life, and most importantly, the quality of schooling. With neighborhood schools, the link between housing and intergenerational mobility is very clear, since poor Black and Latino children attend schools intensely segregated by race and poverty in which few children are ever adequately prepared for postsecondary education and many drop out of high school. Patterns of school opportunity can vary enormously even across small distances near the boundaries of school districts, in effect preparing students for different societies and different economies. District boundaries become social boundaries shaping divergent life chances.[22]

In most metropolitan areas, very few White schools face concentrated poverty.[23] On average, schools with large majorities of Black and Latino students are starkly different in terms of test scores, graduation rates, turnover of enrollment, teacher qualifications and experience, honors and AP courses, and many other important factors affecting school and student success. Sometimes these differences are manifest in deteriorated buildings; at other times they are only apparent when we look carefully to see teachers departing and the curriculum weakening.

Middle-class parents as well as experienced teachers leave schools in areas where a large majority of students are poor.[24] Families looking for housing are likely to find such schools unattractive. Just as the perceived high quality of outlying schools with high test scores is capitalized into housing values in those communities, so value is subtracted from homes in areas where the schools are losing White and middle-class children.[25] The absence of middle-class families with children affects a neighborhood and the socialization of children in manifold ways, and these schools and communities rarely provide students with an effective path to college. We may think that realtors and builders who want to enhance the marketability of local housing would work to keep the school integrated, but typically they simply redirect demand and construction to White areas elsewhere.

Access to the best schools is limited because housing and land-use policies prevent the construction of affordable housing for families in most areas with strong schools.[26] Zoning regulations forbidding multifamily rental construction and setting minimum lot sizes make suburban homes in desirable areas very expensive. Discrimination in the sale, rental, and financing of housing often excludes Blacks and Latinos who could afford it from the highest ranked schools. Although discrimination is illegal, it is quite common and rarely prosecuted.[27] The widely known history of housing discrimination and hostile acts against non-Whites who move into certain all-White neighborhoods limits choice. When families of color have no personal knowledge of or contacts in desirable communities, they are unlikely to seek housing there. The lack of Black and Latino brokers and rental agents in elite suburban areas is yet another barrier. There is also clear evidence that Black and Latino buyers were much more likely to receive "predatory" high-risk, high-interest mortgages than similar White buyers leading up to the housing market crash of 2008.[28] All these forces help create and reinforce segregation.

School segregation tends to intensify the impact of residential segregation. Blacks and Latinos moving into long-established white areas have more school-age children than the older Whites they replace and are less likely to enroll their children in private or parochial schools. Latino families are the youngest and largest compared to other major racial and ethnic groups. When a neighborhood becomes 30 percent nonwhite, its elementary schools may be 60 percent nonwhite. A community that looks integrated in census statistics often is rapidly resegregating in school enrollment, and that process, in turn, stimulates long-term population change.[29] If segregation is not to spread neighborhood by neighborhood, it is essential to reach beyond particular neighborhoods with a plan for school opportunities and housing integration in a much larger residential area that generates stable levels of desegregation. The more localized that school assignments are in a racially segregated residential area, the more intense segregation will be and the more rapidly racial transition will occur.

There is a widespread perception that housing markets are products of free choice and family income. Although this is generally accurate for White and many Asian families, Black and Latino families often face discrimination at many stages of housing choice, and some communities have used their municipal authority in ways that foster segregation by race and income. This means that neighborhood schools usually result in functioning middle-class schools for White and Asian families and segregated schools with substantial concentrations of severely disadvantaged children for Black and Latino students. Since our courts are ending efforts to create nonwhite access to stronger schools,[30] the issue of housing integration has become far more significant to equal opportunity.

SCHOOLS, HOUSING, AND CIVIL RIGHTS

Extensive civil rights enforcement, including race-conscious efforts to desegregate schools and housing, has been essential in successful efforts to break these vicious cycles of inequality. For decades through the 1980s there was substantial progress achieved against what had been totally segregated schooling in the South. In many metropolitan areas, housing became somewhat less segregated for Blacks after the fair housing law was enacted in 1968, despite very little enforcement.[31] Since the late 1980s, however, the Supreme Court has been limiting and reversing civil rights laws. There have been no major urban or housing policy initiatives in the last three decades. New subsidized housing for families is usually located where it feeds into inferior segregated schools.[32] With school desegregation policies blocked, getting Latino and Black children access to better educational opportunities will require a serious attack on housing segregation.

Segregation of Latino students has risen continuously as their population has grown, and many more Latinos are living in communities with few White or middle-class neighbors.[33] Latinos are increasingly isolated with other Latinos (overwhelmingly of Mexican origin in the West) and with poor children than are Blacks, attributable in good part to the enormous growth of the Latino population within segregated metros.

On average, Black and Latino students are attending schools with nearly twice as many classmates who are poor as White students are.[34] By 2006, two-fifths of Black and Latino suburban children were in intensely segregated schools whose student bodies were at least 90 percent Black and Latino, even though the suburbs remain overwhelmingly White.[35] Many of these schools are not thriving. The nation's dropout problem, which afflicts nearly half of males who are Black, Latino or American Indian, is concentrated in a small fraction (about 2,000) of the nation's secondary schools. Robert Balfanz has dubbed them "dropout factories." Most are high-poverty, urban, Black and Latino schools. Similar students in more integrated schools are significantly more likely to graduate.[36]

Housing segregation by race means that poor White children often live in and attend schools in communities with many middle-class families, but Black or Latino children in racially or ethnically segregated schools almost always attend schools with concentrated poverty. Accordingly, children of color are segregated by both race and class.[37] For students of color, even those in the middle class, neighborhood schools usually entail high concentrations of children of impoverished families of color.

Yet, even as isolated and impoverished minorities become a much larger sector of our society, less is done to address the situation. Fears have been stirred by wedge-issue racial politics, perhaps best exemplified by Nixon's Southern Strategy and his denunciation of "forced integration of the suburbs" discussed later. The basic assumption seems to be that nothing can be done about desegregation; it is too hard to achieve and the politics are too negative. Meanwhile, many families of color urgently seek better education for their children because they know it is the only way to secure a safe, middle-class future and that children experience significant downward mobility when they grow up in predominantly low-income communities of color, particularly if their schools are not successful.[38]

Still, racial segregation cannot be explained by income only. People may falsely assume that these problems affect only people who live in inner-city ghettos and hope vainly that they will solve themselves or can simply be postponed. The same attitudes were articulated a half century ago by those resisting the civil rights movement, when African Americans and their allies were struggling to end the American version of apartheid. Martin Luther King faced rock-throwing mobs trying to bring down the color line in Chicago in the 1960s. These attitudes led to neighborhood-by-neighborhood resegregation of our central cities decades ago. The entire struggle over urban desegregation of schools, which began a half century ago, is profoundly related to housing issues.

Although there are stark differences in average income between neighborhoods, many individual neighborhoods exhibit fairly wide ranges in housing prices and in family incomes. Statistical analysis shows that all communities would have significant diversity if money and preferences alone determined outcomes—if race did not factor in.[39] Why does severe housing segregation persist more than four decades after discrimination was forbidden by the federal law and despite positive changes in attitudes? There has been a large increase in suburbanization of racial and ethnic minority families. Some communities that were among the wealthiest two or three decades ago are now rapidly becoming predominantly Black or Latino as metropolitan areas sprawl. Unfortunately, much of this racial change involves the creation of new ghettos, barrios, segregated schools, not the emergence of stable integration.

Integrating housing is inherently far more difficult than integrating schools. A single court order can direct the creation of diverse schools across an entire school district, sometimes across an entire housing market. In contrast, the housing market involves myriad actions of private buyers, sellers, rental agents, lending institutions, and other forces. Housing decisions are individual, multistaged, complex, and hard to document. Changing housing patterns requires a combination of monitoring and enforcement at several transaction levels, such as altering local policies forbidding affordable housing, providing information and support for Black and Latino families who may be interested in moving, and helping communities deal successfully with diversity. The legacy of past discrimination and exclusion is a heavy burden. By subsidizing suburban home ownership for young White families for generations, federal policies compounded the problem.[40] Huge metropolitan areas were usually fragmented into many separate school districts.

For a time at the end of the 1960s it seemed that the public and policy makers recognized that housing is a core civil rights problem and must be addressed systematically. Riots in many urban ghettos, including the nation's capital, showed that something was terribly wrong. Martin Luther King's last major campaign, the Chicago Freedom Movement, attacked housing segregation as a central barrier to rights. President Johnson's riot commission solemnly warned the country in 1968 that "our nation is moving toward two societies, one black, one white, separate and unequal."[41] The commission recommended and Congress enacted the largest program to build housing for poor people outside ghettos and barrios in US history, forbidding the construction of high-rise segregated projects.[42] President Johnson's Model Cities program was meant to produce coordinated federal-local efforts to reverse the decay and destruction of the centers of great cities. Shortly after King's assassination in 1968, Congress passed the fair housing law, which included language requiring that all federal urban programs be administered to advance integration. The pieces were in place for a coherent attack on housing segregation, and the Supreme Court soon ordered systemic districtwide desegregation of southern cities' schools.

Policy was, however, dramatically reversed by the next president. At the beginning of the Nixon administration, the secretary of Housing and Urban Development (HUD), George Romney, planned to require changes in patterns of suburban housing exclusion as a condition for communities to obtain federal grants.[43] Nixon rejected this effort, denouncing "forced integration of the suburbs" and firing Romney.[44] Anti–civil rights leaders, including California's new governor, Ronald Reagan, who had opposed the state's fair housing law, were coming to power in the Republican Party.[45] Federal desegregation assistance was provided by the Emergency School Aid Act under the Nixon and Carter administrations but the act was repealed during the Reagan presidency despite the its popularity and solid evidence of its educational and social benefits.[46] Further, during the Nixon and Reagan administrations many of the urban development and housing programs that could have exerted leverage for major change were abolished, and significant civil rights enforcement was ended.

Decades of conservative appointments transformed the federal courts, limiting remedies for school segregation and other civil rights violations. No significant sanctions against violations of the federal fair housing law existed until 1988 when Congress finally provided some significant enforcement authority. Conservative administrations opposed any systemic attack on racial segregation. In the George W. Bush administration, fewer than 20 of the estimated four million annual incidents of housing discrimination were prosecuted in a given year.[47]

When federal courts seriously investigated cities' racial histories, they found virtually every city guilty of an extensive pattern of intentional discrimination in a variety of local decisions on both school and housing policies.[48] Many of the large black and Latino housing projects, the vertical ghettos that local public housing agencies constructed in poor areas with bad schools, produced social pathology and have now been torn down. Unfortunately HOPE VI, a federal program dealing with the displaced tenants from torn-down projects did not have an explicit commitment to integration and often moved low-income families from one area with weak schools to another, sometimes even fostering resegregation in the receiving neighborhood.

Putting public money into a segregated housing market spreads neighborhood and school segregation unless there is an explicit plan to break these patterns. In the Obama administration, the US Treasury Department has continued to operate the largest federal subsidy for building affordable housing for families, the Low Income Housing Tax Credit. The administration has done this without significant civil rights enforcement, thereby subsidizing the construction of housing in areas with inadequate schools serving predominantly racial and ethnic minority and poor children.[49]

Research conducted by the HUD in the 1970s and early 1980s showed that a substantial share of school segregation in several metropolitan areas was caused by the concentration of subsidized housing in segregated minority communities and the differential access of White and non-White tenants to housing units in neighborhoods.[50] In a short-lived effort to combine school and housing remedies in civil rights enforcement under President Carter, HUD published a regulation requiring that subsidized housing site selection consider its impact on school segregation, but the policy ended after Reagan was elected president.[51]

Since banning the use of federal funds for the construction of high-rise housing projects in 1968, Congress has relied overwhelming on subsidizing housing produced through the private market. Typically, people with a demonstrated need for housing assistance are given market-based rental subsidy certificates or vouchers to find their own housing, but they get little help in finding housing outside areas that are or are becoming ghettos. The experience of implementing a giant remedy for illegal segregation of public housing in Chicago after the 1976 US Supreme Court decision in *Hills v. Gautreaux* showed that even public housing tenants who had always lived in all-black urban neighborhoods could prosper in white suburbia, and many would choose this option if they had good counseling and support

for their moves. In fact, once the program began, the demand for such opportunities far exceeded the available subsidies. Among the program's most important
benefits was giving children access to much stronger schools.[52]

The exit of White middle-class families from the big cities to the suburbs has
been followed by the departure of much of the middle class of color, leaving huge
areas doubly segregated by race and poverty in inner cities and spreading resegregation into suburbia.[53] Middle-class families of color still face, too, a substantial
probability of discrimination. A 2008 report by a national commission headed by
former Republican and Democratic secretaries of HUD, Henry Cisneros and Jack
Kemp, respectively, concluded that there are millions of fair housing violations
each year and only an extremely limited effort to enforce the law.[54]

When housing is severely segregated, a suburb of ambitious and upwardly
mobile neighborhood newcomers can be transformed over a few years into a
ghetto marked by social, economic and political challenges and deepening intergenerational inequality. Segregation creates a social chasm lasting generations and
reinforces racial divisions, producing what Martin Luther King described as a false
consciousness of superiority on the part of the segregators and a false consciousness of inferiority on the part of the segregated.[55]

Educational policy that ignores segregation often unfairly punishes its victims
and those who work with them. Schooling is usually at its worst in the most isolated schools serving the most disadvantaged communities. Many have attempted
to implement a succession of reform theories over the past four decades and have
come under fierce pressure since education policy turned in the 1980s toward
blaming schools and teachers and ignoring community conditions (see chapters 3,
8, and 5, from Kantor and Lowe, Tienken and Zhao, and Rothstein, respectively).

WHAT CAN BE DONE?

Recognizing that residentially segregated communities with segregated neighborhood schools are an absolutely fundamental structure of unequal opportunity is
a first step. But it is easy to look at this deep-rooted system and to conclude that
nothing can be done or that the only practical approach is to accept segregation
and try to make it equal by attempting to raise up the segregated schools and
provide other bridges into middle class, largely white and Asian colleges, jobs, and
opportunities. Those are all worthy efforts that usually have limited support and
success. Much more should be done. The truth is that although no one has any
policy proposal that would end all residential or school segregation, many things
have the potential to diminish it. Integration is no panacea, since we have other

powerful forms of inequality of wealth and position, and widely held prejudices are expressed in discrimination even in diverse settings, but it does have potential to open many opportunities and to create and sustain healthy diverse communities and schools.

Ending School Choice Segregation and Fostering Positive Choice Systems

School choice, one of the most popular approaches to remedying the educational problems that arise from segregation, often does not improve schools and can intensify neighborhood inequality. In the 1960s, unrestricted school choice plans, often designed by desegregation opponents, left minority schools totally segregated, facilitated the departure of Whites from integrated areas, and enrolled token numbers of Black and Latino students in White schools that often did not welcome them. Uncontrolled school choice, like the housing market, tends to deepen inequality because privileged families are able to access the best alternatives, making more informed choices and more skillfully working the system (see also Scott and Wells, chapter 9 in this volume).[56]

Between 1968 and 1971, the Supreme Court ruled that these choice plans were insufficient and ordered mandatory desegregation in the South.[57] The threat of similar orders in the North led to better forms of choice, in which choices that increased segregation were prohibited, and magnet schools with firm desegregation policies were created. This progress, however, was not sustained. Since the Supreme Court decided in 1991 to end many desegregation plans and blocked desegregation controls on transfer and magnet plans in 2007,[58] the nation has reverted to forms of choice that are likely to increase stratification and make racially changing neighborhoods more unstable as Whites choose to leave for whiter schools.[59]

Creating Stable Integrated Neighborhoods

Working toward solutions requires several steps. First, figuring out what is going on in an area and how to effectively surface the real choices that communities face and the very high costs of doing nothing. A second step is organizing concerned citizens and engaging not only the schools but also other local institutions in developing a positive plan. Third, making diversity a public and positive goal addresses fears and triggers positive attitudes. Fourth, seriously integrating and training the staff and the leadership of local institutions helps create understanding and the "equal status interaction" that make interracial institutions fairer and more effective. Fifth, vigorously enforcing the laws against discrimination and obtaining serious penalties especially against realtors, rental agents, and financial institutions engaged in racial steering or mortgage discrimination. Sixth, developing positive housing and school policies to produce and sustain stable integration. Finally, since these issues are inherently regional, we must work actively to secure positive policies from regional, state, and national government institutions. With a serious effort, institutionalized practices and expectations of resegregation can be broken and the possibility of lasting integration with integrated schools substantially enhanced.

Much has been known about the problems of segregated housing and schools for generations, and a variety of approaches to solving them has been attempted or proposed. Although many large-scale efforts have been abandoned and others have proven ineffective, those experiences are nonetheless instructive. Some experiments have suggested workable models, though most have been short term or small scale.[60] An evaluation of what has worked and what has not suggests ways we can transform these persistent but socially constructed patterns. Deeply rooted things can change, and doing nothing only makes the situation worse.

Neighborhoods have continual flows of people moving in and out, often changing their racial composition. This process offers both opportunity and peril; it could facilitate integration but often accelerates segregation. Without supportive school and housing policies and strong enforcement of laws against discrimination in the real estate market, the tendency toward resegregation prevails.

Many racial and ethnic minority families, who prefer interracial neighborhoods and schools, either move into or are steered into neighborhoods that appear to be interracial at the time but are actually in transition.[61] There are many virtually all-white, middle-class options for White families but few stably integrated schools for the many families of all races that would find them acceptable or preferable. The most successful desegregation plans in terms of achieving high levels of lasting desegregation have actually been those that are most radical, involving as much as possible of the metropolitan housing market. By tending to produce relatively stable integration everywhere, they make it harder for Whites to flee to all-white areas[62] and alleviate many Black parents' concern that their children will find themselves in isolated, underresourced schools as resegregation proceeds. A number of metropolitan-wide plans that have existed for three decades actually fostered significant increases in residential integration.[63]

Communities that have remained stably integrated for substantial periods of time, such as President Obama's Chicago neighborhood Hyde Park, tend to be very successful economically and the product of concerted local efforts supported by powerful institutions, in this case the University of Chicago.[64] Yet many of those communities fail to take advantage of the integrative potential of gentrification, making no effort to foster successful school integration when young,

White, middle-class families are moving in or to preserve housing opportunities for the families that have long lived there. Different outcomes will require different strategies.

Recent demographic changes generate new possibilities. In much of the North, black outmigration to the South and the declining size of African American families are reducing the pressure of ghettoization caused by population growth in segregated markets, making stability significantly easier to achieve. The Latino and Asian populations, however, are growing very rapidly, and multiracial neighborhoods may become more stable. A first step in designing a viable policy should be to face the issue and discuss, not only of the dangers of sprawling resegregation, but also the possibility of positive, mutually beneficial outcomes if housing becomes truly integrated. Civil rights organizations, school district leaders, journalists, and researchers at universities should report and analyze the demographic changes that are occurring. People need to understand that racial and class isolation is likely to continue or accelerate unless something is done to prevent resegregation. Discussions of policies and practices that have been successful in other communities are essential. The failures of past political leadership must be challenged.

Many people and institutions in a community are aware that change is happening long before it becomes apparent to most residents. Realtors and banks know who is looking for housing and who is selling. Hospitals and local governments tally births. Kindergartens and elementary schools track rising or falling enrollments and students' shifting racial and class backgrounds. Critical information can be obtained from documents, particularly Census and Home Mortgage Disclosure Act records, and by monitoring real-estate activity involving homes in changing areas. Attention must be paid to what has happened to nearby communities and schools that are resegregated. Making this information public, together with reasonable projections of trends, should occasion serious discussion of both the negative consequences of resegregation and the positive policies available to create a better future. The most important point to get across is that these forces will fundamentally transform many communities and will not stop on their own. Leaders must give up speaking in euphemisms and come up with a plan to achieve stably integrated communities.

Costs of Doing Nothing

Doing nothing about segregation has high social and environmental costs. In housing terms, we risk resegregating and then ghettoizing many viable older suburbs with strong locational advantages and seeing more White and Asian families with children locating farther out in newer suburbs. We cannot afford to continue discarding good communities with good schools one after another and investing money in replicating them 25 miles away at enormous environmental costs simply because we have been unable to develop mutually beneficial ways of living together.[65] Separate local governments in metropolitan areas have been allowed to act as if they were not part of the very metropolitan community that makes them flourish. We must recognize that we are on a destructive path and that there are no good solutions within the existing structure of the housing market and current public policy. It is essential to find the language to discuss racial integration, explain possible solutions to segregation, and develop local, state, and national policies that will produce and sustain stable communities that are desirable to all and that prepare children of all backgrounds for adulthood in a diverse and dynamic society.

Getting Started at the Community and School Level.

How can we get started? Initiatives can begin at the level of localities and metropolitan regions. Healthy suburbs in the early stages of racial change would be good places for proactive policies. They have the resources required to take concrete steps toward stable integration. Many of their residents, both White and of color, experienced destructive racial transitions where they lived before, since the vast majority of neighborhoods that experienced racial diversity in previous generations resegregated, often with considerable social and economic upheaval. These communities usually do not get any help from other levels of government or from other major political, social, and economic institutions. But the members of these communities have power, and civic organizations could be mobilized if citizens understood the consequences of housing resegregation. What must be done is to interrupt and transform the normal processes by which communities are resegregated because of discrimination, lack of knowledge, and interracial fears of hostility. The goal is to maintain a healthy flow of new families, both White and non-White, into neighborhoods. In the housing market, illegal interracial steering must be blocked and interracial communities must be actively marketed to Whites as well as non-Whites. Affluent White and Asian families, who have the most complete freedom to choose housing, need to feel secure in making large long-term investments in homes. The belief that diversity will last and enrich, that all are welcome, and that the neighborhood and schools will remain well integrated should be fostered at all levels.

Racial change is difficult for most Americans to handle well. Racially and ethnically diverse staffs with special training are very helpful in facilitating discussion and effectively addressing issues. Diversifying the faculty and staff of schools and municipal agencies in terms of race, ethnicity, and language is a necessary step. Half of this country's students will soon be children of color, and one-fifth of children are already growing up in homes where English is not the native language. Good training and strong leadership in multicultural education can improve both race relations and the effectiveness of institutions. Since racial issues are highly sensitive in changing neighborhoods, anything bad that happens in a school or neighborhood is likely to have serious effects. Directly and credibly addressing rumors, fears, and stereotypes is very important.

Fair housing enforcement should be proactive, and not wait for complaints. Effective policies include systematic auditing and testing of the practices of local realtors, rental agents, and lending institutions, as well as vigorous prosecution of those who treat people of different races with the same qualifications differently. Realtors should be asked to show potential home buyers of all races houses in neighborhoods where most residents are of another race. Changing market flows at an early stage is much less difficult than when a neighborhood is no longer sought by or shown only to non-White home seekers, and when racial transition in the local elementary schools is far advanced.

Since it is impossible to monitor what is going on at every stage of these transactions, it works best if the real-estate industry becomes convinced that its long-term welfare and the health of the housing market depend on addressing these social issues and that stably integrated communities are desirable for all groups. Community leaders should work with real-estate agents to communicate positive messages about the schools to potential residents of all races, including more and better information about educational opportunities. This information should not be limited to test scores, which say much more about children's backgrounds than about school quality. Concerned citizens must vigilantly address signs of deterioration in diversifying communities and insist that subsidized housing programs are administered in ways that increase rather than diminish diversity and choice.

Local officials should take care that rent subsidy and voucher programs do not direct clients of color into racially changing areas, triggering resegregation. Housing counselors should affirmatively show families of color units in predominantly white areas with strong schools. Construction of family housing receiving any form of public subsidy should be subject to civil rights requirements in both site selection and tenant recruitment. Greatly needed housing for low-income families should not be built where their children would attend inferior segregated schools. Studies conducted during the desegregation era showed that subsidized housing, as it operates normally, almost always contributes to segregated education.[66] Even though it is a very small share of the nation's overall housing market, it is important to low-income, non-White families that integrated subsidized housing significantly increases school opportunities for poor children of color.[67]

Trends toward resegregation do not start or stop at municipal or school district boundary lines, so broader regional strategies are vital. Since families of color account for a continuously increasing share of the population, especially the younger child-bearing population, and Whites are targeted to move out by the marketing of new, virtually all-white developments on the periphery, resegregation is highly likely to continue to spread without a coherent effort extending beyond narrow boundaries.

School and community officials can do more to break the lockstep tie between housing and schooling by broadening school choice in a positive way. If a desegregation strategy means that all the schools in a wider area are relatively similar in demographic composition, more White and middle-class families may be willing to take a chance on a diverse neighborhood because the school will not be directly affected by neighborhood changes in the housing market. Where good desegregated schools are available, housing integration increases and becomes more stable.[68] When schools are diverse and stable, people can move into or remain in a residentially diverse or changing neighborhood without fear that school quality will decline.

Where area-wide school desegregation is impossible, creation of strong choice systems with civil rights policies can help encourage people to live in diverse areas. Special programs that attract families who would not otherwise use public schools or live in highly diverse areas can increase the stability of a school and the desirability of a school district and its neighborhoods. Magnet schools can have diversity policies and admissions priorities that comply with the Supreme Court's 2007 decision in *Parents Involved*. Acceptable policies include special attention to poverty, language, neighborhood composition, and other variables in selecting students that would produce more diverse schools and avoid rapid resegregation of neighborhoods. Local university faculty and scholars in the field could help districts assess possible solutions. Plans like the sophisticated geo-coding of mini-neighborhoods in Berkeley, California, and the choice strategy that was adopted in 2011 in metropolitan Louisville, (Jefferson Country), offer positive possibilities, but they need technical assistance since school districts lack skill in sophisticated demographic analysis and geospatial modeling.

Magnet schools, charter schools, and all other publicly funded schools of choice should be required to have the basic civil rights requirements of diversity goals and recruitment strategies, free transportation, no admissions tests, lotteries when schools are oversubscribed, and service to English language learners and special education students. Regional magnet schools, similar to the model created in Hartford and New Haven, Connecticut could draw students from a number of districts, state-funded regional metropolitan collaborative which have launched a number of very popular advanced magnet curricula. As the operation costs of many small districts propel consolidation, diversity can be promoted. In metropolitan Chattanooga, for example, consolidation has decreased school segregation even in the absence of a desegregation plan.[69]

Because the largest and most segregated minority group in US schools today is Latinos, and since it is still legal to use language in assigning students, there is no barrier to expanding dual-language magnet schools that are planned to be diverse and treat speakers of other languages as resources rather than deficits (see Gándara, chapter 11 in this volume).[70] These schools offer an important opportunity to mitigate the intense segregation that is developing for suburban Latino students in large metropolitan areas and create the kind of equal-status interaction that is optimal for positive outcomes.[71]

Taking Advantage of Gentrification.

Gentrification, the movement of White and middle-class non-White families into poorer neighborhoods in central cities, offers integrative possibilities that are usually ignored.[72] Washington, D.C., the first major US city to become predominantly African American, has been attracting more White residents for several decades, but this shift has had almost no impact on its public schools.[73] Gentrifying neighborhoods have housing stock and neighborhood design that make rehabilitations feasible and attractive. Often located near major employers, such as universities, hospitals, or government agencies, and possessing distinct cultural assets, these neighborhoods may benefit by investment from higher-income residents as well as commercial developers. But the local schools tend to remain virtually all non-White and poor, with very weak academic outcomes, and few middle-class families of any race stay in these neighborhoods after their children reach school age unless they can afford private schools. Schools, city governments, and non-profit organizations should collaborate to create viable diverse schools that offer a clear path to college and to implement scattered-site affordable housing to retain economic and racial diversity as gentrification proceeds.

To achieve that goal, what is required is either a new school or a coherent effort to attract and retain a critical mass of White and middle-class families with children to the existing school by upgrading its academic offerings, which assists the children already attending as well.[74] In central city systems overwhelmed with multiple problems, this proactive response is rarely a priority. It is happening on an ad hoc basis with the small schools movement, but instead of serving an economically diverse population, if there are no integration policies it may create what Jonathan Kozol calls "boutique" schools that serve the privileged.[75] Schools need a strategy to become attractive to newcomers but avoid selection processes that exclude most minority and low-income students. Parents should come to understand that education in diverse schools is not a zero-sum game in which minorities win and middle-class Whites suffer but an across-the-board gain in which minority students gain academically, White students are not harmed academically, and both develop valuable skills for living and working in a diverse society. Addressing gentrification creatively can increase educational opportunity for poor children and the social and political capital of urban public school systems.

State and National Roles.

Beyond local initiatives, some state and federal policies could make major differences. States could require all suburban communities to play a role in providing affordable housing, as has been done successfully in Massachusetts, Connecticut, and parts of California and Maryland. They could sponsor regional magnet schools, like Connecticut, and persuade or require school districts to permit transfers across district boundaries. States could make integration a priority for their mortgage subsidy funds, as was done in Ohio. State civil rights agencies could be more active in testing and enforcing fair housing laws and suspend the licenses of serious violators. They could change their interdistrict school transfer policies and charter laws in ways that would support rather than undermine integration and grant city residents who work in suburban locations the right to enroll their children in school there.

Changing mortgage finance is crucial. Since the Great Recession began almost all mortgages have been federally guaranteed, and there is a vast amount of foreclosed housing that could be used for poor families, so the government has huge potential leverage over housing segregation. Local and federal officials should watch these patterns and severely prosecute mortgage discrimination, which has had especially harmful impacts on Black and Latino families and neighborhoods. Once a community becomes known as stably integrated instead of resegregating or resegregated, it becomes desirable to all racial and ethnic groups, and home buyers will receive good financing.[76]

The driving forces that propelled change during the civil rights era—clear and consistent policies from the courts, Congress, and federal agencies mandating prompt and complete desegregation and providing support for designing and implementing successful plans[77]—have been halted and reversed during the past several decades. Yet, since some progress has been made on residential segregation in spite of the lack of enforcement, largely because of the large outward migration of middle-class minorities; much of that change may turn out to be transitional rather than enduring unless there are effective integration policies, however. Attitudes are changing, the communities are more multiracial, and targeted strategies could do much more.

Judicial policies today are vastly weaker than those that existed four decades ago, but some measures whose effectiveness have been proven could still be undertaken. For example, the federal government could provide funds to help racially changing communities and school districts make positive plans and create appropriate staff training strategies. Today, many school districts strongly desire funds to increase the number of magnet schools. Most importantly, they actively pursue special funding to close racial and socioeconomic achievement gaps, which is now mandated by federal law and is something that is far more difficult to do in segregated schools. In addition to pushing teacher training institutions to ensure that their graduates demonstrate competency on teacher tests, the federal government could press them to ensure that their future teachers more closely resemble the profile of students in their state. It could offer funding for communities eager to create dual-language immersion schools, which take a positive approach to successfully incorporating the vast increase of Latino and Asian EL students in many parts of formerly all-white suburbia.

The US Departments of Justice, Housing and Urban Development, and Education should coordinate the active enforcement of civil rights law and offer legal guidance and technical assistance to communities undergoing demographic change.

The Justice and Education Departments took a first step in December 2011 with the issuance of policy guidance supporting positive school integration initiatives.[78]

Although the federal government is the major source of funding for large-scale educational research, it has not commissioned any serious work on these issues in more than thirty years.[79] The Obama administration's research agenda is about the internal workings of schools, not the outside forces that powerfully shape the schools. Very little basic research has been done on multiracial schools. These issues have remained marginal in the Obama administration's Race to the Top and its Blueprint for education policy, although the widespread interest in its small grant program in 2009 for supporting integrated districts demonstrates that school districts are eager for help. The more fundamental goal should be the crafting of civil rights policies for schools and housing, coupled with initiatives that support stable integrated communities. These measures could substantially expand educational opportunity, prepare members of all groups for a successful multiracial future, and improve the economic and social health of local communities and metropolitan regions.

Finally, any serious effort to address racial and economic segregation in housing and schools will eventually require the reversal of the extremely adverse changes in law based on decisions by the Supreme Court, which has for more than two decades been systematically dismantling race-conscious strategies for dealing with metropolitan inequality. Policies that appear on their face to favor the status quo actually facilitate spreading segregation and undermine the change for successful stable communities. The current 5–4 majority's constitutional doctrines do not reflect the realities of contemporary communities or enable us to address the fundamental challenges of racial transformation and inequality we face. The United States is again becoming a very stratified and segregated country, but it will soon have a nonwhite majority whose children will be largely excluded from essential educational opportunities because of where they live. Rights to equal housing and education, which have been denied by a single vote on the current Supreme Court, must again be fought for and won.

5

Why Children from Lower Socioeconomic Classes, on Average, Have Lower Academic Achievement Than Middle-Class Children

Richard Rothstein

TO MUCH OF the public, it seems self-evident that public schools must be "failing" if they produce large gaps in academic achievement between middle-class White and low-income minority youth. Why, many observers reasonably ask, should the color of a child's skin or how much money his or her family earns affect whether he or she can absorb the instruction of an effective teacher? Many low-income children have been successful in school despite their family hardships. If these children can succeed, all should be able to do so.

'This commonsense attitude suffers from a lack of sophistication about the academic and behavioral differences that are typically produced by social and economic differences. Of course, low-income or minority status do not themselves produce low achievement, but the concrete expressions of these characteristics create impediments to learning that result in average differences in achievement by social class. Some low-income children will always achieve at higher levels than typical middle-class children, and some middle-class children will always achieve at lower levels than typical low-income children. Every human characteristic has a wide distribution. Notwithstanding these distributions, every human characteristic also has a central tendency, or average. It will also always be the case that, on average, lower-class children will achieve at lower levels than children from higher social classes. This is true in every industrialized country. On international tests, every country has an achievement gap comparable to that in the United States.[1]

This chapter describes how social class characteristics operate to produce differences in achievement. It shows why when lower social class characteristics are highly concentrated in particular neighborhoods, achievement is depressed even further. It notes that better schools can elicit higher achievement from disadvantaged children than worse schools, but no matter how good school quality may be, the achievement gap will remain. The chapter recounts the accusation that mere discussion by educators of the relationship between social class and achievement amounts to "making excuses," and responds that failure to acknowledge problems is a certain way to perpetuate them. And the chapter describes some practical programs—such as high-quality early childhood care and education, health clinics in schools, high-quality after-school and summer programs, and policies to promote residential integration by race and class—that could help narrow the achievement gap. Each of these is politically difficult; none is out of reach.

SOCIOECONOMIC DISADVANTAGE DEPRESSES ACADEMIC ACHIEVEMENT

If two groups of children attend equally high-quality schools, the group with greater socioeconomic disadvantage will inevitably have lower average academic achievement than the more fortunate group.[2] Many social and economic manifestations of class have important implications for learning.

First, health matters. Children who can't see well can't read as well as those who can, and lower-class children, on average, have poorer vision than middle-class children.[3] Lower-income children have a higher incidence of lead poisoning,[4] poorer nutrition, and higher rates of iron-deficiency anemia,[5] which result in impaired cognitive ability. They have greater exposure to environmental toxins, air pollution, and smoke,[6] and therefore greater incidence of asthma.[7] Lower-class children have less adequate pediatric care,[8] resulting in more frequent absences from school.

The lack of affordable housing for low-income families is another social class characteristic that has a demonstrable effect on average achievement. Children whose families have difficulty finding adequate housing move frequently, and student mobility is an important cause of low achievement.[9] Teachers cannot work as effectively with children who are in their classrooms for a short time as with those who stay longer. Moreover, the learning of all children attending schools in low-income communities is undermined if their classrooms have high turnover rates because teachers must repeat content for the benefit of newcomers and classes are reconstituted when the influx or departure of students makes classes too large or too small. In such unstable circumstances, even the most skilled teachers cannot ascertain the individual strengths and weaknesses of their students and adapt instruction accordingly.

Poor children, on average, come from families where parents have less education than parents in middle-class families. In consequence, poor children are not read to aloud or exposed to complex language and large vocabularies as often as middle-class children.[10] Their parents have low-wage jobs and are more frequently laid off, causing family stress and more-arbitrary discipline, and when parents are out of work, adolescents are more likely to be delinquent, use drugs, lose faith in the future, and suffer from depression.[11] As children play and walk to school, they face neighborhoods in which crime and drugs are visible, and gainfully employed adults are scarce.[12] Impoverished children more often live in single-parent families and receive less adult attention than their more fortunate counterparts.

Parents of different social classes tend to have different styles of childrearing. They utilize different modes of discipline and communicate their expectations differently.[13] In reading a story to young children, more educated parents are more likely to ask children what they think will happen next or what they would have done in a situation like that in the story. Less educated parents are more likely to ask children to recall what just happened. These differences are not found universally, but they are common enough to influence the average experiences of children from different social classes. Childrearing styles arise from, among other factors, the disparate life experiences of people in the middle and lower classes. Upper-middle-class parents tend to hold jobs that involve collaboration with colleagues, are expected to solve problems, and strive to contribute to the success of the enterprise. They are more likely to instruct their children indirectly, asking their children to understand the reason behind an instruction. Lower-class parents, whose jobs often require them to perform routine tasks, follow instructions, and never question authority, are more likely to instruct their children in a more direct fashion, issuing orders without extensive explanation. Moreover, reading ability depends not only on learning the mechanics but also on having a broad range of experiences in which to situate written material. Children raised in lower-class families whose experiences are narrower are at a disadvantage. Travel, visits to museums and zoos, music or dance lessons, and participation in organized sports all enrich the context for reading, as well as nurturing ambition, cultural awareness, and self-confidence.[14] On average, children who are raised by college-educated parents have more inquisitive attitudes toward the material presented by their teachers than do children who are raised by working-class parents. As children move into higher grades, where critical thinking becomes more important than mere retention of facts or formulas, this difference becomes more serious.[15]

Each of these well-documented social class differences has a palpable though small effect on academic achievement, but the cumulative effect of these disadvantages explains much of the achievement gap.

CONCENTRATING DISADVANTAGE

The negative effects of lower social class status are exacerbated when large numbers of disadvantaged students are concentrated in particular schools. Remediation becomes the norm, and teachers have little time to challenge the exceptional students who can overcome the personal, family, and community hardships that typically interfere with learning.

Nationwide, the isolation of low-income Black and Latino students has been increasing.[16] Integrating these students into schools where more privileged students predominate is an essential prerequisite for narrowing achievement gaps and enhancing the opportunities of low-income Black and Latino students. Racial and socioeconomic integration of schools is a necessary complement to efforts to improve these students' early childhood experiences, health, housing, economic security, and informal learning opportunities. Poorly performing segregated schools cannot be "turned around" if their isolation is not addressed. In high-poverty environments, the problems students bring to school are so overwhelming that policy should never be premised on the assumption that they could be overcome by even the most skilled and dedicated faculty. While schools can make a difference in the lives of these children, they cannot erase the damage done by concentrated poverty.

An investigation of reform in Chicago elementary schools attempted to distinguish the characteristics of schools whose students made dramatic improvements from those of schools whose students stagnated. Schools that had well-developed and aligned curriculum, featured collaboration between teachers and principals, and made a concerted effort to involve parents and the community made substantially greater progress than schools without these characteristics. But the investigators, to their surprise, discovered that well-designed reform programs made little or no difference in schools serving neighborhoods of concentrated poverty, where nearly all students were residentially mobile, African American, and had low-income parents with relatively little formal education and a high likelihood of unemployment. These communities had high crime rates and inadequate community supports, such as health care and social service providers, and few adults exemplified the benefits of educational attainment. In communities of concentrated disadvantage, addressing these contextual factors was essential before school reform could take root. The investigators concluded, "Our findings about schooling in truly disadvantaged communities offer a sobering antidote to a heady political rhetoric arguing that all schools can be improved."[17]

Statistical and qualitative studies document the positive effects of school integration by socioeconomic status and race.[18] Opportunity gaps that segregation produces are indicated by a Texas study of fourth to seventh graders. A team of prominent economists found that, after controlling for a large number of background characteristics, Black student achievement in mathematics declined as the proportion of Black students in a school increased. They concluded that reducing this proportion would improve Black students' achievement, would have no significant harmful effects on White students, and could reduce the Black-White achievement gap by about 10 percent.[19] A literature review of many studies concerning the end of court-ordered desegregation after the 1970s concluded that the "the circumstantial case linking school segregation to the test score gap is compelling."[20] The test-score benefits found in most studies of the deconcentration of poverty and racial isolation are not large, however; rather, the most substantial gains came in rates of graduation, employment, financial self-sufficiency, and avoidance of teen childbearing and delinquency.[21] Econometric studies have compared outcomes that could be attributed to court-ordered school integration programs of the 1960s and 1970s relative to outcomes in the absence of integration orders. Court-ordered desegregation was associated with declining Black student dropout rates, without corresponding increases in White rates.[22] In districts subject to integration orders, Black youths' rate of homicide arrests was cut in half and their rate of homicide victimization also fell by a quarter.[23]

In urban neighborhoods of concentrated poverty, a high proportion of families is made up of female-headed households, lives below the federal poverty line, and receives benefits from the state; many are unemployed, and most are Black or Hispanic. A comparison of low-income Black children living in different types of neighborhoods reveals that those who live in areas of concentrated poverty are three times as likely to drop out of high school as otherwise similar students who live in low-poverty neighborhoods, and half again as likely to drop out as those in moderate-poverty neighborhoods. Living in poorer neighborhoods is a strong predictor of whether teenagers become pregnant and drop out of high school.[24] The risk of these adverse outcomes jumped when fewer than one in twenty employed adults in the neighborhood held professional or managerial jobs.[25] Children raised in neighborhoods of concentrated poverty have, on average, lower verbal ability than socioeconomically similar children raised elsewhere.[26]

Although almost all desegregation efforts since the 1960s have attempted to change student placement policies at the school level through busing, school choice, magnet schools, or modest shifts in attendance zones, two policy initiatives, 35 years apart, attempted to integrate neighborhoods, permitting the measurement of residential integration on student outcomes. Beginning in the late 1970s, under a court order to remedy purposeful racial segregation of public housing, Chicago officials issued Section 8 vouchers to African Americans living in public housing. The vouchers enabled the public housing residents to rent apartments in predominantly White suburbs. Called the Gautreaux program (named for the plaintiff in the original lawsuit), it was studied as a quasi-experiment because families were randomly assigned within the program: the next eligible family on the waiting list was offered the first private apartment that became available, whether it was located in a predominantly White suburb or in a segregated urban neighborhood. Adolescent children who moved to the suburbs fared better than those who stayed in the city, with lower high school dropout rates and greater likelihood of college attendance, especially at four-year colleges.[27]

Officials in Montgomery County, Maryland, recently sponsored a sophisticated experiment to test the effects of integration. The county purchased apartments in suburban Washington, DC, and designated them for families eligible for public housing. Families were randomly assigned to units in more- and less-affluent neighborhoods, permitting a scholar to follow the academic achievement of these families' children on standardized math and reading tests. Nearly three-quarters of the children were African American. Those who attended neighborhood schools in which fewer than 20 percent of the students came from low-income families significantly outperformed similar children who attended schools with greater proportions of low-income students. As the share of children from low-income families increased, the advantage diminished, disappearing when 35 percent or more of students came from low-income families. The benefits of integration alone were greater than the benefits of attending a school that was not integrated but that received substantial additional resources to compensate for children's poverty.[28]

Ethnographic studies of students who have participated in racial integration programs support the expectation that these students will benefit from working together and be better prepared for civic engagement. For example, retrospective interviews with adults who graduated from integrated high schools in 1980 found that Black students who had participated in court-ordered desegregation plans felt more comfortable and confident about their ability to compete in a predominantly White economy.[29]

SCHOOL IMPROVEMENT, TOO

The nexus between concentrated socioeconomic disadvantage and poor educational outcomes does not imply that schools make no difference, or that school improvement is fruitless in the absence of broader social and economic reforms. No matter how serious their problems, disadvantaged students do better in high-quality schools. And in any demographic group, there is a range of ability among individuals; some disadvantaged students outperform typical middle-class students, and some middle-class students fall behind typical disadvantaged students. The achievement gap is a difference in the average achievement of students from disadvantaged and middle-class families.

Because socioeconomic disadvantage is closely correlated with race, the legacy of racial inequality takes its toll as well. In some districts and schools, students are effectively tracked by race, denied the most qualified teachers and the most up-to-date facilities, curriculum, and materials. Failure is expected and accepted. Some educators use students' socioeconomic disadvantage as an excuse for failing to teach well under adverse conditions, whereas others work hard to develop disadvantaged students' talents. But even the most qualified and dedicated teachers cannot marshal the compensatory resources and efforts required when large numbers of disadvantaged students are concentrated in classrooms.

The National Assessment of Educational Progress (NAEP), administered to a national sample of students by the federal government, is generally considered the most reliable measure of US students' achievement. Since 1990, the achievement gap between minority and White students has barely changed, feeding accusations that educators ignore the needs of minority youth. Yet the average math scores of Black fourth graders in 2009 were higher than those of White fourth graders in 1990. If White achievement had been stagnant, the gap would have been closed. Black eighth graders also made substantial gains in math. The gap stagnated only because White students' scores also rose.[30] Reading scores for minority students improved, though not nearly as much as their mathematics scores. (Math achievement is more generally results from classroom instruction, while reading ability more heavily reflects students' home environments.) The dramatic gains in math suggest that efforts to improve instruction may have made a measurable difference for both minority and White students. They also make implausible the claim that most teachers of disadvantaged students have low expectations for these children's performance.

The policy conclusion to be drawn from these observations is that closing or substantially narrowing achievement gaps requires combining school improvement with reforms that narrow the vast socioeconomic inequalities in the United States. Without such a combination, demands such as those made by the No Child Left Behind Act that schools eliminate achievement gaps will not only remain unfulfilled but also cause us to condemn our schools and teachers unfairly.

DISTORTING DISADVANTAGE

Most educators understand that socioeconomic disadvantage lowers average academic achievement. Some policy makers and educators who call themselves "school reformers" resist this logic and throw up a variety of defenses. Some illogically conclude that calling attention to how socioeconomic disadvantage affects achievement is no different from charging that disadvantaged children have a genetic disability, that poor and minority children can't learn.[31] They contend that highlighting the socioeconomic causes of low achievement "blames the victim" and legitimizes racism.[32] Others regard an analysis of the socioeconomic causes of lower achievement dangerous because it "makes excuses" for poor instruction or because demands for social and economic reform "let schools off the hook."[33] Still others say it's simply too difficult to address nonschool problems such as inadequate incomes, health, or housing. The way some school reformers see it, those who call attention to socioeconomic causes want to wait until utopian economic change (or "socialism") becomes a reality before we begin to improve schools.[34]

In reality, many practical reforms could demonstrably improve disadvantaged children's readiness to learn. By insisting that any discussion of social and economic reform is tantamount to postponing school improvement until our economic system is totally transformed, these school reformers make it impossible to weigh the relative effectiveness of practical socioeconomic versus instructional improvements for raising the achievement of disadvantaged children.

The argument of these self-described reformers is at its most incoherent when they themselves insist on the necessity of interventions that might bring disadvantaged children to school more ready to learn, yet simultaneously advocate tough school and teacher accountability systems that take no account of whether those interventions have been attempted. In a 2011 interview, for example, the US secretary of education Arne Duncan recounted his earlier efforts as superintendent of the Chicago Public Schools:

> If children can't see the blackboard, they're going to have a hard time learning so we have to get them eyeglasses. We used to get literally tens of thousands of kids eyeglasses every year. If children aren't fed and are hungry, they're going to have a hard time concentrating, so we fed tens of thousands of kids three meals a day. We had a couple of thousand kids we were particularly worried about so very quietly we would send them home Friday afternoons with a backpack full of food because we worried about them not eating over the weekend.[35]

Yet Duncan proposed a "blueprint" for re-authorizing the Elementary and Secondary Education Act that would hold schools accountable for getting all children "college and career ready" by 2020, whether they can see the blackboard, come to school hungry every day, or eat over the weekend. He designed and implemented the competitive grant program Race to the Top in which states earned points for expanding the charter school sector, developing data systems to tie teacher performance to student test scores, and making other educational changes. But no points were awarded for providing eyeglasses or food, or for implementing any of the multitude of practical programs that might actually improve disadvantaged youths' school readiness and thus their chances of college or career success.[36]

SEEING THROUGH "NO EXCUSES"

The commonplace "no excuses" attack on discussion of the socioeconomic causes of low achievement implies that if educators were to realize that their efforts alone are insufficient to raise student achievement, they would simply give up. Those who make this argument implicitly presume that policymakers like themselves, with Olympian perspectives, can trick teachers into performing at a higher level by making them believe that unrealistically high levels of success are within reach.

This suppression of awareness of how socioeconomic disadvantage lowers student achievement is morally, politically, and intellectually bankrupt. Our first obligation should be to analyze social problems accurately; only then can we design effective solutions. Presenting a deliberately flawed version of reality because of fear that the truth will lead to reduced effort is corrupt and self-defeating. Teachers see for themselves how poor health or family economic stress impede students' learning. Too many educators today have been intimidated and refrain from acknowledging these realities aloud and, in groupthink obedience, repeat the mantra that "all children can learn." But nobody is fooled. Conscientious teachers know that some children's learning is impeded by poor health, poorly educated parents and caregivers, and insecure homes. Suppressing these truths leads only to cynicism and disillusionment. Anecdotal evidence now abounds that too many talented teachers are abandoning the profession, willing to shoulder responsibility for their own instructional competence but not for failures that are beyond their control.

Mythology also prevents educators from properly diagnosing educational failure where it exists. If we expect all disadvantaged students to succeed at levels typical of affluent students, then even the best inner-city teachers look like failures. If we pretend that achievement gaps are entirely within teachers' control, how can we distinguish better from worse classroom practices?

Promoters of the notion that schools can overcome social and economic causes of low achievement assert that claims to the contrary let schools "off the hook." But this myth lets public officials and corporate leaders "off the hook," absolving them from responsibility for narrowing the inequalities that pervade American society. Instead, they should be held accountable for health-care gaps, racial segregation, inadequate housing, and income inequality and insecurity.

Some critics urge that educators' responsibility, authority, and power extends only to classroom practices, so remedying socioeconomic and racial injustice is not their business.[37] According to this reasoning, we should leave the challenge of worrying about inequality to health, housing, and labor experts. Yet we are all citizens in this democracy, and educators have special insight into the damage that deprivation does to children's potential. If educators who face this unfortunate state of affairs daily don't speak up about it, who will? Educators and their professional organizations should publicly insist that social and economic reforms are needed to create an environment in which the most effective teaching can take place. Instead, however, critical voices have been silenced, told they should stick to their knitting, fearing an accusation that denouncing inequality is tantamount to "making excuses."

WHAT WE CAN DO

Modest social and economic reforms that are well within our political reach could have palpable effects on student achievement. For example, we could ensure good pediatric, optometric, and dental care for all students in school-based clinics. We could expand existing housing subsidy programs to reduce low-income families' involuntary mobility. We could provide higher-quality early childhood care so that children are not parked before televisions while their parents are at work. We could increase the earned income tax credit, the minimum wage, and collective bargaining rights so that families of low-wage workers are less financially and emotionally stressed. We could promote the construction of mixed-income housing developments in the suburbs and gentrifying cities to give more low-income students the benefits of attending integrated neighborhood schools. We could fund after-school programs so that inner-city children spend less time in dangerous environments and, instead, develop their cultural, artistic, organizational, and athletic potential.

None of these reforms is utopian. All would send more children to school ready to learn. A broad group of experts and advocates, including both Democrats and Republicans, social scientists and religious leaders, has banded together in a campaign called the "Broader, Bolder Approach to Education" to advocate many of these programs in a package of socioeconomic as well as school interventions.[38] Educators who are unafraid to advocate a balanced set of policies could call the hand of politicians and business leaders who claim that full-service school clinics and full funding of housing voucher programs are too expensive, but at the same time demand school reform so they can posture as the protectors of minority children.

Beyond policies that narrow inequality among families, there is also much that can be done to deconcentrate disadvantage in schools and communities. Massachusetts operates a voluntary integration plan in which predominantly White Boston suburbs receive state subsidies to fill excess school capacity with students voluntarily bused from inner-city neighborhoods; most are African American or Hispanic, and most come from low-income families. Interviews with graduates of the program found that most were prepared to succeed: they had higher rates of college enrollment, better jobs, and higher incomes in adulthood than they could have expected by staying in racially isolated neighborhood schools.[39] Unfortunately, suburban school districts generally offer many fewer places than are needed to accommodate the urban students who apply.

Some school districts have implemented voluntary racial integration programs, usually involving parental choice combined with some race-conscious limitations. However, the US Supreme Court's 2007 decision in *Parents Involved in Community Schools v. Seattle School District* (551 U.S. 701) found that such plans in Louisville and Seattle included an unconstitutional use of race, so the future of these voluntary integration plans is unsettled. Alternatively, some districts are attempting to address concentrated poverty, which implicitly addresses racial segregation. These policies identify students for school assignment by their family incomes or the socioeconomic characteristics of their neighborhoods.[40] For several years, a mandatory busing program in Wake County, North Carolina, which includes Raleigh and Durham, was promoted as the nation's best example of successful socioeconomic integration. In 2010, however, voters effectively repealed the program, returning low-income students to more economically homogenous and racially isolated schools in their home neighborhoods.[41] Subsequently, voters again reversed themselves and replaced the school board's anti-integration majority;[42] at the time of this writing, it remains to be seen what the new pupil assignment policy will be.

The harmful educational effects of concentrated poverty are likely to continue unabated without explicit policies to integrate schools both racially and socioeconomically. While school improvement can partially mitigate the effects of poverty and should be pursued in earnest, a parallel effort focused on both school and neighborhood integration is also necessary. Busing is neither politically feasible nor practical, since the most severely disadvantaged children live far from White, middle-class communities. Effective school integration policy requires increasing the residential proximity of racially and socioeconomically diverse families.[43] The limited exposure today of low-income Black and Hispanic children to middle-class White children is not solely the result of the differential in assets between the White middle-class and low-income minority families. Despite open housing laws, racial discrimination by realtors and mortgage lenders persists.[44] Some suburbs maintain exclusionary zoning rules that require large houses and lots or prohibit development of multifamily structures. Repealing such zoning ordinances would open up these exclusive islands of privilege to low-income families. Federal and state governments could create incentives for metropolitan areas to adopt inclusionary zoning rules that require developers to include affordable units in new private housing projects. This policy must be regional because when individual jurisdictions, especially cities, adopt such ordinances separately, they can simply prompt a shift in development to parts of their metropolitan areas where housing can be built without restrictions regarding affordability. Another positive approach should be expansion of the Section 8 program, which provides vouchers to low-income families that make up the difference between one-third of family income and market rents. The program is currently underfunded, and landlords are not required to participate, making a mockery of the Fair Housing Act's antidiscrimination provisions.

RETICENCE ABOUT RACE

It is puzzling that some critics regard as implicitly racist explanations of why disadvantaged students (who are disproportionately Black) typically achieve at lower levels. Yet, socioeconomic explanations do not blame children and their parents for their lower scores. Instead, they support policies that enhance low-income students' capacity to learn. For example, by reducing the epidemic incidence of asthma in inner-city minority communities—such as, by enforcing prohibitions on the use of high-sulfur heating oil and requiring urban buses to substitute natural gas for diesel fuel—and by providing treatment for its symptoms in school-based clinics, public-health policy can ensure that children suffering from or susceptible to asthma are more likely to attend school regularly and to be more rested when in attendance. Denying the impact of poor health on learning leads critics to blame teachers for circumstances completely beyond their control.

That the conditions responsible for disadvantage disproportionately afflict Black children reflects the history of racial inequality in the United States. Calling attention to these conditions is not racist. But ignoring them and insisting that they have no effect if teaching is competent may well be.

Some self-styled school reformers characterize analyses of social and economic obstacles to learning as being no different from claims that the "culture" of disadvantaged children explains their low achievement. Looking specifically at Black and White students in the United States, there is, indeed, an apparent racial gap in test scores even when poor students are compared with one another or middle-class students are compared with one another. But these deceptively large gaps stem not mostly from culture but from overly broad definitions of poor and middle-class status. Typically, because analysts employ a single cutoff (most often, eligibility for free or subsidized lunches), low-income White students are compared with Blacks who are much poorer, while middle-class Black students are compared with Whites who are much more affluent. Besides current-year income, many other socioeconomic characteristics, with different distributions by race, contribute to social class differences, but are not included in commonplace analyses. Black families have, on average, lower net worth than White families of similar income levels. A typical low-income Black family resides in a neighborhood where average incomes are much lower than average incomes in a neighborhood where a typical low-income White family resides. Low-income Hispanics are more isolated than low-income Whites, but not as isolated as low-income Blacks.[45] If we restricted comparisons to students who were socioeconomically similar on more sophisticated measures of social class, much of the residual racial test-score gap would disappear.[46]

But a gap would probably remain. Many responsible advocates for disadvantaged children have sought to offer assistance, advice, and programs designed to improve the household and neighborhood conditions for low-income Black children. These interventions sometimes focus on educational resources and practices within the home, as well as on other childrearing practices, and sometimes focus as well on raising the status of academic success and reducing the influence of gang role models.[47] While these factors likely constitute only a small contribution to achievement gaps, they should be discussed openly among policy makers and others seeking to improve children's readiness to learn. When a disadvantaged population is isolated in high-poverty, high-crime areas with few employment opportunities and little or no interaction with those living and working outside, it is inevitable that characteristics will develop that present obstacles to success in the mainstream society and economy. Oppositional behaviors and subcultural dialects, for example, can be obstacles to entry into middle-class occupations.[48] The solution should not be a defensive refusal to acknowledge these problems, but reforms that break down the barriers of segregation so all Black children have full opportunities to develop the social and cultural capital necessary for success.

DANCING AROUND THE ISSUE

What about claims that some schools with disadvantaged students have higher achievement, allegedly proving that schools alone can close achievement gaps? Certainly, some schools are superior and should be imitated. But no schools serving disadvantaged students have demonstrated consistent and sustained improvement that closes—not just narrows—achievement gaps. Claims to the contrary are often fraudulent, sometimes based on schools where parents are unusually well educated, whose admissions policies filter out learning-disabled students or those whose family supports are weaker, or where students, although eligible for subsidized lunches, come from stable working-class rather than poor communities.[49]

Some claims are based on schools that concentrate on teaching to the tests rather than on critical thinking, social studies, the arts, science, physical education, and citizenship skills. Increasingly, these claims are based on high proportions of students scoring above state proficiency standards that are themselves defined at a low level. Such tactics reduce apparent achievement gaps without addressing real inequalities. However, responsible analysts define closing the achievement gap as achieving similar score distributions and average scale scores among subgroups. Even No Child Left Behind proclaims the widely ignored goal of proficiency at "challenging" levels for each subgroup.

Frequently, claims that some schools achieve spectacular success with disadvantaged Black students are based on accounts of charter schools. These claims are usually not well founded, based only on minimally "proficient" levels on standardized tests. They are also flawed because charter schools are typically selective in ways that make comparisons with regular schools serving disadvantaged children inappropriate.[50] Although some charter schools enroll children with disabilities, the disabilities are not as severe as those seen in neighborhood schools. While admission to overenrolled charter schools is usually based on a lottery, the pool comprises only children whose parents are sufficiently motivated to apply, frequently because neighborhood school teachers who spot children's unusual potential urge these parents to do so. Typically, "high-performing" charter schools do not hesitate to expel or push out students who do not perform to the schools' behavioral or academic standards.[51] It would be surprising if such schools did not have higher average test scores than regular public schools that serve entire neighborhood populations indiscriminately.

BEYOND EITHER/OR

No educator or policy maker should be forced to choose between advocating for better schools or speaking out for greater social and economic equality. Both are essential. Each depends on the other. Educators cannot be effective if they make excuses for poor student performance. But they will have little chance for success unless they also join with advocates of social and economic reform to improve the conditions from which children come to school.

PART II

Overcoming the Obstacles We Create for Schools

There is no evidence that the added resources [devoted to education in the United States over the 20th century] have improved student performance....

Eric Hanushek, expert for the defense in *Williams v. California*[1]

[My ideal school] would be a classroom with enough tables, enough chairs, enough books, enough materials and a teacher who cares, not just someone who got a GED or whatever.... Enough supplies, enough security, and just enough everything.... You know, just because we're smaller, we are still human beings.

A high school student testifying for the plaintiffs in *Williams v. California*

6

Inequality and School Resources

WHAT IT WILL TAKE TO CLOSE THE OPPORTUNITY GAP

Linda Darling-Hammond

ENORMOUS ENERGY IS devoted in the United States to discussions of the achievement gap.[2] Much less attention, however, is paid to the opportunity gap, the cumulative differences in access to key educational resources that support learning at home and at school: expert teachers, personalized attention, high-quality curriculum opportunities, good educational materials, and plentiful information resources. Systemic inequalities in all of these resources, compounded over generations, have created what Gloria Ladson-Billings has called an "educational debt" owed to those who have been denied access to quality education for hundreds of years (see also Ladson-Billings, Chapter Two of this volume).[3]

Institutionally sanctioned discrimination in access to education is as old as the United States itself. From the time that southern states made it illegal to teach an enslaved person to read, through Emancipation and Jim Crow, and well into the twentieth century, African Americans faced de facto and de jure exclusion from public schools, as did Native Americans and, frequently, Mexican Americans.[4] Even in the North, problems of exclusion, segregation, and lack of resources were severe. In 1857, for example, a group of African American leaders protested to a New York State investigating committee that the New York City board of education spent sixteen dollars per White child and only one cent per Black child for school buildings. While Black students occupied schools described as "dark and cheerless" in neighborhoods "full of vice and filth," White students were taught in "splendid, almost palatial edifices, with manifold comforts, conveniences, and elegancies."[5]

The *Williams v. California* case, a class action lawsuit filed in 2000 on behalf of California's low-income students of color, demonstrated that wide disparities still exist almost 150 years later. The plaintiffs' complaint included many descriptions of schools like this middle school in San Francisco:

At Luther Burbank, students cannot take textbooks home for homework in any core subject because their teachers have enough textbooks for use in class only.... For homework, students must take home photocopied pages, with no accompanying text for guidance or reference, when and if their teachers have enough paper to use to make homework copies.... Luther Burbank is infested with vermin and roaches, and students routinely see mice in their classrooms. One dead rodent has remained, decomposing, in a corner in the gymnasium since the beginning of the school year. The school library is rarely open, has no librarian, and has not recently been updated. The latest version of the encyclopedia in the library was published in approximately 1988. Luther Burbank classrooms do not have computers. Computer instruction and research skills are not, therefore, part of Luther Burbank students' regular instruction. The school no longer offers any art classes for budgetary reasons.... Two of the three bathrooms at Luther Burbank are locked all day, every day.... Students have urinated or defecated on themselves at school because they could not get into an unlocked bathroom.... When the bathrooms are not locked, they often lack toilet paper, soap, and paper towels, and the toilets frequently are clogged and overflowing.... Ceiling tiles are missing and cracked in the school gym, and school children are afraid to play games in the gym because they worry that more ceiling tiles will fall on them during their games.... The school has no air conditioning. On hot days classroom temperatures climb into the 90s. The school heating system does not work well. In winter, children often wear coats, hats, and gloves during class to keep warm.... Eleven of the 35 teachers at Luther Burbank have not yet obtained regular, nonemergency teaching credentials, and 17 of the 35 teachers only began teaching at Luther Burbank this school year.[6]

These inequities are in part a function of how public education in the United States is funded. In most states, education costs are supported primarily by local property taxes, along with state grants-in-aid that are somewhat equalizing but typically insufficient to close the gaps caused by differences in local property values. Rich districts can spend more even when poorer districts tax themselves at proportionally higher rates. In most states there is at least a three-to-one ratio between per pupil spending in the richest and poorest districts.[7]

Disparities also exist among states, with per pupil expenditures in 2008 ranging from nearly $18,000 in Vermont to just over $6,000 in Utah.[8] The federal government has no policies that compensate adequately for these disparities. In fact, the largest federal education program, Title I of the Elementary and Secondary Education Act, which is intended to redress the effects of poverty on children's learning, allocates funds in part based on levels of state per pupil spending, reinforcing rather than ameliorating these wealth-based inequalities.[9]

Funding disparities might not undermine equal educational opportunity if the differentials were due to pupils' needs (such as special education, acquisition of English, or other learning requirements), or if they reflected differences in the cost of living. But differentials do not tend to favor the districts serving the highest-need students, and they persist after differences in the cost of living and pupil needs are taken into account. In California, for example, high-poverty districts spent, on average, $259 less per pupil than low-poverty districts, and high-minority districts spent $499 less than low-minority districts. In higher-spending New York, these differentials were even greater: $2,927 and $2,636, respectively.[10]

EXPLAINING INEQUALITY

Many great schools in this country offer students opportunities to learn in empowering and engaging ways, and more of them are open to a wider range of children than was once the case. The fact that de jure segregation is no longer legal and that some students of color can now attend good schools leads many Americans to assume that inequality has been eliminated from public education. Yet, precisely because de facto segregation currently cordons off poor communities of color from the rest of society, most policy makers, reporters, editorial writers, and concerned citizens don't know how the "other half" experiences school. As Gary Orfield describes in chapter 4 of this volume, school segregation remains pervasive throughout the United States. The assumption that equal educational opportunity now exists reinforces beliefs that the causes of continued low levels of achievement on the part of students of color must be intrinsic to them, their families, or their communities. Educational outcomes for students of color are, however, at least as much a function of their unequal access to key educational resources, both inside and outside of school, as they are a function of race, class, or culture.[11]

Four major resource-linked factors associated account for unequal and inadequate educational outcomes in the United States:

- The high level of childhood poverty coupled with the low level of social supports for low-income children's health and welfare, including their early learning opportunities
- The unequal allocation of school resources, which is made politically easier by the increasing resegregation of schools
- Inadequate systems for providing high-quality teachers and teaching to all children in all communities
- Rationing of high-quality curriculum through tracking and interschool disparities.

Together, as I describe in this chapter, all these factors generate opportunity-to-learn barriers that can sabotage success.

Poverty and Social Supports

The United States not only has the highest poverty rates for children among industrialized nations but also provides fewer social supports for their well-being and fewer resources for their education.[12] Today, about one out of four US children lives in poverty, more than twice the rate of most European nations. Child poverty in America has risen since the early 1970s, when the War on Poverty improved the lives of many children.[13] This country has a much weaker safety net for children than other industrialized countries have, where universal health care, housing subsidies, and high-quality child care are the norm. In other developed countries, schools can focus primarily on providing education, rather than also having to provide breakfasts and lunches, help families find housing and health care, or deal with constant mobility due to factors such as evictions. US schools must also often address the effects of untreated physical and mental illness and the large gaps in children's readiness that exist when they enter school.

The devastating effects of these conditions were brought home poignantly in a recent Congressional briefing by John Deasy, then superintendent of the Prince Georges County Public Schools, an urban district bordering on Washington, DC, who described a nine-year-old child in his district, living within sight of the Capitol building, who had recently died of sepsis from an infected cavity that had gone untreated because the child lacked dental insurance.[14] Disparate access to health care, including maternal prenatal care, contributes to a child mortality rate that is far higher in the United States than in any other wealthy country.[15]

Another contributing factor is unequal access to learning opportunities before children enter school. Many children do not have the kinds of experiences at home or in a preschool that allow them to develop the communication and interaction skills, motor skills, social-emotional skills, and cognitive skills that are required for them to be independent learners when they start school, which undermines their academic success in both the short and the longer run (see Barnett and Lamy, chapter 7, and Rothstein, chapter 5, in this volume).

Nobel prize-winning economist James Heckman points out that "compared to 50 years ago, a greater fraction of American children is being born into disadvantaged families where investments in children are smaller than in advantaged families."[16] The inadequacy of early education and health care negatively affects school success and adult outcomes. Yet, he argues, there is convincing evidence that if interventions occur early enough, they can significantly improve children's health, welfare, and learning.

Although prekindergarten enrollment has been growing recently, low-income children continue to participate in early education at much lower rates than children from higher-income families. In 2000, although 65 percent of children ages three to five whose parents earned $50,000 or more were enrolled in prekindergarten, only 44 percent of children the same ages with family incomes below $15,000 were enrolled. Publicly funded programs, which are the primary source of child care for low-income families, can serve only a minority of those who are entitled to participate.[17] By contrast, in most European countries, publicly supported child care and early education are widely available. In high-achieving Finland, for example, all children have the right to government-subsidized day care until they go to school at the age of seven, and 75 percent are enrolled. Parents also receive subsidies to stay home with their children if they so choose. In addition, over 96 percent of children attend tuition-free preschool at the age of six.[18] These kinds of policies eliminate the achievement gap that otherwise is created before school even begins.

Resegregation and Unequal Schooling

Beyond the large and growing inequalities that exist among families, profound inequalities in resource allocations to schools have been reinforced by increasing resegregation. Although desegregation has enabled many students of color to attend schools they could never before have accessed, many others have been left behind. Progress was made steadily only for about a decade after the passage of the 1964 Civil Rights Act. Segregation began to increase again in the 1980s, when desegregation policies were largely abandoned by the federal government, and courts were asked to end judicial oversight of desegregating districts.[19]

By 2000, 72 percent of the nation's Black students attended predominantly minority schools, up significantly from the low point of 63 percent in 1980. More than one-third of African American and Latino students (37 and 38 percent, respectively) attended schools with a minority enrollment of 90 percent to 100 percent.[20] At the turn of the twenty-first century, the level of segregation in US schools stood almost exactly where it had been 30 years earlier, as the ground gained during the 1970s was lost in a giant ideological tug-of-war.

The situation threatens to become worse as a result of the US Supreme Court's 2007 decision in conjoined cases brought by parents from Jefferson County, Kentucky, and Seattle, Washington. Both districts had placed race-based constraints on their school choice plans, as a way to avoid additional segregation. The court ruled that local school authorities could no longer routinely use individuals' race as a basis for decision making in school assignments.[21] More than 550 scholars signed a social science amicus brief offered by the Civil Rights Project at Harvard, and an additional amicus brief was filed on behalf of the American Educational Research Association (AERA). This case marked the fifth time that social scientists have filed a brief since a few dozen signed a statement about the harms done by segregated schools in connection with the court's consideration of *Brown v. Board of Education* 60 years ago.[22]

The AERA and Civil Rights Project briefs summarized an extensive body of research showing the educational and community benefits of integrated schools for both White and minority students, documenting the persisting inequalities of segregated minority schools, and examining evidence that schools will resegregate in the absence of race-conscious policies. The Civil Rights Project's statement concluded that

> more often than not, segregated minority schools offer profoundly unequal educational opportunities. This inequality is manifested in many ways, including fewer qualified, experienced teachers, greater instability caused by rapid turnover of faculty, fewer educational resources, and limited exposure to peers who can positively influence academic learning. No doubt as a result of these disparities, measures of educational outcomes, such as scores on standardized achievement tests and high school graduation rates, are lower in schools with high percentages of nonwhite students.[23]

Part of the problem is that segregated minority schools are almost always schools with high concentrations of poverty.[24] A number of studies have found that concentrated poverty has an independent influence on student achievement beyond the individual student's own socioeconomic status, confirming the 1966 Coleman Report finding that "the social composition of [a school's] student body is more highly related to student achievement, independent of the student's own social background, than is any school factor."[25]

The phrase "concentrated poverty" is shorthand for a constellation of mutually reinforcing socioeconomic inequalities that affect schooling. These schools typically have less qualified and less experienced teachers and fewer learning resources, lower levels of peer group support and competition, more limited curricula taught at less challenging levels, more serious health and safety problems, much more student and family mobility, and many other factors that seriously affect academic achievement.[26]

High levels of segregation produce linguistic isolation in schools with many native Spanish speakers and few fluent native speakers of English. The lack of opportunity for ongoing conversation with native English speakers impedes students' acquisition of academic English required for success in high school and college.[27] Furthermore, economic segregation reinforces disparities in educational quality. The social capital and clout brought by higher-income parents typically result in higher levels of services from the central administration and greater accountability for performance from schools.

Deepening segregation is closely tied to dwindling resources. Black and Hispanic students are increasingly concentrated in central city public schools, many of which have become majority minority over the past decade while their funding has fallen further behind that of their suburbs (see Orfield, chapter 4 of this volume). In 2005, students of color made up 71 percent of those served by the 100 largest school districts in the country.[28] By the late 1990s, in cities across the nation, a group of schools had emerged that might be characterized as "apartheid schools," serving exclusively students of color in low-income communities. Whether in Compton, California, or Chicago, Illinois, these schools have crumbling, overcrowded buildings, poor libraries and few materials, old and dilapidated texts so scarce that students must share them in class and cannot take them home for homework, and a revolving-door teaching force with little professional expertise.

These conditions arose as taxpayer revolts pulled the bottom out from under state education funding, and the distribution of funds became more unequal.[29] The extent to which many urban and some rural schools serving high proportions of low-income students of color could be abandoned without major outcry was in part a function of their intense segregation. Indeed, this public indifference to deprivation was one of the reasons civil rights advocates sought desegregation in the first place. Their long struggle to end segregation was not motivated purely by a desire to have minority children sit next to White children. Instead, there was strong evidence that the "equal" part of the "separate but equal" principle enunciated by the Supreme Court in its 1896 *Plessy v. Ferguson* decision had never been honored and that predominantly White schools offered better opportunities on many levels—more resources, higher rates of graduation and college attendance, more demanding courses, and better facilities and equipment.

Furthermore, there was a belief that these schools, once integrated, would continue to be advantaged by the greater public commitment occasioned by the more affluent people they serve. This belief seems borne out by the rapid deterioration of resegregated schools in cities that were turning black and brown during the 1980s and 1990s, where the conditions of severe resource impoverishment came to resemble those in underdeveloped nations.[30]

The differences in resources that typically exist between city and suburban schools can strongly influence school outcomes. For example, an experimental study of African American high school youth randomly placed in public housing in the Chicago suburbs rather than in the city found that, compared to their urban peers who started with equivalent income and academic attainment, the students who attended better-funded, largely White suburban schools with higher quality teachers and curriculum had better educational outcomes. They were substantially more likely to have the opportunity to take challenging courses, receive additional academic help, graduate on time, attend college, and secure good jobs.[31]

Finally, not only do urban districts receive fewer resources than their suburban neighbors, but schools with high concentrations of low-income and minority students typically receive fewer resources than other schools within these districts.[32] This disparity occurs for at least two reasons: upper-income parents lobby more effectively for academic programs, computers, libraries, and other supports and tolerate less neglect when it comes to building maintenance and physical amenities. Also, more-affluent schools generally secure more experienced and better educated teachers as schools with better conditions can attract a wider array of applicants.

A recent study of five urban districts found that the disparities in funding between schools in the highest poverty quartile and those in the lowest poverty quartile ranged from 10 percent to 23 percent of a poorer school's budget.[33] A study of the 50 largest California districts found that their high-poverty schools spent an average of $2,576 per teacher less on salaries than low-poverty schools within the same district.[34] This disparity results from the fact that high-poverty schools hire teachers who are less experienced and less well educated.

Unequal Access to Qualified Teachers

More important than the contrasts between up-to-date and dilapidated buildings or even between overflowing libraries and empty shelves are the differences in the teachers children encounter. In the United States, teachers are the most inequitably distributed school resource (see the discussion in Berry, chapter 13 in this volume). As discussed below, this inequity is strongly linked to resources;

financially struggling schools have a very difficult time hiring and retaining experienced, well-trained teachers.

Although federal policies such as service scholarships ended the shortage of teachers by the late 1970s, the cancellation of these policies in the 1980s led to increasing numbers of underqualified teachers being hired in many cities when teacher demand began to increase while resources were declining. In 1990, for example, the Los Angeles Unified School District settled a lawsuit brought by students in predominantly minority schools because their schools were not only more crowded and less well funded than other schools but also disproportionately staffed by inexperienced and unprepared teachers hired on emergency credentials.[35] The practice of lowering or waiving credentialing standards to fill classrooms in high-minority, low-income schools—a practice that is unheard of in high-achieving nations and in other professions—became commonplace in many US states during this period, especially those with large minority and immigrant populations such as California, Texas, Florida, and New York.

A decade later, the entire California system was subjected to legal challenge, as disparities in access to well-qualified teachers had grown even worse. In 2001, for example, students in California's most intensely minority schools were more than five times as likely to have uncertified teachers than those in predominantly White schools. As standards were lowered and nearly half of the state's new teachers entered without training, virtually all of them were assigned to teach in high-need schools. In the 20 percent of schools serving almost exclusively students of color, more than one-fifth of teachers were uncertified, and in some schools they comprised the majority of the teaching force.[36] (See figure 6.1.)

A 1999 episode of the Merrow Report[37] illustrates how debilitating these policies had become for a group of students in Oakland—although the segment could as easily have been about schools in Philadelphia, Los Angeles, Chicago, Newark, Atlanta, or New York City. Zooming into a portable classroom in a middle school comprising entirely of American and Latino students, Merrow interviewed students in an eighth-grade math class that had been without a regular math teacher for most of the year, asking: "How many math teachers have you had this year?" One young man with a good memory started to count: "Let's see, there is Mr. Berry, Miss Gaines, Mr. Lee, Mr. Dijon, Mr. Franklin.... Coach Brown was one of our substitutes one day." A studious-looking girl chimed in: "We had Miss Nakasako; we had Miss Gaines; we had Miss Elmore; we had this other man named...he had like curly hair. His name was Mr. umm...." Merrow remarked: "So you've had so many teachers you can't remember all their names?" The children nodded in agreement.

A few miles away at Oakland High School, a ninth-grade science class had had nothing but substitutes and spent the entire year without a certified science

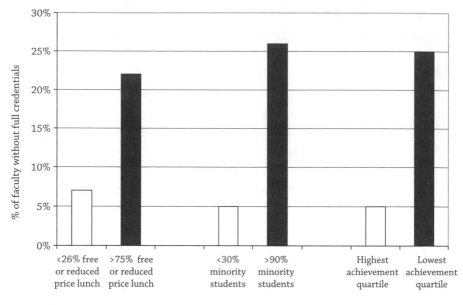

Source: Shields, Humphrey, Wechsler, et al., 2001

FIGURE 6.1 Distribution of Unqualified Teachers in California, 2001

teacher. Merrow asked what it was like having so many teachers. Students' frustration was evident as they answered. Said one boy: "It's just weird. It's like we have to get used to a new teacher every couple of weeks or so." Another added, "I'm feeling short-handed, because this is the third year . . . ever since I got into junior high school, I haven't had a science teacher. . . . [I've had] substitutes all three years." When Merrow asked: "Have you learned much science this year?" the students shook their heads no. One particular Black student, laying his hand on the book in front of him as though it were a life raft, shook his head sadly and answered: "Not really. We haven't had the chance to."

The reporter went on to interview several fully certified science teachers who had applied to teach in the district and had not gotten a call back from the personnel office. Here, as in some other underresourced urban districts, instead of teachers with preparation and experience, uncredentialed teachers and temporary staff were hired to save money. In recent years, Oakland's new leadership has worked heroically to change these practices and to seek out and hire teachers who will become better prepared and stay in the district. Yet the district, like many others in the state, still struggles with the inadequate funding and low salaries that make staffing its schools an uphill climb.

Similar inequalities have been documented in lawsuits challenging school funding in other states, including Massachusetts, New Jersey, New York, South Carolina, and Texas. In Massachusetts in 2002, students in predominantly minority schools were five times more likely to have uncertified teachers than those in the quartile of schools serving the fewest students of color.[38] In South Carolina and Texas they were four times more likely.[39]

By every measure of qualifications—certification, subject matter background, pedagogical training, selectivity of college attended, test scores, or experience— less qualified teachers are found in schools serving greater numbers of low-income and minority students.[40] As noted by Kati Haycock, president of The Education Trust, these statistics on differentials in credentials and experience, as shocking as they are, actually *understate* the degree of the problem:

> For one thing, these effects are additive. The fact that only 25% of the teachers in a school are uncertified doesn't mean that the other 75% are fine. More often, they are either brand new, assigned to teach out of field, or low-performers on the licensure exam.... There are, in other words, significant numbers of schools that are essentially dumping grounds for unqualified teachers—just as they are dumping grounds for the children they serve.[41]

The Influence of Teacher Quality on Student Achievement

All of these aspects of teacher quality matter. Studies at the state, district, school, and individual level have found that teachers' academic background, preparation for teaching, and certification status, as well as their experience, significantly affect their students' achievement.[42] Similar patterns appear around the world. For example, the most significant predictors of mathematics achievement across 46 nations include teacher certification, a major in mathematics or mathematics education, and at least three years of teaching experience.[43]

Teachers' qualifications can have very large effects. For example, a recent study of high school students in North Carolina found that students' achievement was significantly higher if they were taught by a teacher who was certified in the field he or she taught, was fully prepared upon entry, had higher scores on the teacher licensing test, graduated from a competitive college, had taught for more than two years, or was National Board Certified.[44] While each of these traits made teachers more effective, the combined influence of having a teacher with most of these qualifications was larger than the effects of race and parent education combined. That is, the difference between the effect of having a very well-qualified teacher rather than one who was poorly qualified was larger than the average difference in achievement between a typical White student with college-educated parents and a typical Black student with high-school-educated parents. The achievement gap would be significantly reduced if low-income minority students were routinely assigned highly qualified teachers rather than the poorly qualified teachers they most often encounter.

A similar study of teachers in New York City found that teachers' certification status, pathway into teaching, teaching experience, graduation from a competitive college, and math SAT scores were significant predictors of teacher effectiveness in elementary and middle school mathematics.[45] Students' achievement was most enhanced by having a fully certified teacher who had graduated from a university pre-service program, had a strong academic background, and had more than two years of experience. Their achievement was hurt most by having an inexperienced teacher with a temporary license—a teacher profile most common in high-minority, low-income schools.

The good news is that when New York City raised salaries as the result of a school finance lawsuit and adopted policies to distribute teachers more equitably, improvements in these qualifications reduced achievement disparities between the schools serving the poorest and most affluent student bodies by one-fourth within only a few years.[46] Persistence in solving this problem could make a major difference in the opportunities available to students. Indeed, because of public attention to these disparities and to the importance of teacher quality,[47] Congress included a provision in the No Child Left Behind Act of 2002 that states should ensure that all students have access to "highly qualified teachers," defined as teachers with full certification and demonstrated competence in the subject matter fields they teach. This provision was historic, especially because the students targeted by federal legislation—those who are low-income, low-achieving, new English language learners, or identified with special education needs—have in many communities been the least likely to be served by experienced and well-prepared teachers.[48]

At the same time, reflecting a key Bush administration agenda, the law encouraged states to expand alternative certification programs, and regulations developed by the US Department of Education (DOE) allow candidates who have just begun, but not yet completed, such a program to be counted as "highly qualified" classroom teachers. These regulations led parents of low-income, minority students taught by such teachers in California to sue the DOE.[49] They claimed that the rule sanctioned inadequate teaching for their children and masked the fact that they were being underserved, reducing the pressure on policy makers to create incentives that would give their children access to fully prepared teachers.

These alternative programs vary widely. Some well-designed routes for midcareer entrants, such as newly emerging residency programs, provide a tailored pathway for adults who already hold a bachelor's degree that wraps relevant coursework around a carefully supervised practicum over the course of a year under the supervision of an expert teacher. Other programs, generally targeted for high-turnover urban schools, offer only a few weeks of training before teachers step into the classroom with variable access to mentoring or support. These efforts to address shortages in high-need schools by reducing training rather than increasing the incentives to teach have, in many cases, exacerbated staffing problems and undermined efforts to raise student achievement (see Berry, chapter 13 in this volume).

The problems created by underprepared teachers have effects on schools as a whole. A teacher in a California school with a revolving door of underprepared teachers explained the consequences for students and other teachers:

> Teachers who had not been through [preparation] programs had more concerns about classroom management and about effective methods for delivering instruction to the student population at our school than teachers who had been through credential programs. It was a topic that was discussed at the lunch table...the fact we had a class that had had so many substitutes and had had an uncredentialed teacher who was not able to handle the situation and ended up not returning, and that the kids were going to struggle and the teachers who received them the next year would probably have a difficult time with those students because of what they had been through.[50]

Student achievement declines as the proportion of inexperienced, underprepared, or uncertified increases within a school.[51] The high turnover rates of underprepared, inexperienced teachers, which disproportionately affect low-income, high-minority schools, drain financial and human resources.[52] Most important, the constant staff churn consigns a large share of children in high-need schools to a parade of relatively ineffective teachers, leading to higher rates of remediation, grade retention, and dropping out. These longer-term costs are borne by society as well as by individual students. Without additional resources, schools serving the nation's most vulnerable students are ill-prepared to create the working environments and compensation packages needed to attract and retain experienced, well-trained teachers.

Lack of Access to High-Quality Curriculum

In addition to being taught by less expert teachers than their White counterparts, students of color face stark differences in courses, curriculum programs, materials and equipment, as well as in the human environment in which they attend school. High-quality instruction, which is shaped by all these factors and supported by tangible resources, matters greatly for student achievement. For example, when sociologist Robert Dreeben studied reading instruction for 300 Black and White first graders across seven schools in the Chicago area, he found that differences in reading achievement were almost entirely explained, not by socioeconomic status or race, but by the quality of curriculum and teaching the students received:

> Our evidence shows that the level of learning responds strongly to the quality of instruction: having and using enough time, covering a substantial amount of rich curricular material, and matching instruction appropriately to the ability levels of groups.... When Black and White children of comparable ability experience the same instruction, they do about equally well, and this is true when the instruction is excellent in quality and when it is inadequate.[53]

Yet the quality of instruction received by African American students was, on average, much lower than that received by White students, creating a racial gap in aggregate achievement at the end of first grade. In fact, the highest ability group in Dreeben's sample at the start of the study was in a school in a low-income African American neighborhood. These students attended a school that was unable to provide the quality instruction they deserved, and they learned less during first grade than their White counterparts.

In a variety of subtle and not-so-subtle ways, US schools allocate different learning opportunities to different students. Sorting often begins as early as kindergarten or first grade, with decisions about which students are placed in remedial or "gifted and talented" programs. Affluent and poor schools differ sharply in what is offered. Wealthy districts often offer foreign languages early in elementary school, while poor districts offer few such courses even at the high school level; richer districts typically provide extensive music and art programs, project-based science, and elaborate technology supports, while poor districts often have none of these and often offer stripped down drill-and-practice approaches to reading and math rather than teaching for higher-order applications.[54]

For reasons of both resources and expectations, schools serving African American, Latino, and Native American students are "bottom heavy"—that is, they offer fewer academic and college preparatory courses and more remedial and vocational courses that train students for low-status occupations, such as cosmetology and sewing.[55] For example, in 2005 only 30 percent of highly segregated schools serving African American and Latino students in California had a sufficient number of the state-required college preparatory courses to accommodate all their students. These schools, serving more than 90 percent students of color, constitute a quarter of all schools in the state. Furthermore, in a large majority of these highly segregated schools more than one-fifth of the college-preparatory courses they did offer were taught by underqualified teachers.[56] As a result of these conditions, very few African American and Latino high school graduates had taken and passed both the courses and the tests required to be eligible for admission to the state university system.[57]

Tracking is another well-established mechanism used to differentiate access to knowledge (see Tyson, chapter 12 in this volume). In racially mixed schools, the tracks are generally color-coded: honors or advanced courses are reserved primarily for White students, while the lower tracks are disproportionately filled with students of color. Unequal access to high-level courses and challenging curriculum explains much of the difference in achievement between minority students and White students.

Little has changed since Jonathan Kozol eloquently described two decades ago how, within ostensibly integrated schools in New York City, minority children were disproportionately assigned to special education classes that occupy small, cramped corners and split classrooms, while gifted and talented classes, which were exclusively composed of White and Asian students, enjoyed spaces filled with books and computers and learned logical reasoning and problem solving.[58] School pathways locking in inequality can be found in most districts today, as high-quality education is rationed to the privileged few. Furthermore, race and ethnicity are associated with placement in higher or lower tracks independently of students' achievement levels.[59] In addition to inequitable access to knowledge, cross-school segregation and within-school tracking reduce the extent to which different kinds of students have the opportunity to interact with one another and gain access to multiple perspectives.

HOW CAN INEQUALITY BE ADDRESSED?

The resource issues described throughout this chapter all implicate issues of funding. Without adequate and fair funding, little progress can be made in providing the educational resources necessary to address these inequalities. In more than 40 states, poor parents and children have sought redress for the conditions I have described by pursuing equity litigation. These lawsuits, which build in many ways on the foundation laid by *Brown v. Board of Education*, have recently included the argument that if states require all students to meet the same educational standards, they are responsible for providing sufficient resources to allow students a reasonable opportunity of achieving those standards, including a curriculum that fully reflects the standards; teachers well-qualified to teach the curriculum; and the materials, texts, supplies, and equipment needed to support this teaching. The logic is straightforward. Yet the path to educational opportunity through the courts is tortuous, both because of differing interpretations regarding what courts should take on and because our nation's comfort level with inequality often makes the current situation seem tolerable, or even appropriate, to both the public and its judges.

DOES MONEY MAKE A DIFFERENCE?

A recurring argument against school finance reform is that "money doesn't make a difference." Proponents of the school-funding status quo argue that low-cost administrative and governance changes can contribute more to educational quality within districts than financial resources and that no definitive correlation has been shown between money spent and educational quality. It is certainly true that money can be spent unwisely, and dollars spent on patronage, bloated bureaucracies, and sports facilities are less likely to translate into learning than dollars spent on sound instruction.

Moreover, the higher cost of living in many urban areas and the greater educational and noneducational needs of students who live in poverty mean that there is not a one-to-one correspondence between dollars spent and the resources they buy or the net benefits they produce. More money is needed to achieve equivalent outcomes in high-cost locations with high-need students.[60] Opponents of school finance equalization have also pointed to the strong statistical relationships between race, parent education, income, and students' outcomes and argued that greater investments would be wasted on those whom (they implicitly suggest) cannot take advantage of them.[61]

For example, in New Jersey, the state argued more than once in a 30-year litigation process that the urban, minority students in low-spending districts could not profit from the same kind or quality of education as those in wealthy suburbs. In 1990, defendants stated:

> The [basic skills] education currently offered in these poorer urban districts is tailored to the students' present need.... These students simply cannot now benefit from the kind of vastly superior course offerings found in the richer districts.[62]

Although the confluence of race and poverty in the United States, and their relationship to student achievement do indeed complicate analyses of funding and resources, this is no justification for spending less on the education of children living in poverty. Solid analyses show the benefits of increased funding.[63] Indeed, research concerning reforms such as early-childhood education and class-size reduction strongly suggests that less advantaged children stand to benefit the most from such additional resources.[64]

Debates about whether resources make a difference for the schooling of low-income and minority students have been reprised in recent school finance cases. In *Williams v. California*, for instance, the state argued that, despite large, documented differences in expenditures as well as children's access to qualified teachers, textbooks, course offerings, and facilities, these resources are largely unrelated to student achievement. The state also argued that the effects of poverty are what drive disparities in achievement. In a sweeping indictment of educational investments over the last half century, defense expert Eric Hanushek claimed that "there is no evidence that the added resources" devoted to education in the United States over the twentieth century "have improved student performance, at least for the most recent three decades."[65]

Hanushek's research arguing that money makes no difference has been critiqued for its methodology and interpretations by other economists, statisticians, and the courts.[66] His key assertion flies in the face of dozens of studies finding that additional resources contribute to improved student performance. It also ignores the fact that significant expansion in schooling has occurred since the 1960s. For example, the system has greatly expanded access to kindergarten and added prekindergartens.[67] Schools are now required to serve students with disabilities. Attending high school has become nearly universal. Until the 1960s, many communities did not have high schools for African American, Mexican American, or American Indian students, and the segregated high schools that did exist were severely underfunded. By 1970, only 57 percent of White adults and 36 percent of Black adults had finished high school. By 1998, the proportions had leaped to 94 percent and 88 percent respectively.[68]

To make his point about static test scores, Hanushek uses twelfth graders' scores on the National Assessment of Educational Progress (NAEP), which have changed little over several decades even though a great many more educationally disadvantaged students—including special education students, new immigrants and English language learners, students living in poverty, and students of color—now reach the twelfth grade and are part of the testing pool. The fact that their inclusion has not *lowered* the average is a sign that, for most students, achievement has increased. Similarly, SAT scores for students of color rose sharply after 1970 even though more students took the test. Large and visible gains in fourth- and eighth-grade scores on NAEP, especially in mathematics, demonstrate the payoffs from educational investments.

The evidence that increased investments have been accompanied by measurable gains does not mean that all investments have equivalent payoffs. The efficiency argument has merit. Dollars can be wasted or used in counterproductive ways, and bad managerial decisions can create administrative burdens that deflect scarce resources and attention from productive teaching and learning. An effective system must create a means for determining and funding adequacy, as well as incentives to increase the likelihood of funds being wisely spent. Smart policy will be based on investments that produce strong yields in terms of children's well-being and learning.

How Money Makes a Difference

Many studies have documented how specific resources, including better-qualified teachers who are paid competitive salaries; smaller class sizes; and smaller, redesigned schools with advisors, planning time for teaching teams, and support systems for students contribute to student achievement gains.[69]

For example, using data on Texas school districts, Ronald Ferguson demonstrated that expenditure levels make a difference in increasing student performance and that the effect on achievement increases as funding is spent on instructionally crucial resources, such as higher-quality teachers; small-enough class sizes; and rigorous curriculum supported by plentiful, high-quality books, computers, and lab equipment.[70]

The primary driver of achievement in this study was teacher expertise (measured by performance on a statewide certification exam, experience, and master's degrees). The effects were so strong, and the variations in teacher expertise so great, that after controlling for socioeconomic status, the large disparities in achievement between Black and White students were almost entirely accounted for by differences in the qualifications of their teachers. Ferguson concluded: "What the evidence here suggests most strongly is that teacher quality matters and should be a major focus of efforts to upgrade the quality of schooling. Skilled teachers are the most critical of all schooling inputs."[71]

The influences and relative contributions of teacher training and experience levels were also demonstrated by a review of 60 studies, which found that teacher education, ability, and experience, along with smaller schools and lower teacher-pupil ratios, were associated with increases in student achievement across schools and districts.[72]

Ferguson also found that smaller class size was associated with higher achievement, at a critical point of 18 students per teacher. A number of other studies have come to similar conclusions, indicating that smaller classes are more effective, especially in the early grades and for lower-achieving students.[73] Most often cited is the evidence from a randomized experiment, called Tennessee STAR, showing significant gains in achievement as a result of reducing class sizes from 22 to 15 in kindergarten through third grade.[74] Although the costs of reducing class size can be large and the effects of reducing class size are generally smaller per unit of spending than those of improving teacher quality,[75] economist Alan Krueger estimates a benefit-cost ratio of reducing class sizes of nearly 3 to 1 as a function of the earnings expectations of higher achievement.[76]

Other research has found that these kinds of investments also matter in the early childhood years. High-quality preschool programs, such as the Perry Preschool Program and the Abecedarian Program, have been found to reduce the probability of students being retained in grade, needing special education, dropping out of school, being unemployed, and being incarcerated (for descriptions of these programs, see Barnett and Lamy, chapter 7, this volume). They have also shown gains in educational attainment, with more graduates going on to postsecondary education, which boosts later earnings. Indeed, the returns to investment in preschool education have been estimated at $4 to $10 for every dollar spent.[77] High quality programs that produce these kinds of benefits have relied on highly qualified teachers with a bachelor's or master's degree in early childhood education, small class sizes, rich hands-on learning materials, and parent outreach and education.[78]

Each of these investments, of course, costs money.

Funding Equitable Education

Ultimately, the proof is in the pudding. A number of states that have raised and equalized funding as part of systemic reforms have raised student achievement and reduced the opportunity gap.[79] Consider Massachusetts. For the past decade, Massachusetts has led all states in student achievement on the National Assessment of Educational Progress. The meteoric rise began in 1992 with a court decision in *Hancock v. Driscoll* requiring an overhaul of school funding. The school finance formula adopted in 1993 as part of Massachusetts' Education Reform Act led to substantially greater investments in needier schools by equalizing funding and local effort simultaneously and adding funding increments based on the proportions of low-income students and English language learners in a district.

This progressive funding approach was accompanied by new statewide learning standards, curriculum frameworks, and assessments; expanded learning time in core content areas; technology investments; and stronger licensing requirements for teachers. The next year Massachusetts adopted a plan for professional development that provided dedicated funding to districts, led to intensive summer institutes in math and science, and set up continuing education requirements for certification, as well as a new set of standards and expectations for local educator evaluation. The Attracting Excellence to Teaching Program subsidized preparation for qualified entrants to the profession.

In addition, the state quintupled its funding for local early childhood programs, created a Commission on Early Childhood Education to develop a statewide plan, established model preschool programs, and awarded hundreds of Community Partnerships for Children grants to expand access to early education for children in need. By the year 2000, Massachusetts had underwritten these reforms with more than $2 billion in new state dollars for its public schools, greatly expanding the state share of funding and enhancing equity.

Economist Jonathan Guryan found that increased educational funding for historically low-spending districts led to improved student achievement in all subject areas, especially for traditionally low-scoring students.[80] By 2002, the state had dramatically improved overall achievement and sharply reduced its achievement gap. Massachusetts demonstrates how investments, wisely spent in concert with a systemic approach to reform, can make a difference in educational outcomes.

New Jersey provides another, more recent, case. For many years, the state spent about half as much on the education of low-income, minority students in cities like Camden, Trenton, Newark, and Paterson as it did in wealthy districts. After 30 years of litigation and nine court decisions finding the New Jersey school finance system unconstitutional, the state finally agreed to make a major infusion of funding to the 28 highest-need districts to bring them into parity with the per-pupil expenditures in the state's successful suburban districts. The new funding, which began in 1998, was spent to implement a new state curriculum linked to the state standards; support whole school reform; ensure early childhood education for three- and four-year-olds as well as full-day kindergarten; educate preschool teachers; reduce class sizes; invest in technology; ensure adequate facilities; and support health, social services, alternative, and summer school programs to help students catch up. In addition, an early literacy program provided reading coaches and professional development for teachers in kindergarten through third grade.[81]

New Jersey launched a set of new teacher education programs focused on preparing teachers for effective teaching in high-need urban districts, using school-university partnerships to provide both intensive field experiences for teacher candidates and professional learning opportunities for veteran teachers. It developed extensive professional development supports for teaching content area standards and for supporting English language learners and other special needs students, with dedicated funding and assistance in high-needs schools to model effective practices.[82] Gradually, the districts that had become dysfunctional during the lean years began to gain ground.

By 2007, New Jersey had substantially increased its standing on national reading and math assessments, ranking among the top five states in all subject areas and grade levels on the NAEP and first in writing. It was also one of four states that made the most progress nationally in closing performance gaps between White, Black, and Hispanic students in fourth- and eighth-grade reading and math.[83] By 2007, although parity had not yet been achieved, Hispanic and Black students scored between 5 and 10 points above their peers nationwide, depending on the test.[84] The state also reduced the achievement gap for students with disabilities and for socioeconomically disadvantaged students.

Clearly, money well spent does make a difference. Equalizing access to resources creates the possibility that all students will receive what should be their birthright: a genuine opportunity to learn.

7

Achievement Gaps Start Early

PRESCHOOL CAN HELP

W. Steven Barnett and Cynthia E. Lamy

IN THE UNITED STATES, considerable public attention is focused on closing the achievement gap between children from poorer and wealthier families.[1] Typically, this gap first becomes a highly visible public issue when children reach third or fourth grade and take state and national standardized tests for the first time. Concern intensifies again during the high school years, when so many low-income and minority high school students drop out or fail to pass exit exams, and average achievement test scores continue to differ among socioeconomic groups. The achievement gap does not start at third or fourth grade, however. Significant differences in the precursors of academic skills are evident from the earliest years of life and are associated with family circumstances, including income. Efforts to close the achievement gap must begin with efforts to close the opportunity gap that is the source of much of this early difference in abilities.

While group differences in children's abilities and achievement typically are thought of as gaps, we approach this topic from a somewhat different perspective. We recognize that what is commonly thought of as a vast gap between disparate groups—rich versus poor, Blacks and Hispanics versus Whites—can be seen upon closer inspection to be a gradient or gradual slope in which children's abilities steadily increase over the entire family income range. Differences between minorities and Whites similarly can be seen to result from differences in economic and social circumstances and family characteristics that vary within as well as between groups. Recognition that the achievement gap is actually a steady, gradual change along an income or socioeconomic gradient allows us to see that the achievement and opportunity problem is not limited to children in poverty or to minority groups but affects the vast majority of Americans.

To understand achievement gradients it helps to see them. Figures 7.1 and 7.2, based on data from the Early Childhood Longitudinal Study—Kindergarten cohort of 1999, display the gradients for children's cognitive test scores and teacher ratings of children's social abilities by income quintile at kindergarten entry. Viewed this way it is obvious that there is no sharp dividing line between the poor who are in the bottom quintile and everyone else. Instead we see a smooth, steady decline in scores moving from high to low income. Looking at achievement test scores, children at the median income are as far behind children in the top income quintile as poor children are behind those at the median income. Of course, not every child is at the average for their income level; some have higher abilities and others lower. These gradients are very persistent so that they look very much the same at tenth or twelfth grade as at kindergarten. This pattern recurs in the gradient for high school dropout rate by family income.[2]

Ability gradients emerge very early in life. Sizeable differences in children's abilities by family background appear before age five.[3] Hart and Risley found that three-year-olds from low-income families knew only about half as many words as those from higher-income families.[4] More recent studies find Black children far behind their White peers in pre-academic skills by age three.[5] By the time they enter kindergarten, children in poverty can be 12 or 18 months behind the average child.[6] As we noted earlier, inadequate progress is not limited to children in poverty. Across the entire income spectrum, nearly 40 percent of American children at age five are classified as not ready for kindergarten, and most of these children are not poor.[7]

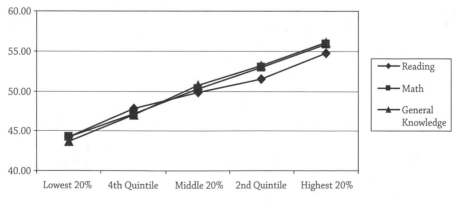

FIGURE 7.1 Median Abilities of Entering kindergarteners by the Family Income

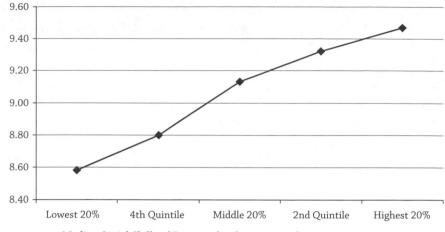

FIGURE 7.2   Median Social Skills of Entering kindergarteners by Income

These very early ability differences emerge from a complex set of family circumstances that vary within and across racial and ethnic groups. The majority of the school readiness "gap" between White children and their African American and Hispanic counterparts can be explained by family background characteristics other than race or ethnicity, particularly family income, parental education, family structure, and the conditions of the neighborhood, as well as by indicators of home experiences that support early learning, such as the number of books or educational toys in the home.[8] When researchers look closely at family behavior, a portion of the difference in early abilities is explained by differences in early parenting, especially how parents talk, read, and play with their children (see also Rothstein, chapter 5, this volume).[9] Variations in children's very early experiences with language—how many words are spoken to them, how often they are spoken to, the extent to which they are encouraged to use their own developing language abilities and emergent preliteracy skills—predict not just their earliest vocabulary but also their later vocabulary in elementary school.[10] A similar relationship is found between early home mathematics experiences and knowledge of mathematics.[11]

Of course, many factors beyond parent-child interaction in the home influence children's early cognitive and social development, including their health, nutrition, exposure to environmental toxins, danger, violence, and emotional stress. Prenatal exposure to tobacco, alcohol, drugs, and maternal stress can affect development before a child is born. Adverse effects on early brain development may impair a child's cognitive, social, and emotional development and mental and physical health over a lifetime.[12] The risk of exposure to these adverse effects steadily increases as income and parental education decline.[13] Racial-ethnic group differences in exposure are partly due to group differences in income and educa-tion. However, discrimination itself also may adversely affect maternal health in ways that harm children's prenatal development.[14]

Even very early ability differences are strongly linked to later achievement. Language development before age three predicts reading comprehension in high school.[15] Early math skills also strongly predict achievement in elementary school and high school.[16] There is very little change in achievement gradients between age five and age eighteen.[17]

In sum, those distressing, attention-grabbing differences in achievement test scores and high school graduation rates can be largely explained by differences in abilities that are evident well before children enter kindergarten. We wish it were otherwise, and it is possible that more equitable opportunities to learn within for-mal schooling could repair much of this early damage, but in the present situa-tion children who begin school substantially behind are unlikely to ever catch up.[18] To be successful, efforts to decrease inequality in achievement and reduce school dropout rates should begin in the first five years, when the problem originates. Of course, such efforts cannot end there as every year of a child's life matters.

EARLY CHILDHOOD PROGRAMS CAN REDUCE ACHIEVEMENT GAPS

The goal of efforts in early childhood to improve children's abilities is to move all children closer to the levels of ability attained by children at the far right (top income quintile) of the ability gradients shown in Figures 7.1 and 7.2. High-quality, publicly provided preschool education has been found to produce just this type of effect on early abilities, thereby also improving children's later academic and over-all life outcomes. Effects tend to be largest for children at the lowest income levels and to decline with income, reflecting differences in the opportunities families have to enhance their children's knowledge and skills. Essentially, such programs shift the entire gradient upward with the amount of upward shift decreasing from left to right. Over the last 20 years, extensive, in-depth research has been con-ducted that helps us understand how support for children's development in the first five years can set them on a more successful trajectory for a lifetime.

A wide range of public programs and policies can contribute to improved oppor-tunities and enhanced child development, including efforts to improve prenatal conditions for the developing child through parent education and support, nutri-tion and health supports from the federal Supplemental Nutrition Program for Women Infants and Children (WIC) to health care reform, paid parental leave, and improved access to high-quality child care and education for young children. We focus here on early education, which is the area of our own expertise. A substantial body of evidence indicates that improvements in early education policy have considerable power to shift the early gradients in opportunities and outcomes that underlie inequality in the United States. Preschool education programs in the first five years of life can substantially enhance cognitive and social development and produce lasting improvements in school success and achievement, as well as a wide range of other adult outcomes including improved health habits and mental health, increased earnings and employment, and decreased involvement in crime.[19]

Solid evidence for short- and long-term cognitive, social, and schooling effects has been summarized by multiple reviews and meta-analyses. A meta-analysis is simply a statistical summary of the research and provides a reasonably objective way to convey a body of research findings on a given topic. A recent meta-analysis of the research on effects of preschool programs in the United States since 1960 finds large initial effects and persistent effects throughout the school years on a broad range of outcomes.[20] For cognitive effects, including achievement, long-term effects are about half the size of short-term effects. Some types of programs are demonstrably more effective than others, and simulations suggest that well-designed preschool education programs could close the entire achievement gap between children from low- and high-income families at school entry and as much as half the gap permanently.[21]

To understand how early education might improve achievement, it is useful to look at the results of specific longitudinal studies. Three rigorous studies provide excellent illustrations of what high-quality preschool programs can do to improve achievement and other educational outcomes, particularly for disadvantaged children. The Perry Preschool Study, the Abecedarian Study, and the Chicago Longitudinal Study carefully measured the effects of high-quality preschool education from early childhood into adulthood.[22] All three focused on children from disadvantaged, primarily low-income African American families. Together they paint a picture of persistent improvements, including higher test scores, better progress through school, and higher rates of on-time high school graduation. These improved educational outcomes led to increased adult economic success, including higher incomes.

In addition, these preschool programs improved children's attitudes, dispositions, and social behaviors. During the school years this improvement translates into better classroom behavior and motivation. Later it yields better health behaviors and (with some differences across studies), improved mental health and decreases in delinquency and crime.[23] These findings offer important evidence that society should provide supports for child development broadly, including character, social behavior, and mental health, and not just for academic achievement narrowly defined.[24] Moreover, well-designed preschool programs support children's social and emotional development with no loss of impact on cognitive development and academic achievement.[25]

The scope and duration of these studies makes it possible to conduct comprehensive benefit-cost analyses, and in all three cases the estimated benefits of preschool education far exceeded the costs.[26] While the children themselves benefit significantly, a substantial portion of the estimated economic benefits accrue to the general public, through increased tax revenues to the government, and through cost savings to educational and criminal justice systems. For example, reduced education costs that are due to the decreased need for special education and reduced grade repetition, as well as less crime and lower criminal justice systems costs, and increased tax revenues due to higher earnings, all contribute to the common good (see also Belfield and Levin, chapter 14 in this volume). A strong case can be made that well-designed policies to publicly provide preschool education can actually pay for themselves over the long term.

Not all preschool programs are equally effective. What makes some programs more (or less) effective than others? Programs emphasizing intentional teaching and individualization (one-to-one and small group interactions) have been more effective.[27] Although the meta-analysis could find no difference in outcomes based on age at start, individual studies as well as the evidence on the emergence of ability differences at very early ages suggest advantages to starting earlier, provided that support continues at least up to kindergarten entry.[28] Unfortunately, the United States has yet to provide truly high-quality early education on a large scale beginning at age three or four, although some states are leading the way with either targeted programs for children from low-income families or universal programs that serve all children.

A detailed review of research reveals that many preschool programs, including major federal programs serving the most disadvantaged children, do not consistently produce impacts comparable to those found in the three studies of exemplary programs or to the average impacts found in the meta-analysis.[29] Typical child care has at best small effects on cognitive development and may even have mild negative effects on cognitive and social development.[30] Head Start has positive impacts, but these are quite small and cease to make much difference after school entry. These results are not surprising, as neither typical child care nor Head Start is characterized by the highly effective approaches of the three programs found to produce the largest gains.

Although it is difficult to balance the need to develop and maintain program quality with the imperative to serve very large numbers of children, it can be done. The programs scrutinized by the Chicago Longitudinal Study, for example, were operated by the Chicago Public Schools. While the effects are smaller than those found in the other two more intensive programs, they were large enough and persistent enough to significantly change the life course of low-income, primarily African American children. While the programs studied in Chicago took place in the 1980s, more recent examples are provided by some of the higher-quality preschool programs funded by states. An eight-state study by the National Institute for Early Education Research (NIEER) found that children attending relatively high-quality state preschool programs scored substantially higher in literacy, language, and math at kindergarten entry than did their peers who had not attended preschool.[31] Results were as favorable for universal programs as for those that targeted low-income children. This study and a separate study of Oklahoma's universal preschool program found effects at school entry quite similar in magnitude to those of the Chicago Longitudinal Study.[32] All of these programs share a focus on education, with well-educated and well-paid teachers, in addition to reasonably small classes and child-staff ratios.

New Jersey's Abbott preschool program, named for a court case in which the State Supreme Court mandated the implementation of high-quality preschool for all three- and four-year-olds in the 31 poorest school districts in the state, has also been rigorously studied. The program has transformed the quality of preschools and had positive effects on children's early elementary school achievement.[33] Test scores were higher at kindergarten entry, and gains persisted at second grade. Early grade retention was decreased by one-third for children who attended preschool for just one year, and by half for those who attended for two years beginning at age three.[34] Here, too, the effects were comparable in size to those found in the Chicago Longitudinal Study.

PRESCHOOL MUST BE HIGH QUALITY TO PRODUCE LARGE LASTING IMPACTS.

Given the differences in outcomes among programs, it is vital that public preschool programs follow the approaches that have been most successful and avoid those that have failed. While academics may disagree on what is absolutely necessary to produce large gains for young children, we can all agree that some approaches have worked quite well. In our view, we simply ought to adopt those approaches that have produced the best results. Our formula for success is based on what has been demonstrated to work and includes the following elements:

- High standards for learning and teaching that are clearly articulated.
- Strong teachers (warm, positive, and pedagogically expert) who are highly educated and adequately paid.

- Strong on-site supervision and coaching with time for teachers to plan and reflect as part of a continuous improvement process.
- A well-defined and broad curriculum that combines intentional teaching with opportunities for child-initiated activities, including a variety of play.
- Small classes with at least two adults in each classroom.

This approach is not inexpensive, but the cost per year is about the same as the cost of a year of good public schooling generally. Moreover, benefit-cost analyses demonstrate that the costs of not providing such programs are far higher. When our society substitutes cheap child care or pays Head Start teachers only about half what public school teachers earn, we lose far more in the long-term than we save.

THERE IS AN OPPORTUNITY GAP IN ACCESS TO HIGH-QUALITY PRESCHOOL.

We believe that because high-quality preschool programs have such positive effects on children's academic and life outcomes, every young child should have access to them. Unfortunately, there is a large opportunity gap in access to high-quality early learning programs for families across the country. About 50 percent of three-year-olds and 75 percent of four-year-olds attend a center-based program, public or private. In addition, many children who are not enrolled in a center-based early learning program typically spend some portion of their time each week in the care of someone outside their immediate family. While center-based programs vary widely in their educational value, this non-center-based care is usually of low educational value.[35] Only center-based preschool programs and intensive parenting interventions have been found to produce the large gains for children that are necessary to significantly improve the achievement of disadvantaged children.

Interestingly, children from wealthier families attend center-based preschool programs at much higher rates than children from low-income families. While about 65 percent of children in poor families attend preschool, about 90 percent of children in high-income families do.[36] Attendance rates are highest for children from the best-educated, most affluent families. Attendance rates are lowest for children from families that are poor or near poor, but only slightly better for children from families that earn around the median income.[37] However, if all families had equal access to preschool programs, research indicates, about 90 percent of children would attend.[38]

Of course, the real need is for broad access to preschool programs that are highly effective. Access does not help if programs are low-quality and ineffective. National data on access to high-quality programs are not available, but a recent Rand study of preschool quality in California provides a useful benchmark.[39] Rand reported the proportion of each type of program (private child care, Head Start, public school, etc.) that could be classified as "good" or better based on a well-known measure of preschool quality, the Early Childhood Environmental Rating Scale—Revised.[40] Although this measure of quality is not perfect, few programs failing to achieve a rating of "good" on the ECERS-R would be highly effective. Combining the Rand estimates with national data on enrollment by type of program, we estimate that an abysmally low 10 percent of children who are poor or low-income attend effective preschool programs at age three. At age four, the percentage attending good programs is 20 percent, still abysmally low. Children in higher-income families fare somewhat better in terms of access to high-quality preschool. Yet, even in the top half of the income distribution most children are not attending good preschool programs.

These disparities and the general lack of access to quality preschool education can be directly traced to shortcomings of our national and state policies. Federal child-care subsidy policy emphasizes low cost and use of informal arrangements with no standards for quality. The Head Start program has emphasized comprehensive services to the family, hiring from the community, and low wages over a strong focus on education, and new federal policies, while an improvement, only partially address the program's limitations.[41] States have primary responsibility for setting child-care standards and for preschool education outside of Head Start, and those child-care standards are uniformly low. Standards for preschool education and the extent to which states provide access to preschool education vary widely. Eleven states have no state preschool program at all, while ten other states serve more than half of their four-year-olds.[42] The needs of three-year-olds for center-based programs are almost uniformly ignored. Only a small handful of states serve a substantial proportion of their three-year-olds (Arkansas, Illinois, New Jersey, and Vermont). Even among states that provide public preschool education to most or all their children at age four, quality standards can be quite low.[43]

HOW CAN WE PROVIDE A STRONG START FOR ALL CHILDREN?

Because children who enter the kindergarten door already behind are highly unlikely to catch up to their better-prepared peers, it is important to provide all children and families the means to adequately support their children's learning and development prior to kindergarten. A wide range of policies and programs have been developed for this purpose, from assistance with prenatal care and nutrition, family-income supports, and home visiting to child-care subsidies. Some have worked better than others. For example, contrary to expectations, the largest impacts and highest rates of return have not been produced by very early interventions during the first three years of life. Programs for infants and toddlers have been more expensive, but often have been ineffective or produced only very small gains.[44] Yet, because there is a strong logic to starting early, our nation needs to develop better, approaches to supporting the development of children under three. Two major federal government initiatives—Early Head Start and the Maternal Infant Early Childhood Home Visiting program (MIECHV)—provide an opportunity to develop better programs if they would focus on learning how to improve services rather than expanding current models.

Research to improve Early Head Start's effectiveness should be a high priority. Early Head Start was recently expanded to enroll over 100,000 low-income pregnant women and children up to the age of three.[45] This program provides a wide range of services aimed at improving early child development and parenting. About half of the families receive child care in centers through Early Head Start, but these are unlikely to be educationally effective. A rigorous national study found that Early Head Start had positive, though very modest immediate effects on children and their parents, and virtually all the effects disappeared by kindergarten entry and did not resurface later.[46] At an average cost of more than $30,000 per child over 2.5 years, these outcomes are unacceptable. One potential approach to improving Early Head Start is to provide much higher quality educational child care in the first three years. We do not in any way mean inappropriately formal schooling for such young children, such as drilling on letters or numbers. Early Head Start should provide engaging, joyful, language-and-concept-rich interactions with responsive caregivers who help children develop knowledge and skills. Essentially, it means offering low-income children the opportunity to grow and learn in the same sort of healthy environment enjoyed by the most advantaged children.

Home visitation for economically disadvantaged children beginning prenatally and continuing up to age five received a boost from 2010 federal legislation providing states with $1.5 billion over five years through the MIECHV program. A variety of home visitation programs show evidence of effectiveness that allows states to fund them under this legislation. Yet, impacts have been for the most part small and uneven, and the production of lasting cognitive benefits is particularly uncertain. Further research should identify approaches that will produce substantive improvements in long-term child development. When highly effective approaches are identified, they should be widely disseminated. Also, because even success-ful programs may not be effective with all low-income parents, it is important to identify the particular families for which strong results can be consistently pro-duced and to develop cost-effective procedures for identifying and enrolling those families.[47]

Finally, we return to preschool programs for children at age three and four. Here the nation already has enough knowledge to create a system of effective programs. The achievement gap is not a discrete gap, but a gradient—a steady decline in chil-dren's abilities as family income falls. Children in poverty are far behind the aver-age child, but children at the median income are similarly far behind those in the highest income families. Not only does the problem of lagging early development afflict many children from low- and middle-income families, but high-quality pro-grams are not available to the vast majority of children. This is a broad societal problem not limited to minority children or children in poverty, though it most severely impacts these groups. Therefore, we call for universal access to high-quality preschool programs for all children rather than targeted programs serving only children from low-income families. A universal approach is also the most effec-tive way to ensure that all disadvantaged children have access to high-quality early education.[48]

Moreover, past experience has shown us that early learning programs targeted to poor families and children have a difficult time accomplishing the critical mission of preparing children for school. There are three basic reasons that targeting fails. First, targeting based on stringent income cutoffs is highly imperfect in practice.[49] For many families, income varies from week to week and month to month. Children who fall below the poverty line or some other standard in the spring when they are identified for enrollment may be just above that line in the fall; conversely, children who are ruled ineligible in the spring may be poorer by the time the program begins. In addition, some families will avoid sending their children to a program that only serves children in poverty, while others will seek to obtain a free preschool educa-tion even if they do not qualify. Second, children learn from one another, and dis-advantaged children in particular gain from attending preschool with peers who are more advantaged.[50] Third, children from middle-income families need and benefit from high quality preschool, and our society needs all children to come to school with the skills that are necessary to succeed in formal education.

Public preschool education provides a means to accomplish this goal, as has been done in statewide in Oklahoma for four-year-olds and in New Jersey's urban centers beginning at age three. States that have sought to provide such services outside public education typically have diluted quality, sometimes to the point that it is debatable whether it can be considered education at all, as in Florida.[51]

The preschool education approach we advocate has been implemented in some 1,300 Schools of the 21st Century, which are based on a model developed by Dr. Edward Zigler, and for thousands more children in New Jersey's Abbott preschool program.[52] These programs add to the formula we provided above—they build relationships with parents, refer children to health services as needed, and offer wraparound child care to ensure that children of working parents are able to participate and are well-cared for until parents can pick them up—without losing their central focus on a quality education.

A system of high-quality universal preschool offered through public education can be highly flexible and might differ in key respects from the K-12 system offered strictly through the public schools. For example, many states allow or even encourage private organizations to deliver public preschool education. This policy can be set up to maximize choice and competition while maintaining high standards and a role for the public schools in quality assurance and support. Within such a system, the intensity of services to children can be based on their individual and community needs. For example, class sizes might be smaller in communities with high concentrations of poverty, and children with disabilities or delays might receive tutoring or additional assistance in the classroom from specialists. Head Start could partner with state programs by providing funding to enhance teacher salaries, decrease class size, and increase the number of mental health and other support professionals in programs serving high-poverty neighborhoods. "Super Head Start" programs with very high standards might operate within a state prekindergarten system serving poor and non-poor together, with federal, state, and local funding in high-need communities.

CONCLUSION: EXPANDING EARLY LEARNING OPPORTUNITIES

In the United States far too many children fail to reach their developmental potential in the first five years of life. By some estimates nearly 40 percent are not ready for kindergarten. Inadequate investments in early childhood development are the source of much of the achievement gap at the other end of the education pipeline and contribute to later inequalities in educational attainment, earnings, and health. A successful strategy to decrease economic and social inequality in educational and other later life outcomes will begin with public investments to improve child development that start very early, even prenatally. A sustained research effort is needed to identify the most effective approaches for children under three, and existing public programs like Early Head Start and home visitation should conduct this work to improve their services.

Although we do not have all the answers regarding the best approaches birth to five, we do already know how to provide high-quality, publicly funded preschool education for older preschoolers. States should move forward to do so. Ideally, they would partner with the federal Head Start program to enhance services for young children who live in communities with the highest concentrations of poverty, providing the most to those who have the least. In addition, Head Start can right now help to ensure that the most disadvantaged children begin quality preschool no later than age three, as many state programs still struggle to serve four-year-olds. It will take time to grow quality programs, but ultimately all children should be served by a public education system that begins at age three. These commitments to a stronger foundation for the development of children would reduce inequality and increase prosperity in a way that unites rather than divides because it is based on the common needs, concerns, and aspirations of all families. With a stronger foundation subsequent educational supports will be able to focus less on remediation of achievement gaps and more on maintaining a higher trajectory of achievement for all of America's children.

8

How Common Standards and Standardized Testing Widen the
Opportunity Gap

Christopher H. Tienken and Yong Zhao

RECENT REVELATIONS OF cheating on standardized tests in the Atlanta Public
Schools (APS) alert us to the fact that high-stakes testing is not a viable solution
to the problem of academic underachievement. A year-long investigation ordered
by the governor of Georgia found that in 44 of 56 schools examined, educators
changed students' answers. A total of 178 educators, including 38 principals, were
named as participants in cheating. The practice had been ongoing for almost a
decade, making it the largest case of cheating in the country. Thousands of children in APS were deprived of educational opportunities they needed because "the
cheating cut off struggling students from the extra help they would have received
if they'd failed."[1] Ironically, the gains in test scores achieved via the cheating also
seemed to add credence to the APS's non-evidence-based policies of increasing the
amount of time devoted to English language arts instruction and mathematics
instruction at the expense of other education programs like the arts. In essence,
the perceived improvement in test scores drove a decrease in overall education
opportunity. Not only did some students not receive the extra help they might
have needed due to the artificially inflated test results, but they were also subjected to a reduced curriculum, driven mainly by two subjects. We use cheating
on high-stakes tests in this chapter as one of many examples to show the cor-
rupting influences of centralized and standardized policy interventions on children's opportunities to participate in intellectually and socially robust education
programs.

That type of deprivation of educational opportunity is the result of the No Child Left Behind Act (NCLB)[2] and similar policy initiatives, such as the centralization of curriculum and assessment across the nation, which ironically were marketed as interventions to provide children with more opportunities. NCLB and the various NCLB waiver schemes approved by United States Department of Education (USDOE) bureaucrats use centralized curricula and high-stakes testing to hold school personnel accountable for improving student learning, particularly for raising the achievement of disadvantaged students to close the achievement gap. The various federal and state laws require schools to make adequately yearly progress (AYP) or achieve some other type of result on standardized tests, and the laws prescribe severe penalties for those students and educators who fail to raise test scores to the mandated level. Schools that serve disadvantaged students have faced tremendous pressure to raise test scores. Most of the actions the schools have taken to raise test scores, however, are counterproductive. Like cheating, they may appear to improve student achievement, but in reality they exacerbate the educational conditions that afflict these children and consequently widen the educational opportunity gap.

OPPORTUNITY TO LEARN

Researchers identified four recurring opportunity-to-learn variables in education and psychology literature, that when cultivated, produce increases in student achievement and overall school success.[3] The variables identified in the literature are: (a) time on task, (b) curriculum quality, (c) effective instructional methods, and (d) depth of instruction. Taken as an interdependent group, the variables can act as one framework from which to loosely gauge how well education policies and systems attend to the opportunity gap.

The opportunity to learn is critical, especially for our neediest students. The opportunity gap increases as the opportunity to learn decreases. For example, as a group, students labeled as economically disadvantaged or poor never score higher on standardized tests than their non-disadvantaged peers in any state on any grade level currently tested under NCLB. As we present, those students more frequently receive a restricted curriculum. The opportunity to experience and learn a broad, quality curriculum cannot be understated.

Like many medicines, education policies and practices carry real risks of unintended side effects and complications, so trade-offs are necessary. Many proposed panaceas for the perceived ills of public education, such as the Common Core State Standards (CCSS)[4] initiative and national high-stakes testing, might not be as effective or safe for certain groups as currently claimed by those who market these initiatives. In fact, those interventions can increase the educational opportunity gap that exists between children of the poor and those of the wealthy. In this chapter we draw on lessons of the past and from other nations to show that the current prescription for closing the achievement gap—common curricular standards and test-based accountability—will not close the opportunity gap but, instead, might widen it.

THE OPPORTUNITY TO RECEIVE EXTRA HELP

Policy perversions, such as cheating, not only deprive struggling students of the extra help they need, but also damage the morale, reputation, and professional working conditions of their teachers. This unethical behavior sets a terrible example for children. As a result of the pressure to raise test scores, cheating has taken place in many different forms and on all levels, but mostly in schools serving low-income, minority students. The NCLB Act and the various waiver programs under the Obama administration prescribe a host of sanctions that must be enacted against educators when their schools fail to make AYP or the goals identified in the state waivers, as measured by student results on state-mandated, high-stakes tests of academic skills and knowledge. Some sanctions include transferring part of schools' Title I funds to private companies to provide tutoring services to eligible Title I students, even if those students "passed" their states' tests. Other sanctions allow for the firing of principals and teachers, converting schools to charter schools, and allowing for-profit and other types of education management organizations (EMOs) to take charge of the local school and local tax dollars. None of these mandated sanctions have been demonstrated empirically to improve educational opportunities for students.

In their book *Collateral Damage: How High-Stakes Testing Corrupts America's Schools*,[5] Nichols and Berliner document various forms of cheating by teachers and administrators, students, and state governments. Unethical activities that would help improve test scores on mandated standardized tests include distributing copies of the test to teachers and/or students in advance, whispering answers to students and asking or encouraging students to change their answers during the test, and changing wrong answers to right ones after the test, which happened in Atlanta. They also document how it is possible for state education bureaucrats and school personnel to "fudge" student performance data to potentially mislead the public.

Cheating is an intolerable form of corruption that can cause severe damage to our students and the entire education system. Although cheating occurs in districts serving wealthy and poor students alike; it unfortunately happens on a larger scale in urban schools that serve impoverished students and students of color. Cheating has been reported in many large urban school systems, including Washington, DC; Baltimore; Los Angeles;[6] Dallas; Houston; Chicago; Oakland; and New York City. In sum, students who are already struggling suffer most from this form of corruption.

THE OPPORTUNITY TO ENJOY A BROAD, BALANCED CURRICULUM

The loss of students' opportunities to experience a broad, well-balanced curriculum because of the imposition of common curriculum standards and high-stakes testing is even more widespread than the loss of access to special academic, social, or emotional services, and the consequences of losing such opportunities might be even more serious. Centralized curriculum and test-based accountability has led to the school curriculum being narrowed down to what is most likely be tested.[7] This happens much more frequently in schools that serve economically disadvantaged students, because their students, historically, score significantly lower on standardized tests. These schools are also under more pressure to improve test performance.

By imposing state standardized testing in math and English language arts, legislation like NCLB and other standardization and centralization schemes resulted in a significant narrowing of the curriculum. For example, five years after the implementation of NCLB, over 60 percent of school districts reported that they had increased instructional time for math and English language arts (ELA), while 44 percent reported that they had reduced time for other subjects or activities such as social studies, science, art and music, physical education, lunch, and/or recess. On average, 32 percent less instructional time was devoted to other subjects.[8] Only two years after the implementation of NCLB, three-quarters of school principles surveyed reported increases in instructional time for math and ELA, one-quarter reported decreases in time for the arts, and one-third anticipated future decreases.[9]

Curriculum narrowing occurs more frequently in schools serving disadvantaged children. More impoverished urban districts (76 percent) increased time for math and ELA and decreased time for other subjects than did suburban districts (69 percent). The Center on Education Policy (CEP) found that 36 percent of principals of high-minority schools reported decreases in instructional time for the arts, while only 21 percent of those in low-minority schools reported decreases. Substantially more districts with at least one school identified under NCLB as needing improvement, corrective action, or restructuring—which are more frequently found in poor and minority neighborhoods—decreased instructional time for subjects other than math and ELA than did districts without any identified schools.[10]

Students from families with low socioeconomic status (SES) are more likely to attend school in districts whose schools have a higher probability of not meeting AYP achievement targets.[11] Nationally, the mean scores on state-mandated tests of math and ELA arts for the subgroup of students categorized as "economically disadvantaged" (ED) are always less than the mean scores of non-ED students at every grade level tested.[12] In some states, the ED subgroup scores below the state's cut-score for proficiency and always scores closer to the proficient cut-score than their non-disadvantaged peers. The ED subgroup actually scores below their states' proficiency cut points in ELA in 11 out of 37 (30 percent) of the states that reported data and below in math in 12 states. The achievement differences are striking in terms of scale score and effect sizes.[13] The effect size differences in mean achievement between the students in the ED subgroup and their non-ED peers ranged from 0.39 to 1.05 in ELA and 0.36 to 1.02 in math. The effect size was 0.50 or higher favoring the non-ED in ELA and math in 27 out of 37 (73 percent) states that reported data.

The schools more often attended by ED students are located in urban and rural areas. Thus, the larger concentration of students who score near or below their states' proficiency cut scores drive aggregate test results lower. Subsequently, the chances that the student scores will not achieve mandated performance goals such as AYP increases and thus, school personnel and students face sanctions. This is what some have documented as the unequal effects of AYP.[14] As noted previously those schools more frequently decrease instructional time for subjects other than math and ELA and reduce the macro-curriculum, in terms of diversity of courses, and the course level micro-curriculum becomes more aligned to what is most likely tested.[15] Curricular reductionism creates a situation of fewer opportunities for students who actually most need to receive broad and diverse educational experiences.[16] Based on the existing literature it is not unreasonable to assume that low SES and racial and ethnic minority students are more likely to experience an educationally impoverished curriculum that in some cases reduces student engagement[17] and offers fewer opportunities to learn a wide array of skills and develop their creative talents than their White, economically privileged counterparts.[18] A regressive, narrow curriculum offers disadvantaged children fewer opportunities to engage with the range of subjects, activities, and experiences that constitute a full, high-quality education.

A measurable gap exists between poor and middle-class students upon entry to preschool and kindergarten. Sociological studies have consistently found that

students who live in impoverished backgrounds come to school with fewer intellectually stimulating life experiences, as well as lower levels of academic achievement.[19] In comparison to their impoverished peers, children of wealthy parents
are more likely to come to preschool and kindergarten knowing their letters and
being able to read. Reading fluency and comprehension correlate with achievement on state standardized tests. A lack of prior experiences also makes it difficult
to make sense of new content, because there is nothing to help children connect to
new learning. Children who live in impoverished environments need the greatest
opportunity to receive the most diverse and enriched curriculum in order to make
sense of and internalize new and challenging content. However, a common curriculum based on a restricted view of learning and achievement does not provide
that opportunity.

A narrow curriculum, focused on a restricted set of test items, detracts from one
of the equalizing functions of public schools: providing the experiences and opportunities that disadvantaged families and communities cannot. Standardization
programs like those carried out under NCLB and the CCSS undermine the socially
just and life-enriching opportunities that a comprehensive curriculum can bring.
A narrow curriculum effectively renders high-quality educational opportunities a
private good, accessible only to those who can afford to purchase or provide it
outside of school.

Subjects and experiences that are not tested are expunged or marginalized. All
that is artistic, emotional, personal, socially conscious, and culturally different
is erased or subjugated at the altar of behaviorist and social-Darwinian policies
in the pursuit of a shallow pool of reproducible skills and knowledge. Those students and teachers who do not bow in reverence are essentially weeded out via
high-stakes testing.

Teachers have responded to this policy environment and, in some cases, direc-
tives from misguided school administrators, by teaching toward what they believe
will be on the tests; they teach only what is likely to be tested, in the formats most
likely to be presented on the tests, and compel students to take practice tests.
Schools that serve mostly poor minority and immigrant children are under more
urgent pressure to raise test scores in order to meet AYP or other state accountability targets and are more likely to reduce instruction to test preparation. This
is the "pedagogy of poverty."[20] This pedagogical chasm will be further widened by
the adoption of the CCSS and the national testing. We fear that linking teacher
and school administrator employment to test results will further bludgeon creativity and innovation out of the curriculum, and thereby increase the opportunity gaps that exist. Middle- and upper-class parents will provide to their children
a wide range of creative and enriching opportunities to create, innovate, design,

strategize, and perform via out-of-school experiences financed out of their pock-etbooks. How will children of poverty access similar types of opportunities if the larger society does not support access?

THE OPPORTUNITY TO GRADUATE

As discussed earlier, an oppressive and regressive form of deprivation of educational opportunities for disadvantaged students results from using common standards and testing as accountability measures: the exclusion of students who might prevent the school from meeting the accountability requirements.[21] "There is considerable evidence that some educators have shaped the test-taking pool in their schools or districts through such exclusionary practices as withdrawing students from attendance rolls," [22] because "if the disaffected or weakest students can be pushed out of schools or allowed to drop out, then the test scores at the school or districts that lose these students will go up."[23]

Accounts of schools pushing out students who are disadvantaged and do not perform well on standardized tests abound.[24] An article in *Time* magazine recounted how one school with high standardized test scores forced or encouraged disadvantaged students to leave the school in order to close the achievement gap.[25] The story explained that an African American student was goaded out of high school after multiple "disciplinary suspensions," and that disciplinary measures were often used to push out underachieving students just prior to the administration dates of the state-mandated test to help the school meet AYP. Unfortunately, most of the students affected by these tactics belong to racial and ethnic minorities and families living in poverty—precisely those whom advocates of standards, testing, and accountability claim to help.

Lower than hoped for graduation rates for impoverished students and students of color have been a persistent concern for American education. Between one-fourth and one-half of students in the 50 largest US cities drop out before graduating high school.[26] "High-stakes testing has simply exacerbated the traditional problem of keeping disaffected youth of all ability levels in school."[27] "Because of high stakes testing, it probably takes much less time today for our K-8 children to develop their academic self-image than in the past, and that image is probably more rigidly held than ever before."[28] Lack of confidence in their abilities induced by a myopic focus on test scores can cause children to disengage from school and eventually lead them to drop out. The most recent data show that graduation rates declined for two consecutive years, from 2005 to 2006 and 2006 to 2007, after the implementation of NCLB.[29]

THE OPPORTUNITY TO DEVELOP INDIVIDUAL
TALENTS AND CREATIVITY

By prescribing rigid grade-level expectations and using high-stakes tests to monitor implementation, the education bureaucrats who manage the education system either assume that all children start at the same point, progress at a uniform pace, and have the same strengths and weaknesses or they choose not to recognize the differences that exist in cognitive, social, and moral development. Should a child not achieve the expected score on one test, he or she is considered at risk. If, as often happens, the child is given remedial education that moves at a slower pace and focuses even more myopically on areas of perceived weakness, the student is denied opportunities to explore a more enriched curriculum and develop his or her creativity and talents, because he or she must participate in the remedial instruction while other students are taking additional electives or attending art and music class. In essence, the standardized system widens the opportunity gap, or perhaps even helps to create it.

Equality of curriculum standards is inherently inequitable when it is interpreted as meaning uniformity of results in a one-size-fits-all approach to instruction and assessment. Compelling all children to follow the same rigid succession of content objectives and perform at the same level of achievement at a given age condemns some to failure, denying them opportunities to learn an array of skills, much less to discover and create. Students who are judged to be at risk based on the results from standardized tests—who disproportionately belong to racial and ethnic minority groups, are English language learners, or have learning disabilities—might possess strengths that are simply not recognized by the standard curriculum and are not assessed by standardized tests.[30] Talents that do not fit into this constricted system are devalued. Children's self-confidence may be severely damaged by being told that they are not good at anything that counts, and they might become alienated from learning.[31] Those students labeled "not proficient" or "in need of improvement" might actually need more choices, more pathways, and more opportunities to develop into free-thinking and self-determined individuals. Standardization of knowledge and performance through rigid curricula and high-stakes testing robs all children—those who are successful within the system, as well as those who are not—of the opportunity to develop freely into creative individuals because standardization marginalizes the talents, skills, emotions, and aspirations that are not valued by the system.

It is fatally misguided to mandate policies that exacerbate the opportunity gap, which already exists between the rich and the poor, by compelling all children to master the same narrow set of academic skills and knowledge and punishing those that do not. It is naïve and irresponsible to think it would actually benefit them or the country. Standardizing knowledge and the ways in which children acquire and demonstrate their mastery of it is an inhumane policy based on a lack of understanding of human diversity and developmental psychology. This approach eschews social scientific research and social-justice principles and, at bottom, forces children to fit into the system instead of designing a system that balances the needs of the child and of society.[32] A policy that is not child-centered will not effectively address these complex and pressing problems.

Curriculum does not operate in a vacuum, as cognitive development theory,[33] ecological systems theory,[34] self-determination theory,[35] sociocultural theory,[36] and Maslow's hierarchy of needs[37] have shown in their various ways. Children's learning is shaped by their personal backgrounds, home environments, cultures, emotions, life experiences, prior knowledge, and stages of cognitive and social development. Standardization assumes that children are blank slates and passive recipients of content, rather than active constructors of meaning who bring their prior knowledge and experiences to the learning situation. Those misguided assumptions are inappropriate for evidence-based policy making in a democratic society.

The standardization of knowledge and thinking denies children educational opportunities that might be more appropriate for their strengths, developmental and learning stages, and interests. Once a standard is established and enforced with high-stakes testing, it is used to include and exclude people. Those who happen to do well on one assessment are considered good and successful and valued more highly, whereas those who do less well are considered at-risk of failure and valued less, regardless of their other strengths. A child who can write imaginative essays or stories but cannot or does not wish to write the way standardized tests require is defined as deficient. These children are then forced to remedy their deficiencies at the cost of losing opportunities to develop their strengths. As a result, their talents are devalued, suppressed, and left to wither.

COMPARATIVE PERSPECTIVES

Many countries that have long histories of centralized curriculum and high-stakes testing have begun reforming their education systems to offer more diverse curricular opportunities, decentralization, and autonomy.[38] Singapore and China, which have been heralded as examples of educational excellence because of their students' performance on international assessments of mathematics, have launched multiple rounds of curriculum reforms to add more flexibility and breadth to their curricula.[39] Creativity and innovation in the Chinese education system has suffered under national standards and high-stakes testing since the invention of *keju*, a national examination system to select government officials, over 2,000 years ago. Although initially *keju* seemed a fair and open mechanism to identify leaders from the commons, it gradually degenerated into a system that rewarded those who mastered the Confucian classics and excluded other more useful talents, especially critical thinking and creativity. *Keju* limited the country's capacity for scientific and technological innovation and was partially blamed for the decline of this great civilization. The *keju* system was abolished in 1905. But its spirit lives on today in the revamped *gaokao*, the college entrance exam. Colleges use it to select students, so it represents the only chance a Chinese youth has to get into college. The stakes are very high, making it a powerful mechanism to enforce national curriculum standards.

In recent years, *gaokao* has been criticized as the root cause of Chinese educational ills: the lack of innovative and creative citizens; unbearable academic pressure and deteriorating health among students, including suicides; widespread cheating and fraud; and massive inequality in educational opportunities. China has now launched a series of efforts to transform its "test-oriented education" into a "quality-oriented education." One of the major strategies is to relax central control of the curriculum and enable more local autonomy.[40] Yet these reforms have not led to a significant expansion in students' curricular opportunities. Innovations are limited, and the educational experiences of the vast majority of students remain confined to what is tested.[41] "As long as principals are held accountable for their schools' performance in national examinations, they cannot afford to stray too far from the mainstream curriculum."[42]

Proponents in the US of the CCSS initiative suggest that they will not develop national high-stakes testing as extreme as China's *gaokao* or that they will develop more innovative assessments rather than utilize the typical multiple-choice questions. That still has not happened. The tests look the same, measure relatively the same skills as the state test they replaced, and are in fact used to make high-stakes, life-changing decisions about children and school personnel. Like their predecessors developed as part of NCLB, the new national tests will also influence some school personnel to cheat or narrow the curriculum to what will most likely be tested. Of course Campbell's Law predicted this.[43] The law tells us that any social indicator used for a high-stakes purpose inevitably becomes corrupted. As occurred with the abuse of the *gaokao* in China, after people in power begin to make consequential decisions on the basis of a national assessment of achievement relative to common core standards, children's opportunities to develop creativity and innovative thinking will be lost, especially for those from impoverished backgrounds.

England's adoption of a national curriculum shows what happens when a standardized curriculum is mandated and monitored with high-stakes tests. England replaced a largely locally controlled curriculum with a national curriculum in the early 1990s. The curriculum is broader than math and literacy, but these subjects, along with science, are considered core subjects and given greater significance through testing. According to "The Cambridge Primary Review," a recent report that received heavy media coverage, the national curriculum deprived public school children of the opportunity to receive a broad and rich education. The problems of the national curriculum include the detachment of curriculum from socio-civic and vocational aims; the loss of the children's entitlement to a broad, balanced, and rich curriculum and the marginalization of the arts, the humanities, and lately, science; the test-induced regression to valuing memorization and recall over understanding and inquiry, and to a pedagogy that rates transmission as more important than the pursuit of knowledge in its wider sense; and the loss of breadth and balance across and within subjects as a result of the pressures of testing, especially at the upper end of the primary school.[44]

THINK GLOBALLY BUT ACT LOCALLY TO CLOSE THE OPPORTUNITY GAP

Curriculum has the greatest influence on student achievement when it is designed locally, with the particular needs of students in mind.[45] It can provide students from impoverished backgrounds with opportunities that their families and communities cannot. When curriculum is handed down from on high, as is the case with the CCSS, it has a much weaker influence. A study of high schools that serve New Jersey's poorest communities found that the more customized the curriculum at the local level, the better the students performed on the state's high school exit exam.[46]

Classic works from the history of education point to the importance of constructing curriculum for specific student bodies; consider the curricular knowledge created by Francis Parker, John Dewey, Horace Mann, Boyd Bode, the Harap Committee, and Hilda Taba. The landmark Eight-Year Study demonstrated that a locally developed, problem-based curriculum can produce better results than traditional programs.[47] As long as they are based on demonstrated research and theories of learning, less standardized, more diverse, locally developed and designed programs offer students greater opportunities to develop their talents. The students from the Eight-Year Study who were educated in the experimental schools performed better in college academically, socially, and civically compared to their traditionally prepared peers. There is no "one best curriculum path" for students in high school, and standardized sequences are not necessary to achieve superior results in elementary and secondary schools.[48]

CONCLUSION

Standardizing the curriculum does not ensure that all children will receive the education they need to be more creative and innovative, as well as proficient learners. The results from the "college prep for all" initiatives beginning in Chicago in 1997, New York State in 2001, and Texas in 2003, as well as the mandated use of universal state standards via the No Child Left Behind Act of 2002, have done little to close the socioeconomically based achievement gap.[49] A mandatory universal curricular program makes no conceptual sense, is intuitively contradictory, and has no empirical backing.

Singling out a few subjects through national standards and testing starves the curriculum and depresses the educational experience. Because the reputation and salary of teachers and administrators are on the line, educators will work toward making sure that students do well on those subjects at any cost, narrowing the curriculum to what is most likely to be tested and reducing teaching to test preparation. In a wrongheaded attempt to lower disparities in test scores, common standards and high-stakes testing actually widen the opportunity gap between the privileged and the disadvantaged, between "normal" children and those who may deviate from the norm, and between those who conform and those who choose to pursue their own individual interests.

We believe that the educational system should provide children with opportunities to develop critical thinking, persistence, empathy, strategize, chances to create rather than imitate, and situations in which students can engage in socially conscious problem-solving. Education policies and practices should foster collaboration, cooperation, and innovation. We value diversity over conformity, creativity over imitation, and informed dissent over blind acceptance. Public schools should provide a safe haven for children to explore their cultures, develop their individual talents to their full potential, and learn how to critically analyze and solve the many issues our society and the people of the planet face. We should open the gates of opportunity to all children without constricting the meaning of education.

Given the weight of the evidence, it seems misguided and downright wrong to support such a massive social experiment as the CCSS, using participants who are compelled to participate without parental consent. Children have a right to high-quality educational opportunities, and educators and policy makers have a duty to help provide them. An old Chinese saying *Yinzhenzhike*, which means drinking poison to quench thirst, warns people not to seek solutions that cause serious damage just because the problem at hand is pressing. We hope this chapter serves as warning to proponents of standards and testing as the cure for the achievement gap in American education.

9

A More Perfect Union

RECONCILING SCHOOL CHOICE POLICY WITH

EQUALITY OF OPPORTUNITY GOALS

Janelle Scott and Amy Stuart Wells

JUDGING FROM RECENT policy trends, many urban school district officials, state leaders, and federal policy makers regard market-based school choice and testing as the most promising interventions for persistently unequal student outcomes. Accordingly, the nation is witnessing an expansion of these interventions into districts serving large numbers of poor students and students of color. At the same time, a political climate that supports widening inequalities of income and wealth; ongoing racial and socioeconomic segregation; unprecedented mass incarceration of people of color; attacks on public employees and their benefits; and tax cuts that depleted federal, state, and local coffers have restricted provisions for services that support the non-rich, including early childhood education, unemployment benefits, and welfare. These cuts place even greater demands on public schools to redress the educational consequences of economic deprivation.

As we explain in this chapter, some forms of school choice can be instrumental in helping to redress educational inequality—but only if those policies explicitly engage the goals of equity and equality of opportunity, and if policy makers provide regulatory mechanisms and incentives to achieve them. Meanwhile, mounting evidence suggests that more market-oriented forms of school choice—for example, most charter school, open enrollment, and voucher policies, particularly when combined with high-stakes testing policies—actually widen inequality and further stratify students' opportunities to learn. This pattern emerges in school systems in which policy makers have adopted school choice with insufficient attention to the types of support systems needed to overcome the extreme level of inequality and the racial and socioeconomic segregation that continue to define residential patterns in the United States.[1]

Indeed, we know from research on various school choice policies—including voluntary, or choice-oriented desegregation plans—that in the absence of provisions or incentives to maintain or achieve equity, schools become increasingly identifiable by race, poverty, and frequently, low performance on standardized assessments.[2] But this evidence runs counter to popular understandings of market-based policies as tools of reform. Advocates argue that parents will transfer their children out of failing schools into schools with higher levels of student achievement and that access to transparent school test-score data and teacher performance metrics will enable them to make informed choices. The process will supposedly lead to the closure of failing public schools as families flee them and they become underenrolled. The market responds to demand for better schools, so the argument goes, and more high-quality schools of choice—usually privately managed charter schools—are opened. This market-based school closing and opening process has, to date, occurred most often in low-income communities where more students had been poorly served by the regular public schools. Supporters see this as the process by which the achievement gaps between students of color and White students and between rich and poor students will be closed.[3]

There are several problems with this market-driven model, however. Most importantly, it ignores the complex political dynamics that shape schools, communities and markets. Indeed, because of the lack of transportation or student-recruitment efforts that transcend segregated communities, the educational "market"—like most markets—is highly segmented both in terms of targets and geography. In other words, educational entrepreneurs are targeting market niches in a manner that may maximize their short-term success and their bottom line, but may not enhance educational opportunities or equality across the board and, in fact, contribute to even greater stratification within low-income and urban communities.

For instance, we know that most market-based[4] choice schools tend to recruit students from geographically specific areas and do not typically provide the transportation needed for students to come to these schools from other communities. They also employ admissions criteria that effectively screen or push out the most disadvantaged and lowest-achieving students, even when they are serving poor communities that have high numbers of such students. We know from research on charter schools in particular that they tend to enroll lower percentages of students who require special education or English language instruction.[5] These restrictions result in many of these schools being more stratified by race, ethnicity, social class, language of origin, and the academic needs of the students than conventional public schools. A number of educational and social theorists and scholars have attempted to articulate a vision for school choice that would negotiate the increasing demand from parents to choose schools for their children (especially poor parents and parents of color) with a broader concern for the implications of individual choices for the public good, arguing that the divide between markets and democracy need not be so pronounced.[6] Even when they advocate for increasing the amount and forms of school choice policies, these scholars tend to be in accord about the need for the state to serve as a regulator and protector of civil rights. In other words, educational market niches often work against democratic principles and "ideals" of the "common" public school.

We are not naïve to the fact that high degrees of stratification and social inequality are also prevalent within the public educational system, and have been since its inception. Still, from the 1960s into the 1980s, the overall trend in public education was toward more inclusion as state-sanctioned segregation systems were dismantled and students with disabilities were finally served by public schools. Thus the democratic ideal of a common public school somewhat offset the stratification of the larger society, especially when public policies such as school desegregation were established to proactively create more equitable schooling.[7] Yet, as race-conscious and equity-minded policies have been scaled back or eliminated and replaced with free-market oriented and deregulatory reforms, we have seen an increase in segregation by race, class, and special needs across schools.[8] The school choice marketplace—as it intersects with a segmented housing market, a new sector of privately run schools that control their admissions and student compositions through attrition, and a rollback of equity-minded policies such as school desegregation—has unequivocally created greater degrees of racial segregation. Indeed, the market facilitates particular high-status options and opportunities for affluent and more-efficacious families, leaving those with the least economic, social, and political power with the fewest opportunities to send their children to high-achieving schools. Families that begin with the most opportunities are further advantaged within a system of unregulated choice.[9]

The response of many market advocates to the lackluster overall performance of their reforms over the last 30 years is that we need more of the same and that we should scale up charter management organizations, which appear to be running the high-achieving networks.[10] Such proposals, while on the surface are appealing, are problematic on several levels, not the least of which is the lack of solid evidence about their success and the large donations from private foundations that sustain many of these high-profile schools. In fact, researchers from Western Michigan University found that the popular Knowledge is Power Program (KIPP) charter school network received on average an additional $5,700 per student compared to comparable schools.[11] This resource dynamic substantially increases the difficulty of any effort to replicate hybridized choice schools on a large scale.[12] In what follows, we provide mounting evidence that market-based models are not working to expand educational opportunity for most children and their families but, rather, are providing more stratified pockets of opportunity for some. Yet despite this evidence, public officials remain committed to market-based policies, and this commitment to school choice, competition, and testing has shifted the policy conversation away from other policy options, especially plans likely to provide more equitable school choices to the most disadvantaged children. For policy makers and citizens concerned about closing the opportunity gap, one key strategy is to engage in careful and deliberate consideration before adopting or expanding school choice programs that could impede progress toward equal educational opportunity. These debates about the structure and dynamics of public education are truly about who will ultimately be able to participate fully in American democracy.

Here we review educational research on both market-based and more democratic school choice policies, within the context of the accountability and testing mechanisms that have defined the terms of educational reform over the last few decades.[13] Yet, we also look at other evidence, when available, that helps explain the more democratic goals (or lack thereof) of different types of school choice plans. We argue that school choice policies *can* advance the democratic goal of greater educational equity if they are conceptualized and constructed in a manner that acknowledges the structural inequality within which public schools exist today and if they include sensible and powerful provisions to counteract its effects. Democratically minded choice plans are not panaceas, but the racial and ethnic and social class diversity they facilitate is a necessary precondition for equalizing opportunities. Otherwise, school choice falls too easily into a market-based policy frame in which some parents and families are advantaged over others, just as they are in the larger social, political, and economic order.

Drawing on the existent research, we offer multiple analyses. First, we compare and analyze market versus democratic forms of school choice policies. Second, we discuss the research literature on student access and equity as it relates to these different types of school choice policies. Third, we unpack issues of testing and assessment in relation to school choice and stratification. Finally, we offer recommendations for policy makers or other stakeholders who seek to promote equity and equality of opportunity.

MARKET VERSUS DEMOCRATIC FORMS OF SCHOOL CHOICE

Many observers of different school choice policies have acknowledged their complicated political histories, as discussed below, and recognized that choice is mainly a means to an end and not an end in itself. What we can accomplish via school choice policy depends on the goals that govern the design of specific programs and policies.[14] In the past, school choice has been employed both as an instrument of segregation and as a tool for desegregation. For instance, in the 1950s and 60s, plans designed to maintain racial segregation enabled White families to choose schools that were very effective at keeping out students of color.[15] Later, policy makers devised voluntary desegregation programs to give students of color more choices and to assure that families of different racial and ethnic backgrounds could and would choose more integrated schools.[16] Concurrently, some racial and ethnic communities regarded choice as necessary for cultural liberation,[17] favoring schools (whether private, independent, or semi-autonomous public) that provided opportunities for self-determination and control over school governance, leadership, and curriculum.[18]

Yet the current landscape represents something very different: a preponderance of racially homogenous schools where key decisions are made by largely White "reformers" on behalf of communities of color. At the same time, the courts have restricted the use of race in student assignment; limiting the ability to craft choice plans that incorporate racial balance and redistribute educational opportunity. Instead, market-based choice plans have become the norm, making no provisions for resource equality, diversity, or access for all students regardless of ability. In terms of equality of opportunity, the political origins, design, and rules governing choice plans matter a great deal. For this reason, any school choice policy's potential to help the most disadvantaged students or to foster greater equality depends on specific guidelines to redress the more stratifying and exclusionary tendencies of markets and capitalist economic systems.[19] Ironically enough, market-based choice policies too often exacerbate these tendencies instead of correcting them, as more democratic and equity-minded models are meant to do.

Unless policy makers maintain an explicit commitment to democratic equity, rather than to laissez faire market principles, school choice plans are likely to exacerbate inequality, leading to more segregation and stratification. Indeed, market-based plans generally stress competition between schools based on narrow standardized test results. Furthermore, they do not target the most disadvantaged students or provide them with meaningful choices in nonpoor schools, nor do they necessarily provide support services, such as transportation or special education, or have guidelines for balancing student enrollments in terms of race, ethnicity, poverty, and English language learners.[20] Perversely, schools are given incentives to accept and retain only the highest-scoring students if they wish to remain viable in a market environment. Here, choice, testing, and stratification become intertwined: the reforms collide in a context in which the value of teachers and schools is measured by narrowly tailored assessments that evaluate performance in just a few subject areas and with metrics whose accuracy, validity, and reliability are highly contested.[21]

The above description points to clear distinctions between market and democratic forms of school choice policies, particularly regarding the means-end relationship. Whereas market adherents believe that the end of school choice policy is unfettered individual choice, adherents to democratic schooling emphasize the greater good. Market adherents would give parents free rein to choose schools and assume that the good of the society as a whole is the sum of these individual choices.[22] Democratic theorists, on the other hand, would privilege our national, collective responsibility for ensuring that all schools are of high quality, have diverse student bodies, are given resources equitably, and achieve academic results that are substantially independent of the socioeconomic differences between students.[23] These distinctions arise from different understandings of the motivations driving parental schooling preferences and from different ideas about how society should be structured.[24]

According to democratic theorist Michael Engel, at least four assumptions about human behavior shape market ideology: (1) human nature is an unchangeable array of traits; (2) society is made up of individuals, and the social order represents the results of their individual choices; (3) people primarily make choices to maximize their personal reward in a self-interested way; and (4) a primary purpose of society should be to protect individual rights to make choices.[25]

Assuming these preconditions, laissez faire choice advocates would argue that there is no need to interfere in the market, as humans will produce according to demand and will strike mutually advantageous bargains. The invisible hand of the market will create pricing that constitutes a beneficial exchange for buyers and consumers. Yet, when market theory is applied to the provision of public education, fissures in its seemingly neat model emerge. For example, although market advocates assume that a baseline support exists for the public provision of schooling, it is not at all clear that everyone will support even minimal public investments in public education even if they enjoy the social benefits it generates. In addition, policy makers increasingly judge the public benefits of schooling in terms of fairly narrow, and as we have argued, problematic test results, and tend to ignore the myriad social benefits not measured by these assessments. High-stakes testing aligns neatly with market-based choice, and becomes the primary tool for determining school quality, ignoring the broader social benefits and costs particular educational forms can bring.

In contrast, adherents of democratic schooling see the purpose of education as both facilitating individual development and providing collective, societal benefits. John Dewey held that preparation for work and preparation for democratic participation are mutually reinforcing; in addition to technical skills, workers need critical thinking skills, as do citizens. Moreover, he argued that human learning takes place in a social context. Engel advocates a holistic-democratic perspective that prioritizes developing well-rounded learners who contribute to a healthy and participatory democracy. He concludes, "A democratic school is one that, above all, tries to enable people to create their own world collectively rather than fit into one that is created for them. It operates on the basis of a faith that people are capable of ... living together democratically. As such, people are valued for who and what they are, not just for what they can produce or return on a financial investment."[26]

We contend that school choice policy, properly designed to achieve equitable ends, can be an important dimension of equal and more-democratic schooling, yet the dominance of market ideologies has greatly constrained that possibility. This conclusion is based on our examination of current research, discussed in the next section, regarding the relationship between school choice policy design and student access to educational opportunities.

ACCESS, EQUITY, AND SCHOOL CHOICE POLICY DESIGN

By the early 1990s, voluntary choice-oriented school desegregation plans were eclipsed by new forms of school choice policy driven by market-based arguments about the efficacy of more competition and less regulation—including racial balancing guidelines—in public education.[27] The goal of school choice shifted abruptly from addressing the collective needs of society by creating a more equal and less segregated educational system to satisfying the self-interests of individual educational "consumers" who demanded "better" schools for their children.[28] These so-called colorblind school choice policies—those with no intent to address racial segregation or resource inequalities—included intra- and interdistrict open enrollment plans, charter schools, and voucher plans. In fact, as part of a larger wave of educational reform that stressed standards, accountability, and testing, these new, market-oriented school choice policies were key components of "neo-Plessyism," or the postdesegregation effort to finally achieve a system of separate but equal education. These policies garnered support from many teachers, parents, and advocates who had long been frustrated with the pace of school reform and had become disenchanted with desegregation efforts, especially when they resulted in tracking and resegregation.[29]

Over the last 20 years, researchers have found a strong correlation between the rapid rise in the number and scope of colorblind school choice policies in the United States and increased racial segregation in public education. We are not suggesting a causal relationship between these two trends, given other policy developments that have coincided with them, especially the rollback of court-ordered school desegregation plans, the changing racial and ethnic demographics within the K-12 population, and ongoing racial segregation in housing across metropolitan areas.[30] But the evidence leaves little doubt that the proliferation of market-oriented school choice policies and their reliance on narrow measures of achievement has contributed to growing racial isolation at the macrolevel and thus to an opportunity gap within the school choice terrain. At the very least, these forms have done little to interrupt racial segregation or to close the growing opportunity gap across the nation's public school systems.

The research on school choice policies suggests that at least part of the explanation for increased racial and socioeconomic segregation is related to the lack of sustained public support within those choice systems, especially for the students who have been most disadvantaged in the educational system.[31] These market-based policies generally do not provide poor students of color with the kind of outreach, information, access, and free transportation that would allow them to transfer to schools in more affluent communities. In sharp contrast, the older, desegregation-oriented plans used such support systems along with racial guidelines to create more integration and equity across schools.[32]

When school choice policies fail to include and enforce racial balancing guidelines and to provide support for disadvantaged students, the decisions parents make in choosing schools for their children are anything but blind to race and socioeconomic status.[33] Absent the sort of public policies that have in the past helped foster and maintain racial balance, parents will generally make demographically conscious choices, leading to greater stratification and segregation.[34] White parents in particular are more likely to choose whiter schools, if they are not provided with reasons to do otherwise.[35]

Black, Latino, and Native American parents often choose more racially homogenous schools as well, either because the cultural characteristics of these schools make them "safe spaces"[36] or because they believe them to be superior to what is offered in the traditional public school system,[37] or because they have little access to more racially diverse schools in more affluent communities.[38] In addition, many parents have become more amenable to market models for schooling.

Many schools tout themselves as beneficial for students of color, especially those a 2008 Fordham Foundation report called "paternalistic schools" that emphasize discipline, curricular basics, and long school days and years.[39]

The fact that parents of color are choosing these schools given their options is not surprising. Communities of color have engaged in historical struggles for high-quality schooling, often fighting for equal access to resources, high-quality teachers, facilities, and diversity among teachers and administrators against recalcitrant policy makers. These struggles predate the current marketized school choice environment.[40] Given their long-standing dissatisfaction with the available public and private schooling options, in the current marketized choice terrain parents of color are often faced with making schooling choices from a choice set that leaves much to be desired, but from which they often choose schools they feel will create safe, culturally representative and responsive, and educationally rich environments.[41] From the standpoint of equal educational opportunity, people of color choosing Afrocentric or Chicano-centric schools is less troubling than are conservative assertions that white paternalism is the best educational model for students of color, or, given the racial history of this country, than White students fleeing racially diverse schools for predominantly white ones.

Still, research on school choice offers no convincing evidence that the educational opportunities available or the academic outcomes of schools that are still segregated in terms of race, ethnicity, and class are better than the similarly segregated schools their students left behind.[42] In fact, some research, as well as common sense, leads us to believe that racially homogenous schools of choice are as enmeshed in the broader context of inequality as regular public schools are. For example, researchers assessing the test scores of high-profile choice schools serving low-income student populations, such as KIPP schools, have found patterns of high student attrition within those networks. Specifically, there are indications of high percentages of lower performing students leaving KIPP schools,[43] and of schools selecting students who are likely to perform well academically.[44]

As Diane Ravitch recently found, many so-called miracle schools—schools serving high-poverty children of color and boasting enviable high school graduation and college acceptance rates actually had lower scores on state assessments than traditional schools, indicating that graduates of such schools are performing poorly on the very measures that market forces say are most important.[45] Rather than miraculously surmounting the real challenges posed by intergenerational poverty and inequality, many choice schools seem to be struggling, despite their hefty private-sector support.

These trends not only require researchers and journalists to scrupulously investigate and place into context the claims of superior results, it also raises questions about high-profile, racially homogenous schools' effect on the traditional public schools that receive students who were counseled out, rejected, or chose to leave such schools. This interaction between selective, "model" schools and traditional public schools is often left unattended by policy makers, and receives insufficient attention from laudatory media accounts of high-profile charter school models. The end result is that separate remains inherently unequal across the nation's traditionally public, private, and marketized choice schools.[46]

When we review the growing body of research on the recent free-market forms of school choice policies—charter schools, open enrollment plans, and voucher plans—we see that their designs do not include important regulations and protections and thus lend themselves to greater racial and socioeconomic segregation, which perpetuates inequality.[47] In most cases, charter schools are more racially and socioeconomically homogeneous than the already highly segregated public schools that students leave behind.[48] While African American students are well represented in charter school enrollment, they tend to go to schools that are majority African American. At the same time, charters tend to enroll comparatively fewer special education students or English language learners.[49]

Like charter schools, statewide intradistrict and interdistrict open enrollment plans are a product of the ideology of market deregulation that became popular during the 1990s. Now enacted in nearly all states, open enrollment laws stipulate that students can transfer from their assigned local public school to either another school in their own district (intradistrict choice) or in another district (interdistrict choice). Although these policies are not targeted specifically toward poor students or students of color, advocates argue that competition will liberate students from low-performing schools, which will then improve or go out of business.[50] Yet the lack of support systems for the most disadvantaged families means that open enrollment plans have disproportionately enabled White and affluent students to transfer to relatively more advantaged school systems, exacerbating inequality between districts.[51]

These plans also allow schools and districts to control the intake of students from other districts. Virtually all evaluations of interdistrict open enrollment choice programs show that low-income students and students of color are the least likely to participate.[52] The other theme to emerge from research on the choices parents and students make is that, as noted above with regard to charter schools, school choice is definitely not colorblind. On the contrary, open enrollment plans consistently lead to greater racial and ethnic stratification and segregation, as White students residing in racially diverse school districts are moving in disproportionate numbers to predominantly white schools and districts.[53]

Finally, in the United States, unlike in most other countries, the handful of, but growing, state-funded tuition voucher programs that give families public money to pay private school tuition are, for the most part, targeted toward low-income families living in urban areas. The largest and longest running programs operate in Milwaukee, Cleveland, and Washington, DC.[54] Given that they are targeted exclusively toward students in these mostly poor and mostly African American and Latino school districts, we should not see the same pattern of greater racial and ethnic segregation that we find in charter schools and open enrollment plans. But once again, this market-oriented school choice policy is associated with greater stratification, including racial segregation.

For instance, in Cleveland, participation in the voucher plan is targeted to low-income families, but the income guidelines include many working-class Whites. These parents, many of whom were already sending their children to racially segregated Catholic schools before the program began, receive a voucher from the state to pay their child's tuition to virtually all-white religious schools.[55] As a result of this dynamic, the Cleveland plan enrolls a disproportionately high number of White students and a disproportionately low number of students from low-income families of color. In fact, whereas only 63 percent of students using the tuition vouchers belong to racial and ethnic minority groups, 82 to 89 percent of students in the city's public schools do.[56] If one compares all eligible Cleveland Public School students based on family income to the program's participants, the racial disparities are even worse. Over time, inequities have grown more severe.[57] Moreover, although the Cleveland voucher plan allows low-income students who live in the city to use their vouchers at private or suburban public schools, no suburban public schools and few selective private schools have accepted city children.[58] Most students end up enrolling in the racially and socioeconomically segregated religious schools in the city.

Even when voucher policies are targeted to low-income families, racial and class inequalities still develop and may become more problematic over time. Three factors contribute to this trend. First, among low-income families of color, students who have more informed parents, with greater formal education, are the most likely to take advantage of voucher plans.[59] Secondly, integration plans based on students' family income, known as socioeconomic (SES) integration plans, are an important step, but alone, they do not necessarily solve the problem of ongoing racial segregation.[60] And finally, overall, private schools are more racially segregated than public schools.[61]

Clearly, the movement of children, identified strictly by family income, into the hypersegregated private sector via vouchers is unlikely to increase racial integration and level the educational opportunity playing field. The tendency of market-driven school choice policies to promote racial and socioeconomic segregation should disturb anyone paying attention to the changing demographics of the

United States. As discussed later, policy makers can design choice policies to alleviate that segregation and inequality, but few policy makers have pursued those promising options.

TESTING, ASSESSMENT, AND SCHOOL CHOICE:
NO ACCOUNTABILITY FOR DIVERSITY

There are complex, but definite, connections between the ways in which parents make choices, the testing and accountability system, and racial as well as socioeconomic segregation. The emphasis on testing has created an environment in which diverse schools, and in particular schools comprising primarily poor students and/ or students of color, are seen as less desirable by those parents with the most choices.[62] The Center for Understanding Race and Education (CURE) at Teachers College, Columbia University is conducting a five-year (2008–2013) research project on metropolitan migration patterns and school district boundaries.[63] The quantitative analysis of Long Island home-purchasing patterns and related housing values coupled with qualitative data from interviews with parents, teachers, and real-estate agents suggest that as the accountability movement becomes a more central feature of educational policy, readily accessible and ubiquitous test-score data are driving separate and unequal housing choices even beyond past housing segregation patterns. School board members and superintendents from Long Island explained that test scores inform real-estate agents' abilities to market houses and also affect housing prices.

Some officials from high-performing school districts even meet with realtors to make sure they are "aware of the status of our budget, our scores, and all of those things that people come and ask them about." A realtor categorized prospective home buyers into "people who are focused on achievement" and those "who are focused on the well being of the child, their emotional, happy, well rounded growth"; "for the achievement-based people it becomes very easy to make a decision. They're looking at the outcome and the numbers tell the story for them." Test scores are not just increasingly important in perceptions of school quality; they are also exacerbating and legitimizing the process by which families sort themselves by race and class across neighborhoods. The extent to which segregation persists and worsens in a supposedly colorblind and postracial era can be partly attributed to the dominance of educational accountability measures that strongly correlate with race and class.

Further evidence that such accountability data influence school and housing choices was found in the Wells et al. study of six high schools that had been racially diverse in the 1970s but that had, in several cases, recently become predominantly Black and Latino.[64] Many of the educators and graduates talked about how these once vibrant racially diverse schools had been undermined by an accountability system that measured "school quality" in a highly simplistic manner that gave predominantly White and affluent schools a huge advantage when parents with means—mostly the White parents—were looking for "good" schools. Indeed, this study demonstrated that even graduates of racially diverse schools who valued their own educational experiences confessed that when it came to choosing schools for their children they felt compelled to put test scores and other narrow measures of academic excellence before diversity.[65] The testing and accountability movement, coupled with market-based choice programs, is working against the creation of racially diverse schools that tend to offer greater access to quality instruction, more equitable resource distribution, and opportunity to interact with a multiracial student body.

THE EVIDENCE ON MORE DEMOCRATIC SCHOOL CHOICE POLICIES

School choice and accountability systems need not perpetuate and intensify inequality and segregation. The rapid expansion of market-based choice programs has curtailed the consideration and widespread implementation of other options that could serve more democratic ends. For policy makers seeking to expand opportunity, we offer some ideas in this section about which school choice policies and programs have the greatest potential for such benefits. We ground these recommendations in a rapidly expanding and increasingly robust body of research that highlights the educational and democratic benefits of race-conscious (as opposed to so-called colorblind) school choice policies that were created and framed around a goal of greater educational equality. It is clear from several reviews of the existing research that the preponderance of this large body of evidence suggests that the academic and social benefits of attending racially diverse schools for students of all racial and ethnic backgrounds is strong. This research is often organized into two bodies of work:

1. The *short-term effects* of attending a racially diverse school, namely, improved academic outcomes, especially for students of color, and enhanced intergroup relations and cross-racial understanding[66]
2. The *long-term effects* of attending a racially diverse school, including greater mobility for graduates of color as well as improved racial attitudes and comfort levels in racially diverse settings for all graduates[67]

This research explains why the Black-White test score gap closed more quickly during the peak years of school desegregation implementation than any other time in our nation's history.[68] It also helps explain improved race relations and racial attitudes in this country over the last few decades as well as the growth of the Black middle class.[69]

At the same time, there is much evidence on the other side of the school desegregation coin—namely. *the harms of racial segregation*—which has received only limited attention since the *Brown* litigation.[70] While it is clear that Black students do not simply need to sit next to White students to learn, the reality is that the broader context of racial inequality in housing, labor, health care, and education has a Jim Crow–like effect on segregated public and charter schools, assuring they remain separate and unequal in many important ways. Programs that emphasize providing greater equality of opportunity as part of their design have demonstrated success, but these plans nonetheless are politically vulnerable and receive much less public and private investment than market-oriented charter schools and similar plans.[71]

All this helps to explain why today, in a country with an extremely diverse school-age population—now only 54 percent White, non-Hispanic—more and more parents are aware that their children are better prepared for our global society in racially and ethnically diverse schools. Indeed, researchers find in both survey data and interviews with parents of all different backgrounds, that there is a growing demand on the ground for high-quality, racially diverse public schools. *What often perpetuates racial segregation in public education today is a lack of leadership at the federal, state, and local levels to create more choices for the growing number of parents who highly value school-level diversity along with school quality.*

SCHOOL CHOICE POLICIES MORE CLOSELY ALIGNED
WITH EQUAL EDUCATIONAL OPPORTUNITY

Here we focus on three examples of more promising school choice policies: magnet schools, interdistrict school desegregation plans, and socioeconomic integration plans that utilize school choice. These programs are far from perfect. They have been subject to many of the same market pressures as other schools, some have tended to be selective, and their reach does not yet extend to all students and families who would like to enroll in them. Still, with adequate support and political cover, these programs' goals provide the foundation to address many of the key concerns discussed in this chapter.

Magnet Schools

In the peak years of school desegregation implementation in the 1970s and 1980s, magnet schools were both extremely popular with parents of all backgrounds and seen by local policy makers as the best way to provide greater choice in education while also meeting school desegregation goals. In more recent years, these more accessible and more expensive schools of choice have been overshadowed by the current menu of more market-driven school choice options. But this shift in popularity may have more to do with politics and spin than reality or perception "on the ground." Magnet schools are public schools that offer special curricular themes or methods of instruction, attract students voluntarily from outside an assigned neighborhood attendance zone, and achieve desegregation by meeting specific racial and ethnic targets.[72] "In the midst of several different national desegregation crises, early magnet schools offered a relatively uncontroversial—and peaceful— means of integrating schools."[73]

Still, magnet schools should not be oversold. Studies have generally found that they have fewer low-income children than other schools in their districts,[74] and when student demographics and initial performance were taken into account, magnet schools seemed to have only minimal effects on performance.[75] Nonetheless, numerous case studies have highlighted the high performance of individual magnet schools and the achievements of individual students within magnet schools.[76] These positive outcomes support a growing body of research that shows significant gains in the life chances of students attending integrated schools.[77]

Magnet schools have fallen prey to standardized measures of school quality, however, and they suffered when the US Supreme Court in 2007 further limited the ability of school districts to take the race of individual students into account in school-assignment plans.. Recognizing the legal risk in using explicit racial quotas in admissions, many districts either adopted a race-blind system, converting the magnet school to a themed school of choice, or used race as only one of several factors considered. Further, when desegregation becomes a secondary goal, resource-rich magnet schools are often the targets of financial cuts.[78] As desegregation takes a backseat to high stakes accountability, equality of opportunity in magnet schools—a goal that was never fully realized—becomes even more diminished.

Interdistrict School Desegregation Plans

The eight existing interdistrict school desegregation plans in the United States have achieved remarkable results, coupling racial diversity with academic improvement.[79]

These programs allow thousands of students to leave poor neighborhoods every day on sometimes long bus rides to more affluent and predominantly White suburban schools. Started through court orders and state laws in places like Rochester, Boston, and St. Louis, these plans were designed to overcome the harms of a segregated and unequal educational system and to provide those families that have historically had the fewest school choices with high-quality educational options.

Interdistrict school desegregation programs have consistently positive outcomes on several key dimensions. Indeed, the research in these programs explains why simply fixing up segregated and poor urban schools will never solve the deep and structural inequalities that define spaces and institutions in our society. These physical divides can only be challenged when disadvantaged students are allowed to cross the barriers and escape the separate and unequal schools that distinguish rich from poor, across race. There are long-term, substantial positive effects on academic achievement of students who transfer to suburbs. The demand for interdistrict transfer programs among city families continues to be strong. Racial and social integration is equally important to the democratic development of children and adults who live in predominantly white and privileged spaces, for these programs improve the racial attitudes and acceptance of the suburban students, educators, and parents.[80] Interdistrict school desegregation programs are not solely about providing low-income students of color with better educational opportunities; they are also about enabling a vast array of people across metropolitan areas to learn to get along in an increasingly diverse society.

Socioeconomic Integration Plans

Given the limitations and legal vulnerabilities of student assignment plans that take race into consideration, reformers have designed school choice plans that focus instead on socioeconomic integration.[81] In 2009, there were 65 school districts with such plans. Like the other options discussed here, this one has limitations. In particular, unless socioeconomic choice plans explicitly incorporate the goal of expanding educational opportunity and do more than simply place students from diverse SES backgrounds in the same school, they will likely have minimal impact on educational inequality, even if they succeed in increasing student diversity.

Nevertheless, while the evidence on the effects of SES integration plans thus far is inconclusive, they offer promising alternatives to the current menu of market-based choice plans. Two exemplary plans have been located in Wake County, North Carolina, and Berkeley, California. The Berkeley Unified School District's plan has been challenged and upheld by the California Supreme Court and could serve as a model for a choice program that foregrounds concern for democratic equality. Key tenets of the plan include a commitment to equalize resources across schools, to circumvent the idea that some schools are inherently more desirable. The plan has resulted in schools that are racially as well as socioeconomically diverse and perceived to be equal in quality, but the choice component is aligned with an overall goal of intradistrict equity. While Berkeley also has a higher than national average rate of private school attendance, parents with children enrolled in Berkeley's schools appear to be satisfied with them.[82]

Conversely, the socioeconomic student assignment plan in Wake County was challenged in 2010 by a newly elected Tea Party–dominated school board, whose president asserted that the plan was tantamount to "social engineering." The plan, in place for over a decade, had ensured that no school enrolled more than 40 percent high-poverty students, it had resulted in dramatic increases in test scores, and parents were largely satisfied with it.[83] A multiracial coalition rallied to preserve the plan, and was able to regain a Democratic majority on the Raleigh School Board, ousting Board Chairman Ron Margiotta in 2011. The events in Raleigh signal the value communities who have such plans in their school districts place on them.

The benefits of socioeconomic integration are many. It creates the conditions for a more equitable distribution of resources and opportunities because it counteracts the tendency to accrue high-status capital in a few schools. In Wake County, it also generated high-performing schools. In this regard, SES integration, while not perfect, more closely adheres to democratic notions of school choice.

DESIGNING SCHOOL CHOICE POLICY TO ADDRESS THE BARRIERS TO EQUAL OPPORTUNITIES

In 2011, Bob Herbert wrote his final columns in the *New York Times* Op-Ed section.[84] On March 21, he lamented the ways in which conversations about the importance of school desegregation had been marginalized in debates on public education. Herbert's final column was a meditation on the unprecedented wealth inequality currently gripping the nation. Public education is feeling the effects of both issues in ways that the supporters of recent, market-oriented school choice and testing policies have largely ignored. Instead, a variety of "no excuses" schools of choice are being developed with substantial private and public support. Policymakers interested in creating and supporting school choice programs that redress racial and socioeconomic inequality should consider the impact of this continued trend, especially given the research we have examined in this chapter that calls into question the results of such approaches.

In the last three decades, public debates about race and educational policy have shifted from a focus on structural inequities to causes and solutions that focus on individual children, families and teachers. As this chapter explains, the conversation about inequality and education must include close attention to the goals we hold for our public schools—the philosophical and political values that support the means and ends we pursue in advancing school choice or other policies.[85] In the civil rights era, there was an explicit and public—albeit deeply contested—discussion about racial isolation, racism, and redistribution; educational policies were often presented as remedies for past discrimination.[86] Such issues are strikingly absent from current discussions of school reform and academic achievement, where freedom of choice almost invariably supplants a broader conversation about the equitable provision of educational resources.

We call for greater investment in choice programs, including magnet schools, interdistrict desegregation plans, and socioeconomic integration plans that have delivered more promising results in terms of equity, access, and student achievement. We do not regard these programs as panaceas. Indeed, the ongoing debates about student achievement in charter schools suggest that no single educational reform is able to redress long-standing racial inequality. Still, policy makers would be wise to look at those particular school choice programs whose origins reside in efforts to increase choice and equity for the most disadvantaged students.

According to 2010 data from the U.S. Department of Education, magnet schools received roughly half of the funding allocated to charter schools.[87] Unless charter school policies are altered to provide less privileged students with the support they need and schools with the oversight that equal educational access requires, other forms of school choice may well be better suited to help ameliorate the racial achievement gap. In the absence of such alterations, we suggest that policy makers, particularly federal policy makers who are in the process of reauthorizing NCLB, turn to other choice forms and invest similar resources as those now given to charter schools.

The research evidence highlights the importance of diverse schools as well as the challenges to maintaining diverse schooling. Accordingly, policy makers should provide clear and meaningful incentives that create diverse and high-achieving schools. Currently, the vast majority of charter school and school voucher policies provide no incentives for maintaining diverse schools, despite a significant research base that finds multiple individual educational benefits for students who attend such institutions and the broader, societal benefits of having citizens who can interact across race and socioeconomic status. By crafting school choice policies that deliberately and effectively address segregation, stratification and inequity, policy makers can take important steps toward closing the opportunity gap, and help to better align choice with equality of opportunity goals.

PART III

Overcoming the Obstacles We Create for Equality

10

Student and School Cultures and the Opportunity Gap

PAYING ATTENTION AND TO ACADEMIC ENGAGEMENT AND ACHIEVEMENT

Prudence L. Carter

OVER THE COURSE of a decade I have spent countless hours interviewing, observing, and surveying students and educators on two different continents, and I understand now that the opportunity gap is fueled, in part, by another form of inequality: the unequal treatment of various student cultures in mainstream schooling.[1] Generally, school reform focuses on changes to the technical aspects of education—what students achieve in learning the proverbial three Rs of schooling. In this chapter, I move beyond the technical, offering evidence-based arguments about conditions that get less attention in policy circles, although their existence powerfully influences educational outcomes: *how cultural behaviors and practices matter to student engagement and achievement.*

In policy and funding circles, the interplay between school and student cultures receives less attention because these relationships are harder to measure. It is also difficult for survey research and intervention studies of this interplay to yield "causal" or "generalizable" claims about their impact on student outcomes, especially test results. Nevertheless, a multitude of researchers who use qualitative methods has documented comprehensively how student-school cultural differences reproduce opportunity gaps.[2]

Schools are not merely places where students learn how to read, to write, and to think critically; they are also major socializing institutions. "[Education is] about ... being able to connect with other people ... being able to question what the teachers are teaching you,"[3] a sage 15-year-old named Judah (a pseudonym) once declared to me when I interviewed him at his affluent, high-performing school on the East Coast. Judah and scores of modest-income African American and Latino students participated in a voluntary desegregation program that had bussed kids like them into the suburbs for decades. While Judah and many of his peers felt that theirs was a good school in terms of its academic outcomes, they struggled with fitting in culturally at the school. Their educational experiences were vastly different from those of their affluent Asian and White peers.

Education is also a system of cultural meanings that educators, students, and communities attach to everyday schooling practices; and these patterns of meaning have serious implications for educational opportunity. We know that connections exist between how students learn and their identities—for example, their race, ethnicity, class, or immigrant status and family culture.[4] Yet, who is defined as a "successful" or "smart" student is often predicated on specific cultural practices of particular social groups in US society, and this often goes above and beyond exhibiting behaviors such as studying or getting good grades. Cultures—shared meanings within groups—can differ.[5] And many ignore the very real tensions between two types of indicators: (1) cultural markers that often have little to do with a person's interest in achievement and success, and (2) cultural markers used by school officials to designate intelligent and competent students. Because of a conflation of these markers, educators, researchers and others have tended to define certain groups' ethnic and racial identities as either oppositional to or congruous with the goals of academic achievement.[6]

Many low-income and racial and ethnic minority students—especially those stereotyped or expected to be low achievers—find their ways of being, language and speech, styles of interaction and tastes, among other cultural factors, pegged as dysfunctional or as signs of lack of motivation, especially when these do not conform to the ways prescribed for academic success by the mainstream. In contrast, students whose fortunes are believed to be steeped in the strong influences of hard-working immigrant parents are attributed a group culture that is depicted with relatively more respect and deference.[7] For instance, some educators now perpetuate the stereotype that all Asian students are highly motivated and successful, when in reality several Asian ethnic groups are, on average, no more motivated or successful than other groups.[8] And more recently, research has portrayed how average-performing Asian American students benefit from the model-minority stereotype as teachers either place them in, or encourage them to take, higher-status classes. That is, these students benefit because they are perceived to be smart based on academic patterns by pan-ethnic Asian identity—what sociologist Jennifer Lee (2012) refers to as "stereotype promise."[9]

Three primary cultural explanations have gained traction concerning the association of students' family and cultural backgrounds with educational outcomes; each is discussed in the sections that follow:[10] (1) oppositional culture; (2) cultural mismatch; and (3) structured school practices that reproduce educational inequality. What we can infer from studies is that there is an interaction between students' and their families' material conditions and the sociocultural demands of schooling. In discussing each, I provide a more detailed summary of these key ideas and their linkages to the opportunity gap through students' daily experiences with teaching and learning. Also, I explore how to address the role of culture differences in education, especially when they threaten to compound the opportunity gap. And I argue that as policy makers, educators, and researchers construct successful approaches for reducing achievement disparities, they need to be aware of not only how the material or resource issues discussed in other chapters of this book are linked to the opportunity gap, but also how cultural inequality, both in wider society and within schools, exacerbates that gap.

OPPOSITIONAL CULTURE AND SCHOOL ACHIEVEMENT

For some, the mere idea that some students behave and speak differently from mainstream groups—tacitly understood as middle class and White in American society—is an indication of cultural differences, and more specifically, "cultural deprivation."[11] A common belief is that if students engage in specific cultural behaviors, from the use of language to the practice of effective study habits and "appropriate" interactional styles, then they will have a higher propensity for school success. This line of thinking has gained much currency in the national mindset, particularly since the overwhelming majority of students who perform less well in school are poor, working class, English Language Learners, or of color. These beliefs are also congruent with the *oppositional culture* argument, which emphasizes how African American, Latina/o and Native American youth are thought to exhibit particular cultural practices that have an adverse impact on their and their peers' academic attainment.[12]

Popularized by the late anthropologist John Ogbu,[13] the oppositional culture thesis declares that the descendants of persons involuntarily incorporated into the social fabric of the United States respond culturally to continual experiences with subjugation, racism, and discrimination.[14] Ogbu wrote that such "involuntary" minorities know what it takes to succeed in the academy, job markets, and elsewhere, but they refuse to fully embrace these requirements because they feel both that they are imposed on them by Whites and that their own cultural and language differences are markers of identity to be maintained and not to be overcome.[15]

The popular expression associated with oppositional culture is "resistance to act-ing white." Signithia Fordham and John Ogbu contended that contemporary Black students avoid behaviors that they associate with whiteness such as embracing the school curriculum, speaking standard English, and spending much time in the library getting good grades. In turn, these students conspire in their own academic underachievement.[16] The resistance to "acting white" notion is one of the most widely used cultural rationales offered to explain the lower academic performances, on average, of African Americans and Latinos. Its currency is evident in the televi-sion and print media and even in the utterances of our public leaders, including then Senator Barack Obama's famous speech at the 2004 Democratic Party Convention.

Nevertheless, serious debates ensue about how oppositional culture explains achievement differences between groups. Some declare its explanatory power,[17] while others find the evidence unconvincing. Survey and ethnographic research reveal that few students disparage education's value, even among the descen-dants of historically disadvantaged groups.[18] More nuanced arguments exist, too. Economists Fryer and Torrelli (2005) argued that the phenomenon of resistance to "acting white" has little to no effect on students who achieve at average lev-els, but such resistance might explain a significant role in the disparities between Black and White students at high achievement levels. Fryer and Torelli's study sug-gested that the linkages between school achievement and "acting white" beliefs are more common in racially diverse schools with a critical mass of White stu-dents than in schools that are predominantly black.[19] Similarly, Tyson, Darity, and Castellino (2005), using interviews and existing data from eight North Carolina secondary public schools, found that Black adolescents are generally achievement oriented. Their analysis showed important similarities in the experiences of Black and White high-achieving students, indicating that dilemmas of high achievement are generalizable beyond a specific racial or ethnic group. High-achieving students, regardless of race, are to some degree stigmatized as "nerds" or "geeks," according to Tyson and her colleagues. The bottom line is that the most recent and in-depth research shows no signs that deviant cultural values or a lack of appreciation for education are significant explanatory factors for racial differences in school achievement. Thus, the opportunity gap cannot be explained by certain youths' lack of belief in or will for doing well in school.

Meanwhile, as explained in chapters throughout this book, few youth or adults can escape the reach of past and present racial and ethnic discrimination and of unfair economic practices in the United States. Further, it is indisputable that youth do indeed racialize different social behaviors, especially when they find that the prevalent images of those engaging in specific activities tend to be from a par-ticular ethnic or racial background. Yet how students classify behaviors as either "black," "white," "Asian" or "Latino" is less an indication of their tastes for achievement than how they view their specific cultural behaviors through the prisms of racial and ethnic identity.

Elsewhere I have argued that for many low-income Black and Latino students, resistance to "acting white" connotes more than anything else these youths' refusal to adhere to the perceived cultural default setting in US society, that which is seen as normative or "natural"—or understood as American, "white," middle-class tastes, speech and interaction styles, dress and physical appearances, music and other attributes.[20] In principle, the embrace or rejection of these particular cultural traits should have little to do with a student's cognitive ability or capacity to learn. Yet they can, precisely because the prescriptions for academic success tend to be based on that which is deemed middle class and "white". Conformity to dominant cultural codes is likely to demarcate who is in the in-group or the out-group, thus reproducing the existent social and economic hierarchies. Not only can these social and cultural boundaries influence academic engagement but also they can limit access to the means of educational mobility. Cultural inequality in schools, therefore, contributes to the opportunity gap.

CULTURAL MISMATCH AND THE
OPPORTUNITY GAP: THE CAPITAL EXPLANATION

Some of the most consistent and convincing research examining student culture and schooling suggests that when students' cultural backgrounds are dissimilar to the backgrounds of their teachers and principals, the disadvantages experienced by those students are due to educators' lack of familiarity with their social backgrounds, which in turn hinders those educators' capacity to engage with the students effectively. This inability of educators to comprehend the social realities, cultural resources, and understandings of Black, Latino, Native American, and other nondominant groups is one of main drivers of the opportunity gap in American education.

We know that secondary and postsecondary education help to cultivate individual skills and abilities (human capital), which can lead to job attainment and the accumulation of material assets (economic capital).[21] And as educator and scholar Lisa Delpit has argued, education and schooling engender a "culture of power," which embodies tastes, styles, dispositions and preferences of the most dominant social groups in society—or the cultural knowledge that is required for moving up the socioeconomic ladder.[22] The culture of power in schools is akin to what is referred to as "cultural capital."[23] Usually, these practices include possessing a particular savviness about how to interact with teachers, how to apply to colleges and universities, and how to use participation in extracurricular activities to broaden one's horizon and impress admission officers.[24] Achievement often depends on the degree to which students can employ this dominant cultural capital.[25]

When some students enter schools in which the dominant cultural codes differ from theirs, a *cultural mismatch* results that may create difficulties in communication, dampen student engagement, and heighten disciplinary issues.[26] Students' assertions of their cultural differences can very well signal their challenges to the educational content and the way that it is offered. For some groups, fundamental differences in worldviews may exist. For example, tribal communities have a strong sense of the connections among education, sovereignty, and self-determination. Yet, according to some thinkers, the values that undergird Native American cultures are rarely recognized among mainstream educational practitioners.[27] That is, many schools tend to espouse assimilation into the dominant culture and tend to render invisible the cultural distinction and viability of other cultures, languages, and knowledge. Rather than recognize the tension between many low-income and/or ethnic minority students' desires for upward mobility and their assertion of legitimate and distinctive cultural identities, a tendency is to focus on how "deviant" these students are from the white, middle-class mainstream. Hence, schooling becomes a "subtractive" process that reduces the chances of mobility for nondominant social groups by ignoring their material, political, and cultural realities—further widening the opportunity gap.[28]

Most conspicuously, the difficulty in handling cultural differences in schooling pertains to bilingual education. As Gándara (chapter 11 in this volume) lays out, a critical mass of American schoolchildren are English Language Learners, but many of them end up performing poorly in school because their schools are unequipped to teach nonnative English speakers effectively. Meanwhile, studies show two things. First, students who maintain, at least, bicultural identities have more positive academic, psychological, and social attainment, compared to their relatively mono-cultural peers.[29] Second, cognitive neuroscience research shows that the regular use of two languages appears to delay the onset of Alzheimer's disease symptoms and shows as well that bilingualism sharpens the minds of children and adults.[30] Culturally flexible students are more likely to possess the ability to interact, participate in, and navigate different social and educational settings; to embrace multiple forms of cultural knowledge; to expand their own understanding of self; and to enhance their overall psychological well-being.[31]Acculturation approaches, however, tend to threaten the cultural integrity and autonomy of many groups of students and to staunch their ability to be culturally flexible. Paying attention to the cultural bases of schooling is not about positioning one culture or a few cultures over others. Rather, it serves concrete educational purposes, and it entails an exposure of all students to a more expansive set of cultural codes and knowledge that represents more fairly what the United States is—a diverse country social and cultural groups.

The role played by cultural mismatch in schooling, nonetheless, may be exaggerated. In particular, some research has questioned the assumption that the academic difficulties of many minority and low socioeconomic status (SES) youth are due to their "outsider" standing relative to the middle-class (white) culture that dominates schools. One survey study of over 800 teachers and students in a large, urban, public school district showed that not all teachers are given to biases related to their social backgrounds. Instead, only teachers from high-SES backgrounds working with low-SES-background students showed a lack of "fit" that may be disadvantageous.[32] Further, low-SES and minority pupils experienced their greatest difficulties in the classrooms of high-SES teachers of all races.[33] High-SES teachers evaluated their lower-status students as less mature, they held lower performance expectations for them, and these teachers scored their classrooms significantly and exceptionally low on perceived school-climate measures. Moreover, year-end marks and standardized test scores of such pupils were depressed by these indicators of pupil-teacher social distance and teacher disaffection.[34] In short, teachers, as cultural gatekeepers, often reward students who embrace the "right" cultural signals, habits and styles; and some educators' judgments of students' noncognitive traits, including their social status, have significant effects on their evaluations of those students.[35]

School officials may fail to see how they discourage academic engagement through their personal interactions with students and through the climate that they create within classes. And the consequences are great when students actively critique or resist the intellectual, political, and cultural girdles of schooling and challenge their teachers. Academic achievement can suffer.[36] The result is another crack that widens the opportunity gap in the educational system, and unless leaders and parents can control the effects of elusive teacher-student bias and cultural mismatch, it can continue to snowball.

HOW STRUCTURED SCHOOL PRACTICES BECOME CULTURAL

By examining practices such as tracking and ability grouping and the curriculum, we can understand the ways in which other aspects of schooling develop meaning. Educators transmit messages to children when they categorize by ability, a practice in some schools that is highly correlated to racial and ethnic background.[37]

And research finds that pedagogic practices that vary among these different class-room groupings are associated with disengagement for students enrolled in the lower-track classes.[38] According to the National Center for Education Statistics, 40 percent of Asian, 19 percent of Black, 15 percent of Latina/o, 11 percent of Native American, and 31 percent of White high school seniors reported enrollment in high-level academic, college preparatory coursework.[39] That is, the representation of high achievement—"the smart kids"—among Asian and White youth is double the representation of African American, Latina/o and Native American students.

Classroom groupings, like adolescent cliques, are labeled. Certain subjects and courses become known as the class for the Black kids or the Asian kids. As Karolyn Tyson explains more extensively in chapter 12, the consequences of track-ing are great and detrimental. Extensive research on track placement already shows that ability groups correspond to significantly different educational out-comes.[40] Generally, lower-tracked students have lower academic achievement, have higher rates of misconduct and truancy, and are less likely to complete college.[41] Lower-tracked students are also more likely to become disengaged from the learn-ing processes. Also when otherwise diverse schools disproportionately place poor students and Black and Latina/o students into lower-track classes, those students are more likely to develop negative impressions of their own low-track classes as well as the higher-track classes that would prepare them more fully to realize their aspirations for college and professional lives beyond. Sorting and stratification in classes transmit messages that become interpreted and symbolized as the turf of one social group or another. Tracking in schools, therefore, bolsters an unbalanced status hierarchy where class, racial and ethnic disproportions exist.

Cultural meanings and signifiers of worthiness are also infused in what stu-dents learn. An analysis of school curricula reveals much about the construction of knowledge in our nation, showing a clear neglect of the historical, political, and economic realities of many communities of color. Sleeter (2002), for example, found that of the 96 Americans who were named for study in the *Framework*'s course descriptions in the State of California, 77 percent were White; 18 percent, African American; 4 percent, Native American; 1 percent Latino; and zero percent, Asian American. All of the Latino and all but one of the Native American names appeared at the elementary level. At the secondary level, 79 percent of the named people were White, mostly either US presidents or famous artists and authors. Meanwhile, many researchers have found strong and positive results on students' academic achievement, attitudes, and engagement when they are exposed to cur-riculum that is more expansive and includes material about their heritages.[42]

The traditionalist perspective views curriculum as neutral and apolitical—merely imparting literacy, numeracy, and critical thinking skills. Former secretary of education William Bennett is representative of this view of the curriculum as a means to pass on to the next generation history, art, and knowledge produced by hallowed Western thinkers and artists.[43] Traditionalists often balk at the challenges that multiculturalists and critical educators bring to curricular reform efforts. Critical education theorists and multiculturalists, in contrast, argue that education is intimately and ideologically linked to power, politics, history, and culture, privileging the descendants of Euro-Americans more than any other group.

Are US elementary and secondary school curricula too exclusive? In many schools, teachers expend much effort to impart the basics to their students. Often well-meaning and well-intentioned, they want their students to be sufficiently exposed to the culture of power. Thus, Euro-American historical and cultural perspectives dominate school curricula and pedagogy.[44] And educators have often categorized additional groups' histories and literature as "other," relegating them to a lesser status, or attending to them symbolically on a particular day or during a certain cultural awareness month. As a result, many US schools fail to provide their schoolchildren with multiple lenses or perspectives through which to view education and society.

The failure to acknowledge, as part of the learning process, the existence of multiple cultural frames of reference for minority children, while simultaneously instilling a relatively unfamiliar and often incongruent Anglo-American cultural purview, is understood by many of these children as stifling, dehumanizing, degrading, and antagonistic.[45] Invisibility in the curriculum can discourage or disengage many students in the educational process. They become bored—a common descriptive I have heard students use to describe their lessons. Others act out, battle with teachers, or engage in other behaviors that lead to underachievement. While some students articulate a sophisticated critique of the unfairness surrounding their schooling, seeing it as a form of subjugation, many merely display nontactical actions that are likely to be reduced to an unreflective, defeatist, or naïve rejection of their formal schooling.[46]

To provide rich opportunities to learn, curricula need to sufficiently reflect the realities of all students. Accordingly, superintendents, curriculum specialists, teachers and principals around the nation should expand the body of knowledge to which American schoolchildren are exposed. This does not mean, however, that low-income and/or Asian, Black, Latina/o, or Native American children cannot read, engage, or learn about the histories of others. Conversely, it does mean that middle-class and affluent White children should read and learn about the discoveries, inventions, and artistic creations of persons of African, Asian, Caribbean, Central and Latin American, and Native American descent. Knowledge and truth lie in the histories and inventions of us all. Frequently, multiculturalists falter on their tendency to balkanize knowledge by labeling it "Asian," "black," "Latino" or "Anglo" history or art, while curriculum traditionalists reveal myopic visions about what constitutes knowledge by demanding an exclusive canon.

As Peter McLaren has written: "[S]chools have always functioned in ways that rationalize the knowledge industry into class-divided tiers; that reproduce inequality, racism and sexism; and that fragment democratic social relations through an emphasis on competitiveness and ethnocentrism."[47] By minding the disparities created by tracking and culturally limited curricula, educators can attack the opportunity gap by encouraging the full participation of students from diverse backgrounds in the classroom.

SOME CREATIVE APPROACHES TOWARD CULTURAL DIFFERENCES IN SCHOOLS

Proponents of what is referred to as "culturally responsive teaching" (CRT)[48] argue for the effective usage of cultural characteristics, experiences, and perspectives of ethnically diverse students as tools for teaching. Some studies demonstrate a correlation among increased reading comprehension, writing performance, self-esteem, and an appreciation of racial and ethnic minority students' own and other's cultures. [49] Other interventions focus on improving the cultural responsiveness of teachers in the classroom, and especially target teachers whose ethnic and racial backgrounds differ from their students. But as several researchers have found, it is not enough to merely change teachers' expectations or attitudes. The teaching profession must also be populated by those with excellent multicultural and culturally responsive skills.[50]

Reporting on a three-year project teaching high school students to respond to literature at Fairgate High School (a pseudonym) in Chicago, Carol Lee (2007) discovered that teachers of students from divergent social backgrounds can succeed if they know the content, practices, and discourse of their discipline and if they have specific knowledge about the language, culture, cognition, motivation, and social/emotional realities of their different students. Lee recommends that educators employ "a framework for the design of learning environments that examines what youth know from [their] everyday settings to support subject matter learning" in school so that "differences between community-based and school-based norms can be negotiated by both students and teachers."[51]

Others have produced related findings. Results from a quasi-experimental study by Brown and Rhoo (2008) showed that minority students learned significantly more about a scientific concept when the researchers built on students' local vernacular and taught content first. That is, they eschewed traditional methods of teaching students to learn and memorize abstract scientific concepts. In this way students were provided with support for publicly displaying the tacit knowledge they possess about how to make sense of a particular problem. They used a language to talk about the problem-solving process that helped them make connections between what they already do and what they are expected to do with "canonical, school based problems."[52] For teachers to facilitate and execute these modes of learning and teaching effectively and responsibly, they must possess both content and pedagogical knowledge. Pedagogical knowledge includes such skills as an understanding of developmental progression, an awareness of multiple routes to maximizing learning, and the ability to assess what students understand and do not understand. Content knowledge refers to the substance of the knowledge at the basis of the discipline taught (e.g., knowing the algebra that one is teaching).[53]

The principles and goals of CRT are laudable, and the approach is supported by research showing it to be an effective school practice to increase opportunities to learn. An evaluation of 45 research articles written about "culturally responsive" and "culturally relevant" teaching found evidence of CRT's enhancement of students' responses to high teacher expectations and increases in their cultural competence.[54] Yet several factors challenge the ability of CRT proponents to declare undeniably that these interventions really affect achievement and attainment positively for many groups. In particular, the vast majority of studies carried out thus far have been relatively small scale, nonexperimental, and carried out in near homogeneous classrooms (e.g., majority African American or Latino classes), all of which limit the generalizability of the findings. Accordingly, we know little about CRT's efficacy in diverse schools and classrooms. Thus, the recommendations for how teachers can successfully enact CRT in multicultural classrooms have been weakly addressed. Further, since CRT clashes with the traditional ways in which education is carried out within our society, the requisite skills and tasks for the implementation of CRT seem herculean to many teachers.[55] Teachers complain that they lack the time and resources to do CRT, and they may argue that they need more time and collaboration with staff and smaller student loads. Finally, changes in the policy context matter. With the rise of standardized curriculum and high-stakes tests, the scale has tipped toward transmission forms of teaching, and consequently student voices are privileged less in the curriculum and structure of the classroom.

Nevertheless, we know from studies around the globe that *peer-assisted*, or *cooperative learning*, approaches aid teachers greatly with diverse student populations. A meta-analysis of several intervention studies on teaching mathematics to low-achieving students, for example, has shown that peer-assisted learning interventions invariably lead to positive effects on student achievement. The average effect size was impressive at .62, with a median of .51 and a range from .34 to 1.26.[56] In addition, cooperative learning techniques used in school interventions for Spanish-dominant English Language Learners nearly always have produced significant effect sizes and positive outcomes on reading achievement when the techniques engaged students in a set of activities related to a story they were reading—including partner reading in pairs, and team activities focused on vocabulary, story grammar, summarization, reading comprehension, creative writing, and language arts.[57]

While adults in the political arena duke it out about what students should and should not be reading, writing, or doing, many youth whose cultural, economic, historical and political experiences are less privileged in the school and classrooms find themselves teetering on the brink of disengagement. Reaching and engaging these students is a crucial part of closing the opportunity gap. The forms and content of knowledge and learning have to be seen as an ongoing struggle over what counts as legitimate culture and forms of educational empowerment.[58]

A QUEST TOWARD A STRONGER CULTURE OF OPPORTUNITY TO LEARN WITHIN SCHOOLS

In sum, to meet the goals of creating a diverse, educated, and productive populace in the remainder of the twenty-first century, it is absolutely necessary that educators, policy makers, and parents attend to the relationship among culture(s), schooling, and learning. The explanations of how culture matters extend into four realms: from the historical and contextual, which capture how members of various racial, ethnic, and class groups have responded to education and achievement based on their economic and political status in society; to the institutional, which explain how schooling reproduces the power of those privileged in society through its everyday practices, organization, and expectations; to the group-specific, which emphasize that students and educators of diverse ethnic backgrounds possess different ways of knowing, understanding, and doing; and finally to the interpersonal, which highlight the incongruence between the lives of select students and their teachers because of their varied cultural sensibilities.

As chapters in this book and beyond have powerfully demonstrated, the opportunity gap is large and will likely continue to expand if we continue with current assumptions and elisions in practices and policy. Many oft-ignored studies have findings that offer evidence-based suggestions for how to improve learning and teaching in diverse classrooms and schools. They indicate that educators would be remiss in ignoring the sociocultural aspects of schooling and thus assuming that a one-size-fits-all model works for all students. If we want to understand why the experiments with equality of opportunity educational policies have not produced certain anticipated returns, we must comprehend why "access" alone is not enough and why the social and cultural "stuff" matter. As I have written elsewhere, some questions that I would encourage policy makers, educators, and parents to ask are:[59]

Does a school practice or policy engender an inequitable pattern by social grouping or identity, for example, race, ethnicity, class, and/or gender?

When should social and cultural identities matter and when should they not matter when it comes to a specific educational practice?

Are there either advantages or disadvantages to having a school practice only affect a certain subgroup(s) in the school?

Can this particular educational practice be deemed egalitarian? Balanced or imbalanced? (Dis)favoring some and not others?

When I discuss the sociocultural matters and power dynamics infused throughout schools, the immediate defensive reaction I often receive is the question of how teachers can be expected to utilize the cultural toolkits of *all* children in a diverse classroom. This response illuminates the limited vision that many of us may have about learning and even knowledge transmission. The composition of a teacher's classroom varies yearly, and excellent teachers have to be regularly equipped with specific skills to accommodate differences in learning and mindsets about education. Some refer to this as building educators' capacity for building "adaptive skills."[60] Although we cannot expect educators to fully supplement or reduce the gaps in the socioeconomic resources of its various student populations, we can expect them to educate more expansively and less selectively. Of course, they cannot do it alone. Schools share the responsibility of education with parents, the community, and our local, state, and national leaders. Policy makers, school bureaucrats, and teachers nevertheless must find the highest common denominator, check their own skepticism and leveled expectations for certain groups of students at the door, and challenge themselves to engage with all learners across diverse social backgrounds. Otherwise, the cultural dissonances that emerge daily behind school doors and from some educational practices will continue to deeply widen the opportunity gap within American education and society.

11

Meeting the Needs of Language Minorities

Patricia Gándara

TODAY, NEARLY ONE in four students (23.7 percent) in US public schools is an immigrant or the child of immigrants. Most come from homes in which a language other than English is spoken.[1] We refer to these students as "language minorities" or "linguistic minorities" (LMs). About half (10.7 percent) are designated by their schools as English learners (ELs)—that is, their English language proficiency is so limited that they are unable to benefit from mainstream instruction without special support.[2] The other half of LM students, while not designated EL, are not necessarily able to compete academically with native English-speaking peers or ready for mainstream instruction without additional support. Many English proficient students who were formerly ELs are still learning the type of English required to succeed in academic settings. For this reason it is common for students who were formerly ELs to fail standardized tests in English Language Arts, even though they are considered proficient based on language proficiency tests.[3] Unfortunately, there is a great deal of confusion among many educators over the difference between being able to understand and respond to directions in English and being able to comprehend and write about complex texts in English or make sense of literary rhetoric. There is also wide variation among the states in the assessments used to identify ELs and in the criteria that are set for proficiency in English. In some states, students with strong oral English skills can pass the proficiency test even if they are unable to read or write well in English. Some researchers are optimistic that the New Common Core standards will allow for more consistent identification and instruction of EL students across states and are working hard toward that end.[4]

One of the most difficult challenges in the education of ELs is the question of when to exit them from the EL category. Enormous opportunity gaps result from the overly rapid reclassification of EL students as proficient in English; from the failure to acknowledge that students who can pass an English proficiency test may still need considerable academic support; and from the failure to provide an adequate education for students who are or have been EL. It takes time to learn a new language. To acquire oral proficiency in English generally takes three to five years; to acquire proficiency in the kind of academic English that is required to succeed in academic instruction generally takes at least four to seven.[5] In a recent review of state-level English proficiency test results, researchers found that EL students seldom reached proficiency sufficient to be reclassified in less than five years.[6] However, a very small proportion of these EL students receives academic instruction in the language they know best. The latest national data show that only about 11 percent of EL students received instruction from a bilingual teacher.[7]

Accordingly, the great majority of EL students are taught all their subjects in a language they are in the process of learning. Most EL and many former EL students do not understand portions of what they are taught, with the result that in mainstream classes the gaps in their understanding grow as instruction moves forward. In specialized classrooms such as those using structured English immersion (SEI), which is the norm in California and Arizona, the opportunities are no better. Instruction is typically modified so that the content students receive is not the same as what their English-speaking peers receive,[8] and the gaps in instructional content continue to grow as students progress from grade to grade.

The undereducation of EL and former EL students has tremendous consequences, not just for the students and their ability to integrate into the American economy, but for the nation as a whole. These students perform worse than any other subgroup except learning disabled students on most academic measures, and they pose significant challenges for teachers and schools that are not prepared to meet their needs. It is unlikely that the United States will be able to compete in a globalizing world if it does not figure out how to meet the needs of this large and increasing proportion of students. Current language-education policies are squandering an asset—students who have the potential to be bilingual and biliterate—and turning it into a deficit.

THE OPPORTUNITY GAP FOR ENGLISH LEARNERS

One way to view the opportunity gap for EL students is to consider the extent to which they are not being prepared to succeed in the mainstream curriculum that

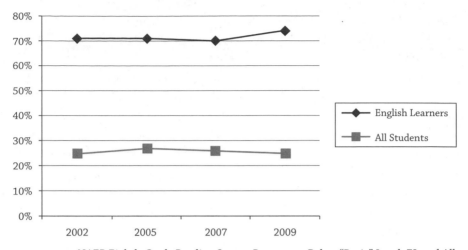

FIGURE 11.1 NAEP Eighth-Grade Reading Scores, Percentage Below "Basic" Level, EL and All Students[9], 2002–2009.

will lead to high school graduation and college. Three things are notable from fig-ure 11.1. There is an enormous gap between EL and non-EL students with respect to the proportion who are unable to achieve reading proficiency in eighth grade; the gap is growing over time (a 46 percentage point gap in 2002 and a 49 percent-age point gap in 2009); and while some improvement is evidenced for non-EL stu-dents, there is a net loss for EL students, increasing the disparity even more.

Because the reading test is in English, and EL students by definition should not be proficient in English, it would be odd not to find a significant gap in reading scores. We therefore turn to mathematics scores at the eighth-grade level (figure 11.2) to see if gaps are significantly different. The same picture emerges. Distressingly, as with reading, the gaps between EL and non-EL students have actually grown over time, from 43 percentage points in 2000 to 45 points in 2009. Similar increases in the gaps are found at twelfth grade math.

Although math tests are somewhat less dependent on language than reading is, it has been well established that math testing is also influenced by English profi-ciency.[10] Because students are tested in English, it is impossible to know to what extent the low proficiency rates are due to language issues and to what extent they reflect inadequate instruction. ELs have much higher dropout rates than the population as whole. For example, only 33 percent of students in the Los Angeles Unified School District who were EL in ninth grade graduated with their class, compared to 54 percent for all other students in 2001.[11]

All LM students face specific hurdles that make learning a challenge in an English-only environment. Being raised in conditions in which English is rarely spoken means that they have few opportunities to learn the language naturally,

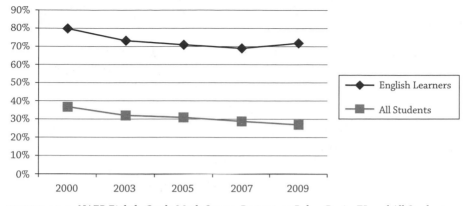

FIGURE 11.2 NAEP Eighth-Grade Math Scores, Percentage Below Basic, EL and All Students, 2000–2009

Source: National Center for Education Statistics, United State Department of Education, The Nation's Report Card, 2011. http://nationsreportcard.gov/math_2011/

through daily interactions with other people. EL students also must contend with the fact that their parents may have significantly less education—and therefore less knowledge of how to support school learning—than the parents of native English speakers. For example, almost 70 percent of Mexican immigrant mothers have less than a high school education, and 45 percent have an eighth-grade education or less. When compared to native-born mothers, fewer than 12 percent of whom lack a high school diploma and almost a quarter (22.5 percent) of whom have a college degree, Mexican immigrant mothers lack not only direct experience with US schools but also the experience of attending secondary schools themselves. Mexican immigrant fathers tend to have even less formal education than mothers.[12] It is understandable that these parents would be reluctant to weigh in on the decisions that schools make about their children's education and know little about how best to support their children's learning other than to encourage them to do well in school, which most do. Importantly, these parents have little knowledge of best pedagogical practices, and in their desire to see their children quickly join the mainstream and learn English, they frequently support schools in pushing their children into English-only settings, where they often flounder.

Exposure to well-educated speakers of any language is a tremendous asset for all students. Children who grow up with well-educated parents tend to have much larger vocabularies than others long before they even enter school.[13] When parents are neither well educated nor encouraged to speak and read to their children in the language they know, children's intellectual growth suffers. When educators fail to encourage reading in the native language and admonish parents to "speak to your children in English," they unwittingly undermine parents' efforts to support their children's academic development.

While most LM students speak Spanish (about 80 percent) and about two-thirds of Spanish speakers are of Mexican descent, there is tremendous diversity in their origins and the languages they speak. But one fact is critical: up to 80 percent of all of these EL students are US-born citizens.[14] These are overwhelmingly *our* children. Further, many of the smaller proportion of students who were born outside the United States were brought to this country at an early age and know no other country as home. Some, reaching the age to apply for a driver's license or some other document, are surprised to find they are not citizens. In any case, we have a constitutional responsibility to educate all children whether they have entered the country with proper documents or not.[15] Hence, all of these LM students are our students through the twelfth grade, and we have both a moral and a legal responsibility to educate them, as well as a very pragmatic imperative to do so.

WHY DO EL STUDENTS FARE SO POORLY ACADEMICALLY?

Although lack of English proficiency distinguishes EL students from others in school, some have argued that English proficiency is not the fundamental problem in these students' academic achievement. Many other students from low-income, historically marginalized communities perform similarly poorly in school, even though English is ostensibly their first language. For example, most Latino students, like many low-income African Americans, are *not* ELs, yet their achievement scores are exceptionally low. And some Asian immigrants who do not begin school speaking English manage to perform exceptionally well. This fact alone suggests that something other than ability to speak English is at work. Moreover, there is a consistent finding that English learners who have a strong education in their primary language (e.g., Spanish) do very well in US schools, often outperforming native English speakers.[16] How could this be true if lack of English proficiency were the primary impediment to learning?

Nearly two-thirds of immigrant children in the United States live near or below the poverty level.[17] In California, the state with the largest number of ELs and where they are primarily Spanish speakers, 85 percent of these students are eligible for free or reduced-price lunches, the schools' best (most available) indicator of poverty.[18] Poverty has devastating effects on children's academic achievement, whether the students are English learners or native-born European Americans (see Rothstein, chapter 5, this volume). Poverty is a major predictor of absenteeism, poor grades and test scores, and high dropout rates.[19] Because LM students, and especially those designated EL, are extremely likely to be poor, they are also likely to attend segregated, underresourced schools with less experienced and qualified teachers and high turnover rates.[20] ELs are commonly found in settings that are segregated by ethnicity, income, and language. For example, 70 percent of all ELs in 2007 were enrolled in only 10 percent of the nation's schools, while half the schools in the country had no ELs at all. Likewise, in schools with high EL populations, 77 percent of peers were minority and 72 percent were poor.[21] Taken together, these factors lead almost inevitably to low achievement.

DIVERSE WITH DIFFERING NEEDS

While middle-class ELs with strong prior education who enter US schools can, after an initial period of adjustment, do well academically, low-income ELs and those with weak or interrupted prior schooling almost always struggle and seldom completely overcome the impediments to their learning. Neither the challenges EL students face nor the means of addressing those challenges are the same for all. Some EL students begin their schooling at kindergarten or the first grade in the United States, and others arrive much later and with weak, interrupted, or no prior education. If they begin early in elementary school, they have time to learn a new language and pass the classes they need to graduate; their chances diminish if they arrive later. But these chances depend on the immigrants' experiences and status. They may arrive as traumatized refugees or as the children of documented immigrants with secure professional jobs. They may come from a language and cultural group with supportive and highly resourced communities in the United States, or they may settle into communities with many challenges and few resources. All these factors influence the way that EL students experience their education, and these factors account for the varied educational trajectories of students from different backgrounds. However, while recognizing this diversity, we should recognize as well that most ELs in the United States face numerous impediments to their schooling.

THE TEACHERS WHO TEACH EL STUDENTS

One factor that most LM and EL students have in common is that they are not likely to be assigned to a teacher who is well prepared to teach them. For students with strong prior schooling and supportive parents and communities, this disadvantage may be overcome. But for the majority of these students, who lack this kind of support system outside of school, this situation can spell disaster. The most recent national survey of the status of EL students and their teachers found that although 40 percent of teachers had at least three EL students in their classes, the typical teacher had attained only four hours of professional development on how to teach these students over the most recent five years.[22] The great majority had no certification related to teaching ELs. Just 18 percent had English as a Second Language (ESL) certification, and only 11 percent had been trained as bilingual teachers. Similarly, a recent study of 5,300 educators of ELs in California found that among teachers whose classes were made up of 50 percent or more ELs, half had received no more than one professional development session related to the instruction of EL students over the most recent five years.[23] Many teachers feel underprepared to instruct these students.

Moreover, there are no agreed-upon national or even state standards as to the critical competencies needed to be an effective teacher of EL students. Although the No Child Left Behind Act (NCLB) requires that all students have a highly qualified (now, highly effective) teacher, it offers no definition of what constitutes a highly qualified or effective teacher of EL students.

CONDITIONS OF EDUCATION FOR EL STUDENTS

In a study conducted for the *Williams v. California* class action lawsuit alleging the failure of the state to adequately meet the needs of English learners and other poor and minority students, researchers found seven ways in which EL students were faring worse than even similarly low-income English-speaking students.[24] Their teachers had less preparation and experience for teaching them and received less relevant professional development. The students were more segregated in their schools than other subgroups. Their educational facilities were inferior. Their textbooks and other materials were less adequate. They had less instructional time in the classroom; and they were given insufficient time to master the tasks they had to master (both the regular curriculum and a second language).

Yet, among the states with large numbers of EL students, California is probably not the most egregiously miserly; it is unlikely that most other states are providing a great deal better for these students. In fact, Arizona has been the subject of a class action suit for almost twenty years for failing to provide adequately for its EL students (*Flores v. Horne*), as has Texas for failing to provide adequately for it secondary-level English learners (*United States v. Texas*).

It is important to note, however, that if the disadvantages of poverty were truly addressed for these students, the additional costs of educating EL and LM students would probably not be very high. A recent study concluded that the additional costs of high-quality materials, translation, and outreach would be small.[25] Employing highly qualified, preferably bilingual teachers generally costs less than the current widespread provision of support staff for teachers who are unable to meet the needs of the EL students in their classes. The largest cost would be in developing a valid and reliable assessment system for these students, a task that the federal government, in collaboration with the states, is now beginning.

A BRIEF HISTORY OF LANGUAGE POLICY
AFFECTING LM AND EL STUDENTS

Unlike other multicultural nations that have adopted policies supporting multilingualism, such as Canada and most of Europe, the United States has consistently sought to maintain English as the only viable language in both educational settings and public life. The European Union encourages a mother tongue plus two additional world languages for all its students. In the United States, however, languages other than English are lost very rapidly. A recent survey by the Pew Hispanic Center found that by the second generation, only 3 percent of Hispanics counted themselves as Spanish-dominant, down from 62 percent who spoke Spanish almost exclusively in the first generation.[26] Indeed, the United States has been described as "a graveyard for languages."[27] Nonetheless, an extreme concern for the survival of English as the language of the United States has driven many policies for educating English learners. Some scholars have concluded that US language education policy is, in reality, driven more by language ideology ("true Americans speak only English in public") than by any real concern that English is about to become extinct.[28]

The Civil Rights Act of 1964 ushered in an era of rights for ELs based on Title VI, which forbids discrimination based on national origin and was interpreted to include language-based discrimination. In 1968, the Bilingual Education Act, the first federal policy designed to address the needs of students who had "limited English proficiency," was passed as Title VII of the Elementary and Secondary Education Act (ESEA). Notwithstanding the title, this legislation did not specifically encourage bilingualism. Inextricably associated with the War on Poverty, it was a compensatory program designed to remediate the language deficits of impoverished students with limited English. In 1974, in *Lau v. Nichols*, the Supreme Court recognized the right of linguistic minority students to have access to the same curriculum as English-speaking students through whatever effective means schools chose to implement, including bilingual education. However, this positive climate toward bilingual education was short-lived. By 1978, the reauthorization of the ESEA included language that barred federal funds from being used for "maintenance" bilingual instruction. In other words, bilingual education was not intended to support bilingualism; rather, it was intended to facilitate students adopting English as the sole language of instruction.

While Americans have been, at best, ambivalent about immigration throughout most of the nation's history, recent steep increases in immigration, especially from Latin America, have been met by hostility and punitive legislation. California and Arizona, two states with particularly high percentages of new immigrants, have been especially fertile sites for anti-immigrant politics. In 1994, California voters passed a law barring most undocumented immigrants from receiving any public services, including schooling, although these provisions of the law were subsequently found to be unconstitutional. In 1998, Californians passed Proposition 227, which was intended to bar bilingual education in most cases. The passage of the initiative, which allowed citizens to sue teachers if they used the students' primary language for instruction, almost immediately reduced the numbers of students receiving such instruction from about 29 percent to about 8 percent of English learners; today, it stands at about 5 percent.

During the same period, Arizonans attempted to pass a series of increasingly restrictive measures against immigrants, and in 2000 it followed California's lead with an antibilingual education law of its own. Proposition 203 was modeled on the California initiative, but included provisions that made it even more difficult for parents to seek waivers to opt out of the prescribed SEI program. In 2004, the state also passed a highly restrictive referendum barring undocumented immigrants from receiving any kind of public social services and made it a crime to fail to report any undocumented person applying for services. Recently, states such as Alabama, Georgia, and Indiana have been competing to pass the most draconian anti-immigrant legislation, including blocking access to public schools for immigrant children. Although such provisions have been ruled unconstitutional in Texas and California, their backers hope the US Supreme Court will revisit the issue.

Current Arizona policy provides that ELs remain in a four-hour, segregated, daily SEI block where "the content . . . emphasizes the English language itself" until they pass the state's English language proficiency test.[29] EL students in Arizona are segregated into classrooms no exposure to English-dominant peers for at least three-fourths of the school day, and in many cases all day. The instruction which they receive focuses on learning English over learning subject matter such as math, science, social studies.[30]

In 2002, Massachusetts also passed an antibilingual education initiative, although the law allowed for the operation of two-way dual language programs that had garnered an important political constituency, particularly in the Cambridge public schools.

Thus, by 2003, three entire states, as well as many local districts, had either legally moved away from instruction in students' primary language or barred it altogether. Several studies from this same time period showed, not surprisingly, an increase in English immersion.[31] This leaves open the question, how are these students, instructed in a language they do not fully understand, supposed to gain access to the curriculum, as required by *Lau v. Nichols*? The answer may be provided by the federal district court in the *Horne v. Flores* decision, which was expected in 2011, but is still pending as of early 2013. The *Horne* court has been asked to rule on the legality of failing to provide students with access to the regular curriculum until they are proficient in English. This "sequential instruction" method—first English then academic instruction— virtually guarantees that EL students will lag behind their English-speaking peers academically. Theoretically, EL students can catch up later; however, since no additional instructional time or resources are typically allotted, and the resulting achievement gap is rarely, if ever, closed.

These initiatives were based on the optimistic but unfounded assumption that EL students would normally become proficient in English within one academic year because the intensive "time on task" in English would result in rapid acquisition of the language. This assumption is especially problematic, as very few students become proficient enough in English within one year to survive academically in mainstream classrooms. A five-year study of the implementation of Proposition 227 in California commissioned by its Department of Education found that the "probability of an EL being re-designated to fluent English proficient status *after 10 years* in California" was less than 40 percent.[32] Several studies commissioned by the Civil Rights Project came to a similar conclusion: English-only policies had failed, and ELs were faring no better in California, Arizona, and Massachusetts than they had prior to the imposition of the English-only laws. In Arizona, EL students have been assigned to special education at higher rates than before passage of the English-only laws, and in Massachusetts dropout rates among EL students have skyrocketed, especially at younger ages.[33] Another consequence of these policies has been the decline in the number of teachers with bilingual credentials. As the population of ELs grows, there are fewer teachers who can speak to the students and their families in a common language.[34] State policies that have sought to limit primary language instruction and impose a single type of SEI instruction appear not to be the panacea—or even beneficial—for addressing the low performance of these students, and these policies are eroding the supply of skilled teachers available to them.

WHY IS SPEAKING ANOTHER LANGUAGE PERCEIVED TO BE A PROBLEM?

Richard Ruiz has argued that if speaking another language were viewed as a resource rather than a problem, instructional policies would build on students' native language with superior educational outcomes.[35] Certainly, the multilingual educational policies of European nations and Canada illustrate this approach. There is also evidence for the viability of this perspective in the growing numbers of dual-language programs cropping up around the country, especially in those states that have limited bilingual instruction. Increasingly, parents of monolingual English speakers are seeking opportunities for their children to be educated in a second language. This trend is not surprising given the consistent finding that students in these programs—both native English speakers and English learners— tend to outperform students in other types of educational programs in both languages of instruction.[36]

A recent newspaper article from Arizona, one of the states most opposed to bilingual education, describes a new dual-language school—Spanish and English— spearheaded by middle-class Anglo parents so that their children can become bilingual.[37] As one parent notes, "this endeavor is all about brain development,"[38] another parent "hopes this chance Gillian is getting to learn about another culture will broaden her horizons for the future." The great irony is that Spanish-speaking children are not allowed to enroll in the program unless they are already proficient in English. Only English-speaking students need apply. No new horizons for Spanish speakers!

WHAT MUST WE DO TO CLOSE THE OPPORTUNITY GAPS FOR LINGUISTIC MINORITY STUDENTS?

We must begin by acknowledging that the source of the problem of underachievement among many children of immigrants is not the students' language, but the way our school system treats language difference. Rather than building on these students' assets, we define them as liabilities and treat them as though their languages and cultures are of no value and need to be replaced.

Focusing on language as the core of the problem allows us to ignore the fundamental issues of poverty, marginalization, and the hostility aimed at immigrants and those who do not speak English, and instead to place the blame on a perceived deficit in the students themselves. We must address the broader needs of LM students that impede their learning—poor health care, poor nutrition, excessive residential mobility, isolated and risky neighborhoods, lack of models of academic success in their communities, and overstressed parents—before assuming that language is the primary problem they face. Immigrant children, by and large, face triple segregation—by ethnicity, by poverty, and by language,[39] and they are among the poorest of the poor in our society.[40] These students face many hurdles before they even get to school.

Teachers are at the core of the educational solution, and while federal legislation requires that all students be taught by an effective teacher, there is no federal definition of an effective teacher for students who do not speak English. There seems to be an assumption that any "qualified" teacher with some orientation to EL students is equipped to meet the students' needs. There is mounting evidence, however, that this is not true.[41] Bilingual teachers are better able to communicate with their students, assess their educational progress more accurately, and reach out to help parents to support students' learning in the home.[42] Incentives for recruiting and training bilingual teachers should be put into place at district, state, and national levels. The fact that so many students come from homes in which another language is spoken means that millions of young people of college age have had the experience of learning English as a second language or at least growing up in a home where other languages were spoken. Many of these young people would welcome the opportunity to become teachers if encouraged to do so.

Policies must also be put into place that help retain strong teachers and principals in schools that serve English learners and other LM students. Too often these schools suffer from high turnover rates among the staff and students. Such churn presents an almost insurmountable obstacle for teachers trying to form strong and meaningful relationships with students and their families, which is key to their effectiveness.

These students also need to be in high-quality schools in strong communities where they can be in contact with mainstream society, not isolated in impoverished institutions (see Rothstein, chapter 5 in this volume). While stabilizing schools that currently serve LM students, we must simultaneously devise policies that encourage the integration of LM students with English-speaking peers. Dual-language magnet schools have proven to be very popular with well-educated, English-speaking parents and to produce superior outcomes for all students.

In order for LM students to benefit from educational opportunities that do exist, their families need to be informed of these opportunities. Having very limited social capital, the families of LM students need strong information networks. Because so many live in isolated circumstances, do not speak English, and feel alienated and uncomfortable in the schools, outreach programs must be established. Bilingual teachers, counselors, and parent liaisons are the most effective ambassadors to these students' homes.

It is in everyone's interest to work toward closing the opportunity gap for EL students. They are our future: in some regions of the United States, English learners form the near-majority of students entering kindergarten. Without a significant change in the way we are educating these students, building on their considerable assets, and integrating them into the mainstream of American life, the future for all of us looks grim.

12

Tracking, Segregation, and the Opportunity Gap

WHAT WE KNOW AND WHY IT MATTERS

Karolyn Tyson

AS THE CHAPTERS in this volume demonstrate, obstacles to providing all students with high-quality educational opportunities are multifaceted and widespread. They exist at various levels of the educational system and schooling process and to different degrees for particular groups of students. But they are not insurmountable. An important first step toward eliminating these obstacles, however, is recognizing and understanding both the antecedents and consequences of each. This is especially true for curriculum tracking—the practice of separating students for instruction based on measures of their achievement or perceived ability. While some scholars identify tracking as a significant obstacle to achieving educational equity, it receives relatively little critical attention outside academic circles. Many educators, parents, and students take for granted that tracking is sound educational practice. However, researchers have long raised concerns about the quality of education students in lower-track classes receive and the fact that lower-income and racial and ethnic minority students are disproportionately represented in those classes. Indeed, recent studies have highlighted the way in which tracking is racialized, resulting in racially segregated classrooms, especially in schools that manage to attain diversity at the school level.[1] This chapter considers the obstacles to educational equity created by racialized tracking and the consequences and day-to-day reality for students. I end by considering alternatives to current tracking practices that have proven effective in narrowing the opportunity gap.

Practices that separate students by race within schools are problematic for a number of reasons. Researchers consistently find that segregation is associated with inequities in the distribution of resources and worse educational achievement and attainment for low-income and racial and ethnic minority students.[2] This is true at both the school and classroom levels, so it is not surprising that questions about the importance of diversity inevitably arise in the context of discussions about tracking. To be clear, the concern with diversity here is about equity and fairness, in terms of both who has access to high-quality learning opportunities and how perceptions of racially distinct classrooms affect students' decision making. As I argue below, the lack of diversity in classrooms works as a sort of self-fulfilling prophecy and a barrier to more equitable opportunities, because it reinforces ideas about a connection between race and intelligence and who is smart and who is not.[3] In the world of adolescents and their all-important peer allegiances and youth cultures, segregated classrooms solidify racial boundaries and create unnecessary social and educational dilemmas for students.

Across the country, Black, Latino, and Native American students are disproportionately underrepresented among those enrolled in advanced courses such as advanced placement (AP), International Baccalaureate (IB), and honors classes, and in gifted programs. White students, on the other hand, and Asians to a lesser extent, tend to be overrepresented in these more academically rigorous courses and programs. This pattern of tracking is an all-too-common feature of public schools and is depicted in countless research monographs and personal accounts of ordinary Americans.[4] For example, in a February 2011 letter to the editor of a Raleigh, North Carolina, newspaper, a high school senior, Jay Zhang, challenged the new superintendent's rosy picture of the Wake County public schools by describing how his school "remains, with few exceptions, separated and unequal within":

> As an attending senior, I can tell you that Enloe Magnet High School is pretty much two schools under one roof. Although it would be far easier to hide behind an ostensible defense of Enloe's diversity, the glaring academic and cultural divide between the magnet and non-magnet students is too obvious to overlook, yet depressing enough to ignore. Statistics simply fail to address the stark separations within. Enloe enrolls many minority students from various ethnic backgrounds, but in all my four years there have never been more than two Black students in any one of my classes. Often there are none.[5]

Zhang is no doubt describing the advanced classes at Enloe, which, in a subsequent article in another local newspaper, fellow students describe as "mostly composed of White and Asian students."[6] I include Zhang's comment here, as I do other select student voices, simply to provide readers with a few concrete examples and pictures of what researchers commonly refer to as second-generation segregation,[7] or racial or racialized tracking.[8] It is important to hear from the students in their own words to get a sense of how some see and experience tracking rather than rely solely on a view that is filtered through the lens of the researcher. While Zhang speaks from a position of privilege within the tracking system at his school, the overall picture he paints for readers of the results of tracking is found in many American schools.

The pattern of within-school segregation Zhang described in 2011 has persisted for decades without much public outcry, even though millions of students, teachers, and administrators observe it at school every day and it has been well documented by researchers. Interestingly, beginning in 2009, the NAACP and some students, parents, and teachers in Wake County waged a vociferous public battle with the school board over its intention to end the school district's 10-year-old diversity plan that assigned students to schools based on socioeconomic status, but no protests have ever been held to address the internal segregation that results from racialized tracking. No doubt the silence on this issue reflects a lack of knowledge about it and the commonplace view that curriculum placements are based on student ability, motivation, and achievement and therefore group differences in placement merely reflect racial differences along these dimensions.

Yet, studies find that the process through which students are assigned to courses is more complicated and involves a host of other factors, including teacher recommendations, course scheduling conflicts, and parents' requests and demands, as well as student socioeconomic status and race.[9] A study of student placement in the Charlotte-Mecklenburg school district, for instance, shows that even when Black and White students are similarly high achieving, Black students are not placed in advanced classes at the same rate as Whites.[10] One set of analyses that compared the placements of Black and White eighth-grade students whose scores on the California Achievement Test placed them in 99th percentile found that while almost three-fourths (72 percent) of Whites in this group were placed in the top English course, less than one-fifth (19 percent) of Blacks were similarly placed. Other studies examining predictors of track placement usually find that the effect of race disappears when prior achievement and background characteristics are taken into account, but some also find an effect of the school's racial composition.[11] Notably, a recent study using a nationally representative sample of students found that increasing school racial diversity increases the chances that White students will be in the college prep track and decreases the chances that Blacks will be in that track.[12] In racially diverse schools, capable Blacks are crowded out of advanced classes by their White counterparts, which may explain some of the racial disparity in student placement found in Charlotte-Mecklenburg.[13]

RACIAL BOUNDARIES AND BLOCKED OPPORTUNITIES

My focus in this chapter on equity and fairness with respect to access to educational opportunities is not intended to ignore or downplay the importance of diversity for society in general. In a US society that is becoming increasingly diverse and global, exposing youth to individuals from other racial, ethnic, and socioeconomic backgrounds who may have experiences, perspectives, and worldviews different from their own is essential. Such exposure provides opportunities for lessons in tolerance and cooperation, as well as for interracial and cross-cultural friendships.[14] The ability to cross cultural borders is becoming a vital necessity whose significance goes beyond career success.[15] Tolerance and respect for difference are fundamental to maintaining a peaceful society, relatively free of intergroup conflict and violence.[16] Schools have a unique opportunity to begin to foster tolerance and respect for diversity in young people in concrete rather than abstract situations. Unfortunately, when institutional practices such as tracking lead to the creation of a school within a school, the benefits of the diverse environment are diminished, or perhaps even lost.[17] However, the problem is that in this context, as some studies have found, diversity can become a liability rather than an asset.[18]

When students are unevenly distributed across curriculum tracks by race and ethnicity or socioeconomic status within a school, stereotypes are born or reinforced and animosity festers. Students generally believe that advanced classes are reserved for the smartest, hardest working among them.[19] In diverse schools in which White students dominate the advanced classes and the ranks of high achievers, Whiteness is projected as the standard for success and connotes privilege and worth.[20] As one education scholar argued in a study of the negotiation and rationalization of advantage among the middle class, "academic and intellectual competencies provide the underpinnings for positive identity. School achievement and attainment signify intelligence; hence, high tracks, good grades, and advanced degrees are valued."[21] Racialized tracking is one means through which the attributes that signify intelligence are funneled to Whites. This achievement hierarchy can raise the ire of the less privileged students, and privileged students become the target of their peers' contempt.[22]

Tracking has long been known to create and reinforce divisions among students, even in the absence of racial diversity,[23] but race exacerbates the problem. According to a 2004 study of a nationally representative sample of tenth-grade students, interracial friendliness decreases as tracking intensifies.[24] This finding is wholly consistent with what many qualitative studies reveal about contemporary American schools: racial boundaries are especially difficult to cross in highly tracked diverse schools. Several ethnographies have documented the palpable tensions that exist among students in schools when racial and ethnic minorities are systematically excluded from advanced classes.[25] Not only do the advanced classes come to be seen as the domain of Whites, but non-White students sometimes feel uncomfortable crossing that institutionally imposed racial boundary. As one Latino student in a study on the formation of race in a racially diverse high school is quoted as saying when asked why he does not work to get into his school's gifted program or higher level classes: "I wouldn't see no Hispanics there. I wouldn't relate to nobody out there."[26] Concerns like this may seem trivial to adults, but for the young people who have to navigate these racialized spaces on a daily basis, they matter a great deal.

Additionally, under certain conditions some non-White students who are enrolled in these classes are challenged on their racial authenticity, accused of acting white or otherwise being uppity by their co-ethnic peers.[27] One study of race, class, and identity among Latina and White girls in a California high school described this particular phenomenon as a "defensive strategy" by the excluded students, "a way of saying, 'I don't understand your success and my failure, so I'll minimize your achievement by accusing you of acting white.'"[28] Again, for some students who find themselves in this position, it is a difficult experience to navigate.

The association of advanced classes and high achievement with White students also has the effect of engendering and perpetuating stereotypes about race and intelligence and other characteristics such as motivation and studiousness. The response of a Latino student to a researcher's question about whether there is a link between race and perceptions about the status of the school's academic programs brings home this point:

Oh, gosh! Yes . . . Well, if society says that . . . you are Latino and lazy, that you are Asian, you are smart, if you are White, Oh God, the best, and if you are Black, you are bad, horrific. If you walk into a class full of Asians and White students . . . you think that this is a really good class, because they are Asian and White. It must be a good class. If you walk into a class that is majority African American and Latino, you know it's bad, because they are lazy and dumb. . . . It is like a pyramid, you know, the supreme of the supreme on top and the rest down the way.[29]

These stereotypes often become part of the conventional wisdom of the school and the explanation for why Black, Latino, and lower-income students are disproportionately underrepresented in advanced classes and among the ranks of high-performing students.[30] Yet these stereotypes obscure more than illuminate the problem of racial disparities in track placement. To be sure, students' motivation and ability and the value they place on education seem like obvious explanations for their placement because, presumably, high school students are able to choose their own courses. In reality, however, students do not have that much choice in course selection.[31] By the time they reach high school, students' choices are constrained by institutional factors including prior placement, course scheduling, prerequisites, and sequencing.[32] Unfortunately, some students experience the effects of these constraints more than others, regardless of their ability, motivation, or how much they value education. Thus, it is important to understand the ways in which school policies may block or limit students' opportunities and why it is that such policies affect some students more than others.

The findings of a few recent studies examining tracking and course placement in North Carolina are especially instructive. One study of tracking systems in 128 North Carolina public high schools found that "across all subjects on average, 37.1 percent of schools use prerequisite requirements that make it impossible for a student who started in the lowest track freshman year to switch to the highest track by senior year."[33] The sequencing of math and science courses, in particular, makes it difficult for students to switch from lower to higher-tracked classes or to enroll in any course they choose. It is reasonable to require that students take algebra before they take geometry, yet because middle-school algebra placement is often restricted to a select few, geometry is closed to many ninth-grade students (unless schools allow students to take such courses simultaneously).[34] This restriction presents a serious barrier to enrollment in advanced math courses in high school, and it is highly unlikely that a student who does not take algebra by the eighth grade will be able to reach calculus by the end of high school. Low-income and minority students are most hurt by this placement predicament, which one researcher refers to as the "algebra obstacle."[35] In a study of racial disparities in algebra placement in North Carolina schools, the researcher found that low-income and Black students were underrepresented in Algebra I in, respectively, 95 percent and 90 percent of the 465 middle schools in North Carolina offering the course, while White students were overrepresented in 90 percent of the schools.[36]

Other constraints on students' course enrollments are prior placement and achievement. Higher-track courses may have minimum grade requirements attached to a prerequisite course, requiring a B+ or better, for example, for enrollment. With respect to prior placement, in some high schools, ninth-grade honors courses are restricted to students previously identified as "gifted."[37] Although this stipulation may be unusual, being identified as gifted is an important part of the unequal opportunity structure of schools. Gifted identification, which typically occurs in elementary school, often marks the start of the process of racialized tracking; White and Asian students are disproportionately overrepresented in these programs, and Black, Latino, and American Indian students are disproportionately underrepresented.[38] Methods of identification, including teacher recommendations and the use of IQ tests or student grades, all of which advantage White students, are implicated in the disproportionality.[39] Moreover, the particular instruments (e.g., tests, grades, teacher recommendations) used to determine giftedness and the cut-offs used to determine who is in and who is out (e.g., scores at the 99th or 95th percentile), vary across schools and districts.[40] These findings provide support for the argument made by some scholars that giftedness is socially constructed.[41]

Gifted identification and placement have substantial and lasting effects on students' subsequent course options and opportunities to learn. The "gifted" label confers both symbolic and material advantages. Students come to believe in their own giftedness and their need for a more demanding curriculum than the standard course of study offers, and school personnel treat them accordingly.[42] Thus, the gifted label is a gateway to advanced classes in later grades. Tellingly, students labeled "gifted" are significantly more likely than others to enroll in advanced classes in high school, even after prior achievement and family background are taken into consideration.[43] Indeed, the "gifted" label can become a self-fulfilling prophecy. The label itself and early exposure to a challenging curriculum better prepare students academically and psychologically for advanced coursework in later grades.[44]

THE CONSEQUENCES OF BLOCKED OPPORTUNITIES TO LEARN

Given all the evidence regarding the effects of school placement policies and of prior learning opportunities on students' course choices, it is clear that stereotypes about racial variation in course enrollment do not reflect the realities of the placement process. Nevertheless, these stereotypes have serious consequences for minority students. In a series of experiments, researchers demonstrated that stereotypes about Blacks' intellectual inferiority pose a significant threat to high-achieving African American college students.[45] When the students were subtly prepared by the researchers to think about race and ability in test-taking situations, they performed less well than when they were not primed to think about those issues before the test. Researchers believe that under the race-primed conditions, Black students (or the group to whom the stereotype applies) become distracted by concerns about confirming the stereotype, which interferes with the cognitive task before them.[46] Stereotype threat, as this phenomenon is called, reminds us how harmful stereotypes can be.[47] Although students may not show outward signs of distress, negative stereotypes—especially those that pertain to a domain with which the student identifies—take a toll on them psychologically and negatively affect their performance.

Beyond the stereotypes, the opportunity gap that results from racialized tracking has implications for the racial gap in test scores. Indeed, one prominent researcher in this area argues that "the relative absence of Black students in higher-level courses and their disproportionate enrollment in lower-level ones is an underemphasized component of the race gap in achievement."[48] Curriculum differentiation is supposed to benefit all students because, in theory, it enables teachers to meet the particular educational needs of students by grouping them with others of similar ability and preparation.[49] Studies of tracking, however, show that tracked classrooms tend to be quite heterogeneous and, more importantly, that students in the lower-level classes tend to be disadvantaged relative to their peers in upper-level classes.[50] Rather than providing enhanced educational opportunities for students who may be struggling academically, students placed in lower-level classes are taught by less experienced teachers, tend to receive lower quality instruction and a less engaging curriculum, and learn less than their peers in higher-level classes.[51] Indeed, there are vast differences in the material that students are exposed to across course levels.[52] These differences make movement from lower- to higher-level classes difficult for many students, so tracking tends to be rigid.

Considering the differences in what students learn in upper- and lower-level courses, we cannot expect students on different tracks to perform equally well. Students cannot know what they have not been taught. To the extent that racial and ethnic minority students and White students are not exposed to the same learning opportunities, racial gaps in achievement on standardized tests will follow, because students who are exposed to a more challenging curriculum tend to score higher on standardized tests than their peers.[53] To understand the magnitude of the effect of exposure to an advanced curriculum, consider that, according to the findings of a 1987 study of tracking, the gap in achievement between students in advanced classes and those in nonadvanced classes is larger than the gap between high school dropouts and non-dropouts. This finding suggests that "cognitive skill development is affected more by *where* one is in school than by *whether or not* one is attending school."[54] Indeed, some scholars argue that tracking is one of the main mechanisms of social reproduction in the United States.[55] Efforts to close the achievement gap must address the opportunity gap.

WHAT CAN BE DONE

Closing these gaps and eliminating some of the obstacles to minority student achievement is not impossible. There are a number of promising avenues toward this goal. First, some schools and school districts have closed the opportunity gap by eliminating tracking and they have significantly reduced if not eliminated achievement gaps. The Preuss School, a charter school affiliated with the University of California, San Diego, is an important example. The school serves approximately 800 students in grades 6 through 12, all of whom are low-income and would be the first in their families to enroll in college. The student body is 59 percent Hispanic, 23 percent Asian, and 12 percent African American. The school has had remarkable success educating students who in other settings are routinely defined as at risk. The Preuss School defies the perception that schools serving high-minority, low-income populations are only failing schools. In a 2011 *Newsweek* ranking, the school placed number 34 among the top 100 high schools in the country, based on, among other things, the graduation rate and the number of students taking AP classes. According to a 2011 *U.S. News and World Report* article that ranks the school number 32 among its "Gold Medal Schools, the AP participation rate is 100 percent."[56] All twelfth grade students had taken at least one AP exam at some point in high school. In addition to relatively small classes and a longer school day and year, the school provides a college preparatory curriculum to all students.[57] Although there is no system of tracking, the school offers tutoring and other supports for students who are struggling academically.[58]

South Side High School in the Rockville Centre district of Long Island, New York, also successfully educates a diverse student body using limited tracking and has substantially narrowed their achievement gap.[59] In the late 1990s, the district began a detracking reform. As part of that process, it eliminated curriculum differentiation where it began in middle school and worked upward with each subsequent grade. The results are a testament to the assertion that "achievement follows opportunity," as the school saw a sharp decrease in the achievement gap along a number of dimensions and an overall rise in student achievement.[60] For example, after one year of heterogeneous grouping, 77 percent of Black and Hispanic students passed the state (Regents) biology exam, compared to just 48 percent the year before.[61] White and Asian students also experienced a boost in achievement, from an 85 percent to a 94 percent pass rate. Similar results were observed for the Regents math exam: under the tracked system, between 1995 and 1997 less than one-quarter of entering ninth-grade Black and Hispanic students passed the algebra-based exam prior to beginning high school, but after tracking was eliminated, three-quarters of Blacks and Hispanics passed. The performance of White and Asian students also improved significantly, with the pass rate for these two groups jumping from 54 percent to 98 percent.[62]

By eliminating curriculum boundaries, the Preuss School and South Side High School ensure that the school's resources are not unequally distributed. All students have access to the same opportunities and resources, including highly qualified teachers and an engaging curriculum. The success these schools achieved without tracking could be replicated elsewhere. A recent meta-analysis of studies of a variety of detracking efforts finds significant positive effects of heterogeneous grouping, especially for lower-ability students.[63] The achievement of higher- and average-ability students generally is not affected by detracking.

It is important to note, however, that simply providing all students with opportunities to learn a high-level curriculum is not sufficient to achieve the kinds of gains made by students at South Side High School or the success of low-income, racial and ethnic minority students at the Preuss School. Although the change in the curriculum structure is a key component of the students' achievements, such change is not likely to be successful without concomitant changes in instructional methods and in the beliefs and dispositions of school and district administrators, teachers, and other adults. Educators must change the way they think about intelligence as well as what they think about students from low-income and minority backgrounds. If the adults at school believe that intelligence is fixed rather than malleable[64] or that race, income, and social class determine students' ability or desire to learn and master a high-level curriculum, detracking is not likely to produce the kinds of gains achieved among South Side or Preuss students. Standards and expectations must be raised for all students, as well as teachers. These types of attitudinal shifts are necessary for the reform to get off the ground, because teachers who doubt their students' ability to learn or their own ability to teach minority and low-income students will not be open to this reform.

Although many studies of detracking reforms focus on secondary schools, elementary schools have also achieved success in closing achievement gaps by expanding opportunities for students to learn a gifted curriculum. An elementary school in Durham, North Carolina, identified ways to place more Black students in its program for academically and intellectually gifted (AIG) students and created a "guest" AIG program to provide more non-AIG Black students access to the challenging gifted curriculum. The result was a narrowing of the achievement gap and a surprising reversal in the passage rate differential between Blacks and Whites on the state's End of Grade tests. Passage rates increased for all cohorts during the five-year tenure of the principal who implemented the changes, but they were most profound for the 2000–2001 third-grade cohort that was the main beneficiary of school's changes: the difference in the passage rate between Whites and Blacks, who made up 66 percent of the school's population, went from a nearly 31 percent White advantage in reading in the third grade, to a 27 percent White advantage in the fourth grade, and then to a slightly higher black passage rate by the fifth grade. To be clear, this was not a zero-sum situation; Black students' improvement was not at the expense of White students' performance. By broadening access to the gifted program and increasing the diversity within the program, more students were able to benefit from the more rigorous curriculum.[65]

In another North Carolina school, researchers developed a program to provide a gifted curriculum to all children and invested in a large-scale professional development component to train teachers to treat all children as gifted.[66] The program, called Project Bright Idea, does with young children what Preuss and South Side have done with older students. The findings of the pilot program, conducted over a five-year period ending in 2009, were impressive. Title I (high-poverty) schools in 11 school districts in North Carolina participated in the program, which involved random assignment of more than 10,000 students in grades K-2 to either a treatment (gifted curriculum) or control (regular curriculum) group. According to a recent evaluation by the US Department of Education, within three years of their participation, from 15 percent to 20 percent of the students who received the gifted curriculum met the district's criteria for gifted status compared to just 10 percent of the control group. Equally interestingly, the evaluation also showed that in the three districts with the highest number of gifted students, among the 19 percent of third graders identified as gifted in 2004 (prior to the program's implementation), not one came from any of the Title I schools included in the study. What we learn from each of these cases is that when the bar is raised and the proper supports are put in place, students and teachers rise to meet the challenge. The expansion of opportunities for students considered at risk for school failure to learn a higher-level curriculum led to significant improvements in achievement.

To be sure, detracking reforms are not politically popular and thus are difficult to implement.[67] Schools districts face serious resistance to these reforms from parents, students, and teachers who benefit from the practice of tracking in its current form, but if the goal is to improve student achievement and close the gap, it is worth the effort.[68] We know from the experience of the Rockville Centre school district that it is possible and that it can significantly improve student achievement.[69]

A range of other options is available to schools and districts to improve learning and achievement for all students and especially those from low-income and minority backgrounds, who have traditionally been underserved. Expanding access to challenging curricular materials and high-quality instruction is a core component of such reforms. Programs like AVID (Advancement Via Individual Determination), a college-readiness program that identifies capable, underperforming minority and low-income students as early as the elementary grades to prepare them academically and socially for challenging coursework, have helped to increase the presence of these underrepresented groups in advanced courses in many suburban school districts. To be effective, any change in the structure of the curriculum also requires fundamental changes in teachers' and students' beliefs about teaching, learning, and student ability.[70] All students should have access to a high-quality education and to educators who see potential in every child. It will be impossible to close the achievement gap if the opportunity gap is not addressed.

CONCLUSION

An advocate of detracking has argued: "Given the more precise understanding of the nature of human intelligence and the wider availability of alternatives to tracking that we now have, it becomes clear that tracking has less to do with ability than we have supposed. At the same time, what is apparent is that tracking has everything to do with opportunity. And the ways in which our institutions, including our public schools, structure opportunity, is a matter for public discussion, debate, and policy."[71]

This chapter has outlined how tracking contributes to a growing opportunity gap between disadvantaged students and their more privileged counterparts and fosters a sense of division and animosity between the two groups. For these reasons, closing the opportunity gap should be a priority among educators and policy makers. Creating conditions within schools to afford more students, and not just a select group, opportunities to learn advanced curricular materials will go a long way toward nurturing a sense of fairness among students and preparing a broader group of young people for a diverse array of opportunities in the labor market. This goal not only serves individual students, but is good for society as a whole. Significantly, no other nation relies as much on tracking in secondary school as the Unites States.[72] For Americans to compete in an increasingly diverse and global world, we must provide opportunities to learn a high-level curriculum, raise the standards and expectations for all students regardless of race or income, and prepare them to live and work in harmony with people from many different backgrounds.

Let's focus on the most important ingredient in the school, and that's the teacher. Let's pay
our teachers more money. Let's give them more support. Let's give them more training.
Let's make sure that schools of education that are training our teachers are up to date with
the best methods to teach our kids. And let's work with teachers so that we are providing
them measures of whether they're effective or not, and let's hold them accountable for being
effective.

President Barack Obama, March 26, 2009

13

Good Schools and Teachers for All Students

DISPELLING MYTHS, FACING EVIDENCE,

AND PURSUING THE RIGHT STRATEGIES

Barnett Berry

A CALL TO ACTION, BUT TAKING THE WRONG POLICY PATHS

From the White House to local communities, Americans are recognizing teacher
quality as the most powerful lever in efforts to improve our public schools.
Students' family backgrounds and the quality of life in their communities strongly
affect their progress and contribute to the opportunity gap (see Rothstein, chapter
5, this volume).[1] However, a substantial body of research points to teachers as the
most important in-school factor that influences academic achievement.[2]

Unfortunately, children in poverty and those of color are much less likely to
be taught by qualified, experienced, effective teachers. Similarly, English learners often find themselves with teachers who are insufficiently trained and inexperienced. High-need schools—those whose students are growing up in poverty,
belong to racial and ethnic minority groups, are learning English, or have learning
disabilities—further disadvantage their students because of the generally lower
quality of their faculty. And, compared to their counterparts who teach in more
affluent communities, teachers in high-poverty schools are far more likely to be
paid less and to work under conditions that undermine their efforts to teach
effectively.[3]

Most Americans want good schools for all students, and over the last few decades polling data have suggested that the public would invest more in teachers and teaching.[4] However, neither positive public opinion nor a growing consensus among researchers and other experts has been sufficient to ensure that low-income students and those of color attend good schools staffed with high-quality teachers.

Instead, the evidence about what makes for good schools and effective teachers is ignored again and again. Our knowledge about how to ensure high-quality teaching and learning for all students means little if policy makers don't take heed. Yet such failure is evident in many of today's policy approaches. Examples include the focus on charter schools to narrow the achievement gap (see Scott and Wells, chapter 9 in this volume), alternative certification programs to recruit a new breed of teachers, and high-stakes tests used to create accountability that have narrowed the curriculum, especially for students with the greatest needs (see Zhao and Tienken, chapter 8 in this volume),[5] while creating perverse incentives for experienced and effective teachers to avoid working in schools that serve them.[6]

Federal policies, from No Child Left Behind to Race to the Top, have placed more emphasis on market tools, incentives, and punishments to drive gains in test scores than on closing opportunity gaps, including opportunities for teachers to share good ideas and practices. The "no excuses" reform rhetoric suggests that teachers must be given incentives to work harder and that their effectiveness has little or nothing to do with their working conditions. Inflammatory language about the profession is now in vogue, exemplified by Steven Brill's scathing exposé of New York's "worst teachers"[7] and Nicholas Kristof's claim that teacher educators are "snake-charmers."[8]

In 2010, President Obama endorsed the firing of all the teachers at the "failing" Central Falls (Rhode Island) High School because "there's got to be a sense of accountability" in a school where only 7 percent of eleventh graders have passed state math tests.[9] But he and Secretary of Education Arne Duncan never acknowledged that the school board had not funded the professional development that teachers need in order to work successfully with English-language learners; one in four students at the school does not speak English. They also ignored the fact that before the "mass firings" administrators had not evaluated teachers for many years and that these same administrators would routinely mandate new curricular programs and then abandon them. The problems at Central Falls had less to do with poor teachers than with a dysfunctional school system and the larger, societal disadvantages of the students served.

Many current policy approaches rest more on myths than on empirical research, so they do not point us toward solutions that ensure all students have access to good schools and effective teachers.

DISPELLING MYTHS AND FACING THE EVIDENCE

The challenges confronting us are long-standing and complex. As H. L. Mencken reminded us, "There is always an easy solution to every human problem—neat, plausible, and wrong."[10] Putting our faith in myths rather than facing reality undermines our best efforts. Like most myths, those about teaching have some truth embedded in them. But hanging onto them keeps us from making much-needed changes and distracts us from more productive approaches. Five common myths about schools and teachers deserve careful scrutiny.

Myth #1: Too few talented individuals enter teaching, primarily because certification barriers discourage them from becoming classroom teachers.

Conventional wisdom, as expressed by former secretary of education Rod Paige, suggests that current teacher certification systems are "broken," imposing "burdensome requirements" and unnecessary pedagogical coursework for talented individuals who would otherwise leave their private-sector careers and enter the profession.[11] In reality, as carefully documented by the Woodrow Wilson Institute, most potential mid-career recruits choose not to teach because of low salaries and poor working conditions, not because of certifications barriers. Most of those surveyed would have chosen to teach in suburban (rather than inner-city) schools, because they perceived they could be more successful teaching there.[12]

Some potential mid-career recruits "know little about teacher preparation programs and what is involved in becoming certified."[13] Some alternative certification programs rightly adapt their pedagogical preparation in light of the recruits' background and experience, but the quality of such programs varies enormously. In 2009, about 62,000 teachers entered the profession through 600 alternative certification programs. Most were trained for a few weeks before assuming full responsibility for classroom instruction and were expected to earn full certification by taking evening courses.[14] In most instances, coursework focused solely on classroom management and how to teach a particular district's prescribed curriculum.[15]

Teacher-education students, as documented by several studies, are actually "getting smarter," with newly minted teachers far more academically qualified today than in the past. For example, the SAT scores of students who enter secondary-level teaching are substantially higher than those of the average college graduate, and teacher candidates in math and science had much higher mean SAT scores in math.[16] The profession would certainly benefit from recruits who are even more academically able, but attracting them will require offering significantly higher salaries and better working conditions.[17]

Myth #2: Teacher preparation and experience matter little for student achievement;
whatever needs to be learned about teaching can be quickly picked up on the job.

Some policies today are somewhat supported by research that suggests that new recruits from Teach for America (TFA) and other alternative certification programs perform about as well as those from traditional, university-based teacher-training programs.[18]

But, studies concerning alternative certification have also shown that the achievement scores of students taught by teachers who had limited coursework in pedagogy actually declined over the course of the academic year.[19] Beginning teachers with more extensive clinical training, including a full-year internship, produced higher student achievement gains than those from either traditional university programs or alternative pathways.[20]

Experience in teaching is also discounted by many of today's policies. Yet a clear finding from study after study is that teacher quality improves during the first several years in the classroom.[21] Whether more than three years of prior teaching experience results in improved student test scores is not clear from the research.[22] But teachers with the same number of years in the classroom nonetheless have different levels of preparation, and their professional development opportunities and working conditions differ over time, which can confound these findings.

Teaching experience of up to 20 years can matter for student achievement when teachers teach the same subjects and grade levels consistently, especially in their first five years of teaching.[23] More experienced, expert teachers know more than novices, organize the content better, have more developed teaching strategies, design varied lessons for the different students they teach, and can apply their knowledge in novel and creative ways.[24] In addition, more seasoned experts are able to overcome some of the stressful working conditions found in many high-need schools, and a stable corps of faculty is needed to maintain long-term school improvement.[25] Overall, then, there is clear value to teaching experience, even after the crucial first years.

Myth #3: The key to improving schools is to eradicate
tenure and remove incompetent teachers.

It is difficult to assess precisely how many teachers are incompetent, by whatever definition. But the best available evidence indicates that the proportion is far lower than media reports suggest. For example, the Teacher Advancement Program (TAP), which includes many thousands of teachers across the United

States, uses both student test results and observational methods to assess teaching effectiveness.

Less than 15 percent are rated less than proficient, and less than 3 percent of TAP teachers are rated ineffective. Over 85 percent have been deemed at least proficient, and almost one-third excel.[26] A New York City administrator reported in 2010 that at most 10 percent of the district's 80,000 teachers were ineffective. Further, in half of those cases the district was at fault because the ineffective teachers were not sufficiently prepared or supported to succeed in classrooms with many students of color, who live in poverty, are learning English as a second language, or have special needs. Many others are required to teach grade levels or subjects for which they have not been trained.[27]

The difficulty of removing ineffective teachers has much less to do with tenure rules and much more to do with badly trained administrators who lack the skills and tools to assist beginning teachers and to distinguish between excellent, acceptable, and poor teaching.[28] Poor evaluation procedures, and not tenure, are more likely to account for a school district's inability to fire poor performers.[29] In fact, nations with the highest scores on internationally benchmarked student assessments have highly unionized teaching workforces, and no qualms about teacher tenure.[30]

*Myth #4: Sound business principles should be applied to
education, and merit pay is key to motivating teachers.*

Research on the effects of linking teachers' pay to their students' performance has, as yet, yielded little conclusive evidence.[31] A few studies suggest a positive connection between merit pay and student learning, but the effects are very small and do not appear to last.[32] In the most rigorous study to date, a team of scholars from Vanderbilt University and the RAND Corporation concluded that "rewarding teachers with bonus pay, in the absence of any other support programs, does not raise student test scores."[33] An even more recent evaluation of New York City's $56 million bonus-pay system, again by RAND, also yielded no positive effect on either student performance or teachers' attitudes toward their jobs. A significant percentage of teachers believed the rating system was unfair because of its overreliance on standardized-test scores, while others reported they did not understand how the payouts were determined.[34]

Effective performance-based pay systems include the following components: teachers must be involved in their design and implementation; the cost needs to be known and made public prior to the program's adoption; the system cannot take a one-size-fits-all approach (districts and schools must be able to adapt it to local circumstances); and one or two direct measures of student learning cannot be the only basis for rewarding teachers.[35]

Despite the myth, merit pay is far from universal in privately owned business-es.[36] In fact, only 16 percent to 30 percent of all workers in America receive some type of merit pay, and only about 6 percent are paid for performance on an ongoing basis.[37] Merit pay plans are generally found in sales-related occupations, such as finance and real estate. The product of education is not a tangible good or a service; it is about what students learn and can do, which cannot be so neatly quantified. Merit pay systems are seldom found in organizations where well-prepared individuals need to work together to develop and apply their skills.[38] Schools need more sophisticated performance management systems than those that are commonly used, but their emphasis should be on developing talent and spreading best practices.[39] Teachers, like other knowledge workers in high-involvement organizations, have to apply a wide variety of information and strategies in nonroutine, adaptive ways. Accordingly, the current push for using value-added test-score data to assess teachers may undermine efforts to increase teaching effectiveness. Today's systems for measuring teacher effects on student test-score gains can provide useful information, but the data are not always reliable enough to guide high-stakes decisions.[40] If these data are used in a comprehensive performance pay system, they must be supplemented by a wider array of measures to ensure that accurate personnel decisions are made.[41]

Myth #5: Charter schools, by forcing traditional educators to compete for students and funding, have become key levers for school improvement.

Advocates often claim that charter schools, freed from the bureaucratic constraints of traditional public schools as well as contracts with teachers' unions, are more efficient and more effective with low-income children.[42] Charter schools currently enroll approximately 3.5 percent of the nation's public school students.[43] On average, they perform no better (and perhaps worse) than comparable traditional public schools,[44] even while often benefiting from substantial donations and grants[45] and generally serving fewer students with special needs and English language learners.[46] But their policy influence has far outstripped those numbers and results. Charter schools have been lionized by the popular media,[47] and with the recent documentary *Waiting for Superman*, the media has sometimes engaged in "distortions" and the promotion of "half-truths."[48]

A number of charter schools that employ teachers who do not work under collective bargaining agreements push them to work considerably longer hours. In doing so, they lose about three times as many teachers as public schools;

some have annual turnover rates that exceed 80 percent.[49] Students in such schools are relegated to novices who come and go, rather than a well-prepared faculty who know the community and can support long-term school improvement efforts.

GOOD SCHOOLS AND TEACHERS FOR ALL

Fortunately, the research evidence base does provide a road map for policy makers to use in efforts to improve schools and teaching for all students, and especially to close the opportunity gap between white, middle-class students and those who are growing up in poverty, belong to racial and ethnic minority groups, are English-language learners, or have special needs. This research clarifies what it takes to staff schools that enroll a diverse student body as well as the conditions that enable staff to teach effectively. The evidence suggests five strategies that will work for students: seriously prepare teachers for the realities of teaching; develop standards for new teachers; pay teachers as professionals; create positive school conditions; and connect teachers to out-of-school supports.

Strategy #1: Seriously prepare teachers for the realities of teaching.

Those who enter with inadequate preparation are more likely to leave the profession than teachers who have a thorough grasp of the fundamentals of teaching, and they are also less likely to be effective over time.[50] This is particularly important because the shortage of teachers is largely due to attrition from the profession, not to a failure to prepare skilled teachers in the first place.[51]

To prepare teachers for the classroom, government at the local and national levels must create incentives and build capacity for higher education and K-12 schools, as well as community-based organizations, to fuse their resources in jointly training new recruits for the profession. In fact, research evidence, much of it synthesized of late, suggests a "broader and bolder" approach to education reform is needed.[52] For example, a critical mass of teachers, up to 25,000 per year (representing 1 in 10 new hires), will need to be prepared to work in high-need schools as well as assume leadership roles. They should be trained for a variety of urban and rural communities and develop the skills required to work effectively with administrators and policy makers. A substantial internship in a community-based organization would enable them to understand how students and their families live. An internship in a virtual teacher network would enable them to learn specific skills in using multiuser virtual environments to educate students as well as to spread expertise among teaching colleagues. Pedagogical preparation should use a mix of live and digitally recorded "lesson studies" in which teams of candidates critique teaching and assess student learning. Each person should have specific tasks to accomplish plus performance assessments to measure when and what they are ready to teach. Competency, not time spent sitting in college classrooms, should determine when teachers are ready to teach independently, in what schools and under what conditions.

A number of school-university partnerships are beginning to apply these principles to teacher education.[53] Federal and state policies, through existing tools such as the Teacher Quality Enhancement grants under Title II of the Higher Education Act, should promote the dissemination and application of these ideas and practices on a larger scale.

Nations whose students excel on international assessments, such as Finland and Singapore, recruit top students to teaching; they make sure these teachers are well prepared at government expense, and they pay novices while they are learning to teach.[54] It is time for the United States to do the same.

Strategy #2: Develop standards for new teachers, moving away from the long-standing policy of allowing underprepared teachers to teach independently, often in disadvantaged communities.

To count as truly "qualified," teachers should complete a full preparation program and should be able to meet state certification standards in their field. Teachers in training should be accurately identified, equitably distributed, and adequately supervised by expert teachers who have time and training to mentor them. The nation now has almost 100,000 National Board Certified Teachers, many of whom would surely be willing to serve as mentors for recruits who need their guidance and supervision in their early years of teaching. High teacher turnover, caused in large part by lack of preparation as well as by poor working conditions, costs our nation's schools about $5 billion annually.[55] More comprehensive support for new teachers would cost the system more in the short run but would improve student achievement and save public education dollars in the long run.

Most top-performing nations offer new recruits reduced teaching loads so they can continue to learn how to teach under the tutelage of seasoned, expert teachers.[56] By adopting such practices, American schools can help ensure that new recruits in our high-need schools have a teaching load that allows them to serve their students effectively.

Strategy #3: Pay teachers as professionals, with a premium for
spreading their expertise to their colleagues.

Without a doubt, teachers' salaries remain too low to attract and retain enough talented, well-prepared professionals to fill our nation's high-need classrooms.[57] In 2005 Lou Gerstner, former IBM CEO, called for raising teacher salaries between 10 and 30 percent, at a total estimated cost of $30 billion, in order to pay all teachers as professionals and those who are more effective considerably more.[58] And more recently, Secretary of Education Arne Duncan called for our nation's teachers to have a starting salary of $60,000, with opportunities to earn up to $150,000, based on performance.[59] American teachers are underpaid compared to teachers in top-performing nations and to other professionals with similar training and responsibility; on average, they earn 60 percent less than other college graduates.[60]

Performance pay plans have the potential to make a difference in student achievement, but only if they are designed to improve the school climate and encourage collaboration among teachers.[61] If carefully planned and implemented, bonuses can be effective motivators of best practices.[62] Teacher involvement in designing and monitoring performance-based compensation systems improves their likelihood of success.[63]

Looking toward the future, teaching will require new teacher leadership roles, including master or mentor teachers, assessment designers, learning architects, and guides to multi-user virtual environments.[64] Since these specialists and generalists will be organized horizontally as well as vertically, performance pay should support a career lattice or matrix for many teachers, not a hierarchical ladder for a few of them. As growing numbers of teachers are suggesting, pay supplements should be designed to encourage and reward best teaching practices—accelerating the achievement of local, state, national, and international school improvement goals—and to reward the hybrid teacher-leader roles that a comprehensive teacher development system requires.[65]

Implementing these strategies will take more money, but it will be money well spent. Today $300 billion of public funds are lost each year due to the cost of dropouts, incarceration linked to illiteracy and school failure, and low productivity in the workforce.[66] A 2005 a poll by the bipartisan Teaching Commission found that more than 81 percent of Democrats and 61 percent of Republicans favored tax increases to pay teachers more.[67] It is time for policy makers to act on what the American people want for their schools and students and for the teachers who serve them.

Strategy #4: Create school conditions that allow for effective teaching.

The cutting-edge research of Tony Bryk and his colleagues concludes that "good schools" are built upon five "essential supports." These conditions for effective teaching include: strong leadership from principals who are "strategic, focused on instruction, and inclusive of others in their work;" a welcoming attitude toward parents and the formation of connections with the community; a learning climate that is safe, stimulating, and nurturing to all students; robust instructional guidance and curricular materials; and the development of professional capacity among teachers, especially in teams.[68] All these school conditions matter for effective teaching.

Teacher collaboration seems to make a difference for student achievement. A recent study found that students achieve more in mathematics and reading when they attend schools characterized by higher levels of teacher collaboration for school improvement.[69] Two decades ago, Susan Rosenholtz's landmark study concluded that "learning-enriched schools" were characterized by "collective commitments to student learning in collaborative settings ... where it is assumed improvement of teaching is a collective rather than individual enterprise, and that analysis, evaluation, and experimentation in concert with colleagues are conditions under which teachers improve."[70] New research has found that teachers are more likely to have greater gains in student achievement when they are in schools with others whose students progress as well.[71]

Other conditions, including class size and student load, are essential for teachers to personalize teaching and get to know the children and adolescents they teach. In top-performing nations such as Singapore, teachers spend about 15 hours per week working with colleagues, involved in joint planning, action research, lesson study, and observations in one another's classrooms.[72] These conditions allow teachers to teach effectively. However, few policy makers appear to grasp the importance of "teacher time" in effective teaching. If accountability is going to drive school improvement, then assessment measures should indicate not just which schools, teachers, and students are performing at higher or lower levels. Those measures should also indicate the reasons for the success or failure. The capacity now exists for policy makers to use evidence to assess the conditions that allow teachers to teach effectively; they should do so.[73]

*Strategy #5: Connect teacher teams to other support
providers that serve students and families.*

Teacher quality may be the most important in-school factor influencing student achievement, but it is not the most powerful one overall. Even Rick Hanushek, a leading proponent of high-stakes teacher evaluations using student test scores, estimates the individual teacher effects component of measured student achievement to be only between 7 and 10 percent.[74] Poverty, family background, and the neighborhood environment, as well as access to quality health care, can mightily affect student achievement (see Rothstein, chapter 5 in this volume). Low-income students often lose ground after school and during the summer.[75] If they do have access to extended learning opportunities, there is often a disconnect between the school curriculum and the services offered in after-school programs. Effective extended learning opportunities should encompass cultural, artistic, and athletic activities that more privileged families typically provide for their own children.

The much-praised Harlem Children's Zone in New York City offers not just the traditional school curriculum but also early childhood programs, parent training and engagement, and social and health services, including prenatal care.[76] If President Obama's Promise Neighborhood proposals[77] are expanded, more teachers must be trained to create connections between academic standards and the social and health care supports children need to meet them. The federal government should offer special scholarships to prepare professional educators to serve in hybrid roles as teachers and community organizers, building bridges between schools and neighborhoods and the lives of students in and out of school.

Few policies are in place to ensure the alignment and connection of out-of-school supports with the traditional in-school curriculum and to prepare teachers for these new roles. Powerful results and considerable efficiencies could be created if our nation's school finance system integrated the work and staffing of health care and social work inside the schools that serve specific communities. New federal legislation, including significant changes to the Elementary and Secondary Education Act (currently known as the No Child Left Behind Act), is needed so partnerships of school districts, universities, and nonprofit organizations, as well as other agencies, can use Title I, Supplemental Educational Services (SES), and other funding streams, such as the 21st Century Community Learning Centers Fund and the Child Care and Development Fund, to coordinate more comprehensive services for students.

CONCLUSIONS

The Race to the Top initiative has offered state and local policy makers a new opportunity to identify, prepare, and reward teachers in ways that "elevate the teaching profession and help recruit and retain great teachers and principals for underserved schools and communities."[78] However, too many policy approaches are built more on myths than on facts. As Linda Darling-Hammond has argued, ensuring good schools and teachers for all students will require nothing short of a Marshall Plan for teaching.[79]

Many reformers lament that when it comes to international measures of student achievement, the United States finds itself in the bottom third of developed countries, while it "still lacks trained, motivated, accountable talent at the front of the class."[80] As documented by a number of recent analyses, current policy ideas (most of which are associated with these same reformers) are "out of sync with high-performing nations."[81] The National Center for Education and the Economy pointed out that top-scoring countries do not rely on high-stakes standardized tests, as the United States does; instead, they provide opportunities for well-prepared teachers to develop and assemble evidence on student and school performance.[82] Finland and Singapore have no equivalent to Teach for America, for example, with its five-week boot camp for teaching a two-year stint in a high-need school. Instead, they recruit top college students to teaching and prepare them for this career at government expense.[83]

As a nation, we need to build a system of teaching and learning to enable millions of well-prepared administrators and teachers to do the extraordinary work of public education. Today, almost 100,000 schools are facing enormous financial challenges and a "funding cliff,"[84] just as America's 55 million students are expected to meet internationally benchmarked standards. Children who have special needs, are growing up in poverty, belong to racial or ethnic minority groups, or are English language learners will not progress adequately unless we devote additional resources and expertise to ensuring equal opportunity for all.

The common good for our nation depends on good schools and teachers for all students. We have the technical knowledge to do so. Now is the time to dispel the myths, face the evidence, and pursue the right strategies.

PART IV

Solutions/Conclusion

14

The Cumulative Costs of the Opportunity Gap

Clive Belfield and Henry M. Levin

WHAT ARE THE consequences, for individuals and for society, of neglecting to provide everyone with an adequate education? This chapter examines the opportunity gap in terms of diminished lifetime opportunities for employment and income, as well as the social costs of having an undereducated workforce, when students do not complete high school or beyond. We take an economic approach, but we also might pose the issue in terms of equity or fairness. Why should individuals' prospects in life be significantly diminished as a result of personal circumstances, low-quality schooling, and public policies over which they have limited control? It makes no economic sense to have large proportions of young people enter adult hood without sufficient preparation. Reducing the opportunity gap might not only be considered just, it would also bring tremendous social benefits.

We present our calculations of the economic burden associated with the opportunity gap—the cost that is paid later when current educational investments are insufficient. Education develops human capital, the skills and knowledge that equip people to be productive workers and capable citizens. The individual gains in terms of higher incomes and more secure employment, as well as in a host of other ways. Equally importantly, when individuals are more educated, taxpayers gain, since those who earn more pay more in taxes and rely less on public services. Society gains, too; individuals who earn more are healthier, less likely to commit crimes, and more likely to participate actively in the democratic process.[1]

Conversely, when students fail to acquire adequate skills, the economic costs are considerable. The skills required for stable employment are multiplying. In *The*

Race between Education and Technology, Claudia Goldin and Lawrence Katz demonstrate that wage levels and economic growth depend on how well workers can keep up with changes in the complexity of job tasks.[2] In the twentieth century, increasing proportions of young people attended high school and, later, college. Jobs were available for high school dropouts, but these are now being replaced by physical capital (machines) or outsourced. Current high school and college graduates will need to be more flexible, and to keep up with technological changes, they will need a strong foundation of literacy and numeracy. Yet, many students lack this foundation. People who acquired very little human capital during high school are clustered in urban areas, where demographic changes intersect with low-quality schooling.[3] Helping these individuals gain credentials that have strong value in the labor market is vital for the economy over future decades.

Alternatively, we could ask whether the educational opportunities available to students are fair or equitable (see Moses and Rogers, chapter 15 in this volume). Usually, the economic efficiency and equity approaches are expressed in terms of a trade-off: efficiency can be increased at the expense of equity. However, in this case enhancing educational opportunities not only would reduce inequities in lifetime economic outcomes, but would be more efficient from a societal perspective. Both the moral and economic perspectives make clear the urgency of addressing the opportunity gap.

In this chapter, we first describe educational attainment across groups of students. Next we calculate the economic consequences associated with inadequate education. We define inadequate education as failure to graduate from high school; this is our baseline, even though many students would benefit from college. We describe the benefits associated with education and provide monetary estimates of what these benefits are worth. Finally, we consider the implications for education policy.

THE ECONOMIC VALUE OF EDUCATION

Defining Human Capital

Education promotes human capital, the behaviors, knowledge, and skills that make individuals more productive. In measuring human capital, many researchers emphasize traits that go beyond years of schooling and test scores to encompass so-called soft skills or critical thinking.[4] Although we agree that these are important, we calculate human capital in terms of educational attainment. Test scores seem to us an overly narrow depiction of human capital; they fail to capture many valuable noncognitive attributes, such as diligence, and may be very

TABLE 14.1

Demography of the 2005 Cohort of High School Students

	High school dropout	High school graduate (incl. GED)	Some college	College graduate (BA+)	N (millions)
Males					2.252
White + other	15%	27%	35%	23%	1.593
Black	28%	35%	27%	12%	0.301
Hispanic	49%	34%	11%	6%	0.358
Females					1.983
White + other	8%	27%	32%	33%	1.404
Black	21%	32%	26%	21%	0.296
Hispanic	35%	29%	19%	17%	0.283

weakly correlated with productive behaviors. For example, people who pass the General Education Development (GED) test have cognitive skills that match those of regular high school graduates; but their incomes are lower. Completed years of schooling encompass cognitive skills, such as passing achievement tests, and or noncognitive competencies, which may well be just as valuable. Finally, our society regards high school graduation as a threshold for adulthood; those who do not graduate cannot go on to college and are not eligible for military service.

Table 14.1 shows the distribution of educational attainment by race and gender across a single age cohort.[5] Each high school class has approximately 4 million students. Of these, one in five fails to graduate from high school. In addition, many high school graduates are unprepared for college and do not finish. As we see, there are significant differences by race and gender. These differences may arise from many causes, heavily mediated by family circumstances, and as such are outside the strict purview of schools. However, school quality undoubtedly plays a role; and, where family circumstances are impoverished, the capacity of schools to promote human capital is further undermined.

The Benefits of Human Capital

Copious evidence attests to the economic benefits of high school graduation. We might ask whether the link between education and income is merely a correlation or a matter of causation. For example, would more talented individual students get better jobs even if they did not stay in school longer? Most of the research on this question points to the conclusion that more education produces higher

earnings. Similarly, other researchers have found strong linkages between more
education and better health, less involvement in crime, and greater satisfaction
with life. Investments in education yield significant benefits that would not otherwise have occurred.[6]

To ascertain the lifetime consequences of education, we look at the situation
from the perspective of an individual who is aged 18 and is just about to complete
(or drop out of) high school. We use data from the Current Population Survey,
an annual survey of households across the United States, from the years 2006
through 2010 to show the substantial differences in economic status by educational level (see table 14.2). Adults who did not graduate from high school are
much more likely to be out of the labor force (42 percent) and unemployed (8
percent) than high school graduates (26 percent and 6 percent, respectively) and

TABLE 14.2

Labor Market Status: US Adults (aged 18–65)

	High school dropouts		High school graduate (incl. GED)		Associate degree or some college		BA degree or above	
Not in labor force	0.42		0.26		0.23		0.15	
Unemployed	0.08		0.06		0.04		0.02	
In school	0.12		0.03		0.13		0.01	
Annual earnings	$12,932	(21,784)	$25,008	(31,527)	$29,952	(36,126)	$60,427	(71,452)
State tax (net cr.)	$246	(1,219)	$651	(2,158)	$893	(2,741)	$2,156	(5,141)
Federal tax (net cr.)	$816	(3,767)	$2,193	(6,192)	$3,224	(8,118)	$8,439	(15,976)
Pension plan	0.15		0.35		0.43		0.58	
Private health insurance	0.39		0.64		0.75		0.88	
Food stamps	$538	(1,553)	$255	(1,082)	$148	(816)	$27	(338)
Welfare amounts	$81	(713)	$39	(484)	$27	(422)	$4	(183)
Supplemental Security Income	$384	(1,763)	$174	(1,258)	$97	(1,008)	$35	(639)
N	89,377		198,817		191,144		180,607	

Source: Current Population Survey, March Supplements 2006–2010 pooled.
Notes: All adults (male and female). Sample includes persons with zero earnings, tax payments, and
welfare receipt. Standard errors in brackets. Federal tax does not include FICA.

college graduates (15 percent and 2 percent). Dropouts earn much less than high school graduates ($13,000 compared to $25,000) and are less likely to have a pension plan or private health insurance. Finally, they are much more likely to rely on food stamps, welfare, and supplemental security incomes.

Over a lifetime, these differences add up. To show this we have created lifetime profiles from age 18 to age 65 by education level for earnings, tax payments, and government expenditures. We can estimate the economic value of the opportunity gap by imagining movements across the education levels, for example, from being a high school dropout to being a high school graduate.[7]

CALCULATING THE CUMULATIVE COSTS OF THE OPPORTUNITY GAP

Earnings Gains from Education

We first calculate the lifetime earnings associated with each level of education. Gross earnings are derived directly as averages from the Current Population Survey data pooled over the five years from 2006 to 2010. Gross earnings, including tax payments and employer contributions, are analyzed in order to calculate the social differences in output by education level, not the net income to the individual. The full productivity of a worker is the amount that the employer has to pay to compensate that worker.

Lifetime earnings by educational level are shown in figure 14.1. The estimates are averages, based on calculations weighted according to sex and race.[8] Relative to dropouts, high school graduates gain over $300,000 more in lifetime earnings; the

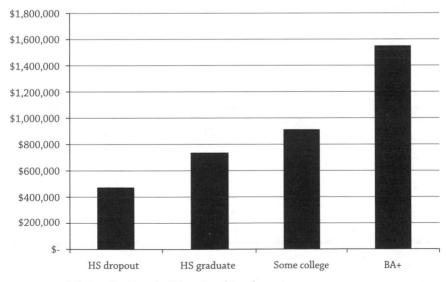

FIGURE 14.1 Lifetime Earnings by Educational Level

gains are more than $1.2 million for those with at least a college degree. Over the lifetime, a college graduate earns approximately four times that of a high school dropout. For the individual student, additional education has a very large payoff.

Tax Payments

These substantial differences in earnings by educational level translate into differences in tax payments and the costs of government services. Most income taxes accrue to the federal government, although states also collect revenues through state income taxes, sales taxes, corporate taxes, and other taxes.[9] Using declared tax payments from the Current Population Survey (CPS), we derive lifetime values of total federal and state tax payments by educational level.[10] Table 14.3 shows that, at every level, those with more education contribute substantially more in taxes.

DIRECT GOVERNMENT EXPENDITURES BY EDUCATION LEVEL

We now examine other influences of education on lifetime economic well-being. We focus on health, crime, and welfare, which are those most salient to the fiscal burden of education, and we also include additional expenditures on public education, including remediation. For each domain we calculate the lifetime profiles by educational level.

The relationship between education and both health behaviors and health status is strong and appears to be increasing over time. More-educated persons follow healthier diets, exhibit fewer risky behaviors, and appear to internalize

TABLE 14.3

Current Cohorts of Students: Federal and State Tax Payments Lifetime Present Value by Education Level

	High school dropout	High school graduate (incl. GED)	Associate degree or some college	BA degree or above
Federal tax	$62,640	$100,630	$132,730	$246,130
difference over dropout	-	$37,990	$70,100	$183,490
State tax (Ts)	$45,170	$64,990	$103,150	$129,070
difference over dropout		$19,820	$57,980	$83,900

Source: Current Population Survey, March Supplements 2006–2010 combined.

Notes: Includes all persons, employed or not. Dollars rounded to nearest 10.

health-related and medical information more effectively. They are more likely to have jobs with private health insurance.[11] Education-related differences in health status render government expenditures for the less educated to be much higher than they are for the more educated.[12]

Education levels are strongly correlated with criminal activity. The link is both direct—additional education lowers the likelihood of criminal conviction—and indirect—higher incomes reduce it. High school dropouts are at greater risk of being arrested and incarcerated. National data show that 68 percent of state prison inmates do not have a high school diploma and that only 12 percent have any post-secondary education.[13] When crime is lower, the pressure for spending on policing, the criminal justice system, and incarceration is lessened.[14]

Similarly, the link between education and reliance of welfare programs is well documented. Not only does additional education reduce the risk of poverty, but welfare programs are means tested.[15] However, the lifetime differences are not large because welfare assistance is often time limited and tied to the presence of children in the household.[16]

The lifetime economic consequences in terms of health, crime, and welfare expenditures are shown in table 14.4. For each domain, government expenditures

TABLE 14.4

Federal and State Expenditures on Health Care, Crime, Welfare, and Education Lifetime Present Values by Education Level

	High school dropout	High school graduate (incl. GED)	Associate degree or some college	BA degree or above
Federal spending (Gf):				
Health	$51,350	$23,790	$14,380	$4,130
Crime	$18,750	$12,080	$5,560	$2,200
Welfare	$16,010	$5,750	$3,220	$670
Education	$(1,350)	$0	$540	$18,880
Total	$84,760	$41,620	$23,700	$25,870
State spending (Gs):				
Health	$43,720	$19,980	$12,200	$3,380
Crime	$37,940	$24,610	$11,290	$4,470
Welfare	$5,370	$1,910	$1,080	$220
Education	$(12,230)	$0	$7,060	$42,010
Total	$74,800	$46,510	$31,630	$50,070

Notes: Present values with 3.5% discount rate. Education expenditures net of K-12 spending until high school completion.

on high school dropouts significantly exceed those on graduates and persons with college education. They are especially large in health. The costs of crime are also significant, although these are concentrated among males.

We also account for the public subsidies that persons with more education receive because they stay in school longer. The cost savings associated with not educating students up to high school graduation should be subtracted from the amounts in table 14.3. But these are only short-run savings; by not educating students we avoid spending taxpayer dollars, but we are creating greater social expenditures in the future.

We should also consider the resource implications of remediation in post-secondary education. Many students who graduate from high school and enroll in college are not prepared for college-level work and must take remedial courses.[17] There is a cost to the student in terms of fees and time away from the labor market, compounded by the fact that many students in remedial classes never progress to complete college credits.[18] There is also a fiscal cost to the extent that these courses are subsidized by the state. One way to understand the cost of remediation is to ask: what proportion of the costs of the higher education system reflects inadequate K-12 schooling? National estimates suggest that at least 11 percent of community college budgets and around 5 percent of four-year college budgets reflect inadequate preparation.[19] However, because we cannot be sure that the remediation costs will fall as the number of graduates increases, remediation is not included in our overall total.

THE OVERALL CONSEQUENCES OF THE OPPORTUNITY GAP

Total Fiscal Impacts

We now summarize the full tax and expenditure impacts across educational levels. These show significantly greater taxes paid by persons with more education and significantly lower government expenditures incurred on their behalf.

The average high school dropout will impose a substantial fiscal burden, while the high school graduate generates an even greater net gain and the college-educated person produces four times as much net revenue for the government. The critical values are given in the final row of table 14.5, which shows the marginal fiscal saving associated with moving an individual from being a high school dropout to a higher level of attainment. These figures show that, were a high school dropout to graduate from high school, the savings would be at least $129,230.[20] If that high school graduate then goes on to college, the taxpayer would save at least $200,000. The opportunity gap is very costly to taxpayers.

TABLE 14.5

Total Fiscal Impacts Lifetime Present Values by Education Level

	High school dropout	High school graduate (incl. GED)	Associate degree or some college	BA degree or above
Net fiscal impact:				
Federal government (Tf-Gf)	$(22,120)	$59,010	$109,030	$220,260
State government (Ts-Gs)	$(29,630)	$18,480	$71,520	$79,000
Total	$(51,750)	$77,490	$180,550	$299,260
Saving over HS dropout		+$129,230	+$232,300	+$351,010
Saving per graduate+		$187,700		

Notes: 2011 dollars. Discount rate of 3.5%. Present values at age 18. See tables 14.1 and 14.3 for values of Tf, Gf, Ts, and Gs. Graduate+ is a high school graduate who is expected to progress to some college with probability = 0.34 and complete college with probability = 0.17.

Social Impacts

These calculations offer only a partial accounting of the economic value of education. The development of human capital confers many social benefits as well. Here we consider four of the most important.[21] Unfortunately, we cannot estimate them as precisely as we do the fiscal benefits: the economic value of these effects of education is not easily calculable. So these figures should be treated with caution.

The primary social benefit of education is the positive economic spillover from having a more educated workforce. Workers learn skills from one another, and firms are more likely to locate in areas with larger pools of skilled workers; hence the rise of the so-called creative class.[22] Studies have estimated that the spillover is worth at least 37 percent more than the simple income gains.[23]

Second, there are wide benefits from reduced crime. Indeed, the main benefit from a lower crime rate is not that spending on the police force is lower, but that fewer people are victimized by crime. Victims bear a heavy loss in terms of reduced quality of life and monetary losses, such as time off work. Everyone pays in devoting resources to avoid being a victim of crime. Current estimates of the social costs of crime, however, do not include the psychic costs to criminals and their families from incarceration. As an approximation, we follow Miller, Cohen, and Wiersema, who calculate that the social burden of crime is at least 2.5 times the size of the fiscal burden.[24]

Finally, raising revenue for government programs imposes an economic distortion. Since income taxes rise with incomes, people will work less if income taxes increase. This distortion is necessary to raise tax revenue, but it carries a social

TABLE 14.6

Total Social Impacts Lifetime Present Values by Education Level

	High school dropout	High school graduate (incl. GED)	Associate degree or some college	BA degree or above
Income gains + Productivity spillovers (Y)	$ 648,040	$ 1,006,140	$ 1,248,650	$ 2,126,270
Health burden (H)	$ 94,070	$ 43,770	$ 26,580	$ 7,510
Crime burden (C)	$ 198,410	$ 128,430	$ 59,000	$ 23,320
Education burden (E)	$(13,580)	$ 0	$ 7,590	$ 60,890
Tax distortion (M)	$ 53,310	$ 78,070	$ 120,410	$ 161,070
Totals (=Y-H-C-E+M)	$421,440	$ 912,010	$ 1,275,890	$ 2,195,630
Difference over dropout		$ 490,560	$ 854,440	$ 1,774,180
Difference per graduate+		$ 760,830		

Notes: 2011 dollars. Discount rate of 3.5%. Social benefits exclude welfare transfers and count gross earnings. Crime burden includes victim costs. QALY benefits are not included. Tax distortion calculated as 13 cents per dollar of tax payments (table 14.1).

cost. In raising a dollar of tax revenue, the government might impose a distortion of 28 cents or even more. We use a conservative estimate: the distortion imposed by a dollar of tax is 13 cents.[25]

The social value of better health is greater than the amount that the government spends to alleviate poor health. For example, someone who is sick may have to take time off work. Given the difficulty of making reliable estimates of the social value of health, however, we have not included this factor in our calculations.[26]

As table 14.6 shows, including these social costs greatly magnifies the differences by educational level. The total social benefit of a high school graduate over a dropout is approximately almost half a million dollars. If someone progresses from being a dropout to attending and completing a four-year degree, the social benefit amounts to $1.77 million. If we adjust for the possibility that a high school graduate will attend college, the estimated social value is $760,830. These social impacts make an extremely compelling case for greater investments in education.

Aggregate Fiscal and Social Impacts

These calculations are for individuals. In order to calculate the aggregate cost of the opportunity gap we need to count the relevant populations of students. As shown in table 14.1, there are approximately 800,000 high school dropouts in each year cohort. Therefore the aggregate fiscal burden is $150 billion and the aggregate social burden is $610 billion.

It is not likely, however, that the opportunity gap can be closed for all students by educational interventions alone, nor is it likely that all dropouts would gain the same benefit (see Rothstein, chapter 5 in this volume). Many students face personal challenges that cannot be fully remedied by more schooling. It will be necessary to commit additional resources to reforms that will close the opportunity gap, so it is important to demonstrate that effective interventions exist. In other work, we have reviewed numerous interventions, including preschool, reductions in class size, and increasing teacher wages. We have estimated the costs of delivering these interventions and have found that their costs are far below the marginal value of each new high school graduate: in sum, they cost far less than $200,000 per student. (Indeed, the entire K-12 funding of many students—particularly those in disadvantaged communities—is less than $200,000). Some of these interventions are targeted at particular groups of students, so we cannot assume they would work for all students. But others are generally applied and might help a large proportion of all students who face an opportunity gap. If we assume that one-third of the opportunity gap might be closed, the economic consequences would be $50 billion in fiscal savings and $200 billion in savings from society's perspective. By point of comparison, total taxpayer spending on K-12 education is approximately $570 billion.

Our calculations of the economic burdens of inadequate education rely on many different research studies and modeling assumptions. Although the studies we use are the best available, it is important to consider how sensitive our calculations are to alternative assumptions.[27] We have reason to believe that the full economic burden is significantly above our estimates. First, we use conservative assumptions.[28] Second, we do not count benefits that might occur before high school graduation, such as reduced rates of special education and grade retention, as well as declines in juvenile crime.[29] A preschool program might reduce the need for special education. We also omit some important effects of dropping out, such as teenage pregnancies and single motherhood, as well as the social repercussions of mass incarceration.

An argument may be made that we have overstated the benefits. First, increasing the number of high school graduates might mean that they have to take jobs that dropouts used to take. However, most studies of the labor market find skill-biased technological change; as the educational levels of the workforce increase, firms use more technologically complex processes. Second, if there were more high school graduates, their wages might decline. This outcome might result if the expansion were very large relative to the total workforce, but it is not. Even if we anticipate 0.8 million new high school graduates, they would amount to just one-half of one percent of the labor force. Many of these new graduates would go on to college rather than immediately enter the labor market. The appropriate analogy is a race, rather than a zero-sum game in which one skilled worker deprives another of employment. Third, it may not be appropriate to assume that the benefits of education will accrue to the same extent across all dropouts. In general, we assume that a person who becomes a graduate is likely to get the benefits typically found for graduates. If this person requires a lot more extra schooling to graduate, that fact would have implications for the costs of education reform, but not the benefits. Finally, we assume that the benefits of education that exist today will be perpetuated for current cohorts of graduates. If the future for more-educated persons is bleaker, we will have overstated the benefits. But the Great Recession (officially dated from June 2007 to December 2009) has not affected graduates more than it did dropouts; those who have been hit hardest are those with the weakest skills. We would have overstated the burden if the gains from education decrease, but most evidence suggests that the gains will actually increase.[30] Therefore, it is likely that the costs of inadequate education to taxpayers and to society are larger than these estimates.

INVESTMENTS TO CLOSE THE OPPORTUNITY GAP

The case for closing the opportunity gap might be expressed in terms of fairness. Much of the difference found in educational and life outcomes is associated with the socioeconomic, immigrant, or racial and ethnic group membership of families. Other chapters in this volume illustrate the multidimensional and cumulative nature of the opportunity gap. Such a gap is inconsistent with a just and democratic society. Our economic findings strengthen that case by showing how important that gap continues to be in adulthood and by comparing the amount that is currently being invested with the amount that is being jeopardized by a failure to invest adequately. Powerful social and economic interventions have been shown to close this gap and these are inexpensive compared to what is being cumulatively jeopardized. Indeed, the number and diversity of potential interventions and reforms is growing. It includes not only school-based reforms—some of them very substantial (e.g., raising teacher quality) and others more targeted (such as Talent Search)—but it also encompasses out-of-school youth programs such as Job Corps and National Guard Youth Challenge. But perhaps the broadest solution to the opportunity gap is to make the high fiscal and social gains widely known and generally believed. This would affect the climate of opinion and make decision makers aware that the investment in human capital is worth it. Although the investment of public resources in the interest of fairness is often viewed as a cost to society; our economic analysis highlights the substantial benefits that result from this investment.

Education then, beyond all other devices of human origin, is a great equalizer of the conditions of men,—the balance wheel of the social machinery...and, if this education should be universal and complete, it would do more than all things else to obliterate factitious distinctions in society.

Horace Mann, 1848

15

Enhancing a Nation's Democracy through Equitable Schools

Michele S. Moses and John Rogers

AS DOCUMENTED THROUGHOUT this book, public education in the United States is not fulfilling its promise of ensuring equal educational opportunities for all students. Too often, the neighborhood in which a child grows up determines the quality of educational resources in her local public school. Young people living in low-income communities of color, on average, attend schools with less qualified teachers, poorer facilities, and less rigorous coursework than their White and affluent counterparts. The opportunity gap has serious consequences for students' academic achievement and for young people's civic skills and commitments. The implications of these equality of opportunity issues are not new. Nineteenth-century social reformer Horace Mann raised them more than a century and half ago, contending that public schooling ought to decrease social inequality. In this chapter, we examine that normative claim and argue for an increased public focus on the democratic purposes of schools.

What is the relationship between the quality and distribution of learning opportunities and the role of public schools in promoting democracy and eradicating social inequality? Why do learning opportunities matter for the broad public and democratic purposes of education? We argue for a public education system that prepares young people both to participate in existing democratic structures and to challenge an unequal, segregated social context.

We explore how more racially integrated, robust, and equitable learning opportunities for all students, particularly students from non-dominant communities, serve democracy. Our arguments are based on three guiding assumptions: that a set of key learning opportunities matters for the development of civic capacity and commitments; that racially, ethnically, and socioeconomically diverse classrooms can enhance students' preparation for democratic deliberation; and that the quality of learning conditions in particular schools conveys powerful symbolic lessons about fairness and about how much the state cares about the well-being of different communities. In sum, the quality of our democracy is shaped by decisions about who attends school together and how we distribute learning opportunities across different students and different schools.

Addressing gaps in education is not, in itself, sufficient for tackling the problems associated with social inequalities related to race and ethnicity and socioeconomic status. Nevertheless, the education system should not exacerbate those inequalities. Indeed, under the right conditions, as Mann suggested, education may combat those inequalities; education is important although it should not be seen as the sole cause or solution.

As the title of this book suggests, policy and policy discussions will benefit from shifting beyond a narrow focus on achievement to a more expansive consideration of opportunity. Attending to opportunity turns the conversation to why and how public schooling should be improved, and concerns about democracy should be central to that endeavor. In addition, we want to emphasize a complementary reconceptualization of what educational outcomes matter. The current achievement orientation highlights economic ends and the instrumental purposes of education, with a focus on narrow indicators of performance on standardized tests in math and English language arts (see Zhao and Tienken, chapter 8 in this volume). Accountability systems that overemphasize high-stakes testing push out other important educational domains, including civic education. For example, some research suggests that elementary schools serving large numbers of low-income students of color are more likely to have reduced the amount of time devoted to social studies in the wake of accountability pressures from the No Child Left Behind Act.[1] Without access to a robust social studies curriculum, students may not develop critical understandings of the history and principles of American democracy or how community members may participate in civic life.

ATTENDING TO THE DEMOCRATIC PURPOSE OF PUBLIC EDUCATION

Why should public schools devote valuable time to civic development? Proponents of civic education often note that building democratic skills and commitments has been central to public education since the nation's founding.[2] We make two other claims about why civic goals should shape the work of public schools today. First, we need to prepare students to deliberate in a pluralistic society characterized by conflicts of values and goals. Second, we need to develop young people's commitments to and skills for democratic participation, which will yield benefits including expanding the capacity of students to address declining and unequal rates of civic engagement as well as broader forms of economic and social inequality.

Contemporary political life necessarily includes moral disagreements and conflicts related to values and politics. This pluralism requires democratic structures and practices that place moral discussion at the center of political life.[3] Deliberative democracy is characterized by three conditions that regulate and structure the deliberative process of politics: reciprocity, by which reason giving and justification for mutually binding policies are seen as a mutual endeavor; publicity, which stipulates that policy makers, researchers, officials, and members of the public should have to justify their decisions and actions in public; and accountability, which requires those who make policy decisions to answer to those who are bound by those policies. The idea of reciprocity is key here. According to Amy Gutmann, "Reciprocity among free and equal individuals [means] citizens and their accountable representatives owe one another justifications for the laws that collectively bind them. . . . To the extent that democracy is not deliberative, it treats people as objects of legislation, as passive subjects to be ruled, rather than as citizens who take part in governance."[4] A deliberative perspective encourages greater public participation in and understanding of public debates by demanding that citizens[5] abide by the principles of reciprocity, publicity, and accountability.

Citizens need to develop both capacities for and commitments to democratic deliberation. Deliberative capacities include skills of listening, weighing evidence, and communicating with people from diverse backgrounds. Deliberative commitments are ways of thinking and being that collectively constitute a democratic character. Gutmann explained that children "must learn not to just *behave* in accordance with authority but to *think* critically about authority if they are to live up to the democratic ideal of sharing political sovereignty as citizens."[6] In addition, the development of democratic character is linked with the ability to reason morally, which is intimately connected with deliberation. As Gutmann pointed out, "People adept at logical reasoning who lack moral character . . . use moral arguments to serve whatever ends they happen to choose for themselves. . . . But people who possess sturdy moral character without a developed capacity for reasoning are ruled only by habit and authority. . . . Education in character and in moral reasoning are therefore both necessary, neither sufficient, for creating democratic citizens."[7] For example, individuals might use moral reasons to rationalize unacceptable or even unjust acts, for example, the educational administrators in Atlanta who pressured teachers to falsify test scores to avoid sanctions if their students performed below certain standards. They justified their actions as being in the best interests of the students and their schools.[8]

The need for public schools to educate students for democratic participation has grown in recent years. Voting has declined over several decades, particularly among younger adults, and there has been a significant drop-off in civic engagement beyond electoral politics, such as participation in civic associations and volunteering in community activities.[9] A committee convened by the American Political Science Association recently reported that "Americans have turned away from politics and the public sphere in large numbers, leaving our civic life impoverished."[10]

Political scientists also have highlighted growing inequalities in civic life. The likelihood of voting, belonging to civic groups, making political contributions, and participating in protest activities is strongly related to race, level of education, and social class.[11] According to the American Political Science Association Task Force on Inequality and American Democracy:

> Generations of Americans have worked to equalize citizen voice across lines of income, race, and gender. Today, however, the voices of American citizens are raised and heard unequally. The privileged participate more than others and are increasingly well organized to press their demands on government. Public officials, in turn, are much more responsive to the privileged than to average citizens and the least affluent. Citizens with lower or moderate incomes speak with a whisper that is lost to the ears of inattentive government officials, while the advantaged roar with clarity and consistency that policy makers readily hear and routinely follow.[12]

Inequalities in political participation both result from and lead to growing economic inequality. Since the early 1970s, almost all growth in real incomes has accrued to the wealthiest Americans, producing higher levels of income inequality than at any time since the Great Depression.[13] Wealth increasingly shapes the ability of citizens to have their voices heard (a trend that likely will become more pronounced in the wake of the Supreme Court's 2010 ruling in *Citizens United*).[14] Legislators have responded to moneyed voices with policies that disadvantage the poor, including tax cuts for the wealthiest Americans and more stringent requirements for bankruptcy.[15] When political scientist Larry Bartels examined the votes of United States senators between 1989 and 1994 in light of the preferences their constituents expressed in survey data from this same period, he found that senators' votes are most closely aligned with interests of their wealthiest constituents and that the policy preferences of the citizens in the bottom third of the income distribution had no demonstrable effect on their votes.[16]

As Gary Orfield observes in chapter 4 of this volume, economic and political inequality has a spatial dimension. Americans increasingly live in economically segregated communities. Since 1970, the proportion of middle-income neighborhoods in metropolitan areas has declined dramatically.[17] Although racial and ethnic residential segregation has moderated during this period, race remains a significant predictor of where people live.[18] These patterns of residential segregation limit interchange across social class and race and often leave low-income communities of color politically isolated.[19]

Civic education cannot, in and of itself, eradicate political, economic, or social inequality. Yet policy makers also cannot ignore these threats to democratic life. Working amid structures of inequality, public schools must prepare students for forms of civic engagement that include critique and social change as well as social cooperation and deliberation. Later we share some ideas of how schools might approach this challenge.

LEARNING OPPORTUNITIES THAT SHAPE
CIVIC CAPACITY AND COMMITMENT

An array of social science research suggests that the civic capacity and commitment of adults are, in part, a product of their earlier experiences in schools. Ronald La Due Lake and Robert Huckfeldt argue that the "positive relationship between education and political participation is one of the most reliable results in empirical social science."[20] In general, higher levels of formal education are associated with greater political understanding, skills, and civic participation.[21]

What sorts of learning opportunities matter to the civic development of young people? A first answer to this question comes from testimony provided in *The Campaign for Fiscal Equity v. New York*, a school finance lawsuit filed in 1993. The New York State Court of Appeals (the state's highest court) said that the state's guarantee of a "sound basic education" meant that young people needed to "function productively as civic participants capable of voting and serving on a jury."[22] As an expert witness, Linda Darling-Hammond analyzed the cognitive demands on these forms of participation and related them to state curriculum standards. She found that voters and jurors need to be able to read statistical tables, understand economic concepts, demonstrate analytic reading skills, and possess "a reasoning process of understanding evidence and applying it to a conclusion."[23] Darling-Hammond concluded that civic participation demands levels of literacy, numeracy, and problem solving that can only be developed in schools that provide ample educational opportunities.

A set of civic learning opportunities has been shown to promote civic knowledge and commitment including instruction in the history and principles of American democracy, classroom discussion of current events that make a direct and tangible difference in young people's lives, community service, participation in civic organizations that address meaningful issues, and participation in public forums and democratic governance in school and in the larger community.[24]

While these practices promote civic development, they are not always provided to all students, and the implications are serious. Access to high-quality civic learning opportunities in school is more consequential than student race or parental engagement in civic life in predicting students' civic commitments.[25] Moreover, low-income students, Latino and African American students, and students enrolled in low academic tracks have less access to these civic learning opportunities than their peers.[26] These inequalities play out both between and within schools (see Tyson, chapter 12 in this volume, for a discussion of within-school opportunity gaps).

JOHN DEWEY AND RELATIONSHIPS WITH DIVERSE OTHERS

Relationships among young people from diverse backgrounds provide a critical component in fostering deep democratic engagement. Young people who go to school together have an opportunity to learn from one another, form understandings of community, and build their capacity for and commitment to working in diverse settings.

American philosopher John Dewey pointed out that the interests and values of a community can only be truly shared when all group members have "an equable opportunity to receive and take from others,"[27] that is, to learn and participate in the formulation and negotiation of the common values and interests. In explaining why education is so important in a democracy, Dewey stressed that citizens need to be informed enough to participate in the democratic process. Democracy is not only a form of government, however; more fundamentally, it is "primarily a mode of associated living, of conjoint communicated experience."[28] He concluded: "A society which makes provision for participation in its good of all its members on equal terms and which secures flexible readjustment of its institutions through interaction of the different forms of associated life is in so far democratic. Such a society must have a type of education which gives individuals a personal interest in social relationships and control, and habits of mind which secure social changes."[29] Further, Dewey was concerned that students develop unity, not uniformity of outlook: "The intermingling in the school of youth of different races, different religions, and unlike customs creates for all a new and broader environment. Common subject matter accustoms all to a unity of outlook upon a broader horizon than is visible to the members of any group while it is isolated."[30]

Values such as those Dewey described are transmitted by providing students "with the kinds of experiences that make their values real and significant for their own lives," preparing them "for democratic life by involving them in forms of democratic living appropriate for their age."[31] Dewey envisioned teachers encouraging students to reconsider and revise their beliefs and values.[32] Education ought to provide experiences that equip students for intelligent, well-considered rethinking. Learners are to be seen as inquirers who make good use of conflicts or problematic encounters in order to grow.[33]

Dewey also highlighted the importance of communication for democracy, civic participation, and community life. Through education, citizens would learn that they must consider their own actions as affecting the larger community and their own good as inextricably linked to the good of others.[34] Accordingly, he believed that education should move beyond mere acquisition of academic content to include the development of social attitudes conducive to participation in a democratic society, including "the willingness to rethink one's own beliefs and traditions when encountering others who think and act differently, a commitment to considering the bearing on the community as a whole of one's own actions, a belief that one's own good cannot be separated from the good of others, the willingness to make every effort to resolve conflict through public discourse."[35] These attitudes and experiences contribute to dispositions toward equality and justice.[36]

Dewey's insights about the educational benefits of learning environments in which educators purposefully incorporate diversity are echoed in an array of social science research. These settings improve students' learning experiences, problem-solving abilities, critical thinking skills, capacity for democratic citizenship, and preparation for life in a diverse society.[37] Amy Stuart Wells, Jennifer Holme, Anita Revilla, and Awo Atanda studied the experiences of people who attended racially and ethnically integrated schools. They concluded, "African Americans and Latinos who have led desegregated lives can attest to the importance of crossing color lines and reaching across the racial divide. They argue that such connections across race make for a more democratic society."[38] Elizabeth Anderson extended this point, arguing that policies that promote racial segregation represent "a loss suffered by the American public at large because they limit the ability of citizens from all origins [to] exchange ideas and cooperate on terms of equality—which is the indispensable social condition of democracy itself."[39]

UNDERSTANDING SOCIAL INEQUALITY AND SOCIAL CHANGE

Following Dewey and Gutmann, we argue that the democratic purposes of education ought to be centrally invoked in calls for more equitable schooling, and education's role in fostering a more racially integrated, equitable, and democratic society ought to be highlighted in the quest for educational improvement.

Another domain that is crucial in fostering an education that prepares students to take part in remedying inequity involves the relationship of young people to power, authority, and social change. Just as positive learning conditions contribute to the development of students' civic skills and commitments, exposure to poor or inequitable conditions can lead to civic despair or alienation. Consider, for example, the statements from students who participated in focus groups Michelle Fine conducted as part of the *Williams v. California* adequacy litigation. These focus groups brought together young people from public schools that were dramatically understaffed, lacked learning materials, and had dilapidated facilities. Describing conditions in her high school, Alondra Jones explained:

> It make you feel less about yourself, you know, like you sitting here in a class where you have to stand up because there's not enough chairs and you see rats in the buildings, the bathrooms is nasty, you got to pay. And then you, like I said, I visited Mann Academy, and these students, if they want to sit on the floor, that's because they choose to. And that just makes me feel real less about myself because it's like the State don't care about public schools. If I have to . . . stand in the class, they can't care about me.[40]

Fine argues that the powerful sense of injustice that Jones articulates leads many young people to become alienated from the public sphere. Opportunity gaps send similar messages to parents about how little the state values their children's future. These messages are particularly consequential for immigrant parents whose primary relationship to the state is framed by their children's public school.

Students can learn democratic capabilities in public schools. Even though many students face dismal and discriminatory conditions, some learn how to navigate systems and are resilient in the face of obstacles to social change. Joel Westheimer pointed out that the "purposeful nurturing of a sense of community and hopefulness" is a significant factor in helping students negotiate systems and achieve positive outcomes.[41] When students encounter obstacles to political action, they have the opportunity to gain "an understanding of power relations, obstacles to change, and resistance,"[42] which helps to fulfill the democratic aims of education. The most successful democratic projects in schools nurture hopefulness in the face of difficulties, preparing students to struggle even within an unequal society. As such, we want to put forward three ideas that could be implemented to help prepare students for civic life and democratic participation.

1) The civic learning opportunity index. We note that schools provide differential civic learning opportunities to different groups of students. We also argue that current accountability structures focus narrowly on English language arts and math and ignore civic capacities. To address these concerns, we propose a civic learning opportunity index that reports on (a) classroom civic opportunities such as current events, service learning, and speakers from the community; (b) opportunities to participate in extracurricular activities that support working in groups and addressing community issues; and (c) opportunities for diverse students to participate in decision making in the school or school district.

2) Restorative justice programs. Students can work with school administrators to negotiate and resolve appropriate school discipline and leadership issues, instead of administrators making all such decisions. We argue that students should be taught about working to make change even within unjust systems, and participatory justice programs may provide important opportunities for such learning.

3) The senior civic portfolio. We note that policies should encourage schools to focus attention on developing civic capabilities. We propose a graduation requirement that calls on students to produce a civic portfolio, including some project through which students demonstrate a capacity to deliberate and work in groups to identify and address problems in the local community. An additional requirement must be paired with additional supports. It is essential to ensure that all students are provided with the learning conditions necessary to complete the senior portfolio.

Of course, the details for these proposals will need to be worked out within specific school contexts. In addition, there is the overall need for a broad approach to change. We argued above that civic education cannot, in and of itself, eradicate political, economic, or social inequality. Promoting social mobility and civic equality requires policy changes in housing, labor, and civil rights in addition to changes in education.

Unfortunately, and as Zhao and Tienken describe in this volume, the current emphasis on accountability in education does not recognize the importance of education for democratic capabilities. A reconceptualization of these policies would help students throughout the nation, allowing policy makers and educators to invoke an expansive sense of educational accountability that focuses on the central importance of creating citizens. Students currently have disparate opportunities to learn about and practice democracy. Rather than holding educators accountable primarily for their students' scores on standardized exams, we should hold them—as well as policy makers—accountable for helping students develop democratic capabilities that can be used effectively within an inequitable and unjust social context.

16

Building Opportunities to Achieve

Prudence L. Carter and Kevin G. Welner

FOR MORE THAN a half century, Americans have been told that our international competitiveness depends on a strong educational system.[1] For even longer, we have been told that America is the land of opportunity—a place where a child's success does not depend on the happenstance of being born to well-off parents. But the reality is not so evenhanded. Some groups of students must run in the proverbial race of academic and economic success in lanes replete with hurdles, potholes, and broken glass, while for others the lanes are unobstructed, well-paved, and smooth. The lanes assigned to different children are terribly predictable based on their racial, ethnic, and class backgrounds. Of course, many members of historically disadvantaged groups have made it, and we as a nation cheer for those Horatio Alger heroes who overcome daunting obstacles. We as a nation also pretend that such stories are common or even the norm. All the while, we unquestioningly treat as natural those barriers themselves as well as the overwhelming number of children who never come close to clearing them. These children lose opportunities to thrive, and the nation loses the chance to develop its most valuable resource: its youth.

The evidence amassed by the illustrious collection of scholars and researchers in this book paints a grim picture of a wide and deep opportunity gap arising from the accumulated impact of many factors: segregation in housing as well as segregation between and within schools; differences in resources between poor children and wealthier children; differences in access to high-quality early childhood education; between-school differences in teacher training, teacher experience, and teacher quality, as well as between-school differences in other resources, such as technology, safe buildings with heating and air conditioning, textbooks, working bathrooms, and class size; differences in the provision of engaging, deep, project-based learning versus instruction focused on raising test scores; stratified school opportunities arising from the types of school choice policies that are now in vogue; the widespread provision of culturally unresponsive curriculum and instruction; and the failure to value and build on the strengths of language minority children. The opportunity gap is also widened by factors not covered by the chapters in this book, such as student discipline policies that push children out of school—and that disproportionately harm lower-income children and youth of color;[2] grade retention policies that do not increase achievement but are instead associated with a substantially increased likelihood of dropping out—again disproportionately harming lower-income children and youth of color;[3] and very different levels of access to enriching learning activities during nonschool hours.[4] While some readers may occasionally quibble with elements of the opportunity gap, offering "yeah, but ... " retorts to a particular contention, the cumulative evidence presented in the preceding chapters is overwhelming and distressing. We as a nation have created and perpetuated a system that denies fair opportunities to millions—arguably tens of millions—of our children every year. American education is perfectly un-American as long as these deep inequities exist.[5]

Educational opportunities, however, are not just about formal education. Schools do not exist as an independent social institution, somehow separate from larger society. Instead, our schools and students are steeped within the folds of formidable economic, political, cultural, and social contexts. We deceive ourselves if we believe that we can insulate schooling outcomes from poverty or wealth, from unemployment or wages, or from racism and discrimination. While some schools serve highly functioning neighborhoods, families, and communities, others lie within areas of concentrated poverty with crumbling infrastructure. Some schools are able to employ and retain high-quality, knowledgeable, and socially conscious educators, while others suffer from constant churn or from mediocre teachers with low expectations for the vulnerable youth put in their charge. Is it a surprise that children will fare best if they have access to the greatest combinations of these resources—if they have rich opportunities to learn?

The millions of youth attending schools across the nation will never be the same on every dimension, and we should never want them to be. Fair opportunity is very different from being identical on every dimension of life's circumstances. Some differences are fair, natural, and good; they add to the mosaic of diversity in a vibrant society. Other differences, however, are harmful. This is especially true of those pertaining to the grossly disparate resource levels provided to many low-income US schoolchildren, who are disproportionately of color. Decades of widening inequality compound the glaring divide between children who have and succeed and those who have not and fail.

The national response to that widening inequality, over the past three decades in particular, has been to provide minor treatments for the proverbial symptoms as opposed to getting to the roots of an undeniable disease. If we continue to follow that feeble approach, we will see unequal opportunities continue to ravage our youth. But we have a choice. We can start along the path to giving every child a fair chance at success. This start requires that policy makers of various political stripes acknowledge that our collective health is systemic—acknowledge the ecology of opportunity in US society. A balance in one part of the social system is connected to well-being in another part of it.

The US Congress will soon determine the future of the Elementary and Secondary Education Act (ESEA), whose current incarnation is referred to as No Child Left Behind[6]. Originally passed in 1965, ESEA was a critical piece of the Great Society's War on Poverty. While ESEA was never perfect (see Kantor and Lowe, chapter 3 of this volume), it was a key part of a larger effort to address the poverty and disadvantage that severely limited the life chances of America's youth. Yet since the Johnson administration, US policy makers have repeatedly waved a white flag in the War on Poverty. In 2012, the United Nations Children's Fund (UNICEF) issued a report looking at child poverty rates within 35 affluent, or "developed," nations. The United States—one of the world's wealthiest nations[7]—had the second highest poverty rate, with 23.1 percent of children living in poverty, behind only Romania's 25.6 percent but well ahead of Latvia (18.8 percent) and Bulgaria (17.8 percent).[8]

Meanwhile, ESEA has undergone multiple transformations and has emerged as something very different from its original incarnation. Changes to the law have increasingly contracted education's focus and purposes, and an outcome-based accountability system has been put in place. These changes and others have strained teachers' relationships with school officials, parents, and students, as stringent standards seek to identify who is to blame for students' academic outcomes. Schooling now revolves around accountability and test scores—our current conventional and narrow measure of school success. Blame and test-based accountability are supplanting learning resources as the federal government's tool of choice.

Shifting US educational and social policy toward a path designed to close opportunity gaps will not be easy. But that new path is not hidden; it is systematically mapped out by decades of established social science research. The authors of the preceding chapters provide an array of worthwhile and evidence-based recommendations. In this final chapter we offer our own summation, drawn from those

chapters. Our goal is not to recount every one of our expert authors' recommendations. Instead, it is to embrace the experts' ideas and consider them as a whole.

The broad conception of education set forth by our authors suggests multiple
ways for us to understand how schooling can enhance children's ability to learn
and thrive. As a first step, lawmakers must discard notions that treat our children's educational well-being like a game or competition. The paramount need
for equitable educational opportunities must not be sacrificed to any approach
that fosters economic or educational inequality. Such inequality did lessen over
the course of the mid- to late twentieth century, and the nation saw educational
opportunity correspondingly improve for groups previously disenfranchised and
undereducated.[9] But as economic inequality increased from the late 1990s to the
early twenty-first century, the divide between successful and low-achieving school
children has widened.[10] That disparity compounds what already existed in terms
of the "educational debt" that Gloria Ladson-Billings discusses in chapter 2. Class
matters, as does race—and the two have long been inextricably linked.

Our lawmakers must also face the reality that schools have never been able to do
the work of closing the opportunity gap alone. This does not deny the existence of
excellent schools serving disadvantaged youth, nor does it deny the benefits that
those schools can impart. Children attending schools that provide rich opportunities to learn see substantially improved academic and life chances. Their odds are
improved. Many of them will enter higher education, and many will become productive members of society. But their chances of success are still far below those
of their more advantaged counterparts with economically and socially secure lives.
The obstacles we erect in front of these children are much more difficult to clear.

A related reality is that school resources and school quality have never been independent of community resources. Schools in poor communities are more likely to
flounder precisely because they have fewer financial resources to draw on, because
they have less political power that can be exercised to gain other resources, and
because they are forced to contend with the emotional, social, and academic fallout of youth whose families, as Rothstein describes in chapter 5, can barely keep it
together in terms of basic survival—poverty, unemployment, and whatever psy-
chosocial challenges that ensue from often-traumatic economic circumstances.
These realities mean that policy cannot sensibly focus on schools alone. Economic
and social welfare policies are also extraordinarily important, with parental
employment playing a crucial role.[11] Wise policies do not prop up children's schools
while ignoring the employment needs of those children's parents.

Local, state, and federal government officials must also face the fact that separate has never been and will never be equal. Since long before *Plessy* and continuing
to the present day—with only a decade or two pause around the 1970s—separate

but (never really) equal has been the nation's dominant approach toward race and schooling. And it has failed. Thick racial, ethnic, class, and religious boundaries undermine democracy and thwart equity. Where and how we raise and educate our children also hinder the realization of a truly postracial and open society. School integration, as described by Orfield in chapter 4, was meant to offer better edu-cational opportunities and to provide African Americans and other racial minori-ties with the human capital needed for economic advancement in the developing post–World World II capitalist economy. While some schools did pursue genuine racial integration, many others resegregated within schools, using racial tracking as described by Tyson in chapter 12.

Even this minor progress was, however, short-lived. By the close of the twenti-eth century, the courts were well on their way to systematically dismantling any remaining integrationist efforts. As part of this retrenchment, White parents—steeped in a zero-sum game mentality and fearful that others are taking what is "rightfully" theirs—sued school districts with race-conscious, integration- and equity-focused policies. The US Supreme Court sided with those parents in 2007, by a margin of five to four, in cases arising out of Seattle and Louisville (the "PICS" cases), where the districts had used racial classifications to avoid severe racial seg-regation arising out of school choice policies.

Schools are critical spaces of shared learning, socialization, and citizenship building for society, and Asian, Black, Latino, Native American, and White public school students usually have little to no daily contact with each other across racial lines. The areas of damage include achievement but also include intergroup rela-tions as well as the students' choices of segregated or integrated working and liv-ing environments as adults.[12] De facto segregation casts a pall over society—over schools that ask their students to utter "with liberty and justice for all" to begin each school day.

We all pay the price for this social myopia, even those of us who live in safe, com-fortable, homogeneous neighborhoods with our segregated albeit high-performing schools (in terms of test scores and college-going rates). In chapter 14, Clive Belfield and Hank Levin calculate how much we already lose from potential earnings and contributions to the national treasury when our fellow citizens are not properly educated: closing just one-third of the opportunity gap would yield annual eco-nomic benefits of $50 billion in fiscal savings and $200 billion in savings from soci-ety's perspective (e.g., the benefits of a better-educated workforce). Moreover, as Moses and Rogers explain in chapter 15, the opportunity gap also damages our civic responsibilities and the health of our democracy. Tolerance of segregation, inequality, and social division undermine long-standing policy goals and basic American principles. Opportunity gaps stubbornly reproduce boundaries between the "us" and the "them." They also reproduce a blinkered understanding of the meaning of merit, success, and achievement.

These realities also make clear the need for just and sensible policies related to immigrants. Just as children face additional educational hurdles when their families are mired in poverty or unemployment, immigration- and language-related fears and impediments destabilize children's lives and undermine their ability to succeed academically. Latino immigrants—a diverse, pan-ethnic, Spanish-speaking group of people of various national origins—have been the largest group over the past half century. Many of these immigrants are poor with very limited formal education. They want the American Dream, and they want the best for their children, but many have difficulty communicating with their children's teachers and principals for various reasons, particularly because of a language barrier.

From a policy perspective it is disconcerting to see these needs met by a renewed national push for monolingualism (namely, English only). By comparison, in the era of increased globalization, significant percentages of students in other advanced, industrialized nations speak at least one other language.[13] Here again, we see limited social and cultural boundary spanning; we see one-way acculturation as the dominant cultural assertion. We should, it seems, all speak and behave the same. If this approach is not modified, the opportunity gap for children in immigrant families will remain in place, and additional generations of talent will be lost. The primacy of English as the main language that bridges people of various social backgrounds across the United States does not have to be lost. At the same time, policies designed to encourage multilingualism will help American citizens and employees of the next generation prepare to be more effective global citizens.

The irony of xenophobic policies should not be overlooked. With the exception of Native American citizens, all of us are the descendants of persons "foreign," whether forcibly or willingly. Significant cultural and religious differences prevailed among early immigrants to this land; equally as many differences existed among indigenous peoples. These are sources of strength to be embraced, not feared. Today immigrant students comprise a significant percentage of our nation's schools, and they are projected to continue to do so.[14] As Gándara explains in chapter 11, their school success is critical to the nation's overall well-being. Wise policy must recognize the need for just and fair immigration policies and language policies, in tandem with strong educational practices. Policies that promote the development of a strong corps of well-trained bilingual teachers are one way to tend to the United States' educational future.

Because opportunities to learn arise out of outside-school as well as within-school resources, we also must reconceptualize how we define student achievement and success. As noted earlier, the policies currently in vogue have changed the daily experience of schooling such that it now revolves around accountability and test scores. Good tests used sparingly can be integral to sound teaching. But when testing supplants teaching, students suffer. And those students, particularly as they get older, are well aware of the futility of the exercise. Darlene, a 15-year-old African American student attending a high performing high school in the American South told one of us in an interview: "They don't really care about us. All they care about is how well we perform on the test so they can look good." Darlene and several of her schoolmates divulged that they put little effort into taking the test. Disillusioned and alienated, they held little regard for test's worth and its relevance to their lives. Similarly, a *New York Times* article concerning the limitations of test scores quoted Nikita Thomas, a high school graduate: "Passing the Regents don't mean nothing. The main focus in high school is to get you to graduate; it makes the school look good. They get you in and get you out." Nikita had passed the New York state exam and made it into college but, because of the lack of preparation at her high school, she was forced to take remediation courses in college.[15]

Notwithstanding the tests' severe limitations, as discussed by Zhao and Tienken in chapter 8, student test-score success has become almost synonymous with teacher quality. Policies linking teacher evaluations to students' scores will cost thousands of teachers their jobs—many of whom are effectively engaging students in learning. Related "turnaround" policies will result in a churn in school leadership, in teaching staff, and even in the closing and reopening of schools themselves. This will all happen disproportionately in low-income communities of color. One result is that we as a nation have forsaken some of the most integral connections between schools and society. We are losing sight of solid evidence showing that there are more effective ways to assess students and teachers. Very few states use, in their requisite high-states tests, extended response items or a performance assessment linked to higher-order thinking skills.[16]

Obviously, we as a society must act to staunch the serious inequities that exist between and within schools. The impetus for our current testing fixation is the academic achievement disparity—the much-discussed "achievement gap"—between students of different race and class backgrounds. Yet a misguided definition of academic success may very well threaten the well-being of millions of school-aged children who do not possess the family, neighborhood, and material resources that we know improve test scores. If the achievement gap is defined narrowly as "a test score gap that is due to schools' failure," then the opportunity gaps that arise outside of schools never get addressed and, in fact, contribute to our misunderstanding of the opportunity gaps that arise inside of schools. To illustrate, imagine two children, Elena and Daniel. While Elena benefits from the resources available from her upper-middle class family and community, Daniel has few educational resources available outside of his school. That is, before even considering formal schooling, an opportunity gap already separates these two children. If, as is likely, Elena's local school has greater resources than does Daniel's, the opportunity gap becomes wider. And if, as is again relatively likely, the test-based accountability system declares Daniel's school to be failing and in need of radical "turnaround" measures instead of simply assistance and capacity building, then he and his class-mates will be subjected to instability and churn when what they really need is stability and resources. Misdiagnosing—confusing an achievement gap with an opportunity gap—can lead to treatments that are unhelpful and even genuinely harmful.

Politicians may score points when they demand that poor children perform as well as middle-class and affluent ones. This is "no excuses" rhetoric and is rarely accompanied by supports such as current textbooks, high-quality teachers, safe schools, one-on-one tutors, and expensive test-prep programs. Emphasizing test-ing and outcomes over teaching and opportunities to learn has put the cart before the horse.

It is not our goal to be alarmist here, but we do entreat lawmakers and others to consider what the evidence reveals. There exist thoughtful and evidence-based approaches for improving the chances for our children and enriching our educa-tional system. Rich opportunities arise from a correspondingly worthy and infor-mative catalog of forward-looking policies, such as the following:

- Instead of policies that lead to segregation and stratification of students and their families, we can turn to policies demonstrated to promote affordable and more integrated housing, policies that create integrated magnet schools, and policies that enforce existing civil rights laws, and school choice policies that prioritize diversity. While the United States has a long history of segregation, the nation also has a long history of policies proven effective at addressing segregation. As discussed by Orfield (chapter 4) and by Scott and Wells (chapter 9), the problem is not a lack of good ideas; the problem is a lack of sustained commitment to effective ideas that compel us to work together as a nation, as communities, and as fellow citizens.
- Similarly, Tyson (chapter 12) outlines the segregation and educational harms arising from tracking and ability grouping. Tracking is a rationing of opportunities to learn; it says to students, "Yes, we know how to provide a challenging and engaging class, but we're only going to provide that to a select group of you." But Tyson also presents policies that promote universal acceleration and detracking. We are also impressed with the strategy

of "linked learning,"[17] which combines the idea of detracked, universal acceleration—a college preparatory curriculum offered to all students— with the idea of career-relevant, applied learning for all students.

- Instead of "no excuses" demands leveled at children and their teachers, lawmakers should address their very real needs for health care, eye care, dental care, a healthy diet, jobs for their parents, high-quality early childhood education, safe housing, and communities with basic resources and transportation.

- Instead of continuous batteries of high-stakes tests, the focus should be on low-stakes, informative testing that enables teachers to understand how well their students are learning. The focus should also be on a portfolio of work that expects students to use a range of critical thinking skills.

- Instead of policies that treat language minority students as simply deficient in English, policies can build on and invest in the native language skills these children already possess. Current policy leaves most of these students behind, not just with lesser English skills but also with lesser skills in core academic areas and with ever-decreasing skills in their native languages. Policies that treat these native languages as a resource can cultivate multilingual students who will have brighter academic futures and who are better able to contribute to our society and economy.

- Instead of rewarding the accumulation of disconnected knowledge, the focus should be on opportunities to learn in the most engaging contexts, just as students are taught in elite schools. Places like Sidwell Friends School (attended by the daughters of presidents Clinton and Obama), as well as many public schools in upper-middle class and wealthy neighborhoods, cultivate a deep appreciation of knowledge and learning. Students at these more elite schools are provided with a culture where schooling is much more than a means to an ends—a mere credential for work mobility. In contrast, many teachers at nonelite schools are now compelled to teach to tests and are using a "banking" approach; a term popularized by the progressive educational theorist and practitioner Paulo Freire. (That notion of "banking" reemerges in the widely touted film *Waiting for Superman*, when the narrator walks the audience through an animation where—and the film presents this in a positive light—teachers are literally opening the heads of children and pouring liquid knowledge into them.)

- Healthy reform would create incentives for committed and talented individuals to enter teaching, including those who otherwise would make excellent teachers but who end up choosing another career path because of the present challenging conditions of public education and the lack of respect for the teaching force. Healthy reform would develop a cadre of well-trained teachers who are bolstered by access to ample learning tools and other resources. These teachers and others involved with schools would move forward with a deep understanding of students' diversity, bridging the injurious communicative divides among and between students and teachers who differ in areas such as race, ethnicity, culture, and socioeconomic status. By creating and maintaining a culture of high expectations for all students, by developing critically conscious and historically accurate pedagogy and curricula, and by vigilantly preventing new forms of segregation within schools, these educators would work to ensure that all students have equal opportunities to learn. While we are inspired by schools and their communities that are already pursuing these goals, they are working within a larger system that hinders the pursuit for many others.

• Perhaps most importantly, instead of an either/or debate that pits advocates of policy attention to schooling opportunities to learn against advocates of broader opportunities to learn, any serious discussion of K-12 education must address both areas of need. Similarly, attention to these opportunity gaps does not mean that lawmakers should ignore achievement gaps. We need a healthy balance between input-focused policies and output-focused policies. An imbalanced focus on outputs has led to a harsh and unfair blaming of schools and educators for many factors beyond their control. It has also led to impotent policies that cruelly and harmfully ignore children's genuine needs. But an imbalanced focus on inputs—one that fails to carefully evaluate outcomes—would likely lead to unchecked investment in many inefficient and ineffective approaches. Wise policies heed both ends of the process.

We hope that this book serves to jump-start a new type of conversation in the United States about its educational system, its investment in its youth, and its overall well-being. To give all children a fair chance at educational success, Americans must commit to wise, evidence-based, and equity-focused policies and practices. The failed policies of the past need not be continued; for our next generations, we can choose to veer away from paths that waste the talent of our youth, particularly in communities of color and those in poverty. Children in these communities can reach their full potential and can indeed "close the gap" in achievement. To steer toward this promising path, however, we all have a role to play. As a society, we must provide all children with equitable and meaningful *opportunities* to reach that full potential. As students, children in communities of color and those in poverty have the same responsibility as children in more advantaged communities: to seize those opportunities. When those opportunities are equal—inside and outside of schools—then we can fairly expect the outcomes to be equal. We can close the achievement gaps. Meanwhile, the headlines scream, and the warning bells shriek. Dare we be bold enough to act differently and give all American children even chances to succeed?

NOTES

CHAPTER 1

1.   For a discussion of the idea of "effectively maintained inequality," whereby addressing specific inequitable structures merely leads to alternative approaches for creating those inequities, see Lucas (2001).

2.   OECD, 2010. In addition to describing the lack of intergenerational movement, the OECD report points to specific education policies associated with better outcomes—noting in particular three policies highlighted later in this book: pre-school opportunities, detracking, and increased diversity: "Education policies play a key role in explaining observed differences in intergenerational social mobility across countries. For example, higher enrolment in early childhood education is associated with a lower influence of parental background on students' achievement in secondary education. By contrast, school practices that group students into different curricula at early ages come with less social mobility in educational achievement. Moreover, increasing the social mix within schools appears to boost performance of disadvantaged students without any apparent negative effects on overall performance." (chapter 5, 5–6.)

3.   KewalRamani, et al., 2007. Note that throughout this volume we capitalize race terms when they refer directly to individuals or a group of people. When the descriptive is used to assign racial meaning to an abstract concept, thing, or object, we use the lower case.

4.   NCES, 2013. See also Swanson, 2011a.

5.   NCES, 2013. See also Swanson, 2011a.

6.   Oakes, 2005.

7.   NAACP Legal Defense and Educational Fund, 2006.

8.   Ibid.

9. Losen, 2011.

10. Mann, 1848/1868, 669.

11. See U.S. Census Bureau, 2008.

12. Huber, et al., 2006; Mullen, Goyette, & Stuart, 2011.

13. Long, 2004; St. John & Asker, 2003.

CHAPTER 2

1. DeLange & Alter, 1947.

2. Reckdahl, 2011.

3. Louisiana Council on the Social Status of Black Boys and Men, 2010.

4. Lakoff & Johnson, 2003.

5. Tyack, 1974.

6. Anderson, 1988.

7. Denton, 2001; Fix & Struk, 1993.

8. Schwartz, 1976, 407.

9. Linville, 1970, 9.

10. Kozol, 2005.

11. Epstein, 2011, 7.

12. The Education Trust, 2006.

13. Bowen & Bok, 1998.

14. Ibid.

15. Gill, 2000.

16. Robinson, 2000, 74.

17. Takaki, 1998, 21.

18. Guggenheim, 2010.

19. Shanker, 1985.

20. Ladson-Billings, 2009.

21. Feldman, 1989.

22. Payne, 2005.

CHAPTER 3

1. Social provision includes all forms of publicly provided welfare benefits, from such universal programs as Social Security and Medicare to means-tested programs such as food stamps and subsidized housing.

2. See Cohen, 2005; Katz, 2010; Garfinkel, Rainwater, & Smeeding, 2010; Kantor, 1991; Kantor & Lowe, 2006.

3. Hofstadter, 1955, chap. 7; Kennedy 1999, chap. 12, Brinkley, 2003.

4. Tyack, Lowe, & Hansot, 1984.

5. Katznelson, 1989; Quadagno, 1999; Brinkley, 1998; Mileur, 2005.

6. Matusow, 1984; Dallek, 1998; Bell, 2004.

7. Lichtenstein, 1989; Stevens, 1990; Klein, 2003.

8. Goluboff, 2007; Sullivan, 2009; Tushnet, 1987.

9. Kantor and Lowe, 1995.

10. Brauer, 1982; Davies, 1996; McKee, 2011.

11. Steensland, 2008; O'Connor, 1998; Morgan, 2001; Rose, 2010, chap. 2.

12. Davies, 2007, chap. 4.

13. Steensland, 2008, chap. 6; Patterson, 1998.

14. Davies, 2007, chap. 9; Michael, 2008, chap. 5.

15. O'Connor, 1998; Schulman, 1998: Schulman, 2001, chap. 5.

16. Katznelson, 2005; Lieberman, 1998; Brown, 1999, chap. 5; Oliver & Shapiro, 2006. For more positive assessments of New Deal policies on race, see Sitkoff, 1978; Sullivan, 1996; Mettler, 2005.

17. Skrentny, 2002.

18. Quadagno, 1994, p. 4; Cloward & Piven, 1975.

19. Wolman & Thomas, 1970; Wilkerson, 1965.

20. Bailey & Mosher, 1968, pp. 143–56; Halpern, 1995, chap. 3.

21. Jeffrey, 1978, pp. 107–14; Orfield, 1969, chaps. 6, 7; Kotlowski, 2005.

22. Orfield, 1978, chap. 9.

23. Cohen and Moffitt, 2009, 185.

24. Kaestle & Smith, 1982, pp. 396–400.

25. Cottrol, Diamond, & Ware, 2003; Patterson, 2001; Klarman, 2004; Katz, 2012, chap. 2.

26. Lassiter, 2003; Lassiter, 2004; Kantor & Brenzel, 1993; Patterson, 2001.

27. McGuinn, 2006.

28. Vinovskis, 2009; Finn, 1988. Also see Harvey Kantor, "Sustaining the Liberal Educational State: Title I of ESEA and the Politics of Federal Education Policy, 1965 1994," unpublished paper, 2002.

29. Katz, 2001; Soss, Hacker, & Mettler, 2007; Gilbert, 2002; Hacker, 2006.

30. Gilbert & Gilbert, 1989; see also Quadagno, 1999; Gilbert, 2002.

31. Katz, 2001; Garfinkel, Rainwater, & Smeeding, 2010.

32. Gilbert, 2002, chap. 1; Berger, 2007.

33. Reider, 1987; McGirr, 2001; Weir, 2005.

34. Fine, 2009; Plotke, 1992; Vogel, 1989, chaps. 7, 8; Ackard, 1994; Hacker & Pierson, 2010; Martin, 1999.

35. Hacker 2004, p. 257.

36. Ventry, 2000; Hacker, 2004.

37. Miller, 1989.

38. Hess & McGuinn, 2002; Stockman, 1986; Wllentz, 2008, chap. 5 and epilogue.

39. Cuban, 2004; Jennings, 1998; Goldberg & Traiman, 2001; Borman, Castenell, & Gallagher, 1993; Timpane & McNeill, 1991.

40. Wells & Holme, 2004; Feigenbaum, Henig, & Hamnett, 1999.

41. Welner, 2008.

42. See http://www.edreform.com/_upload/CER_charter_numbers.pdf.

43. Fuller, 2000; Henig, 2009.

44. Davies, 2007; McGuinn, 2006; DeBray, 2006; Cohen & Moffitt, 2009; Vinovskis, 2009.

45. DeBray, McDermott, & Wohstetter, 2005.

46. DeBray-Pelot and McGuinn, 2009.

47. Coleman et al., 1966; Jencks, 1972.

48. Edmonds, 1979; Stedman, 1985.

49. Liebman & Sabel, 2003; Taylor, 2003; DeBray-Pelot & McGuinn, 2009.

50. Perlstein, 2008; Center on Educational Policy, 2006, pp. 95–96; Meier & Woods, 2004.

51. Ryan, 2010.

52. Holme & Wells, 2008.

53. Ryan, 2010, pp. 198–202, 222–225.

54. Smith, 2006.

55. Obama, 2010a.

56. "Text of Obama's Second State of the Union," *New York Times*, February 25, 2011; Sam Dillon, "Obama Proposes Sweeping Change in Education Law," *New York Times*, March 14, 2010, 1; Jeff Zeleny, "Obama Backs Rewarding Districts That Police Failing Schools," *New York Times*, March 1, 2010.

57. Ravitch, 2010.

CHAPTER 4

1. Orfield & McArdle, 2006.

2. Logan & Oakley, 2012.

3. Ready & Silander, 2011.

4. James Coleman, et al., 1966; Duncan & Magnuson, 2005; Rothstein, 2004.

5. Freeman, Scafidi & Stoquist, 2005.

6. Mickelson, 2008.

7. National Commission on Excellence in Education, 1983, Orfield & Eaton, 1996.

8. NAEP, 2009.

9. Swanson, 2011.

10. Bonilla-Silva, 2006, Newport, 2009.

11. Anderson, 1999.

12. Bonilla-Silva, 2003.

13. O'Connor, Tilly, & Bobo, 2003.

14. Pew Research Center, 2011, 123.

15. Clotfelter, 2004.

16. Sunderman, 2008.

17. Orfield & McArdle, 2006.

18. World Public Opinion.Org, 2008, www.worldpublicopinion.org.

19. Wells, 2009.

20. Reardon & Yun, 2003; Boger & Orfield, 2005; Frey, 2011.

21. Pfeiffer, 2009.

22. Weiher, 1991.

23. Orfield, 2009. All the reports of the Civil Rights Project cited in this chapter can be found on its website, www.civilrightsproject.ucla.edu.

24. Orfield & McArdle, 2006.

25. Orfield, 1985.

26. DiPasquale, 1996.

27. National Commission on Fair Housing and Equal Opportunity, 2009.

28. Institute on Race and Poverty, 2009; Taylor, Kochhar, Fry, et al., 2009.

29. Frankenberg & Orfield, 2012.

30. *Parents Involved*, 2007.

31. National Commission on Fair Housing and Equal Opportunity, 2009; Scommegna, 2011; Logan & Stults, 2011; McArdle et al., 2011; Farley, 2011.

32. Pfeiffer, 2009.

33. Orfield, 2009.

34. Ibid.; These figures were computed by the Civil Rights Project from the Common Core of Data of the National Center for Education Statistics.

35. Orfield, 2009.

36. Balfanz & Legters, 2004.

37. Cottrell, 2011.

38. Patillo-McCoy, 1999.

39. Kain, 1986; Harris & McArdle, 2004.

40. Orfield, 1975.

41. National Advisory Commission on Civil Disorders, 1968, 1.

42. See National Commission on Urban Problems, 1968b; the 1969 Housing and Urban Development Act of 1968, 12 U.S.C. Sec. 1715z.

43. Lamb, 2005.

44. Nixon Press Conference, December 10, 1970; Lamb, 2005.

45. Orfield, 1988.

46. Crain, 1973.

47. NFHA, 2007.

48. CNPR, 1977.

49. Pfeiffer, 2009. Institute on Race and Poverty, 2009.

50. Orfield & Fischer, 1981.

51. Citizens Commission on Civil Rights, 1983, 55–56; Orfield & Eaton, 1996, 53–72.

52. Polikoff, 2006.

53. Reardon, Yun, & Chmielewski, 2012.

54. National Commission on Fair Housing and Equal Opportunity, 2009.

55. Martin Luther King Jr., "Facing the Challenge of a New Age," address to NAACP Emancipation Rally, Atlanta, January 1957, in *The Papers of Martin Luther King, Jr.*, vol. 4 (Berkeley: University of California Press, 2000), 76.

56. Fuller, Elmore, & Orfield, 1996.

57. *Green v. New Kent County*, 391 U.S. 430 (1968); *Swann v. Charlotte-Mecklenburg*, 420 U.S. 1 (1971).

58. *Parents Involved in Community Schools* (*PICS*), 551 U.S. 701 (2007).

59. Mickelson, Bottia, & Southworth, 2012.

60. Saltman, 1990; Goodwin, 1979; Briggs, 2005.

61. Surveys over many years consistently show a very low Black and Latino preference for living in a neighborhood that is all of their own race or ethnicity and there has been a massive move to suburbia from segregated city neighborhoods but segregation is rapidly spreading in the suburbs, especially for students. (See Frankenberg & Orfield, 2012; Charles, 2003.)

62. Clotfelter, 2004; Orfield, 2006.

63. Siegel-Hawley, 2011; Pearce, 1979; Institute on Race and Poverty, 2009; Clotfelter, 2004.

64. Orfield, 1985; Taub, Taylor, & Dunham, 1984.

65. Camagni, Gibelli, & Rigamonti, 2002.

66. Orfield & Fischer, 1981.

67. Ibid.

68. Orfield & Luce, 2009; Pearce, 1979; Siegel-Hawley, 2011.

69. Siegel-Hawley, 2011.

70. Watanabe, 2011.

71. Allport, 1954; Pettigrew & Tropp, 2011.

72. Washington, DC, is the most notable example; the proportion of residents who are Black has been declining for several decades (Morello & Keating, 2011).

73. Washington, DC was becoming whiter for three decades and lost its black majority in 2011, after becoming the first major city to become black majority back more than a half century earlier (Tavernise, 2011). Though the share of White population was much higher, the public schools were still only 10 percent White (District of Columbia Public Schools, n.d.) and the large system of public charter schools were 3 percent White (Annie E. Casey Foundation, n.d.).

74. Gentrifying neighborhoods can gain value, generate jobs, and create wealth, but they are occupied mostly by young people without children, gays, empty nesters, and the elderly. This limited market tends to create communities with a great deal of transiency and very little connection with or support for public schools.

75. Kozol, 2005.

76. Orfield, 1985. Hyde Park-Kenwood in Chicago, which has been stably integrated and very prosperous for a half century even though it is surrounded by nonwhite low-income communities, is a classic example.

77. Orfield, 1981.

78. U.S. Depts. of Justice and Education, 2011.

79. The only large national study was the Coleman Report, commissioned by Congress in the l964 Civil Rights Act. The author was the chair of the academic advisory committee of last major federal effort to commission such research, at what was then the National Institute of Education, which held meetings with scholars across the country, issued a call for proposals, developed consensus among researchers of widely differing ideologies about what needed to be learned, and selected the best proposals. All of this research was cancelled and the staff fired by the incoming Reagan administration which only commissioned white flight studies to be used to dissolve desegregation plans. No successive administration has produced a national study on school desegregation. The federal government even stopped publishing regular statistics on the extent of school segregation by the early l970s. Almost all such studies since that time have been conducted outside of government. In meetings with leaders of the Obama administration's educational research staff, the author of this chapter was informed that this issue was not on the agenda.

CHAPTER 5

1. Carnoy and Rothstein, 2013
2. Rothstein, 2004 Berliner 2009.
3. Egbuonu and Starfield, 1982; Starfield, 1982; Gould and Gould, 2003; Orfield, 2007; Orfield, Basa, & Yun, 2001; Harris, 2002.
4. General Accounting Office (hereafter GAO) of the United States, 1999.
5. Centers for Disease Control (CDC), 2002; Koch, 2002.
6. Whitman, Williams, & Shah, 2004.
7. Forrest et al., 1997; Halfon & Newacheck, 1993; GAO 1983; Collin & Collin 1997.
8. Hoffman et al., 2003.
9. Kerbow, 1996; Bruno & Isken, 1996; Wang, Haertel, & Walberg, 1994; GAO, 1994.
10. Hart & Risley, 1995.
11. McLoyd, 1990; McLoyd et al., 1994; Flanagan & Eccles, 1993.
12. Wilson, 1987.
13. Lareau, 2003.
14. Ibid.

15. Hart & Risley, 1995; Lareau, 2003.

16. Orfield, chapter 4 in this volume.

17. Bryk et al., 2010, 210.

18. Mickelson & Bottia, 2010; Linn & Welner, 2007.

19. Hanushek, Kain, & Rivkin, 2006; Haushek & Rivkin, 2009.

20. Vigdor & Ludwig, 2008.

21. Tyson, in this volume. The benefits in test scores as well as other outcomes might be greater if students were not segregated within these nominally desegregated schools.

22. Guryan, 2004.

23. Weiner, Lutz, & Ludwig, 2010.

24. Harding 2003, 681, table 1.

25. Crane, 1991.

26. Sampson, Sharkey, & Raudenbush, 2008

27. Kaufman & Rosenbaum, 1992. Sanbonmatsu et al., 2006, describe efforts by the federal government to duplicate this experiment in several cities; the results were disappointing, although the differences between experimental and control conditions were less carefully developed than the naturally occurring difference in Gautreaux.

28. Schwartz, 2010.

29. Wells et al., 2009

30. Rothstein, 2011.

31. Haycock, 2005. Referring to my previous work on this topic, Haycock opined: "Rothstein and his ilk demean the countless educators who have worked so hard to produce spectacular results among the very children who aren't supposed to be able to learn." See also Klein, Rhee, et al., 2010; Rothstein, R. 2010.

32. For example, the Hoover Institution's Williamson Evers, US Assistant Secretary of Education for Planning, Evaluation, and Policy Development during the George W. Bush administration, argued: "For decades, excuse-making apologists for the public-school establishment have whispered behind closed doors that poor and minority children can't 'make it.' These children, said the educrats, come from households where English isn't spoken or parents aren't highly educated. Some of these children come from broken families or were born out of wedlock. 'Don't you see,' said the educrats, 'we can't teach these children.' We'd better not hear this racist nonsense any longer." Evers, 2002.

33. "When poor and minority families hear the argument that their children can't achieve as highly as others because of their impoverished backgrounds, their response, [Katie] Haycock says, is 'How dare you!' They don't want poverty to be an excuse for not holding their children up to the same standards as everybody else." Russlynn Ali, formerly the director of Education Trust–West and later US Assistant Secretary of Education for Civil Rights, said: "There is great danger in sending messages to education stakeholders that the achievement gap cannot be closed. Teachers and administrators will hear leaders decry the sheer impossibility of closing gaps and ask why they should even try to teach poor and minority kids to high levels.... Effective educators are demeaned by messages that suggest their work is a fool's errand." EdSource, 2002; Ali, 2007; Hardy, 2006. In a summary of reactions to Rothstein (2004), Lawrence Hardy, editor of the *American School Board Journal*, writes: "Critics say Rothstein's position lets schools off the hook: They can blame societal factors for the failure of disadvantaged students without turning a mirror on themselves."

34. Chester Finn (2004) asks rhetorically: "Do we quit trying to fix the schools we've got for the kids we've got while we wait for radical social changes to be made? Is this not a counsel of

despair that plays right into the tendency of some educators to say 'We're doing all that should be expected of us, given the kids we're being sent from the homes they're being sent from, so stop demanding more from us?'" Michael Petrilli (2005) opines: "Should [Democrats] lurch to the loopy left and embrace the arguments of Richard Rothstein, the unions, and others who declare education improvement impossible until poverty is eradicated?" Kevin Carey (2006) writes: "Creating better schools is one part of a larger challenge to give marginalized, disadvantaged students better nutrition, housing, health care, and ultimately better lives. To set those individual goals against one another—to argue that one should be ignored until some far–off day when all the others are solved—harms no one more than the students themselves." Kati Haycock (2005) asserts that an analysis like that in this chapter "argues that it is impossible to substantially narrow the achievement gap without fixing all of society's problems" and adds that the analysis says to educators that before they can improve instruction, "Gee, you've got to wait until all those things outside your school are fixed" (2007a). Amy Wilkins (2005), a principal partner at Education Trust, agrees: "Faced with damage that racism and poverty inflict, too many educators have simply given in and given up on these children, insisting that as much as they care about these kids, they are powerless to change their life chances until someone else acts to improve the conditions of their families and their communities. And they back up these claims and their inaction with quotes from people like Messrs Mishel and Rothstein. In a very real sense these educators—with rhetorical support from Mishel and Rothstein—have surrendered to racism and poverty."

35. Duncan, 2011.

36. Peterson & Rothstein, 2010.

37. For example, Kati Haycock (2007b) attacks *Education Week* for including indicators of socioeconomic disadvantage in its *Quality Counts* compendium: "The annual report also appears to have made the mistake of focusing on what we, as educators, cannot change, instead of what we can do to ensure all students succeed. The report's 'Chance-for-Success Index' is based on many indicators that cannot be directly affected by educators or education policymakers in the near term. The resulting message to states is clear: If you have large numbers of poor or undereducated adults, just forget it."

38. See www.boldapproach.org.

39. Eaton, 2001.

40. Kahlenberg, 2006.

41. Khadaroo, 2010.

42. Sturgis, 2011.

43. Orfield, chapter 4 in this volume.

44. Yinger, 1998; Galster & Godfrey, 2005.

45. Logan, 2011, table 2.

46. According to Phillips et al., 1998, 138, "Even though traditional measures of socioeconomic status account for no more than a third of the [Black–White] test- score gap, our results show that a broader index of family environment may explain up to two-thirds of it." Other differences, for example in health and housing, might explain even more of the gap.

47. Ferguson 2005; Noguera 2008; Phillips et al., 1998; Ogbu, 2003.

48. Wilson, 1987; Massey & Denton, 1993; Moss & Tilly, 1996; Leventhal & Brooks-Gunn, 2000; Turner & Garcia, 2006; Sampson, Sharkey, & Raudenbush, 2008; Anderson 2010.

49. Rothstein, 2001.

50. See Scott & Wells, chapter 9 in this volume, for a discussion of these choice issues.

51. For a discussion of the implicit selection bias in the lotteries of the highly acclaimed KIPP charter schools, see Carnoy et al., 2005, 51–65. For a discussion of attrition from KIPP,

see NEPC, 2010; Miron, Urschel, & Saxton, 2011. For journalistic account of attrition at the Harlem Success Academies, another highly acclaimed group of charter schools, see Winerip, 2011a.

CHAPTER 6

1. The *Williams* class action litigation sought equal access to instructional materials, safe and decent school facilities, and qualified teachers. The case was settled in 2004, with the state acknowledging its responsibility for ensuring quality and an equal education to all California's students and agreeing to provide an additional $138 million to give low-outcome schools extra books and other instructional materials, $50 million to assess and make emergency repairs at those schools, and another $800 million for critical facilities investments.

2. This chapter draws in part on Linda Darling-Hammond, *The Flat World and Education: How America's Commitment to Equity Will Determine Our Future* (New York: Teachers College Press, 2010), and Linda Darling-Hammond, "Inequality and the Right to Learn: Access to Qualified Teachers in California's Public Schools," *Teachers College Record*, 106(10) (October 2004), 1936–1966.

3. Ladson-Billings, 2006.

4. Tyack, 1974, 109–125; Kluger, 1976; Meier, Stewart, & England, 1989; Schofield, 1995.

5. Quoted in Tyack, 1974, 119.

6. Williams et al. v. State of California, Superior Court of the State of California for the County of San Francisco, 2001, Complaint, 569–66.

7. Darling-Hammond, 2010.

8. Baker, Sciarra, & Farrie, 2010.

9. Liu, 2008.

10. Education Trust, 2006.

11. See Rothstein, chapter 5, this volume, and Darling-Hammond, 2010.

12. Bell, Bernstein, & Greenberg, 2008.

13. DeNavas-Walt, Proctor, & Lee, 2005; US Census Bureau, 2006.

14. Darling-Hammond, 2010.

15. UNICEF, 2001, 3.

16. Heckman 2008, 49.

17. Children's Defense Fund, 2001.

18. Sahlberg, 2011.

19. Rumberger & Palardy, 2005; see also Orfield, chapter 4, this volume.

20. Orfield, G., 2001.

21. *Parents Involved in Community Schools v. Seattle School District No. 1*, 551 U.S. 701 (2007).

22. See Linn & Welner, 2007.

23. Civil Rights Project (2006), amicus brief filed in Parents Involved in Community Education v. Seattle School District No. 1, pg. 3.

24. Orfield, 2001.

25. 1966 Coleman Report, p. 325. For a recent review of this evidence, see Kahlenberg, 2001.

26. Schofield, 1995; Anyon, 1997; Dawkins & Braddock, 1994; Natriello, McDill, & Pallas, 1990

27. Lee, 2004; Horn, 2002; See also the discussion in Gándara, chapter 11, this volume.

28. Garofano, Sable, & Hoffman, 2008.

29. Resnick, n.d.

30. Darling-Hammond, 2010.

31. Kaufman and Rosenbaum, 1992.

32. Education Trust West, 2005.

33. Roza & Hill, 2004.

34. Education Trust–West, 2005.

35. Darling-Hammond, 2004.

36. Shields et al., 2001.

37. John Merrow Reports are available from Learning Matters at http://learningmatters.tv/.

38. Darling-Hammond, 2004.

39. Analyses of teacher distribution data were conducted by the author.

40. NCES, 1997; Lankford, Loeb, & Wyckoff, 2002.

41. Haycock, 2000, 11.

42. These findings are documented in Betts, Rueben, & Dannenberg, 2000; Boyd et al., 2006; Clotfelter, Ladd, & Vigdor, 2007; Darling-Hammond, 2000; Darling-Hammond, Holtzman, Gatlin, & Heilig, 2005; Ferguson, 1991; Fetler, 1999; Goldhaber & Brewer, 2000; Goe, 2002; Hawk, Coble, & Swanson, 1985; Monk, 1994; Strauss and Sawyer, 1986.

43. Akiba, LeTendre, & Scribner, 2007.

44. Clotfelter, Ladd, & Vigdor, 2007.

45. Boyd, Lankford, Loeb, Rockoff, & Wyckoff, 2008.

46. Boyd et al., 2006.

47. NCTAF, 1996.

48. Ibid.

49. Renee v. Duncan, 623 F. 3d 787 (2010). The court ruling favored the plaintiffs, but Congress subsequently wrote the department's regulations into law, for a time period that currently extends until June 2013. This means that, until that time, teachers-in-training will be considered "highly qualified."

50. Darling-Hammond, 2003, 128.

51. Betts, Rueben, & Dannenberg, 2000; Darling-Hammond, 2000; Fetler, 1999; Fuller, 1998, 2000; Goe, 2002; Strauss & Sawyer, 1986.

52. Shields, Humphrey, Wechsler, et al., 2001.

53. Dreeben, 1987, 34.

54. Kozol, 2005; Darling-Hammond, 2010.

55. College Board, 1985; Pelavin & Kane, 1990; Oakes, 2005.

56. Oakes et al., 2006.

57. California Postsecondary Education Commission, 2007.

58. Kozol, 1992.

59. Oakes, 1993, 2005; Welner, 2001.

60. Downes & Pogue, 1994; Duncombe, Ruggiero, & Yinger, 1996.

61. Darling-Hammond, 2010.

62. Abbott v. Burke, 1990, 364.

63. See Baker & Welner, 2011, as well as the research discussion below.

64. Barnett, 2008; Finn & Achilles, 2003

65. Hanushek, 2003, 4

66. For methodological critiques, see Greenwald, Hedges, & Laine, 1996b; Hedges, Laine, & Greenwald, 1994; Krueger, 2003; Rebell, 2007; Taylor, 1997. Courts have raised additional

concerns. In an Alabama case, the court criticized Hanushek's failure to control for "variables that could affect student scores[,] such as race, socio-economic status, and parental education" and his use of average rather than actual test scores. *Opinion of the Justices,* 624 So. 2d 107, 140 (Ala. 1993). When Hanushek's data were reanalyzed using actual scores, there was "a statistically significant positive correlation between expenditures and achievement" (140 n34). Similarly, the trial court judge in *Lobato v. Colorado* wrote, "Dr. Hanushek's analysis that there is not much relationship in Colorado between spending and achievement contradicts testimony and documentary evidence from dozens of well-respected educators in the State, defies logic, and is statistically flawed" (Hoover, 2011).

67. NCES, 2000, 15.

68. Ibid.

69. Baker & Welner, 2011; Darling-Hammond, 2010; Darling-Hammond, Ross, & Milliken, 2007; Ferguson, 1991; Greenwald, Hedges, & Laine, 1996b; Grissmer et al., 2000; Krueger, 2000.

70. Ferguson, 1991.

71. Ibid., 490.

72. Greenwald, Hedges, & Laine, 1996a.

73. See Finn & Achilles, 2003; see also Glass et al., 1982; Walberg, 1982; Educational Research Service, 1980.

74. Mosteller, 1995; Krueger, 2003.

75. Greenwald, Hedges & Laine, 1996a; Darling-Hammond, 2000.

76. Krueger, 2003.

77. Reynolds and Temple, 2006, 50.

78. Bueno, Darling-Hammond, & Gonzales, 2009.

79. Baker & Welner, 2011; Darling-Hammond, 2010.

80. Guryan, 2001.

81. Assistant Commissioner Jay Doolan and State Assessment Director, Timothy Peters, Presentation to the New Jersey State Board of Education, *NAEP 2007: Reading and Mathematics, Grades 4 and 8,* October 17, 2007.

82. See "New Jersey's Plan for Meeting the Highly Qualified Teacher Goals," submitted July 7, 2006, to the US Department of Education, http://liberty.state.nj.us/education/data/hqt/06/plan.pdf.

83. NCES, *Top Four States in Closing Achievement Gap.* Retrieved on August 2, 2008, from http://www.fldoe.org/asp/naep/pdf/Top-4-states.pdf.

84. NCES, 2007.

CHAPTER 7

1. Ceci & Papierno, 2005; Coleman et al., 1966; Duncan & Murnane, 2011.

2. Chapman, Laird, & KewalRamani, 2010.

3. Halle et al, 2009; Lee & Burkham, 2002.

4. Hart and Risley, 1995.

5. Burchinal et al., 2011.

6. Ibid.; Dickinson, 2011.

7. Hair, Halle, Terry-Humen, Lavelle & Calkins, 2006.

8. Duncan & Magnusson, 2005.

9. Burchinal et al., 2011.

10. Dickinson, 2011.

11. Levine, Suriyakham, Rowe, Huttenlocher & Gunderson, 2010.

12. Hertzman, 1999; Hertzman & Boyce, 2010; Shonkoff, 2011.

13. Duncan & Magnuson, 2005.

14. Mays, Cochran, & Barnes, 2007.

15. Burchinal et al., 2011; Dickinson, 2011.

16. Duncan et al., 2007; National Mathematics Advisory Panel, 2008; Verhoeven, van Leeuwe, & Vermeer, 2011.

17. Cunha, Heckman, Lochner, & Masterov, 2006; Heckman, 2006.

18. Duncan et al 2007; Lee & Burkham, 2002.

19. Barnett, 2008, 2011a.

20. Camilli, Vargas, Ryan, & Barnett, 2010.

21. Barnett, 2011a; Camilli et al., 2010.

22. Campbell & Ramey, 1995; Campbell, Ramey, Pungello, Sparling & Miller-Johnson, 2002; Reynolds, Temple, Robertson & Mann, 2002; Reynolds, Temple & Ou, 2010; Schweinhart et al, 2005.

23. Barnett & Masse, 2007; Muennig, Schweinhart, Montie, & Neidell, 2009; Muennig et al., 2011, Reynolds, Temple, White, Ou, & Robertson, 2011.

24. Heckman, 2006.

25. Barnett et al., 2008; Bishop-Josef & Zigler, 2011.

26. Barnett & Masse, 2007; Reynolds et al., 2011.

27. Camilli, Vargas, Ryan, & Barnett, 2010.

28. Barnett, 2011a; Cunha et al., 2006.

29. Barnett, 2008, 2011a.

30. Barnett, 2011a.

31. Barnett, Jung, Frede, Hustedt & Howes, 2011.

32. Gormley, Phillips & Gayer, 2008.

33. Frede & Barnett, 2011.

34. Frede, Barnett, Jung, Lamy, & Figueras, 2010; Frede, Jung, Barnett, & Figueras, 2009.

35. Barnett & Frede, 2010.

36. Barnett, 2011b.

37. Ibid.

38. Applewhite & Hirsch, 2003.

39. Karoly, Ghosh-Dastidar, Zellman, Perlman, & Fernyhough, 2008.

40. Harms, Clifford, & Cryer, 1998.

41. Haskins & Barnett, 2010.

42. Barnett et al., 2011.

43. Ibid.

44. Reynolds et al., 2011.

45. Haskins & Barnett, 2010.

46. Zill, 2010.

47. Daro & Dodge, 2010; Kahn & Moore, 2010; Olds, 2010.

48. Barnett, 2011b.

49. Ibid.

50. Neidell & Waldfogel, 2010; Schechter & Bye, 2007.

51. Barnett et al., 2010.

52. Frede & Barnett, 2011; Zigler, 2011.

CHAPTER 8

1. Vogell, 2011.
2. No Child Left Behind [NCLB] Act of 2001, 2002.
3. Aikin, 1942, 4–16; Brophy & Good, 1986, 328–375; Cohen, 1987, 16–20; Fisher et al., 1980, 7–22; Good et al., 1978, 72–75; Mosteller et al., 1996, 797–828; Osafehinti, 1987, 193–197; Tanner & Tanner, 2007; Tyler, 1949.
4. Common Core State Standards Initiative, 2010.
5. Nichols & Berliner, 2007.
6. *USA Today*, 2011.
7. Hout & Elliot, 2011.
8. McMurrer, 2007.
9. Zastrow & Janc, 2004.
10. Center on Education Policy, 2008.
11. Hursh, 2007, 493–518.
12. Tienken, 2011, 257–271.
13. Ibid.
14. Brown & Clift, 2010, 774–798.
15. Au, 2011, 25–45; Au, 2007, 258–267; Booher-Jennings, 2005, 231–268.
16. Amrein & Berliner, 2002, 1–74; Au, 2011, 25–45.
17. Anagnostopolous, 2003, 177–212.
18. Pacheco, 2010, 292–317; Srikantaiah & Kober, 2009.
19. Hart & Risley, 4–9.
20. Haberman, 290–294.
21. Hursh, 2007, 493–518; Nichols & Berliner, 2007.
22. Nichols & Berliner, 2007, 57.
23. Ibid.
24. Ibid.
25. *Time* magazine, 2007.
26. Swanson, 2009.
27. Nichols & Berliner, 2007, 60.
28. Ibid., 59.
29. Swanson, 2009.
30. Sternberg, 1996.
31. Nichols & Berliner, 2007.
32. Tyler, 1949.
33. Piaget, 1963; Vygotsky, 1978.
34. Bronfenbrenner & Evans, 2000, 115–125.
35. Ryan & Deci, 2000, 68–78.
36. Vygotsky, 1978.
37. Maslow, 1954.
38. Zhao, 2009.
39. Jiaoyubu, 2001; Ministry of Education, 2005; Tan, 2010, 50–58; Tan & Gopinathan, 2000, 5–10; Zhao, 2009.
40. Zhao, 2009.
41. Ibid.
42. Tan & Gopinathan, 2000, 8.

43. Campbell, 1976.

44. Alexander, 2009.

45. Wang et al., 1993, 249–294.

46. Ibid; Tramaglini, 2010.

47. Aikin, 1942, 4–16.

48. Jersild et al., 1941, 307–309; Thorndike, 1924, 1–22; Wrightstone et al., 1939, 423–432; Wrightstone, 1936, 242–243.

49. Allensworth et al., 2009, 367–391.

CHAPTER 9

1. See Reardon & Bischoff, 2011; Sethi & Somanathan, 2004.

2. See Scott, 2005; Mickelson, Bottia, & Southworth, 2012; Wells & Roda, 2008; Wells, Warner, & Grzesikowski, in press.

3. Moe & Hill, 2011; Bulkley, Henig, & Levin, 2010.

4. We use "market-based choice" to refer to most charter schools, school voucher plans, tuition tax credits, and, increasingly, as we will discuss, some magnet schools. We recognize that there is much institutional diversity among schools of choice, and many schools of choice that operate within a marketized regulatory framework strive to serve students equitably.

5. Scott, 2005.

6. See, for example, Brighouse, 1996; Forman, 2005.

7. See Orfield & Lee, 2007.

8. Mickelson et al., 2012; Wells & Roda, 2008.

9. Scott, 2011; Winerip, 2011b.

10. Whitman, 2008.

11. Miron, Urschel, & Saxton, 2011.

12. Scott & Home, 2002; Scott, 2009.

13. For a more detailed discussion of testing policies and their effects on the opportunity gap, see Zhao & Tienken, chapter 8 in this volume.

14. Wells, 1993; Wells, Warner, & Grzesikowski, in press.

15. Lassiter & Davis, 1998.

16. Wells, 1993; Willie, Edwards, & Alves, 2002.

17. Scott, 2011.

18. Shujaa, 1993

19. Arsen, Plank, & Sykes, 1999.

20. See for example, Frankenberg, Siegel-Hawley & Wang, 2011, for a discussion of these issues in relation to charter school policies.

21. Rothstein, 2010.

22. Friedman, 1962.

23. Engel, 2000; Howe, 1997.

24. Stone, 2002.

25. Engel, 2000.

26. Ibid., 65.

27. Wells, 1993.

28. Henig, 1994.

29. For a discussion of tracking by perceived ability, see Tyson, chapter 12, this volume; for a discussion of school segregation, see Orfield, chapter 4 in this volume.

30. Orfield & Lee, 2007; Sethi & Somanathan, 2004.

31. Scott & Holme, 2002; Holme & Wells, 2008.

32. Wells, Warner, & Grzesikowski, in press.

33. Holme & Wells, 2008; Johnson & Shapiro, 2003; Wells & Roda, 2009; Lauder & Hughes, 1999.

34. Sinkkink & Emerson, 2007; Wells & Holme, 2005; Roda & Wells, in press.

35. Lankford & Wyckoff, 2005; Mickelson, Bottia, & Southworth, 2012; Wells & Roda, 2008, 2009.

36. Wells, Lopez, Scott, & Holme, 1999.

37. Scott, 2011.

38. Mickelson et al., 2012.

39. Whitman, 2008.

40. Anderson, 1988; Siddle-Walker, 1996.

41. Bell, 2009; Wilson Cooper, 2005.

42. Rouse & Barrow, 2009.

43. Miron, Urschel, & Saxton, 2011; David et al., 2006.

44. Winerip, 2011b.

45. Ravitch, 2011.

46. Wells et al., 1999.

47. Wells & Frankenberg, 2007.

48. Wells, Roda, Warner, Hill, & Fox, in press.; Mickelson et al., 2012; Wells et al., 2000.

49. Fuller et al., 2003; Frankenberg, Siegel-Hawley, & Wang, 2010.

50. Chubb & Moe, 1990.

51. See Holme & Wells, 2008.

52. Ibid.

53. For a review of the evidence on open enrollment plans, see Holme & Wells, 2008.

54. Welner (2008) has also documented the rise of "neovouchers," which mimic vouchers but create funding through tuition tax credit mechanisms, exist in eight states and provide more vouchers than conventional voucher policies.

55. Metcalf et al. 2003; Plucker et al., 2006.

56. Metcalf et al., 2006.

57. Plucker et al., 2006.

58. Ibid.; Wells & Roda, 2008.

59. Mickelson et al., 2012; Lankford & Wyckoff, 2005; U.S. General Accounting Office, 2001.

60. Reardon, Yun, & Kurlaender, 2006.

61. Yun & Reardon, 2005.

62. See Zhao & Tienken, chapter 8, this volume.

63. Wells et al., in press.

64. Wells et al., 2009; Wells & Home, 2005.

65. Wells et al., 2009.

66. See, for instance, Hanushek, Kain, & Rivkin, 2006; Borman, Eitle, T., Michael, Eitle, D. J., Lee, Johnson, Cobb-Roberts, Dorn, & Shircliffe, 2004; Mickelson, 2001.

67. See, for instance, Braddock, 1980; Braddock & McPartland, 1987; Eaton, 2001; Wells & Crain, 1994; Wells, Duran, & White, 2008; Wells, Holme, Revilla, & Atanda, 2009.

68. See Harris & Herrington, 2006.

69. See Towles-Schwen & Fazio, February, 2001; Wells et al., 2009.

70. See Armor, 2006; Wells & Frankenberg, 2007.

71. Wells et al., in press.

72. Rossell, 2003.

73. Rossell, 2005.

74. Sapporito, 2003; Smrekar & Goldring, 1999.

75. Adcock & Phillips, 2000.

76. Archbald, 2004; Crain, Allen, Thaler, Sullivan, Zellman, Warren Little, & Quigley, 1999; Cullen, Jacob, & Levitt, 2005; Flaxman, Guerrero, & Gretchen, 1999; Smith et al., 2002

77. Eaton, 2001.

78. Rossell, 2005.

79. There are interdistrict plans in Rochester, Boston, East Palo Alto, Hartford, Indianapolis, St. Louis, Milwaukee, and Minneapolis.

80. Wells et al., in press.

81. Kahlenberg, 2001, 2002.

82. Chavez & Frankenberg, 2009.

83. Silberman, 2002.

84. Bob Herbert, "Losing Our Way," *New York Times* online, May 25, 2011, accessed May 27, 2011, http://www.nytimes.com/2011/03/26/opinion/26herbert.html?ref=bobherbert.; Bob Herbert, "Separate and Unequal," *New York Times* online, May 21, 2011, accessed May 25, 2011, http://www.nytimes.com/2011/03/22/opinion/22herbert.html?ref=bobherbert.

85. See also Moses & Rogers, chapter 15 in this volume.

86. See for example, The United States Commission on Civil Rights, 1967; Kerner Commission, 1968; Kantor & Lowe, chapter 3 in this volume.

87. The Magnet Schools Assistance Program received $100,000,000. Funding for the MASP has been in decline since 2002. Charter schools, including several federal charter initiatives (Replication, VPSC, CSP, Credit Enhancement, National Leadership Activities) received $225,000,000. This figure does not include funds distributed through the I3 or Race to the Top programs, which have provided charter schools with additional support.

CHAPTER 10

1. Carter, 2012.

2. Conchas, 2006; Deyhle, 1995; Gutierrez & Rogoff, 2003; Lareau, 2003; Lewis, 2003; Pollock, 2004; Tyson, 2011; Warikoo, 2011.

3. Carter 2012, 2.

4. See King, 2005; Lee, 2007; Nasir & Hand, 2006.

5. It is important to state that not all individuals of particular ethnic or racial groups agree on what cultural practices, ideas, or traditions define groups, and indeed collective narratives about specific groups risk naturalizing or making it feel as if the only way to be a member of that group is to engage in those cultural behaviors (see Gutierrez & Rogoff 2003: Appiah, 1996; Brubaker & Cooper, 2000; Hollinger, 1995).

6. Warikoo & Carter, 2009.

7. See Warikoo & Carter, 2009; for a similar discussion, see also Slaughter-Defoe, et al., 1990.

8. S. Lee, 1996.

9. J. Lee, 2012.

10. For some reviews of the research on culture and education, see (Ngo & Lee, 2007; O'Connor, Lewis, & Mueller, 2007; Small, Harding, & Lamont, 2010; Warikoo & Carter, 2009).

11. Moynihan, 1965; Murray & Herrnstein, 1994; Sowell, 1981.

12. Fordham, 1996; Fordham & Ogbu, 1986; Lewis, 1969; Ogbu & Simons, 1998.

13. J. Ogbu, 1978, 1987, 1988; J. U. Ogbu & Simons, 1998.

14. J. Ogbu, 1978, 1987, 1988; J. U. Ogbu & Simons, 1998.

15. J. U. Ogbu & Simons, 1998.

16. Fordham and Ogbu, 1986.

17. Farkas, Lleras, & Maczuga, 2002.

18. Ainsworth-Darnell & Downey, 1998; Cook & Ludwig, 1997; Harris, 2011; Solorzano, 1992; Tyson, 2002.

19. In addition, Wells and Crain (1999) have argued that academic achievement is not considered "acting white" in schools that more critically examine racial and ethnic relations locally, nationally, and globally.

20. Carter, 2005.

21. Becker, 1964.

22. Delpit, 1995.

23. Bourdieu, 1977, 1986; Bourdieu & Passeron, 1977.

24. DiMaggio, 1982; DiMaggio & Mohr, 1985.

25. Bourdieu, 1977, 1986.

26. Ferguson, 2000; Foley, 1991; Hale, 1986; Irvine, 1990; Kochman, 1981; Rist, 1973.

27. Castagno & Brayboy, 2008.

28. Valenzuela, 1999.

29. Carter 2005; Darder 1991; Gibson 1988; Mehan et al., 1994; Phinney & Devich-Navarro, 1997.

30. Bialystok et al., 2004; Kovács & Mehler, 2009.

31. Carter, 2012; Sussman, 2000.

32. Alexander et al., 1987.

33. Ibid. More current studies show how new or inexperienced teachers of color also grapple with cultural challenges in the classroom. See Achinstein & Aguirre, 2008.

34. Alexander et al., 1987

35. Bowles & Gintis 1976; DiMaggio 1982; Farkas, Grobe, Sheehan, & Shuan, 1990; Ferguson 1998.

36. Fine, 1991; Fordham, 1993.

37. Gamoran, 1987; Oakes, 2005.

38. Bernstein, 1971; Bowles & Gintis, 1976

39. High-level academic coursework consists of four years of English; three years of mathematics (including at least one year of a course higher than algebra II); three years of science (including at least one year of a course higher than biology); three years of social studies (including at least one year of US or world history); and two years of a single non-English language enclose in parentheses (National Center for Education Statistics, 2010).

40. Gamoran, 1987; Lucas, 1999; Oakes, 2005.

41. Kao & Thompson, 2003.

42. For a review of these studies, see Sleeter, 2011.

43. Bennett, 1988; D'Souza, 1995.

44. J. E. Hale, 2001; Hilliard, 1978; Spencer, Swanson, & Cunningham, 1991.

45. A. Wade Boykin, 1984.

46. Apple, 1999.

47. McLaren, 1988, 160–161.

48. Culturally responsive teaching is based on the assumption that when academic knowledge and skills are situated within the lived experiences and frames of reference of students,

they are more personally meaningful, have higher interest appeal, and are learned more easily and thoroughly.

49. For a review of these studies, see Gay, 2000. See also Brayboy & Castagno, 2009.

50. Sleeter, 2001.

51. C. Lee, 2007, 15.

52. See also ibid., 61.

53. C. Lee, 2007.

54. Morrison et al., 2008.

55. Ibid.

56. Baker et al., 2002. Generally, the authors calculated effect sizes as the differences between the experimental and control groups' means divided by a pooled standard deviation.

57. Cheung & Slavin, 2012.

58. Freire, 2001 (1970).

59. Carter, 2012.

60. Darling-Hammond & Bransford, 2005.

CHAPTER 11

1. The 2000 census shows that 72 percent speak a language other than English at home (Hernandez, Denton, et al., 2009). This number has likely increased over time.

2. Migration Policy Institute (MPI), 2011.

3. Lillie et al., 2012; Garcia et al., 2006.

4. See http://ell.stanford.edu/content/our-work.

5. Hakuta, Butler, & Witt, 2000.

6. ELL Working Group, 2011.

7. Zehler et al., 2002.

8. On Arizona, see Lillie et al., 2011.

9. "All students" for NAEP reporting purposes includes all students reporting scores, whether their subgroup was reported separately or not; thus ELs are also included in the "all students."

10. Abedi et al., 1998; Lewis et al., 2012.

11. Silver, Saunders, & ZáNewrate, 2008.

12. Hernandez et al., 2009.

13. Hart & Risley, 2003.

14. Urban Institute, 2006.

15. The Supreme Court found in 1982 (Plyler v. Doe, 457 U.S. 202) that these students could not be held responsible for the actions of their parents and that it did not serve them or the nation well to maintain them as a "permanent underclass."

16. August & Hakuta, 1997.

17. NCES, 2009.

18. LAO, 2007.

19. Rothstein, 2004; Berliner, 2006.

20. Orfield, Siegel-Hawley, & Kucsera, 2012.

21. Cosentino de Cohen & Clewell, 2007.

22. Zehler et al., 2002.

23. Gándara, Maxwell-Jolly, & Driscoll, 2005.

24. Gándara et al., 2003.

25. Gándara & Rumberger, 2008.

26. Pew Hispanic, 2004.

27. Rumbaut, Massey, & Bean, 2006, 448.

28. Schmidt, 2000; Wright, 2007.

29. Arizona English Language Learner Task Force, 2007.

30. Gándara & Orfield, 2013.

31. Zehler et al., 2003; Kindler, 2002.

32. Parrish et al., 2006, ix.

33. Gándara & Hopkins, 2010.

34. Hopkins, 2011.

35. Ruiz, 1984.

36. See Genesee et al., 2006, for an excellent review of this research.

37. Silverman, 2011.

38. The parent is actually quite right about this. A series of studies have now shown that bilinguals are advantaged in a number of ways, including cognitive flexibility, better intergroup relations, and later onset of dementia. See, for example, Genesee & Gándara, 1999; Bialystock, 2001; Bialystock et al., 2004.

39. Gándara & Orfield, 2011.

40. Hernandez et al., 2009.

41. See, for example, Gándara, Maxwell-Jolly, & Driscoll, 2005.

42. Hopkins, 2011.

CHAPTER 12

1. Several studies cite evidence showing that some school districts used tracking as a way to keep Black and White students separate when they were ordered to desegregate; see McNulty, 2002; Welner, 2002.

2. See Kozol, 1992; Logan, Minca, & Adar, 2012; Mickelson, 2005; Mickelson & Heath, 1999; Rumberger & Palardy, 2005; Street, 2005.

3. See Bettie 2003; Conchas, 2010; Staiger, 2006; Tyson 2011.

4. See Ansalone, 2006; Bettie, 2003; Carter, 2005; Clotfelter, 2004; Lee, 1996; Lucas, 1999; Metz, 1978; Oakes, 2005; Oakes & Guiton, 1995; Perry, 2002; Schofield, 1989; Staiger, 2006; Tyson, 2011; Tyson, Darity, & Castellino, 2005; Warikoo, 2011; Welner, 2001.

5. Jay Zhang, Enloe's racial divide, letter to the editor, *Raleigh News and Observer*, February 3, 2011. Blacks, at 39 percent of the student population, are the largest racial-ethnic group at Enloe; Whites make up 34 percent, Asians 12 percent, and Hispanics 9 percent.

6. Jane Stancill, Enloe in spotlight: Much is separate, perhaps unequal, at system's premier high school, *Cary News*, March 2, 2011. Retrieved July 2011 from http://www.carynews.com/2011/03/02/29281/enloe-in-spotlight.html.

7. Meier, Stewart, & England, 1989.

8. Welner, 2002.

9. See Gamoran, 1987; Oakes, Wells, Jones, & Datnow, 1997; Perry, 2002; Riehl, Pallas, & Natriello, 1999; Welner, 2001.

10. See Mickelson, 2005.

11. See Gamoran & Mare, 1989.

12. See Lucas & Berends, 2007.

13. Previous studies have also found that tracking is more intense in racially diverse schools, those between 30 and 60 percent Black; see Clotfelter, 2004.

14. Pettigrew, 1997.

15. See Carter, 2012.

16. The recent mass murders in Norway by a self-proclaimed right-wing Christian who railed against multiculturalism and the growing racial/ethnic and religious diversity in Europe is a frightening example of the potential costs of intolerance.

17. Students from different racial and ethnic backgrounds have opportunities to meet in other noncore or elective classes, such as band and PE, and through involvement in extracurricular activities such as sports and student government, but these classes and activities tend to be segregated as well; see Clotfelter, 2004; Moody 2001. When students have choices, they tend to prefer settings in which they will not be isolated from friends; see Staiger, 2006; Tyson, 2011; Warikoo, 2011.

18. This may also be the case when students are grouped by race *within* classrooms; see Schofield, 1989.

19. See Staiger, 2006; Tyson, 2011.

20. While social class tends to be equally important in these situations, it is seldom as visible as race or ethnicity.

21. Brantlinger, 2003, 75.

22. See Bettie, 2003; Tyson 2011.

23. See Rosenbaum, 1976.

24. See Stearns, 2004; also Moody 2001.

25. See Bettie, 2003; Conchas, 2010; Lee, 1996; Staiger, 2006.

26. Staiger 2006, 57.

27. See Carter 2005; Horvat & Lewis, 2003; Staiger, 2006; Tyson, 2011; Warikoo, 2011.

28. See Bettie, 2003, 181.

29. Conchas, 2010, 163.

30. See Bettie, 2003; Dehyle, 1995; Tyson, Darity, & Castellino.

31. See Kelly & Price, 2011.

32. See ibid.; Riehl, Pallas, & Natriello, 1999; Staiger, 2006.

33. See Kelly & Price, 2011, 576.

34. The National Council of Teachers of Mathematics recommends teaching algebra in grade 8. Some states, including California, have adopted this standard.

35. See Diette, 2005.

36. Ibid.

37. Parents can override this requirement. See Kelly & Price, 2011; Tyson, 2011.

38. See Ford, 1995; Irvine, 1990; Jolla, 2005; Kornhaber, 1999; Tyson, 2008.

39. See Kornhaber, 1999.

40. See Kelly & Price, 2011; Tyson, 2011.

41. Privileged White and middle-class parents, who tend to be in the know (Oakes, Welner, Yonezawa, & Allen, 1998), are often able to push beyond the formal placement procedures and criteria to have their children placed in gifted programs; see Margolin,; Staiger, 2004.

42. See Tyson, 2011.

43. Danielle Evans's short story "Robert E. Lee is Dead" in *Before You Suffocate Your Own Fool Self*, depicting the experience of gifted placement and racialized tracking for the Black protagonist Crystal, has uncanny similarities to the experiences described by students of color in research reports; see Bettie, 2003; Tyson, 2011.

44. See Tyson, 2011.

45. See Steele, 1992; Steele & Aronson, 1995; Steele, 1997.

46. See Steele, 2010.

47. See Steele, 1992.

48. Mickelson, 2005, 88.

49. See Hallinan, 1994.

50. See Lucas 1999; Oakes, 2005; Welner, 2001.

51. See Oakes, 2005; Wheelock, 1992.

52. See Bettie, 2003; Oakes, 2005; Staiger, 2006.

53. See Diette, 2005; Gamoran, 1987; Sorenson & Hallinan, 1977.

54. Gamoran, 1987, 150.

55. Oakes, 2005.

56. Retrieved July 2011 fromhttp://education.usnews.rankingsandreviews.com/best-high-schools/listings/california/the-preuss/school-ucsd.

57. Retrieved July 2011 from http://preuss.ucsd.edu/about.model.php.

58. The school has an application process for admission, but it is not merit based, so it is not necessarily selecting the highest-achieving students.

59. See Burris & Welner, 2005.

60. See Burris, Wiley, Welner, & Murphy, 2008.

61. Burris & Welner, 2005, p. 4.

62. See Burris & Welner, 2005.

63. See Rui, 2010.

64. See Resnick, 1995.

65. Jolla, 2005.

66. See http://today.duke.edu/2011/03/darity.html, accessed July 23, 2011. Personal communication with Margaret Gayle, July 15, 2011.

67. See Oakes, Wells, Jones, & Datnow, 1997.

68. See Wells & Serna, 1996.

69. For more on the process of detracking, see Burris & Garrity, 2008. For other examples of successful detracking, see Rubin, 2006; Wheelock, 1992.

70. Burris & Welner, 2005; Rubin, 2006.

71. Wheelock, 1992, 15.

72. Burris, Welner, & Bezoza, 2009.

CHAPTER 13

1. Rothstein, 2004.

2. Boyd et al., 2007; Ferguson, 1991; Hanushek, 1996; Rivkin et al., 2005; Rockoff, 2004; Sanders & Rivers, 1996.

3. Adamson & Darling-Hammond, 2011.

4. Educational Testing Service, 2002; Public Education Network, 2004; The Teaching Commission, 2005; Bushaw & NcNee, 2009.

5. McMurrer, 2007.

6. Clotfelter et al., 2008.

7. Brill, 2009.

8. Kristof, 2006.

9. Speech by Barack Obama to the US Chamber of Commerce on March 1, 2010. Retrieved from http://projects.washingtonpost.com/obama-speeches/speech/190/.

10. Mencken, 1949.

11. US Department of Education, 2002.

12. Peter D. Hart Research Associates, 2008.

13. Ibid.

14. Feistritzer & Harr, 2010.

15. Chait & McLaughlin, 2009.

16. Gitomer, 2007.

17. Tucker, 2011.

18. Decker et al., 2004; Xu et al., 2011.

19. Corcoran & Jennings, 2009.

20. Boyd et al., 2008.

21. Murnane & Steele, 2007.

22. Ibid.

23. Ost, 2009.

24. Shulman, 1987; Berliner, 1988; Sternberg & Horvath, 1995.

25. Garmston,1998.

26. Jerald & Van Hook, 2011.

27. Arons, 2010. Personal interview.

28. Weisberg et al., 2009.

29. Snowden, 2009.

30. Organization for Economic Co-operation and Development, 2011.

31. Hulleman & Barron, 2010.

32. Springer, 2009.

33. Springer et al., 2010.

34. Marsh et al., 2011.

35. Ibid.

36. Adams et al., 2009.

37. Hulleman & Barron, 2010.

38. Lawler, 2008.

39. Ibid.

40. Goldhaber, 2008; McCaffrey et al., 2003; Berry et al., 2009; Sass, 2008; Jennings & Corcoran, 2009; Hill et al., 2010.

41. Hill, H. et al., 2010.

42. Brooks, 2010.

43. Seehttp://www.edreform.com/Issues/Charter_Connection/?All_About_Charter_Schools.

44. A study published in June 2009 by the Center for Research on Education Outcomes (CREDO) at Stanford University analyzed data from charter schools enrolling 70 percent of all US charter school students and compared those schools and students to matched (similar) conventional public schools. Only 17 percent of the charters had results that were significantly better than the matched school, while 37 percent had results significantly worse than students would have attained (on average) had they remained in conventional public schools. Similarly, a study by Mathematica Policy Research, commissioned by the US Department of Education, found that "on average, charter middle schools that hold lotteries are neither more nor less successful than traditional public schools in improving student achievement, behavior, and school progress; however, impacts varied widely across schools." (CREDO, 2009)

45. Baker & Ferris, 2011.

46. Frankenberg, E. et al., 2011; Miron et al., 2010; Miron & Urschel, 2010.

47. Henig, 2008.

48. Ayers, 2010.

49. Thevenot, 2010; Newton et al., 2011.

50. Constantine et al., 2009; Darling-Hammond, 2009.

51. Ingersoll, 2003.

52. See http://www.boldapproach.org/index.php?id=01.

53. National Council for the Accreditation of Teacher Education, 2010.

54. Darling-Hammond, 2010.

55. Alliance for Excellent Education, 2005.

56. Darling-Hammond, 2010.

57. Murnane & Steele, 2007; Adamson & Darling-Hammond, 2011.

58. The Teaching Commission, 2004.

59. see   http://www.huffingtonpost.com/2011/07/29/duncan-boosts-merit-pay-a_n_913608.html.

60. Organization for Economic Co-operation and Development, 2011.

61. See Barnett et al., 2007.

62. Heneman & Milanowski, 1999.

63. Center for Teaching Quality, 2008.

64. Berry, B. & the TeacherSolutions 2030 Team, 2011.

65. Center for Teaching Quality, 2007.

66. Darling-Hammond, 2010.

67. Peter D. Hart Research Associates, Inc. and Harris Interactive, 2005.

68. Bryk et al., 2010.

69. Goddard & Goddard, 2007.

70. Rosenholtz, 1989.

71. Jackson & Bruegmann, 2009.

72. Kang & Hong, 2008; Darling-Hammond, 2010.

73. Viadero, 2008.

74. Rivkin et al., 2005.

75. Entwisle et al., 1998.

76. See http://www.hcz.org/.

77. Obama, 2008.

78. United States Department of Education, 2009.

79. Darling-Hammond, 2007.

80. Green, 2010.

81. Sawchuck, 2011.

82. Tucker, 2011.

83. Organization for Economic Co-operation and Development, 2011.

84. Jennings, 2011.

CHAPTER 14

1. For more detail on these relationships and frameworks, see Belfield & Levin, 2007; Sum et al., 2009).

2. Goldin & Katz, 2008.

3. On the demographics of education and the opportunity gap, see Tienda & Alon, 2007.

4. See, Magnuson & Duncan, 2011.

5. These figures are adapted from the 2005 Current Population Survey estimates of Belfield and Levin (2007). They account for delayed completion of high school, as well as race-specific adjustments for GED and institutionalization.

6. On incomes and education, see Rouse (2007). On health and education, see, Cutler & Lleras-Muney (2010). On life satisfaction and education, see, Oreopoulos & Salvanes (2011).

7. This modeling framework is developed by Belfield and Levin (2007). It was applied for California by Belfield and Levin (2008) and Brady et al. (2005) and for Connecticut by Sum et al. (2009). This literature follows methodological and empirical work that extends back to Levin (1972). To make all comparisons consistent, we report all dollar amounts in 2011 prices and present values at twelfth grade. Present valuation means that the amounts are adjusted for the fact that money amounts that accrue later are valued less than those that accrue earlier; we use a 3.5 percent discount rate, and different discount rates are applied as part of the sensitivity testing. The justification for a 3.5 percent discount rate is given in Moore et al. (2004).

8. No adjustments are made for labor market participation, GED receipt, or incarceration rates. Labor market activity begins at age 18 (conditional on not being in college) and lasts to age 65. We generate estimates that vary with assumptions about health and pension benefits (average or zero); discount rate (3.5 percent–7.5 percent); and productivity growth (1 percent–2 percent).

9. See www.taxadmin.org/fta/rate/tax_stru.html.

10. An alternative method is to insert the earnings estimates directly into the National Bureau of Economic Research tax calculator, TAXSIM9. However, TAXSIM calculations exclude expense exemptions, mortgage interest tax relief, and employer tax contributions.

11. Cutler & Lleras-Muney, 2010; Adler & Stewart, 2010.

12. To calculate the expenditure consequences, we adapt estimates from Muennig (2007).

13. On the general relationship between education and crime, see Lochner & Moretti (2004) and Oreopoulos & Salvanes (2011). On the education levels of the prison population, see WolfHarlow (2003).

14. A number of studies have calculated the lifetime economic consequences of being either an offender or a chronic offender; we adapt these to estimate the lifetime crime-related consequences of education and its public costs. See DeLisi et al. (2010); Cohen & Piquero (2009).

15. See Waldfogel et al., 2007.

16. We use estimates from Waldfogel et al. (2007) to calculate differences in the receipt of welfare benefits by educational level.

17. NPSAS:04 data show that nationally 43 percent of community college students take at least one remedial course (Horn & Nevill, 2006, table 6.2). Rates cited in Bailey et al. (2010, 257) are even higher. In addition there is nontrivial remediation at the four-year level: using the national average rate from NPSAS:04 data, however, the rate is 15 percent (Horn & Nevill, 2006, table 6.2).

18. Bailey et al. (2010) estimate that up to two-thirds of students in remediation fail to complete the required sequence of courses. These students are simply repeating high school classes even as they are recognized as high school graduates.

19. This only counts the expenditure on providing remedial courses. This falls far short of a full accounting of the costs of remediation, which should include additional screening and counseling, dilution of college-level course content, and the substantial burden on discouraged students.

20. This estimate is a lower bound because graduating from high school also gives individuals the opportunity to enroll and or complete college. If we adjust for the probability that each high school graduate would progress to higher education, the net fiscal impact per new high school graduate is $187,700 (we call this "graduate+" in table 14.5). This estimate assumes that the new graduates progress on to college and complete college at the same rate as those persons in the lowest tercile of socioeconomic status, that is, at rates below the average transition from high school to college.

21. We do not count any general social benefits from having a more educated population (e.g., on civic participation).

22. Florida, 2002.

23. On the 37 percent estimate, see McMahon (2006). However, some studies find that the effect depends on how human capital spillovers are measured (e.g., Moretti, 2004).

24. Miller et. al.,1996. Also, there are tax losses from crime when victims are unable to work.

25. Allgood & Snow, 1998.

26. Two recent studies have calculated this broader social value associated with better health. Muennig et al. (2010) calculate the remaining quality-adjusted life years (QALYs) of persons aged 18. A QALY is a scale to measure health status, with perfect health given a score of 1 and specific conditions translating into QALYs of less than one. Muennig et al. (2010) estimate that a high school graduate reaps an extra 2.4 years of life in full health. Schoeni et al. (2011) estimate annual education-driven differences: relative to a dropout, a high school graduate experiences .03 extra QALYs each year and a college graduate experiences .062 QALYs more. These two estimates are not close together and it is unclear whether these values include some portion of the fiscal benefits of health. Therefore, we omit this effect from our calculation.

27. For each domain (earnings, taxes, crime, health and welfare) we have used a range of estimates. Thus, some sensitivity testing is implicitly incorporated in our framework.

28. For example, in some models we use a discount rate above that recommended by Moore et al. (2004); this reduces the value of any benefits of education that happen in the future. Perhaps the most critical of these is that we are assuming that the valuation of non-work time is equivalent across education levels even as the opportunity cost of leisure rises. Because of data limitations we are almost certainly undervaluing the income gains from education and under-adjusting for employment probabilities.

29. See Belfield & Levin, 2008.

30. There are other reasons why the differential between graduates and dropouts is likely to grow. The earnings gains from education have increased over recent decades, not least because of the decline in routine, noncognitive jobs that are typically open to dropouts. Future demographic and labor market changes are likely to amplify these trends (Kirsch et al., 2007). Finally, the costs of health care and of incarceration have been growing at rates much faster than general inflation.

CHAPTER 15

1. Valenzuela, 1999; McNeil, 2000.

2. Rothstein, Wilder, & Jacobsen, 2007; Gibson & Levine, 2003.

3. This description of deliberative democracy is based primarily on Gutmann & Thompson (1996, 2004).

4. Gutmann, 1999, xii.

5. We use an expansive view of the concept of a "citizen" that includes all people who live in a nation, not just those that have achieved official citizenship.

6. Gutmann, 1987, 51.

7. Ibid.

8. Mayer & Watson, 2011; Severson, 2011.

9. Putnam, 2000; Skocpol, 2003.

10. Macedo et al., 2005, 1.

11. Verba, Schlozman, & Brady, 1995; Jacobs & Skocpol, 2005.

12. American Political Science Association Task Force on Inequality and American Democracy 2004, 1.

13. Levy & Temin, 2007; Saez, 2009.

14. In a 5–4 decision, the United States Supreme Court held in Citizens' United v. Federal Election Commission (558 U.S. 50, 2010) that political spending is speech protected by the first amendment and that government cannot place restrictions on the amount of money that corporations or unions spend to support or criticize candidates for public election.

15. Christopher Jencks (2002) argues that the high level of income inequality in the United States is directly related to differences between public policies in the United States and most nations in Western Europe; those related to wages and to social welfare are the most important.

16. Bartels, 2008.

17. Booza, Cutsinger, & Galster, 2006.

18. Massey et al., 2009.

19. Anderson, 2010; Orr, 1999.

20. Lake & Huckfeldt, 1998.

21. Nie, Junn, & Stehlik-Barry, 1996.

22. Campaign for Fiscal Equity, 1995, 306.

23. Darling-Hammond, 1999.

24. Galston, 2004; Gibson & Levine, 2003; Schultz, 2008.

25. Kahne & Sporte, 2008.

26. Kahne & Middaugh, 2008.

27. Dewey 1916, 71.

28. Ibid., 73.

29. Ibid., 83.

30. Ibid., 21.

31. Noddings, 2006, 36.

32. Dewey 1916, 1938.

33. Robertson, 1992.

34. Ibid.; Moses, 2002.

35. Robertson, 1992, 375.

36. Dewey, 1916, 1927, 1938.

37. E.g., Antonio et al., 2004; Chang, 1999; Chang, 2001; Chang, Witt, Jones, & Hakuta, 2003; Gurin, 1999; Gurin, Dey, Hurtado, & Gurin, 2002; Gurin, Nagda, & Lopez, 2004.

38. Wells et al., 305.

39. Anderson 2002, 1270–1271.

40. Fine et. al., 2004, 2199.

41. Westheimer 2011, 1.

42. Ibid., 2.

CHAPTER 16

1. See National Defense Education Act of 1958; National Commission on Excellence in Education, A Nation at Risk: The Imperative for Educational Reform, April 1983; Auguste, Hancock, & Laboissière, 2009.

2. Losen, 2011.

3. Jimerson, S. R., Anderson, G. E., & Whipple, A. 2002; Jacobs, B. A. & Lefgren, L. 2004; Nagaoka, J. & Roderick, M. 2004.

4. Cooper et al., 1996; McCombs et al., 2011.

5. Duncan & Murnane, 2011.

6. ESEA was slated for reauthorization in 2008, but for the past five years Congress has failed to agree on new legislation. The law, however, has a provision that automatically extends existing law (NCLB), and Congress has continued to provide funding.

7. First in gross domestic product (GDP), and seventh in GDP per capita. http://www. forbes.com/sites/bethgreenfield/2012/02/22/the-worlds-richest-countries/.

8. http://www.unicef-irc.org/publications/660.

9. Lee, 2002; Long, Kelly, & Gamoran, 2011.

10. Reardon, 2011.

11. Ananat et. al., 2011; Ransdall, 2011; Orr, 2003.

12. Linn & Welner, 2007.

13. Grosjean, 2010.

14. Passel & Cohn, 2008.

15. Winerip, 2011c.

16. Darling-Hammond, 2010.

17. Saunders & Chrisman, 2011; http://nepc.colorado.edu/publication/linking-learning.

REFERENCES

Abedi, J., Lord, C., & Hofstetter, C. (1998). *Impact of selected background variables on students' NAEP math performance*. Los Angeles: University of California, Center for the Study of Evaluation/National Center for Research on Evaluation, Standards, and Student Testing.

Achinstein, B., & Aguirre, J. (2008). Cultural match or culturally suspect: How new teachers of color negotiate sociocultural challenges in the classroom. *Teachers College Record, 110*(8), 1505–1540.

Ackard, P. (1994). Corporate mobilization and political power: The transformation of U.S. economic policy in the 1970s. *American Sociological Review, 57*, 597–615.

Adams, S., Heywood, J., & Rothstein, R. (2009). *Teachers, performance pay, and accountability: What education leaders should learn from other sectors*. Washington DC: Economic Policy Institute.

Adamson, F., & Darling-Hammond, L. (2011). *Addressing the inequitable distribution of teachers: What it will take to get qualified, effective teachers in all communities?* Washington, DC: Center for American Progress.

Adler, N. E., & Stewart, J. (2010). Health disparities across the lifespan: Meaning, methods, and mechanisms. *Annals of the New York Academy of Sciences, 1186*, 5–23.

Adock, E. P., & Phillips, G. W. (2000). Accountability evaluation of magnet school programs: A value-added model approach. Paper presented at the annual meeting of the American Educational Research Association, New Orleans, Louisiana, April 24–28.

Aikin, W. M. (1942). *The story of the eight-year study*. New York: Harper.

Ainsworth-Darnell, J. W., & Downey, D. B. (1998). Assessing the oppositional culture explanation for racial/ethnic differences in school performance. *American Sociological Review, 63*(4), 536 553.

Akiba, M., LeTendre, G. K., & Scribner, J. P. (2007). Teacher quality, opportunity gap, and national achievement in 46 countries. *Educational Researcher, 36*(7), 369–387.

Alexander, K. L., Entwisle, D. R., & Thompson, M. S. (1987). School performance, status relations, and the structure of sentiment: Bringing the teacher back in. *American Sociological Review*, 52(5), 665–682.

Alexander, R. J. (2009). *Towards a new primary curriculum: A report from the Cambridge Primary Review. Part 2: The future*. Cambridge: University of Cambridge Faculty of Education.

Ali, R. (2007). The danger of ignoring the achievement gap. *Los Angeles Times*, November 26, on-line blog. Retrieved from http://www.latimes.com/news/opinion/la-op-dustup26nov26,0,2403101.story?page=2&coll=la-promo-opinion.

Allensworth, E., Takako, N., Montgomery, N., & Lee, V. E. (2009). College preparatory curriculum for all: Academic consequences of requiring algebra and English I for ninth graders in Chicago. *Education Evaluation and Policy Analysis*, 31(4), 367–391.

Allgood, S., & Snow, A. (1998). The marginal cost of raising tax revenue and redistributing income. *Journal of Political Economy*, 106, 1246–1273.

Alliance for Excellent Education. (2005, August). *Teacher attrition: A costly loss to the nation and to the states, Issue brief*. Retrieved from http://www.all4ed.org/files/archive/publications/TeacherAttrition.pdf.

Allport, G. (1954). *The nature of prejudice*. Boston: Addison-Wesley.

Amrein, A. L., & Berliner, D. C. (2002). High-stakes testing, uncertainty, and student learning. *Education Policy Analysis Archives*, 10(18), 1–74. Retrieved from http://epaa.asu.edu/epaa/v10n18.

Anagnostopolous, D. (2003). Testing and student engagement with literature in urban classrooms: A multi-layered perspective. *Research in the Teaching of English*, 38(2), 177–212.

Ananat, E. O., Gassman-Pines, A., Francis, D. V., & Gibson-Davis, C. (2011). Children left behind: The effects of statewide job loss on student achievement. National Bureau of Economic Research (NBER) Working Paper 17104. Retrieved from http://www.nber.org/papers/w17104.

Anderson, J. (1988). *The education of blacks in the south, 1860–1935*. Chapel Hill: University of North Carolina Press.

Anderson, E. (1999). *Code of the street: Decency, violence and the moral life of the inner city*. New York: W.W. Norton.

Anderson, E. (2002). Integration, affirmative action, and strict scrutiny. *New York University Law Review*, 77, 1195–2002.

Anderson, E. (2010). *The imperative of integration*. Princeton, NJ: Princeton University Press.

Annie E. Casey Foundation (n.d.). *Racial/ethnic composition of public school student body: White, non-Hispanic (percent)—2009–10*. Washington DC, Data Center, Kids Count. Washington DC: Author. Retrieved from http://datacenter.kidscount.org/data/bystate/Rankings.aspx?order=a&loct=3&dtm=11143&state=DC&tf=809&ind=4774&ch=816%2ca&by=a.

Ansalone, G. (2006). Tracking: A return to Jim Crow. *Race, Gender and Class*, 13(1/2), 144–153.

Antonio, A. L., Chang, M. J., Hakuta, K., Kenny, D. A., Levin, S., & Milem, J. F. (2004). Effects of racial diversity on complex thinking in college students. *Psychological Science*, 15(8), 507–510.

Anyon, J. (1997). *Ghetto schooling: A political economy of urban educational reform*. New York: Teachers College Press.

Appiah, K. A. (1995). The uncompleted argument: DuBois and the illusion of race. In *Overcoming Racism and Sexism*, ed. L. Bell and D. Blumenfeld, 59–78, Landam, MD: Rowman and Littlefield Publishers, Inc.

Apple, M. (1999). *Power, meaning, and identity: Essays in critical educational studies*. New York: P. Lang.

Applewhite, E., & Hirsch, L. (2003). *The Abbott preschool program: Fifth year report on enrollment and budget*. Newark, NJ: Education Law Center.

Archbald, D. A. (2004). School choice, magnet schools, and the liberation model: An empirical study. *Sociology of Education*, 77, 283–310.

Arizona English Language Learners Task Force (2007). Minutes of March 29, 2007. Retrieved from http://www.ade.state.az.us/ELTaskForce/.

Armor, D. J. (2006). "Lessons learned from school desegregation." In *Generational change: Closing the test score gap,* ed. Paul Peterson, 115–142. Lanham, MD: Rowman & Littlefield.

Arons, B. (2010). Personal interview. July 15.

Arsen, D., Plank, D., & Sykes, G. (1999). *School choice policies in Michigan: The rules matter*. East Lansing: Michigan State University.

Au, W. (2011). Teaching under the new Taylorism: High-stakes testing and the standardization of the 21st century curriculum, *Journal of Curriculum Studies*, 43(1), 25–45.

Au, W. (2007). High-stakes testing and curricular control: A qualitative metasynthesis. *Educational Researcher*, 36(5), 258–267.

August, D., and Hakuta, K. (1997). *Improving schooling for language minority children: A research agenda*. Washington, DC: National Research Council, Institute of Medicine.

Auguste, B. G., Hancock, B., & Laboissière, M. (2009). The economic cost of the US education gap. *McKinsey Quarterly*. Retrieved from http://www.mckinseyquarterly.com/The_economic_cost_of_the_US_education_gap_2388.

Ayers, R. (2010). *"Waiting for Superman" schools documentary is a slick marketing piece full of half-truths and distortions*. Alternet. Retrieved from http://www.alternet.org/media/148299/'waiting_for_superman'_schools_documentary_is_a_slick_marketing_piece_full_of_half-truths_and_distortions/.

Bailey, Stephen, & Mosher, Edith. (1968). *ESEA: The Office of Education administers a law*. Syracuse: Syracuse University Press.

Bailey, T., Jeong, D. W. & Cho, S. W. (2010). Referral, enrollment and completion in developmental education sequences in community colleges. *Economics of Education Review, 29*, 255–270.

Baker, B. D., & Ferris, R. (2011). *Adding up the spending: Fiscal disparities and philanthropy among New York City charter schools*. Boulder, CO: National Education Policy Center. Retrieved from http://nepc.colorado.edu/publication/NYC-charter-disparities.

Baker, B. D., Sciarra, D., & Farrie, D. (2010). *Is school funding fair? A national report card*. Newark, NJ: Education Law Center.

Baker, B. D. & Welner, K. G. (2011). School finance and courts: Does reform matter, and how can we tell? *Teachers College Record, 113*(11), 2374–2414.

Baker, S., Gersten, R., & Lee, D.S. (2002). A synthesis of empirical research on teaching mathematics to low-achieving students. *Elementary School Journal, 103*(1), 51–73.

Balfanz, R. & Legters, N. (2004). "Locating the dropout crisis: Which high schools produce the nation's dropouts." In *Dropouts in America*, ed. Gary Orfield, 57–84. Cambridge, MA: Harvard Education Press.

Barnett, J. H., Ritter, G. W., Winters, M. A., & Greene, J. P. (2007). *Evaluation of year one of the Achievement Challenge Pilot Project in the Little Rock School District*. Fayetteville: University of Arkansas, Department of Education Reform. Retrieved from http://www.uark.edu/ua/der/Research/merit_pay.html.

Barnett, W. S. (2008). *Preschool education and its lasting effects: Research and policy implications*. Boulder, CO: National Education Policy Center. Retrieved from http://nepc.colorado.edu/publication/preschool-education.

Barnett, W. S. (2011a). Effectiveness of early educational intervention. *Science*, 333, 975–978.

Barnett, W. S. (2011b). Four reasons the United States should offer every child a preschool education. In *The pre-k debates: Current controversies and issues*, ed. E. Zigler, W. Gilliam, & W. S. Barnett, 34–39. Baltimore, MD: Brookes Publishing.

Barnett, W.S., Carolan, M.E., Fitzgerald, J., & Squires, J.H. (2011). *The state of preschool 2011: State preschool yearbook*. New Brunswick, NJ: National Institute for Early Education Research.

Barnett, W. S., Epstein, D. J., Carolan, M., Fitzgerald, J., Ackerman, D. J., & Friedman, A. (2010). *The state of preschool 2010: State preschool yearbook*. New Brunswick, NJ: National Institute for Early Education Research (NIEER).

Barnett, W. S., & Frede, E. C. (2010). The promise of preschool: Why we need early education for all. *American Educator, Spring*, 21–29.

Barnett, W. S., & Masse, L. N. (2007). Early childhood program design and economic returns: Comparative benefit-cost analysis of the Abecedarian program and policy implications. *Economics of Education Review*, 26, 113–125.

Barnett, W. S., Jung, K., Frede, E., Hustedt, J., & Howes, C. (2011). *Effects of eight state pre-kindergarten programs on early learning*. New Brunswick, NJ: Rutgers University/ National Institute for Early Education Research.

Berry, B., Daughtrey, A., & Wieder, A. (2009). *Strategic management of human capital: A lens for understanding how effective teachers make effective schools*. Hillsborough, NC: Center for Teaching Quality.

Bartels, L. (2008). *Unequal democracy: The political economy of the new gilded age*. New York: Russell Sage Foundation.

Becker, G. S. (1964). *Human capital*. New York: National Bureau of Economic Research.

Belfield, C. R., & Levin, H. M., eds. (2007). *The price we pay: The economic and social costs of inadequate education*, 1–20. Washington, DC: Brookings Institution Press.

Belfield, C., & Levin, H. (2008). *The Return on Investment for Improving California's High School Graduation Rate*. Monograph, California Dropout Research Project, UC Santa Barbara. Retreived from http://www.cdrp.ucsb.edu/pubs_reports.htm

Bell, C. A. (2009). All choices equal? The role of choice sets in the selection of schools. *Peabody Journal of Education*, 84(2), 191–208.

Bell, J. (2004). *The liberal state on trial: The Cold War and American politics in the Truman years*. New York: Columbia University Press.

Bell, K., Bernstein, J., & Greenberg, M. (2008). Lessons for the United States from other advanced economies in tackling child poverty. In *Big ideas for children: Investing in our nation's future*, ed. First Focus, 81–92. Washington, DC: First Focus.

Bennett, W. J. (1988). *Our children and our country: Improving America's schools and affirming the common culture*. New York: Simon & Schuster.

Berliner, D. (1988). *The development of expertise in pedagogy*. Paper presented to the American Association of Colleges for Teacher Education, New Orleans, LA.

Berliner, D. (2006). Our impoverished view of educational reform. *Teachers College Record*, 108, 949–995.

Berliner, D. (2009). *Poverty and potential: Out-of-school factors and school success*. Education Public Interest Center. March. Retrieved from http://nepc.colorado.edu/files/PB-Berliner-NON-SCHOOL.pdf.

Berry, B. & the TeacherSolutions 2030 Team (2011). *TEACHING 2030: What we must do for our students and our public schools . . . now and in the future*. New York: Teachers College Press.

Bernstein, B. (1971). Social class, language and socialisation. In *Class, codes, and control*, vol. 1, ed. B. Bernstein, 170–189. London: Routledge & Kegan Paul.

Bettie, J. (2003). *Women without class: Girls, race, and gender*. Berkeley: University of California Press.

Betts, J. R., Rueben, K. S., Danenberg, A. (2000). *Equal resources, equal outcomes? The distribution of school resources and student achievement in California*. San Francisco: Public Policy Institute of California.

Bialystock, E. (2001). *Bilingualism in development: Language, literacy, and cognition*. New York: Cambridge University Press.

Bialystok, E., Craik, F. I. M., Klein, R., & Viswanathan, M. (2004). Bilingualism, aging, and cognitive control: Evidence from the Simon task. *Psychology and Aging, 19*(2), 290–303.

Bishop-Josef, S. J., & Zigler, E. (2011). The cognitive/academic emphasis versus the whole child approach: The 50-year debate. In *The pre-k debates: Current controversies and issues*, ed. E. Zigler, W. Gilliam, & W. S. Barnett, 83–88. Baltimore, MD: Brookes Publishing.Bonilla-Silva, E. (2003). *Racism without racists: Color-blind racism and the persistence of racial inequality in the United States*. Lanham, MD: Rowman and Littlefield.

Boger, J., & Orfield G., eds. (2005). *School resegregation: Must the South turn back?* Chapel Hill: University of North Carolina Press.

Booher-Jennings, J. (2005). Below the bubble: "Educational triage" and the Texas accountability system. *American Educational Research Journal, 42*(2), 231–268.

Booza, J., Cutsinger, J., & Galster, G. (2006). Where did they go? The decline of middle-income neighborhoods in metropolitan America. In *Living Cities Census Series*. Washington, DC: Brookings Institution Press. Retrieved from http://www.brookings.edu/~/media/research/files/reports/2006/6/poverty%20booza/20060622_middleclass.pdf.

Borman, K., Castenell, L., & Gallagher, K. (1993). Business involvement in school reform: The rise of the Business Roundtable. In *The new politics of race and gender*, ed. Catherine Marshall, 69–83. 1992 Yearbook of the Politics of Education Association. Washington, DC: Falmer.

Borman, K. M., Eitle, T. M., Michael, D., Eitle, D. J., Lee, R., Johnson, L., Cobb-Roberts, D., Dorn, S., & Shircliffe, B. (2004). Accountability in a post-desegregation era: The continuing significance of racial segregation in Florida's schools. *American Educational Research Journal, 41*(3), 605–631.

Bourdieu, P. (1977). Cultural reproduction and social reproduction. In *Power and Ideology in Education*, ed. J. Karabel & A. H. Halsey, 487–510. New York: Oxford University Press.

Bourdieu, P. (1986). The forms of capital. In, *Handbook of Theory and Research for the Sociology of Education*, ed. J. G. Richardson, 241–258. New York: Greenwood Press.

Bourdieu, P., & Passeron, J. C. (1977). *Reproduction in education, society and culture*. Beverly Hills: Sage.

Bowen, W. G. & Bok, D. (1998). *The shape of the river: Long-term consequences of considering race in college and university admissions*. Princeton, NJ: Princeton University Press.

Bowles, S., & Gintis, H. (1976). Schooling in capitalist America: Educational reform and the contradictions of economic life. New York: Basic Books.

Boyd, D., Grossman, P., Lankford, H., Loeb, S., and Wyckoff, J. (2006). How changes in entry requirements alter the teacher workforce and affect student achievement. *Education Finance & Policy, 1*, 176–216.

Boyd, D., Lankford, H., Loeb, S., Rockoff, J., & Wyckoff, J. (2007). *The narrowing gap in New York City teacher qualifications and its implications for student achievement in high-poverty schools*, National Bureau of Economic Research Working Paper No. 14021. Cambridge, MA: NBER 2007.

Boyd, D., Grossman, P., Lankford, H., Loeb, S., & Wyckoff, J. (2008). *Teacher preparation and student achievement*. National Bureau of Economic Research Working Paper No. W14314. Washington, DC: NBER. Retrieved from http://ssrn.com/abstract=1264576.

Braddock, J.H. II. (1980). The perpetuation of segregation across levels of education: A behavioral assessment of the contact-hypothesis. *Sociology of Education, 53*, 178–186.

Braddock, J. H. II, & McPartland, J. (1987). How minorities continue to be excluded from equal employment opportunities: Research on labor market and institutional barriers. *Journal of Social Issues, 43*, 8–12.

Brady, H., Hout, M., & Stiles J. (2005). Return on investment: Educational choices and demographic changes in California's future. Working paper. University of California, Berkeley.

Brantlinger, E. (2003). *Dividing classes: How the middle class negotiates and rationalizes school advantage*. New York: Routledge/Falmer.

Brauer, C. M. (1982). Kennedy, Johnson, and the war on poverty. Journal of American History, 69, 98–119.

Brayboy, B. M. J., & Castagno, A. (2009). Self-determination through self-education: culturally responsive schooling for Indigenous students in the USA. *Teaching Education, 20*(1), 31–53.

Brighouse, H. (1996). Liberal egalitarians and school choice. *Politics and Society, 24*(4), 457–486.

Brill, S. (2009). The battle over New York City's worst teachers. *The New Yorker*. Retrieved from http://www.newyorker.com/reporting/2009/08/31/090831fa_fact_brill.

Brinkley, A. (1998). *Liberalism and its discontents*. Cambridge, MA: Harvard University Press.

Brinkley, A. (2003). The New Deal experiments. In *The achievements of American liberalism: The New Deal and its legacies,* ed. W. Chafe, 1–20. New York: Columbia University Press.

Briggs, X. d. S. (2005). *The geography of opportunity: Race and housing choices in metropolitan America*, Washington: Brookings Institution.

Bronfenbrenner, U. I., & Evans, G. W. (2000). Developmental science in the 21st century: Emerging questions, theoretical models, research designs and empirical findings. *Social Development, 9*(1), 115–125.

Brooks, D. (2010). Teachers are fair game. *Atlantic Monthly*. Retrieved from http://www.theatlantic.com/magazine/archive/2010/07/teachers-are-fair-game/8155.

Brophy, J., & Good, T. (1986). Teacher behavior and student achievement. In *Handbook of Research on Teaching*, ed. M. Wittrock, 328–375. New York: Macmillan.

Brown, A. B., & Clift, J. W. (2010). The unequal effect of adequate yearly progress: Evidence from school visits. *American Education Research Journal, 47*(4), 774–798.

Brown, M. K. (1999). *Race, money, and the American welfare state*. Ithaca, NY: Cornell University Press.

Brubaker, R., & Cooper, F. (2000). Beyond identity. *Theory and Society, 29*(1), 1–47.

Bruno, J. & Isken, J. (1996). Inter and intraschool site student transiency: Practical and theoretical implications for instructional continuity at inner-city schools. *Journal of Research and Development in Education, 29*(4), 239–252.

Bryk. A., Sebring, P.B., & Allensworth, E. (2010). *Organizing schools for improvement: Lessons from Chicago*. Chicago: University of Chicago Press.

Bueno, M., Darling-Hammond, L., & Danielle Gonzales, D. (2009). *Pre-k 101: Preparing teachers for the pre-k classroom*. Washington, DC: PreK Now.

Bulkley, K., Levin, H. M., & Henig, J. eds. (2010). *Between public and private: Politics, governance, and the new portfolio models for urban school reform*. Cambridge, MA: Harvard Education Press.

Burchinal, M., McCartney, K., Steinberg, L., Crosnoe, R., Friedman, S. L., & McLoyd, V. (2011). Examining the Black–White achievement gap among low-income children using the NICHD Study of Early Child Care and Youth Development. *Child Development, 82*(5), 1404–1420.

Bushaw, W. J., & NcNee, J. A. (2009). *The 41st annual Phi Delta Kappa/Gallup poll of the public's attitudes toward public schools*. Bloomington, IN: Phi Delta Kappan International/Gallup.

Burris, C. C., & Garrity, D. T. (2008). *Detracking for excellence and equity*. Alexandria, VA: Association for Supervision and Curriculum Development.

Burris, C. C., & Welner, K. (2005). Closing the achievement gap by detracking. *Phi Delta Kappan*, 86(8), 594–598.

Burris, C. C., Welner, K., & Bezoza, J. (2009). *Universal access to quality education: Research and recommendations for the elimination of curricular stratification*. National Education Policy Center. Retrieved from http://nepc.colorado.edu/publication/universal-access.

Burris, C. C., Wiley, E., Welner, K., & Murphy, J. (2008). Accountability, rigor, and detracking: Achievement effects of embracing a challenging curriculum as a universal good for all students. *Teachers College Record*, 110(3), 571–608.

California Postsecondary Education Commission. (2007). *College-going rates: A performance measure in California's higher education accountability framework* (Commission Report No. 07–04). Sacramento, CA: Author.

Camagni, R., Gibelli, M. C., & Rigamonti, P. (2002). Urban mobility and urban form: The social and environmental costs of different patterns of urban expansion, *Ecological Economics, 40*, 199–216.

Camilli, G., Vargas, S., Ryan, S., & Barnett, W. S. (2010). Meta-analysis of the effects of early education interventions on cognitive and social development. *Teachers College Record*, 112(3), 579–620.

Campaign for Fiscal Equity Inc. v. State, 86 N.Y.2d 306, 1995.

Campbell, D. T. (1976). *Assessing the impact of planned social change*. Hanover, NH: Public Affairs Center, Dartmouth College.

Campbell, F. A., & Ramey, C. T. (1995). Cognitive and school outcomes for high-risk African-American students at middle adolescence: Positive effects of early intervention. *American Educational Research Journal*, 32(4), 743–772.

Campbell, F. A., Ramey, C. T., Pungello, E. P., Sparling, J. J. & Miller-Johnson, S. (2002). Early childhood education: Young adult outcomes from the Abecedarian project. *Applied Developmental Science, 6*, 42–57.

Carey, K. (2006). Rothstein redux. *The Quick and the Ed*. August 9. Retrieved from http://www. quickanded.com/2006/08/rothstein-redux.html.

Carnoy, M., Jacobsen, R., Mishel, L., & Rothstein, R. (2005). *The charter school dust-up: Examining the evidence on enrollment and achievement*. Washington, DC: Economic Policy Institute.

Carnoy, M., & Rothstein, R. (2013). What do international tests really show about U.S. student performance? Washington, D.C.: Economic Policy Institute. http://www.epi.org/files/2013/EPI-What-do-international-tests-really-show-about-US-student-performance.pdf

Carter, P. (2005). *Keepin' it real: School success beyond black and white*. New York: Oxford University Press.

Carter, P. (2012). *Stubborn roots: Race, culture, and inequality in U.S. and South African schools*. New York: Oxford University Press.

Castagno, A., & Brayboy, B. M. J. (2008). Culturally responsive schooling for indigenous youth: A review of the literature. *Review of Educational Research*, 78(4), 941–993.

Ceci, S. J., & Papierno, P. B. (2005). The rhetoric and reality of gap closing: When the "have-nots" gain but the "haves" gain even more. *American Psychologist, 60*, 149–160.

Center for National Policy Review (CNPR). (1977). *Why must northern school systems desegregate? A summary of federal court findings in recent cases*. Washington, DC: Catholic University Law School.

Center for Teaching Quality (2008). *Improving student learning through strategic compensation.* Hillsborough, NC. Center for Teaching Quality. Retrieved from http://catalog.proemags. com/showmag.php?mid=ggfgt#/page0/.

Center for Teaching Quality (2007). *Paying teachers for performance: Design a system that students deserve.* Carrboro, NC: Author.

Center on Educational Policy. (2006). *From the capital to the classroom: Year 4 of the No Child Left Behind Act.* Washington, DC: Author.

Center on Education Policy. (2008). *Instructional time in elementary schools: A closer look at specific subjects.* Washington, DC: Author.

Centers for Disease Control and Prevention (CDC). (2002). *Pediatric nutrition surveillance 2001 report.* Washington, DC: US Department of Health and Human Services.

Chait R., & McLaughlin, M. (2009). *Realizing the promise: How state policy can support alternative certification programs.* Washington, DC: Center for American Progress.

Chang, M. J. (1999). Does racial diversity matter? The educational impact of a racially diverse undergraduate population. *Journal of College Student Development, 40*(4), 377–395.

Chang, M. J. (2001). The positive educational effects of racial diversity on campus. In *Diversity challenged: Evidence on the impact of affirmative action,* ed. G. Orfield with M. Kurlaender, 175–186. Cambridge, MA: Civil Rights Project, Harvard University and Harvard Education Publishing Group.

Chang, M. J., Witt, D., Jones, J., & Hakuta, K., eds. (2003). *Compelling interest: Examining the evidence on racial dynamics in colleges and universities.* Palo Alto, CA: Stanford University Press.

Chapman, C., Laird, J., and KewalRamani, A. (2010). *Trends in High School Dropout and Completion Rates in the United States: 1972–2008* (NCES 2011–012). National Center for Education Statistics, Institute of Education Sciences, US Department of Education. Washington, DC. Retrieved from http://nces.ed.gov/pubsearch.

Charles, C. Z. (2003). Processes of racial residential segregation. In *Urban Inequality Evidence from Four Cities,* ed. Alice O'Connor, Chris Tilly, & Lawrence D. Bobo, 217–271. New York: Russell Sage.

Chavez, L., & Frankenberg, E. (2009). *Integration defended: Berkeley Unified's strategy to maintain school diversity.* Berkeley: Chief Justice Earl Warren Institute on Race, Ethnicity, and Diversity, Boalt Law School, University of California, Berkeley.

Cheung, A. C. K., & Slavin, R. (2012). Effective reading programs for Spanish-dominant English language learners (ELLs) in the elementary grades: A synthesis of research. The Best Evidence Encyclopedia. Retrieved from www.bestevidence.org.

Children's Defense Fund. (2001). *Children's Defense Fund calculations, based on data from U.S. Bureau of the Census.* June.

Chubb, J., & Moe, T. (1990). *Politics, markets, and America's schools.* Washington, DC: Brookings Institution.

Citizens Commission on Civil Rights. (1983). *A decent home: A report on the continuing failure of the federal government to provide equal housing opportunities.* Washington, DC: Citizens Commission.

Civil Rights Project (2006). *Brief of 533 Social Scientists as Amici Curiae in Support of Respondents.* Filed in U.S. Supreme Court. Retrieved from http://civilrightsproject.ucla.edu/ legal-developments/court-decisions/statement-of-american-social-scientists-of-research-o n-school-desegregation-submitted-to-us-supreme-court/amicus_parents_v_seatle.pdf

Clotfelter, C. (2004). *After* Brown: *The rise and retreat of school desegregation.* Princeton, NJ: Princeton University Press.

Clotfelter, C., Glennie, E., Ladd, H., & Vigdor, J. (2008). Teacher bonuses and teacher retention in low performing schools: Evidence from the North Carolina $1,800 teacher bonus program. *Public Finance Quarterly*, 36(1), 63–87.

Clotfelter, C. T., Ladd, H. F., & Vigdor, J. L. (2007). Teacher credentials and student achievement: Longitudinal analysis with student fixed effects. *Economics of Education Review*, 26(6), 673–682.

Cloward, R., & Piven, F. F. (1975). *The politics of turmoil: Poverty, race, and the urban crisis.* New York: Vintage Books.

Cohen, D., & Moffitt, S. (2009). *The ordeal of equality: Did federal regulation fix the schools?* Cambridge, MA: Harvard University Press.

Cohen, M. (2005). Reconsidering schools and the welfare state. *History of Education Quarterly*, 45, 511–537.

Cohen, M., & Piquero, A. (2009). New evidence on the monetary value of saving a high-risk youth. *Journal of Quantitative Criminology*, 25(1), 25–49.

Cohen, S. A. (1987). Instructional alignment: Searching for the magic bullet. *Educational Researcher*, 16(8), 16–20.

Coleman, J. S., Campbell, E. Q., Hobson, C. J., McPartland, J., Mood, A. M., Weinfeld, F. D., York, R. L. (1966). *Equality of educational opportunity.* Washington, DC: US Government Printing Office.

College Board (1985). *Equality and excellence: The educational status of Black Americans.* New York: College Entrance Examination Board.

Collin, R. W., & Collin, R. M. (1997). Urban environmentalism and race. In *Urban planning and the African American community: In the shadows*, ed. June Manning Thomas & Marsha Ritzdorf, 200–236. Beverly Hills, CA: Sage Publications.

Common Core State Standards Initiative. (2010). *National Governors Association and state education chiefs launch common state academic standards.* June 2. Retrieved from http://www.corestandards.org/articles/8-national-governors-association-and-state-education-chiefs-launch-common-state-academic-standards.

Conchas, G. (2006). *The Color of Success: Race and High-Achieving Urban Youth.* New York: Teachers College Press.

Conchas, G. (2010). Structuring failure and success: Understanding the variability in Latino school engagement. In *Beyond stereotypes: Minority children of immigrants*, ed. R. Saran and R. Diaz, 155–182. Rotterdam, The Netherlands: Sense Publishers.

Constantine, J., Player, D., Silva, T., Hallgren, K., Grider, M., & Deke, K. (2009). *An evaluation of teachers trained through different routes to certification.* Princeton, NJ: Mathematica Policy Research. Retrieved from http://ies.ed.gov/ncee/pubs/20094043/pdf/20094043.pdf.

Cook, P., & Ludwig, J. (1997). Weighing the "burden of 'acting White'": Are there race differences in attitudes toward education? *Journal of Policy Analysis and Management*, 16(2), 256–278.

Cooper, H., Nye, B., Charlton, K., Lindsay, J., & Greathouse, S. (1996). The effects of summer vacation on achievement test scores: A narrative and meta-analytic review. *Review of Education Research*, 66(3), 227–268.

Corcoran, S. P., & Jennings, J. L. (2009). *Review of "An evaluation of teachers trained through different routes to certification: Final report."* Boulder, CO: National Education Policy. Retrieved from http://nepc.colorado.edu/thinktank/review-evaluation-of-teachers.

Cottrell, M. (2011). In Chicago, even wealthy black families live in poor neighborhoods. *Chicago Muckraker*, Chicago Reporter, August 8.

Cottrol, R., Diamond, R, & Ware, L. (2003). *Brown v. Board of Education: Caste, culture, and the Constitution.* Lawrence: University Press of Kansas.

Cosentino de Cohen, K., & Clewell, B. (2007). Putting English language learners on the map. Washington, DC: Urban Institute. Retrieved from http://www.urban.org/UploadedPDF/311468_ell.pdf.

Crain. R. L. (1973). *Southern schools: An evaluation of the effects of the emergency school assistance program and of school desegregation.* Chicago: National Opinion Research Center.

Crain, R., Allen, A., Thaler, R., Sullivan, D., Zellman, G., Little, J.W., & Quigley, D. (1999). *The effects of academic career magnet education on high schools and their graduates.* Berkeley: National Center for Research in Vocational Education, University of California.

Crane, J. (1991). The Epidemic Theory of Ghettos and Neighborhood Effects on Dropping Out and Teenage Childbearing. *American Journal of Sociology,* 96(5), 1226–1259.

CREDO. (2009). *Multiple choice: Charter school performance in 16 states.* Palo Alto, CA. Retrieved from http://credo.stanford.edu/reports/MULTIPLE_CHOICE_CREDO.pdf and http://www.mathematica-mpr.com/publications/PDFs/education/charter_school_impacts.pdf.

Cuban, L. (2004). *The blackboard and the bottom line: Why schools can't be businesses.* Cambridge, MA: Harvard University Press.

Cullen, J., Jacob, B. A., & Levitt, S., (2005). The impact of school choice on student outcomes: An analysis of the Chicago Public Schools. *Journal of Public Economics,* 89(5–6), 729–760.

Cunha, F., Heckman, J. J., Lochner, L. J., & Masterov, D. V. (2006). Interpreting the evidence on life cycle skill formation. In *Handbook of the economics of education,* ed. E. A. Hanushek & F. Welch, 697–812. Amsterdam: North-Holland.

Cutler, D., & Lleras-Muney, A. (2010). Understanding differences in health behaviors by education. *Journal of Health Economics,* 29, 1–28.

D'Souza, D. (1995). *The end of racism: Principles for a multicultural society.* New York: Free Press.

Darder, A. (1991). *Culture and power in the classroom: A critical foundation for bicultural education.* New York: Bergin & Garvey.

Dallek, R. (1998). *Flawed giant: Lyndon Johnson and his times, 1961–1973.* New York: Oxford University Press.

Darling-Hammond, L. (1999). Testimony before the Supreme Court of the State of New York in *Campaign for Fiscal Equity v. State of New York.* December 14. Retrieved from http://finance.tc-library.org/ContentTypes.asp?cgi=5.

Darling-Hammond, L. (2000). Teacher quality and student achievement: A review of state policy evidence. Educational Policy Analysis Archives, 8 (1). Retrieved from http://epaa.asu.edu/epaa/v8n1.

Darling-Hammond, L. (2003). Access to quality teaching: An analysis of inequality in California's public schools, *Santa Clara Law Review,* 43, 101–239.

Darling-Hammond, L. (2004). Inequality and the right to learn: Access to qualified teachers in California's public schools. *Teachers College Record,* 106(10), 1936–1966.

Darling-Hammond, L. (2007). A Marshall Plan for teaching: What it will really take to leave no child behind. *Education Week.* Retrieved from http://www.edweek.org/ew/articles/2007/01/10/18hammond.h26.html.

Darling-Hammond, L. (2009). *Educational opportunity and alternative certification: More evidence and more questions.* Palo Alto, CA: Stanford Center for Opportunity Policy in Education, Stanford University. Retrieved from http://edpolicy.stanford.edu/pages/pubs/pub_docs/mathematica_policy_brief.pdf.

Darling-Hammond, L. (2010). *The flat world and education: How America's commitment to equity will determine our future.* New York: Teachers College Press.

Darling-Hammond, L., & Bransford, J., eds. (2005). *Preparing teachers for a changing world: What teachers should learn and be able to do*. San Francisco, CA: Jossey-Bass.

Darling-Hammond, L., Holtzman, D., Gatlin, S. J., & Heilig, J. V. (2005). Does teacher preparation matter? Evidence about teacher certification, Teach for America, and teacher effectiveness. *Education Policy Analysis Archives*, 13(42). Retrieved from http://epaa.asu.edu/epaa/v13n42/.

Darling-Hammond, L., Ross, P., & Milliken, M. (2007). High school size, organization, and content: What matters for student success? In *Brookings Papers on Education Policy 2006/07*, ed. Frederick Hess, 163–204. Washington, DC: Brookings Institution Press.

Daro, D., & Dodge, K. A. (2010). Strengthening home-visiting intervention policy: Expanding reach, building knowledge. In *Investing in young children: New directions in federal preschool and early childhood policy*, ed. R. Haskins & W. S. Barnett, 79–88. Washington, DC: Center on Children and Families at Brookings and the National Institute for Early Education Research.

David, J., Woodworth, K., Grant, E., Lopez-Torkos, A., & Young, V. (2006). *Bay Area KIPP Schools: A study of early implementation, first year report 2004–205*. Menlo Park, CA: SRI International.

Davies, G. (1996). *From opportunity to entitlement: The transformation and decline of Great Society liberalism*. Lawrence: University Press of Kansas.

Davies, G. (2007). *See government grow: Education politics from Johnson to Reagan*. Lawrence: University Press of Kansas.

Dawkins, M. P., & Braddock J. H. (1994). The continuing significance of desegregation: School racial composition and African American inclusion in American society. *Journal of Negro Education*, 63(3), 394–405.

DeBray, E. (2006). *Politics, ideology, and education: Federal policy during the Clinton and Bush administrations*. New York: Teachers College Press.

DeBray, E., McDermott, K., & Wohstetter, P. (2005). Introduction to the special issue on federalism reconsidered: The case of the No Child Left Behind Act. *Peabody Journal of Education*, 80, 1–18.

DeBray-Pelot, E., & McGuinn, P. (2009). The new politics of education: Analyzing the federal education policy landscape in the post-NCLB era. *Educational Policy*, 23, 15–42.

Decker, P. T., Mayer, D. P., & Glazerman, S. (2004). *The effects of Teach for America on students: Findings from a national evaluation*. Princeton, NJ: Mathematica

Dehyle, D. (1995). Navajo youth and Anglo racism: Cultural integrity and resistance. *Harvard Educational Review*, 6(3), 403–444.

DeLange, E. & Alter, L. (1947). Do you know what it means to miss New Orleans? [Performed by Louis Armstrong and sung by Billie Holiday]. Debuted in *New Orleans* [Motion Picture].

DeLisi, M, Kosloski, A., Sween, M., Hachmeister, E. Moore, M. & Drury, A. (2010). Murder by numbers: Monetary costs imposed by a sample of homicide offenders. *Journal of Forensic Psychiatry and Psychology*, 21, 501–513.

Delpit, L. (1995). *Other people's children: Cultural conflict in the classroom*. New York: New Press. Distributed by W.W. Norton.

DeNavas-Walt, C., Proctor, B. D., & Lee, C. H. (2005). Income, poverty, and health insurance coverage in the United States: 2005. In *Current Population Reports*. Washington, DC: US Department of Commerce.

Denton, N. (2001). The persistence of segregations: Links between residential segregation and school segregation. In *In pursuit of a dream deferred: Linking housing and educational policy*, ed. J. Powell, G. Kearney, & V. Kay, 89–119. New York: Peter Lang.

Dewey, J. (1916). *Democracy and education*. New York: Macmillan.

Dewey, J. (1927). *The public and its problems*. New York: Capricorn.

Dewey, J. (1938). *Experience and education*. New York: Collier.

Deyhle, D. (1995). Navajo youth and Anglo racism: Cultural integrity and resistance. *Harvard Educational Review*, 65(3), 403–444.

Dickinson, D. K. (2011). Teachers' language practices and academic outcomes of preschool children. *Science*, 333, 964–967.

Diette, T. (2005). The algebra obstacle: Access, race, and the math achievement gap. Unpublished PhD diss., University of North Carolina, Chapel Hill.

DiMaggio, P. (1982). Cultural capital and school success: The impact of status culture participation on the grades of U.S. high school students. *American Sociological Review*, 47(April), 180–201.

DiMaggio, P., & Mohr, J. (1985). Cultural capital, educational attainment, and marital selection. *American Journal of Sociology*, 90(6), 1231–1261.

DiPasquale, D., & Wheaton, W. C. (1996). *Urban Economics and Real Estate Markets*, Englewood Cliffs, NJ: Prentice Hall.

District of Columbia Public Schools (n.d.). *Facts and Statistics: 2011–2012. General Data about DCPS: Schools, Demographics and Performance*. Retrieved from http://dc.gov/DCPS/About+DCPS/Who+We+Are/Facts+and+Statistics.

Downes T. A., & Pogue, T. F. (1994). Adjusting school aid formulas for the higher cost of educating disadvantaged students. *National Tax Journal*, 47(1), 89–110.

Dreeben, R. (1987). Closing the Divide: What Teachers and Administrators Can Do to Help Black Students Reach Their Reading Potential, *American Educator*, 11(4), 28–35.

Duncan, A., interviewed by Rotherham, A. J. (2011). Back-to-School Special: Arne Duncan goes off script. *Time*, August 25. Retrieved from http://www.time.com/time/nation/article/0,8599,2090299,00.html.

Duncan, G. J., & Magnuson, K. (2005). Can family socioeconomic resources account for racial and ethnic test score gaps? *Future of Children*, 15, 35–52.

Duncan, G. J., & Murnane, R. (2011). *Whither opportunity? Rising inequality, schools, and children's life chances*. New York: Russell Sage Foundation.

Duncan, G. J., Dowsett, C., Claessens, A., Magnuson, K., Huston, A., Klebanov, P., et al. (2007). School readiness and later achievement. *Developmental Psychology*, 43, 1428–1446.

Duncombe,W., Ruggiero, J., & Yinger, J. (1996). Alternative approaches to measuring the cost of education. In *Holding schools accountable: Performance-based reform in* education, ed. H. F. Ladd, 327–356. Washington, DC: Brookings Institution.

Eaton, S. (2001). *The other Boston busing story: What is won and lost across the boundary line*. New Haven, CT: Yale University Press.

EdSource. (2002). *Is California on the right track?* EdSource Report. May.

Edmonds, R. (1979). Effective schools for the urban poor. *Educational Leadership*, 37, 15–24.

Educational Testing Service (2002). *A national priority: Americans speak on teacher quality*. Princeton, NJ: Educational Testing Service.

Education Trust. (2006). *Funding gaps 2006*. Retrieved from http://www.edtrust.org/sites/edtrust.civicactions.net/files/publications/files/FundingGap2006.pdf.

Egbuonu, L., & Starfield, B. (1982). Child health and social status. *Pediatrics*, 69, 550–557.

ELL Working Group Recommendations for the Reauthorization of ESEA (2011). Retrieved from http://ellpolicy.org/wp-content/uploads/ESEAFinal.pdf.

Engel, M. (2000). *The struggle for control of public education: Market ideology vs. democratic values*. Philadelphia: Temple University Press.

Entwisle, D. R., Alexander, K. L., & Olson, L. S. (1998). *Children, schools, and inequality*. Boulder, CO: Westview Press.

Epstein, D. (2011). *Measuring inequity in school funding*. Report. Washington, DC: Center for American Progress.

Farkas, G., Lleras, C., & Maczuga, S. (2002). Does oppositional culture exist in minority and poverty peer groups? *American Sociological Review, 67*(1), 148–155.

Evans, D. (2010). Robert E. Lee is dead. In Evans, *Before you suffocate your own fool self*, 199–229. New York: Riverhead Books.

Evers, W. (2002). No more excuses, *NW Brainstorm*, February 2002, 22–24, as cited in Bracey, http://www.america-tomorrow.com/bracey/EDDRA/k0610bra.pdf.

Farkas, G., Grobe, R. P., Sheehan, D., & Shuan, Y. (1990). Cultural resources and school success: Gender, ethnicity, and poverty groups within an urban school district. *American Sociological Review, 55*, 127–142.

Farley, R. (2011). The waning of American apartheid? *Contexts, 10*(3), 36–43. Retrieved from www.psc.isr.umich.edu/pubs/pdf/rp617.pdf.

Feldman, R. [writer/producer]. (1989). Harriet Tubman Elementary, Newark, NJ. [Television series episode]. In *Against all odds: A tale of two cities*. Seacaucus, NJ: WWOR TV.

Feigenbaum, H., Henig, J., & Hamnett, C. (1999). *Shrinking the state: The political underpinnings of privatization*. Cambridge: Cambridge University Press.

Feistritzer, E. C. & Harr, C. K. (2010). *Alternative routes to teacher certification*. Washington, DC: National Center for Alternative Certification. Retrieved from http://www.teach-now.org/RESEARCH%20ABOUT%20ALTERNATE%20ROUTES.pdf.

Ferguson, A. A. (2000). *Bad boys: Public schools in the making of black masculinity*. Ann Arbor: University of Michigan Press.

Ferguson, R. F. (1991). Paying for public education: New evidence on how and why money matters. *Harvard Journal on Legislation, 28*(2), 465–498.

Ferguson, R. (1998). Teachers' perceptions and expectations and the black-white test score gap. In *The Black-White Test Score Gap*, ed. C. Jencks & M. Phillips, 273–317. Washington, DC: Brookings Institution Press.

Ferguson, R. F. (2005). *Toward skilled parenting and transformed schools inside a national movement for excellence with equity*. Prepared for the Achievement Gap Initiative (AGI) and O'Connor Project at Harvard University. October 13. Retrieved from http://devweb.tc.columbia.edu/manager/symposium/Files/71_Ferguson_paper.ed.pdf.

Fetler, M. (1999). High school staff characteristics and mathematics test results. *Education Policy Analysis Archives, 7* (March 24). Retrieved from http://epaa.asu.edu.

Fine, K. P. (2009). *Invisible hands: The making of the conservative movement from the New Deal to Reagan*. New York: Norton.

Fine, M. (1991). *Framing dropouts: Notes on the politics of an urban public high school*. Albany: State University of New York Press.

Fine, M., Burns, A., Payne, Y., & Torre, M. (2004). Civics lessons: The color and class of betrayal. *Teachers College Record, 106*(11), 2193–2223.

Finn, C. E. Jr. (1988). Education policy and the Reagan administration: A large but incomplete success. *Educational Policy, 2*, 343–360.

Finn, C. E. Jr. (2004). Short reviews of new reports and books. *Education Gadfly, 4*(22). June 3. Retrieved from http://www.edexcellence.net/publications-issues/gadfly/national/gadfly060304.html.

Finn, J. D., & Achilles, C. M. (2003, Fall). Class size: Counting students can count. *Research Points: Essential Information for Education Policy*, 1(2), 1–4. Washington, DC: American Educational Research Association. Retrieved from http://www.aera.net/uploadedFiles/Journals_and_Publications/Research_Points/RP_Fall03.pdf.

Fisher, C. E., Berliner, D. C., Filby, N. N., Marliave, R., Cahen, L. S., & Dishaw, M. M. (1980). Teacher behaviors, academic learning time and student achievement: An overview. In *Time to learn*, ed. C. Denham & A. Lieberman, 7–22. Washington, DC: National Institute of Education.

Fix, M., & Struyk, R., eds. (1993). *Clear and convincing evidence: Measurement of discrimination in America*. Washington, DC: Urban Institute Press.

Flaxman, E., Guerrero, A., & Gretchen, D. (1999). *Career development effects of career magnets versus comprehensive schools* (MDS-803). Berkeley: National Center for Research in Vocational Education, University of California.

Florida, R. 2002. *The rise of the creative class*. New York: Harper Business.

Foley, D. E. (1991). Reconsidering anthropological explanations of ethnic school failure. *Anthropology and Education Quarterly*, 22(1), 60–86.

Ford, D. (1995). Desegregating gifted education: A need unmet. *Journal of Negro Education*, 64(1), 52–62.

Fordham, S. (1993). Those loud black girls: (Black) women, silence, and gender passing in the academy. *Anthropology and Education Quarterly*, 24(1), 3–32.

Fordham, S. (1996). *Blacked out: Dilemmas of race, identity, and success at Capital High*. Chicago: University of Chicago Press.

Fordham, S., & Ogbu, J. (1986). Black students' school success: Coping with the 'burden of acting white'. *Urban Review*, 18, 176–206.

Forman, J. (2005). The secret history of school choice: How progressives got there first. *Georgetown Law Journal*, 93, 1287.

Forrest, C. B., Starfield, B., Riley, A. W., & Kang, M. (1997). The impact of asthma on the health status of adolescents. *Pediatrics*, 99(2), February, E1.

Frankenberg, E., & Orfield, G., eds. (2012). *The resegregation of suburban schools: A hidden crisis in american education*. Cambridge, MA: Harvard Education Press.

Frankenberg, E., Siegel-Hawley, G., & Wang, J. (2011) Choice without equity: Charter school segregation. *Educational Policy Analysis Archives*, 19(1). Retrieved from http://epaa.asu.edu/ojs/article/view/779.

Frede, E. C., & Barnett, W. S. (2011). New Jersey's Abbott pre-k program: A model for the nation. In *The pre-k debates: Current controversies and issues*, ed. E. Zigler, W. Gilliam, & W. S. Barnett, 191–196. Baltimore: Brookes Publishing.

Frede, E. C., Barnett, W. S., Jung, K., Lamy, C., & Figueras, A. (2010). Abbott Preschool Program Longitudinal Effects Study: Year one findings. In *Childhood programs and practices in the first decade of life: A human capital integration*, ed. A. J. Reynolds, A. J. Rolnick, M. M. Englund, & J. A. Temple, 214–234. New York: Cambridge University Press.

Frede, E. C., Jung, K., Barnett, W. S., & Figueras, A. (2009). *The APPLES Blossom: Abbott Preschool Program Longitudinal Effects Study (APPLES) Preliminary results through 2nd grade*. New Brunswick, NJ: National Institute for Early Education Research.

Freeman, C. E., Scafidi, B., & Sjoquest, D. L. (2005). Racial segregation in Georgia public schools, 1994–2001: Trends, causes, and impact on teacher quality. In *School Resegregation: Must the South turn back?* ed. John Charles Boger & Gary Orfield, 48–163. Chapel Hill: University of North Carolina Press.

Freire, P. (2001 [1970]). *Pedagogy of the oppressed.* 30th anniversary edition. New York: Continuum.

Friedman, M. (1962). *Capitalism and freedom.* Chicago: University of Chicago Press.

Frey, W. H. (2011). *America's diverse future: Initial glimpses at the U.S. child population from the 2010 census.* April. Washington, DC: Brookings Institution Metropolitan Studies Program.

Fuller, B., ed. (2000). *Inside charter schools: The paradox of radical decentralization.* Cambridge, MA: Harvard University Press.

Fuller, B., Elmore, R., & Orfield, G. (1996). *Who chooses? Who looses?* New York: Teachers College Press.

Fuller, B., Gawlik, M., Gonzalez, E. K., Park, S., & Gibbings, G. (2003). *Charter schools and inequality: National disparities in funding, teacher quality, and student support.* Working Paper Series 03-2. Berkeley: Policy Analysis for California Education.

Galster, G., & Godfrey, E. (2005). By words and deeds: racial steering by real estate agents in the U.S. in 2000. *Journal of the American Planning Association, 71*(3), 251–268.

Galston, W. (2004) Civic education and political participation. *PS Online,* April. 263–266. Retrieved from http://www.apsanet.org/imgtest/CivicEdPoliticalParticipation.pdf.

Gamoran, A. (1987). The stratification of high school learning opportunities. *Sociology of Education, 60*(3), 135–155.

Gamoran, A., & Mare, R. (1989). Secondary school tracking and educational inequality: Compensation, reinforcement or neutrality? *American Journal of Sociology, 94*(5), 1146–1483.

Gándara, P., Rumberger, R., Maxwell-Jolly, J., & Callahan, R. (2003). English learners in California schools: Unequal resources; unequal outcomes. *Educational Policy Analysis Archives.* Retrieved from http://epaa.asu.edu/epaa/v11n36/.

Gándara, P., Maxwell-Jolly, J., & Driscoll, A. (2005). *Listening to teachers of English learners.* Santa Cruz, CA: Center for the Future of Teaching and Learning.

Gándara, P., & Rumberger, R. (2008). Defining the resource needs for English learners. *Education Finance and Policy, 3,* 130–148.

Gándara, P., & Hopkins, M. (2010). *Forbidden language: English learners and restrictive language policies.* New York: Teachers College Press.

Gándara, P. & Orfield, G. (2013). Segregating Arizona's English learners: A return to the Mexican Room? *Teachers College Record, 114*(9), 2–3. Retrieved from http://www.tcrecord.org ID Number 16600.

Garcia, G., McKoon, G., & August, D. (2006). Language and literacy assessment of language-minority students. In *Developing literacy in second-language learners: Report of the National Literacy Panel on Language-Minority Children and Youth,* ed. D. August & T. Shanahan, 597–625. Mahwah, NJ: Lawrence Erlbaum Associates.

Garfinkel, I., Rainwater, L., & Smeeding, T. (2010). *Wealth and welfare states: Is America a laggard or leader?* New York: Oxford University Press.

Garmston, R.J. (1998). Becoming expert teachers (part 1). *Journal of Staff Development, 19*(1). Retrieved from http://www.nsdc.org/library/publications/jsd/garmston191.cfm.

Garofano, A., Sable, J., & Hoffman, L. (2008). *Characteristics of the 100 largest public elementary and secondary school districts in the United States: 2004–05.* US Department of Education, National Center for Education Statistics. Washington, DC: US Government Printing Office.

Gay, G. (2000). *Culturally responsive teaching: Theory, research, and practice.* New York: Teachers College Press.

General Account Office (GAO) of the United States. (1983). *Siting of hazardous waste landfills and their correlation with racial and economic status of surrounding communities.* Washington, DC: US Government Printing Office.

General Accounting Office (GAO) of the United States. (1994). *Elementary school children: Many change schools frequently, harming their education.* GAO/HEHS-94-45. Washington, DC: ED 369-526.

General Accounting Office (GAO) of the United States. (1999). *Lead poisoning: Federal health care programs are not effectively reaching at-risk children.* GAO/HEHS-99-18. Washington, DC: Author.

General Accounting Office of the United States (2001). *School vouchers: Publicly funded programs in Cleveland and Milwaukee: Report to the Honorable Judd Gregg, U.S. Senate.* Washington, DC: Author.

Genesee, F., & Gándara, P. (1999). Bilingual education programs: A cross-national perspective, *Journal of Social Issues, 55,* 665-686.

Genesee, F., Lindholm-Leary, K., Saunders, W., & and Christian, D. (2006). *Educating English language learners: A synthesis of research evidence.* New York: Cambridge University Press.

Gibson, C., & Levine, P. (2003). *The civic mission of schools.* New York: Carnegie Corporation of New York and Washington, DC: the Center for Information and Research on Civic Learning.

Gibson, M. (1988). *Accommodation without assimilation.* Ithaca, NY: Cornell University Press.

Gilbert, N. (2002).*Transformation of the welfare state: The silent surrender of public responsibility.* New York: Oxford University Press.

Gilbert, N., & Gilbert, B. (1989). *The enabling state: Modern welfare capitalism in America.* New York: Oxford University Press.

Gill, D. (2000). *Becoming good: Building moral character.* Downers Grove, IL: Intervarsity Press.

Gitomer, D. (2007). *Teacher quality in a changing policy landscape: Improvements in the teacher pool.* Princeton, NJ: Educational Testing Service.

Glass, G. V, Cahen, L. S., Smith, M. L, Filby, N. N. (1982). *School class size: Research and policy.* Beverly Hills, CA: Sage.

Goddard, Y., & Goddard, R. D. (2007). A theoretical and empirical investigation of teacher collaboration for school improvement and student achievement in public elementary schools. *Teachers College Record, 109*(4) (April), 877-896.

Goe, L. (2002). Legislating equity: The distribution of emergency permit teachers in California. *Educational Policy Analysis Archives online, 10*(42). Retrieved from http://epaa.asu.edu/epaa/v10n42/.

Goldberg, Milton, & Traiman, Susan. (2001). Why business backs education standards. In *Brookings Papers on Education, 2001,* ed. Diane Ravitch, 75-127. Washington, DC: Brookings Institution Press.

Goldhaber, D. (2008). Teachers matter, but effective teacher quality policies are elusive. In *Handbook of Research in Education Finance and Policy,* ed. H. F. Ladd & E. B. Fiske, 146-65. New York: Routledge.

Goldhaber, D. D. & Brewer, D. J. (2000). Does teacher certification matter? High school certification status and student achievement. *Educational Evaluation and Policy Analysis, 22,* 129-145.

Goldin, C., & Katz, L. F. (2008). *The race between education and technology.* Cambridge, MA: Harvard University Press.

Goluboff, Risa. (2007). *The lost promise of civil rights.* Cambridge, MA: Harvard University Press.

Good, T., Grouws, D. A., & Beckerman, T. M. (1978). Curriculum pacing: Some empirical data in mathematics. *Journal of Curriculum Studies, 10*, 72–75.

Goodwin, C. (1979). *The Oak Park strategy.* Chicago: University of Chicago Press.

Gormley, W. T., Phillips, D., & Gayer, T. (2008). Preschool programs can boost school readiness. *Science, 320*, 1723–1724.

Gould, M. C., & Gould, H. (2003). A clear vision for equity and opportunity. *Phi Delta Kappan, 85*(4) (December), 324–328.

Green, D. (2010). *Summary of* "The teachers' unions' last stand: How Obama's Race to the Top could revolutionize public education," *by Steven Brill.* Retrieved from http://www.drdoug-green.com/wp-content/Unions-Last-Stand.pdf.

Greenwald, R., Hedges, L.V., & Laine, R. D. (1996a). The effect of school resources on student achievement. *Review of Educational Research, 66*(1), 361–396.

Greenwald, R. Hedges, L.V., & Laine, R.D. (1996b). Interpreting research on school resources and student achievement: A rejoinder to Hanushek. *Review of Educational Research, 66*(3), 411–416.

Grissmer, D. W., Flanagan, A., Kawata, J., & Williamson, S. (2000). *Improving student achievement: What NAEP state test scores tell us.* Santa Monica, CA: RAND Report. Available online. http://www.rand.org/publications/MR/MR924.

Grosjean, F. (2010). *Bilingual: Life and reality.* Cambridge, MA: Harvard University Press.

Guggenheim, D. (Director). (2010). *Waiting for Superman* [motion picture]. Los Angeles: Paramount Vantage.

Gurin, P. (1999). Selections from the compelling need for diversity in higher education: Expert report of Patricia Gurin. *Equity & Excellence in Education, 32*(2), 36–62.

Gurin, P., Dey, E. L., Hurtado, S., & Gurin, G. (2002). Diversity and higher education: Theory and impact on educational outcomes. *Harvard Educational Review, 72*(3), 330–366.

Gurin, P., Nagda, B. A., & Lopez, G. E. (2004). The benefits of diversity in education for democratic citizenship. *Journal of Social Issues, 60*(1), 17–34.

Guryan, J. (2004). Desegregation and Black dropout rates. *American Economic Review, 94* (September), 919–943.

Guryan, J. (2001). *Does money matter? Regression-discontinuity estimates from education finance reform in Massachusetts.* NBER Working Paper 8269. Cambridge, MA.

Gutierrez, K., & Rogoff, B. (2003). Cultural ways of learning: Individual traits or repertoires of practice. *Educational Researcher, 32*(5), 19–25.

Gutmann, A. (1987). *Democratic education.* Princeton, NJ: Princeton University Press.

Gutmann, A. (1999). *Democratic education,* 2nd ed. Princeton, NJ: Princeton University Press.

Gutmann, A., & Thompson, D. (1996). *Democracy and disagreement.* Cambridge, MA: Harvard University Press.

Gutmann, A., & Thompson, D. (2004). *Why deliberative democracy?* Princeton, NJ: Princeton University Press.

Haberman, M. (1991). The pedagogy of poverty versus good teaching. *Phi Delta Kappan, 73*(4), 290–294.

Hacker, J. (2004). Privatizing risk without privatizing the welfare state: The hidden politics of social policy retrenchment in the United States. *American Political Science Review, 98*, 243–260.

Hacker, J. (2006). *The great risk shift.* New York: Oxford University Press.

Hacker, J., & Pierson, P. (2010). *Winner-take-all politics: How Washington made the rich richer and turned its back on the middle class.* New York: Simon and Schuster.

Hair, E., Halle, T., Terry-Humen, E., Lavelle, B., & Calkins, J. (2006). Children's school readiness in the ECLS-K: Predictions to academic, health, and social outcomes in first grade. *Early Childhood Research Quarterly, 21,* 431–454.

Hakuta, K., Butler, G., & Witt, D. (2000). *How long does it take English learners to attain proficiency?* Policy Report. Santa Barbara: Linguistic Minority Research Institute, University of California, Santa Barbara.

Hale, J. E. (1986). *Black children: Their roots, culture and learning styles.* Baltimore, MD: Johns Hopkins University Press.

Hale, J. E. (2001). Learning while Black: Creating educational excellence for African American children. Baltimore, MD: Johns Hopkins University Press.

Halfon, N., & Newacheck, P. W. (1993). Childhood asthma and poverty: Differential impacts and utilization of health services. *Pediatrics, 91*(January), 56–61.

Halle, T., Forry, N., Hair, E., Perper, K., Wandner, L.,Wessel, J., & Vick, J. (2009). *Disparities in early learning and development: Lessons from the Early Childhood Longitudinal Study–Birth Cohort (ECLS–B).* Washington, DC: Child Trends.

Hallinan, M. (1994). Tracking from theory to practice. *Sociology of Education, 67*(2), 79–91.

Halpern, S. (1995). *On the limits of the law: The ironic legacy of Title VI of the Civil Rights Act.* Baltimore, MD: Johns Hopkins University Press.

Hanushek, E. A. (1996). *School resources and achievement in Maryland.* Baltimore: Maryland State Department of Education.

Hanushek, E. A. (2003). The structure of analysis and argument in plaintiff expert reports for *Williams v. State of California.* Retrieved from http://www.decentschools.org/expert_reports/hanushek_report.pdf.

Hanushek, E. A., Kain, J. & Rivkin, S. (2006). *New evidence about Brown v. Board of education: The complex effects of school racial composition on achievement.* NBER Working Paper No. 8741.

Hanushek, E. A., & Rivkin, S. G. (2009). Harming the best: How schools affect the Black-White achievement gap. *Journal of Policy Analysis and Management, 28*(Summer), 366–393.

Harding, D. J. (2003). Counterfactual models of neighborhood effects: The effect of neighborhood poverty on dropping out and teenage pregnancy. *American Journal of Sociology, 109*(3), 676–719.

Hardy, L. (2006). Children at risk. *American School Board Journal, 193*(12), 17–21.

Harlow, C. W. (2003). *Education and correctional populations.* Bureau of Justice Statistics, Special Report: US Department of Justice, NCJ 195670.

Harms, T., Clifford. R. & Cryer, D. (1998). *The Early Childhood Environmental Rating Scale— Revised.* New York: Teachers College Press.

Harris, A. (2011). *Kids don't want to fail: Oppositional culture and the Black-White achievement gap.* Cambridge, MA: Harvard University Press.

Harris, D. J., & McArdle, N. (2004). *More than money: The spatial mismatch between where homebuyers of color can afford to live and where they actually reside.* Cambridge, MA: Harvard Civil Rights Project.

Harris, D. N., & Herrington, C. D. (2006). Accountability, standards, and the growing achievement gap: Lessons from the past half-century. *American Journal of Education, 112*(2), 209–238.

Harris, P. (2002). Learning-related visual problems in Baltimore City: A long-term program. *Journal of Optometric Vision Development, 33*(2), 75–115.

Hart, B., & Risley, T. (1995). *Meaningful differences in the everyday experience of young American children.* York, PA: Maple Press.

Hart, B., & Risley, T. (2003). The early catastrophe. The 30 million word gap by age 3. *American Educator, Spring*, 4–9.

Haskins, R., & Barnett, W. S. (2010). *Investing in young children: New directions in federal preschool and early childhood policy*. Washington, DC: Brookings Center on Children and Families, and New Brunswick, NJ: National Institute for Early Education Research.

Hawk, P., Coble, C. R., and Swanson, M. (1985). Certification: It does matter, *Journal of Teacher Education*, 36(3), 13–15.

Haycock, K. (2000). No more settling for less. *Thinking K-16*, 4(1), 3–8, 10–12. Washington, DC: Education Trust.

Haycock, K. (2005). A "can do" or "can't do" profession? *The School Administrator*, April, guest column.

Haycock, K. (2007a). Can educators close the achievement gap? *Journal of Staff Development*, 28(1).

Haycock, K. (2007b). Letter. Report adds fuel to belief in "demographic" destiny. *Education Week*, 26(March 7), 29.

Heckman, J. J. (2006). Skill formation and the economics of investing in disadvantaged children. *Science*, 312, 1900–1902.

Heckman, J. J. (2008). The case for investing in disadvantaged young children. In *Big ideas for children: Investing in our nation's future*, ed. First Focus, 49–66. Washington, DC: First Focus.

Hedges, L. V., Laine, R. D., & Greenwald, R. (1994). Does money matter? A meta-analysis of studies of the effects of differential school inputs on student outcomes. *Educational Research*, 23(3), 5–14.

Heneman, E. G. III, & Milanowski, A. T., (1999). Teacher attitudes about teacher bonuses under school-based performance award programs. *Journal of Personnel Evaluation in Education*, 12(4), 327–341.

Henig, J. (1994). *Rethinking school choice: Limits of the market metaphor*. Princeton, NJ: Princeton University Press.

Henig, J. (2008). *Spin cycle; How research is used in the public debates: The case of charter schools*. New York: Russell Sage Foundation.

Henig, J. (2009). Education policy from 1980 to the present: The politics of privatization. In *Conservatism and American political development*, ed. Brian Glenn & Steven Teles, 291–317. New York: Oxford University Press.

Herbert, B. (2011). Separate and unequal. *New York Times*, March 21. Retrieved from: http://www.nytimes.com/2011/03/22/opinion/22herbert.html?ref=bobherbert.

Herbert, B. (2011). Losing our way. *New York Times*, May 25. Retrieved from http://www.nytimes.com/2011/03/26/opinion/26herbert.html?ref=bobherbert.

Hernandez, D., Denton, N., & McCartney, S. (2009). School-age children in immigrant families: Challenges and opportunities for America's schools. *Teachers College Record*, 111, 615–658. Retrieved from http://www.tcrecord.org ID Number: 15331.

Hertzman, C. (1999). The biological embedding of early experience and its effects on health in adulthood. *Annals of the New York Academy of Sciences*, 896, 85–95.

Hertzman, C., & Boyce, T. (2010). How experience gets under the skin to create gradients in developmental health. *Annual Review of Public Health*, 31, 329–347.Hess, F., & McGuinn, P. (2002). Seeking the mantle of "opportunity": Presidential politics and the educational metaphor, 1964–2000. *Educational Policy*, 16, 72–95.

Hill, H., Kapitula, L., & Umland, K. (2010). A validity argument approach to evaluating teacher value-added scores. *American Educational Research Journal*, 20(10), 1–38.

Hilliard, A. (1978). Equal educational opportunity and quality education. *Anthropology and Education Quarterly*, 9, 110–126.

Hoffman, K., Llags, C., & Snyder, T. (2003). *Status and trends in the education of Blacks*. NCES 2003–034. Washington, DC: US Department of Education, Office of Educational Research and Improvement.

Hofstadter, R. (1955). *The age of reform: From Bryan to FDR*. New York: Vintage Books.

Hollinger, D. A. (1995). *Postethnic America: Beyond multiculturalism*. New York: Basic Books.

Holme, J. J., & Wells, A. S. (2008). School choice beyond district borders: Lessons from the reauthorization of NCLB from interdistrict desegregation and open enrollment plans. In *Improving on No Child Left Behind Act: Getting education reform back on track*, ed. Richard Kahlenberg, 139–215. New York: Century Foundation Press.

Hoover, J. (2011). Denver judge's ruling on school funding levels blisters state's witnesses. *Denver Post*, December 11. Retrieved from http://www.denverpost.com/legislature/ci_19520710

Hopkins, M. (2011). Building on our teaching assets: Bilingual educators' pedagogy and policy implementation. Unpublished PhD diss., University of California, Los Angeles.

Horn, C. (2002). *The intersection of race, class and English Learner status*. Working Paper. Prepared for National Research Council.

Horn, L., & Nevill, S. 2006. *Profile of undergraduates in U.S. postsecondary education institutions: 2003–04*. Washington, DC: US Department of Education, National Center for Education Statistics.

Horvat, E. M., & Lewis, K. (2003). Reassessing the "burden of acting white": The importance of peer groups in managing academic success. *Sociology of Education*, 76(4), 265–280.

Hout, M., & Elliott, S. W. (Eds.). (2011). *Committee on Incentives and Test-Based Accountability in Public Education*. Washington, DC: National Research Council.

Howe, K. R. (1997). *Understanding equal educational opportunity: Social justice, democracy, and schooling*. New York: Teachers College Press.

Huber, L. P., Huidor, O., Malagón, M. C., Sánchez, G., & Solorzano, D. G. (2006). *Falling through the cracks: Critical transitions in the Latina/o educational pipeline*. CSRC Research Report No. 7. Los Angeles: University of California, Los Angeles, Chicano Studies Research Center.

Hulleman, C. E., & Barron, K. E. (2010). Performance pay and teacher motivation: Separating myth from reality. *Phi Delta Kappan*, 19(8), 27–31.

Hursh, D. (2007). Assessing "No Child Left Behind" and the rise of neoliberal education policies. *American Educational Research Journal*, 44(3), 49–18.

Ingersoll, R. (2003). *Is there really a teacher shortage?* Seattle, WA: Center for the Study of Teaching and Policy. Retrieved from http://www.boldapproach.org/index.php?id=01.

Institute on Race and Poverty. (2009). *Communities in crisis: Race and mortgage lending in the Twin Cities*. Minneapolis: University of Minnesota.

Irvine, J. J. (1990). *Black students and school failure: Policies, practices, and prescriptions*. Westport, CT: Greenwood Press.

Jackson, C. K., & Bruegmann, E. (2009). *Teaching students and teaching each other: The importance of peer learning for teachers*. National Bureau of Economic Research Working Paper No. 15202. Washington, DC: NBER. Retrieved from http://www.nber.org/papers/w15202.

Jacobs, B. A., & Lefgren, L. (2004). Remedial education and student achievement: A regression-discontinuity analysis. *Review of Economics and Statistics*, 86(1), 226–244.

Jacobs, L., & Skocpol, T. (2005). American democracy in an age of rising inequality. In *Inequality and American democracy: What we know and what we need to learn*, ed. Lawrence Jacobs and Theda Skocpol, 1–18. New York: Russell Sage Foundation.

Jeffrey, J. R. (1978). *Education for children of the poor: A study of the origins and implementation of the Elementary and Secondary Education Act of 1965.* Columbus: Ohio State University Press.

Jencks, C. (2002). Does inequality matter? *Daedalus, Winter, 131*(1), 49–65.

Jencks, C., Smith, M., Acland, H., Bane, M. J., Cohen, D., Gintis, H.,. Heynes, B., & Michelson, S. (1972). *Inequality: A reassessment of the effect of family and schooling in America.* New York: Basic Books.

Jennings, J. (2011). *Report: School districts at funding cliff.* Retrieved from http://www.washingtonpost.com/blogs/answer-sheet/post/report-school-districts-at-funding-cliff/2011/06/28/AGmGl2pH_blog.html.

Jennings, J. F. (1998). *Why national standards and tests: Politics and the quest for better schools.* Thousand Oaks, CA: Sage.

Jennings, J. L., & Corcoran, S. P. (2009). Beware of geeks bearing formulas: Reflections on growth models for school accountability. *Phi Delta Kappan, 90*(9) (May), 635–639.

Jerald, C. & Van Hook, K. (2011). *More than measurement: The TAP system's lessons learned for designing better teacher evaluation systems.* January. Retrieved from http://www.tapsystem.org/publications/eval_lessons.pdf.

Jersild, A. T., Thorndike, R. L., & Goldman, B. (1941). A further comparison of pupils in "activity" and "non-activity" schools. *Journal of Experimental Education, 9,* 307–309.

Jiaoyubu (Ministry of Education). (2001). *Yiwu Jiaoyu Kecheng Shezhi Fang'an (Curriculum Framework for Compulsory Education).* Retrieved from http://www.edu.cn/ke_cheng_775/20060323/t20060323_109425.shtml.

Jimerson, S. R., Anderson, G. E., & Whipple, A. (2002). *Winning the battle and losing the war: Examining the relation between grade retention and dropping out of high school. Psychology in Schools, 39*(4), 441–457.

Johnson, H. B., & Shapiro, T. M. (2003). Good neighborhoods, good schools: Race and the good choices of white families. In *White out: The continuing significance of racism,* ed. A. Doane, & E. Bonilla-Silva, 173–187. New York: Routledge.

Jolla, A. (2005). Closing the achievement gap by increasing access to the AIG (Academically and Intellectually Gifted) program: A case study of Southwest Elementary School. Unpublished Master's thesis, University of North Carolina at Chapel Hill.

Kaestle, C., & Smith, M. (1982). The federal role in elementary and secondary education, 1940–1980. *Harvard Educational Review, 52,* 384–408.

Kahlenberg, R. D. (2001). *All together now: Creating middle class schools through public school choice.* Washington, DC: Brookings Institution Press.

Kahlenberg, R. D. (2002). *Divided we fail: Coming together through public school choice: Report of the Century Foundation Task Force on the Common School.* New York: Century Foundation Press.

Kahlenberg, R. D. (2006). *A new way on school integration.* The Century Foundation. Retrieved from http://www.tcf.org/publications/education/schoolintegration.pdf.

Kahn, J., & Moore, K. A. (2010). What works for home visiting programs: Lessons from experimental evaluations of programs and interventions. *Child Trends Fact Sheet, 2008.* Washington, DC: Child Trends.

Kahne, J., & Middaugh, E. (2008). *Democracy for some: The civic opportunity gap in high school.* CIRCLE Working Paper 59. Washington, DC: The Center for Information and Research on Civic Learning. Kahne, J., & Sporte, S. (2008). Developing citizens: The impact of civic learning opportunities on students' commitment to civic participation. *American Educational Research Journal, 45*(3), 738–766.

Kain, J. F. (1986). The influence of race and income on racial segregation and housing policy. In *Housing desegregation and federal policy*, ed. J. Goering, 99–118. Chapel Hill: University of North Carolina Press.

Kang, N., & Hong, M. (2008). Achieving excellence in teacher workforce and equity in learning opportunities in South Korea. *Educational Researcher*, 37(4), 200–207.

Kantor, H. (1991). Education, social reform, and the state: ESEA and federal education policy in the 1960s. *American Journal of Education*, 100(November), 47–83.

Kantor, H., & Brenzel, B. (1993). Urban education and the "truly disadvantaged": The roots of the historical crisis. In *The "underclass" debate: Views from history*, ed. Michael B. Katz, 366–402. Princeton, NJ: Princeton University Press.

Kantor, H. & Lowe, R. (1995). Class, race, and the emergence of federal education policy: From the New Deal to the Great Society. *Educational Researcher*, 24, 4–11, 21.

Kantor, H., & Lowe, R. (2006). From New Deal to no deal: No Child Left Behind and the devolution of responsibility for equal opportunity. *Harvard Educational Review*, 70 (Winter), 474–502.

Kao, G., & Thompson, J. S. (2003). Racial and Ethnic Stratification in Educational Achievement and Attainment. *Annual Review of Sociology*, 29, 417–442.

Karoly, L. A., Ghosh-Dastidar, B., Zellman, G. L., Perlman, M., & Fernyhough, L. (2008). *Prepared to learn: The nature and quality of early care and education for preschool-age children in California*. Santa Monica, CA: RAND Corporation.

Katz, M. B. (2001). *The price of citizenship: Redefining the American welfare state*. New York: Henry Holt.

Katz, M. B. (2010). The American welfare state and social contract in hard times. *Journal of Policy History*, 22, 508–529.

Katz, M. B. (2012). *Why Don't American Cities Burn?* Philadelphia: University of Pennsylvania Press.

Katznelson, I. (1989). Was the Great Society a lost opportunity? In *The rise and fall of the New Deal order, 1930–1980*, ed. Steve Fraser and Gary Gerstle, 185–211. Princeton, NJ: Princeton University Press.

Katznelson, I. (2005). *When affirmative action was white: An untold history of racial inequality in twentieth century America*. New York: Norton.

Kaufman, J. E., & Rosenbaum, J. E. (1992). Education and employment of low-income Black youth in White suburbs. *Educational Evaluation and Policy Analysis*, 14(3), 229–240.

Kelly, S., & Price, H. (2011). The correlates of tracking policy: Opportunity hoarding, status competition, or technical-functional explanation? *American Educational Research Journal*, 48(3), 560–585.

Kennedy, D. (1999). *Freedom from fear: The American people in depression and war, 1929–1945*. New York: Oxford University Press.

Kerbow, D. (1996). Patterns of urban student mobility and local school reform. *Journal of Education for Students Placed At Risk*, 12, 147–169.

Kerner Commission (1968). *Report of the National Advisory Commission on Civil Disorders*. Washington, DC: US Government Printing Office.

KewalRamani, A., Gilbertson, L., Fox, M. A., & Provasnik, S. (2007). *Status and trends in the education of racial and ethnic minorities* (NCES 2007–039). Washington, DC: National Center for Education Statistics, Institute of Education Sciences, US Department of Education.

Khadaroo, S. T. (2010). Busing to end in Wake County, N.C. Goodbye, school diversity? *Christian Science Monitor*, March 24. Retrieved from http://www.csmonitor.com/USA/Education/2010/0324/Busing-to-end-in-Wake-County-N.C.-Goodbye-school-diversity.

Kindler, A. L. (2002). *Survey of the states' Limited English Proficient students and available educational programs and services: 2000–2001 summary report.* Washington, DC: National Clearinghouse for English Language Acquisition and Language Instruction Educational Programs.

King, J. E., ed., (2005). *Black education: A transformative research and action agenda for the new century.* Mahwah, NJ, Lawrence Erlbaum Associates.

Kirsch, I., Braun, H., Yamamoto, K., & Sum, A. (2007). *America's perfect storm. Three forces facing our nation's future.* Educational Testing Service Policy Brief. Princeton, NJ: ETS.

Klarman, M. (2004). *From Jim Crow to civil rights: The Supreme Court and the struggle for racial equality.* New York: Oxford University Press.

Klein, J. (2003). *For all these rights: Business, labor, and the shaping of America's public-private welfare state.* Princeton: Princeton University Press.

Koch, K. (2002). Hunger in America. *CQ Researcher, 10*(44), 1034–1055.

Kochman, T. (1981). *Black and White styles in conflict.* Chicago: University of Chicago Press.

Kotlowski, D. (2005). With all deliberate delay: Kennedy, Johnson, and school desegregation. *Journal of Policy History, 17,* 155–192.

Kovács, A. M., & Mehler, J. (2009). Cognitive gains in 7-month-old bilingual infants. *Proceedings of the National Academy of Sciences of the United States of America, 106*(16), 6556–6560.

Kornhaber, M. (1999). Enhancing equity in gifted education: A framework for examining assessments drawing on the theory of multiple intelligences. *High Ability Studies, 10*(2), 143–161.

Kozol, J. (1992). *Savage inequalities: Children in America's schools.* New York: Harper Perennial.

Kozol, J. (2005). *The shame of the nation: The restoration of apartheid schooling in America.* New York: Crown Books.

Kluger, R. (1976). *Simple justice.* NY: Vintage.

Kristof, N. (2006). Opening classroom doors. *New York Times,* April 30, 2006. Retrieved from http://select.nytimes.com/2006/04/30/opinion/30kristof.html?_r=1.

Krueger, A. B. (2000). Economic considerations and class size, Paper 447. Princeton University, Industrial Relations Section. Retrieved from www.irs.princeton.edu/pubs/working_papers.html.

Krueger, A. B. (2003). Economic considerations and class size. *Economic Journal, 113,* 485, F34–F63.

Ladson-Billings, G. (2006). From the achievement gap to the education debt: understanding achievement in U.S. schools. *Educational Researcher 35*(7), 3–12.

Ladson-Billings, G. (2009). *The dreamkeepers: Successful teachers of African American children,* 2nd edition. San Francisco: Jossey Bass.

Lake, R., & Huckfeldt, R. (1998). Social networks, social capital, and political participation. *Political Psychology, 19,* 567–584.

Lakoff, G., & Johnson, M. (2003). *Metaphors we live by,* 2nd ed. Chicago: University of Chicago Press.

Lamb, C. (2005). *Housing Segregation in Suburban America since 1960: Presidential and Judicial Politics.* New York: Cambridge University Press.

Lankford, H., Loeb, S., & Wyckoff, J. (2002). Teacher sorting and the plight of urban schools: A descriptive analysis. *Education Evaluation and Policy Analysis, 24*(1), 37–62.

Lankford, H. & Wyckoff, J. (2005). Why are schools racially segregated? Implications for school choice policies. In *School choice and diversity: What the evidence says,* ed. J. Scott, 9–26. Teachers College Press.

Lareau, A. (2003). *Unequal childhoods: class, race, and family life.* Berkeley, CA: University of California Press.

Lassiter, M. (2003). Suburban strategies: The volatile center in postwar American politics. In *The democratic experiment: New directions in American political history*, ed. Meg Jacobs, William Novak, & Julian Zelizer, 327–349. Princeton, NJ: Princeton University Press.

Lassiter, M. (2004). The suburban origins of "color-blind" conservatism: Middle-class consciousness in the Charlotte busing crisis. *Journal of Urban History, 4*, 549–582.

Lassiter, M., & Davis, A. (1998). Massive resistance revisited: Virginia's white moderates and the Byrd organization. In *The moderate's dilemma: Massive resistance to school desegregation in Virginia*, ed. Lassiter and Davis, 1–21. Charlottesville: University Press of Virginia.

Lauder, H., & Hughes, D. (1999). *Trading in futures: Why markets in education don't work*. Buckingham: Open University Press.

Lawler, E. E. (2008). *Strategic talent management: Lessons from the corporate world*. Paper presented to the Consortium for Policy Research in Education at the Wisconsin Center for Education Research. May 2. University of Wisconsin at Madison.

Lee, C. D. (2007). *Culture, literacy, and learning: Taking bloom in the midst of the whirlwind*. New York: Teachers College Press.

Lee, C. (2004). *Racial segregation and educational outcomes in metropolitan Boston*. Cambridge, MA: The Civil Rights Project at Harvard University.

Lee, J. (2002). Racial and ethnic achievement gap trends: Reversing the progress toward equity? *Educational Researcher, 31*(1), 3–12.

Lee, J. (2012). Asian American exceptionalism and stereotype promise. The Society Pages online. Retrieved from http://thesocietypages.org/papers/asian-american-exceptionalism-and-stereotype-promise/.

Lee, S. (1996). *Unraveling the "model minority" stereotype: Listening to Asian American youth*. New York: Teachers College Press.

Lee, V., & Burkham, D. (2002). *Inequality at the starting gate: Social background differences in achievement as children begin school*. Washington, DC: Economic Policy Institute.

Legislative Analysts Office (LAO). (2007). *Analysis of the 2007–08 budget: Education*. Sacramento: LAO. Retrieved from http://www.lao.ca.gov/analysis_2007/education/ed_11_anl07.aspx.

Leventhal, T., & Brooks-Gunn, J. (2000). The neighborhoods they live in: The effects of neighborhood residence on child and adolescent outcomes. *Psychological Bulletin, 126*(2), 309–337.

Levin, H. M. (1972). *The cost to the nation of inadequate education*. Select Senate Committee on Equal Educational Opportunity, 92nd Congress, US Government Printing Office.

Levine, S. C., Suriyakham, L. W., Rowe, M. L., Huttenlocher, J., & Gunderson, E. A. (2010). What counts in the development of young children's number knowledge? *Developmental Psychology, 46*(5), 1309–1319.

Levy, F., & Temin, P. (2007). Inequality and institutions in 20th century America. MIT Department of Economics Working Paper No. 07–17. Cambridge, MA. Retrieved from SSRN, http://ssrn.com/abstract=984330.

Lewis, A. E. (2003). *Race in the schoolyard: Reproducing the color line in school*. New Brunswick, NJ: Rutgers University Press.

Lewis, J., Ream, R., Boclan, K., Cardullo, R., Hammond, K., & Fast, R. (2012). Con cariño: Teacher caring, math self-efficacy, and math achievement among Hispanic English learners. *Teachers College Record, 114*(7). Retrieved from http://www.tcrecord.org ID Number: 16472.

Lewis, O. (1969). The culture of poverty. In *On understanding poverty*, ed. D. P. Moynihan, 187–199. New York: Basic Books.

Lichtenstein, N. (1989). From corporatism to collective bargaining: Organized labor and the eclipse of social democracy in the postwar era. *In Rise and fall of the New Deal order*, ed. Steve Fraser and Gary Gerstle, 122–52. Princeton: Princeton University Press.

Lieberman, Robert. (1998). *Shifting the color line: Race and the American welfare state.* Cambridge, MA: Harvard University Press.

Liebman, James, & Sabel, Charles. (2003). The federal No Child Left Behind Act and the post-desegregation civil rights era. *University of North Carolina Law Review, 81,* 1703–1749.

Lillie, K., Markos, A., Arias, M. B., & Wiley, T. G. (2012). Separate and not equal. The implementation of structured English immersion in Arizona. *Teachers College Record, 114.* Retrieved from http://www.tcrecord.org/content.asp?contentid=16588.

Linn, R., & Welner, K. eds., (2007). *Race-conscious policies for assigning students to schools: Social science research and the Supreme Court cases.* Washington, DC: National Academy of Education.

Linville, J. (1970, Dec.) Troubled urban interstates, *Nation's Cities, 8,* 8–11.

Liu, G. (2008). Improving Title 1 funding equity across states, districts, and schools, *Iowa Law Review, 93,* 973–1013.

Lochner, L. (2011). Non-production benefits of education: Crime, health, and good citizenship. National Bureau of Economic Research Working Paper No. 16722.

Logan, J. R. (2011). *Separate and unequal: The neighborhood gap for Blacks, Hispanics and Asians in metropolitan America.* US2010 Project, Brown University, July. Retrieved from http://www.s4.brown.edu/us2010/Data/Report/report0727.pdf.

Logan, J. R., & Oakley, D. (2012). Schools matter: Segregation, unequal educational opportunities and the achievement gap in the Boston region. In *Schools, Neighborhoods and Communities,* ed. William F. Tate IV, 103–123. Lanham, MD: Rowman and Littlefield,

Logan, J. R., & Stults, B. (2011). *The Persistence of segregation in the metropolis: New findings from the 2010 Census.* March. Project US2010 Census Brief. Retrieved from www.s4.brown.edu/us2010.

Long, B. T. (2004). How have college decisions changed overtime? An application of the conditional logistic choice model. *Journal of Econometrics, 121*(1/2): 271–296.

Long, D. A., Kelly, S., & Gamoran, A. (2011). Whither the virtuous cycle? Past and future trends in black–white inequality in educational attainment. *Social Science Research, 41*(1), 16–32.

Logan, J. R., Minca, E., & Adar, S. (2012). The geography of inequality: Why separate means unequal in American public schools. *Sociology of Education, 85*(3), 287–301.

Losen, D. J. (2011). *Discipline Policies, Successful Schools, and Racial Justice.* Boulder, CO: National Education Policy Center. Retrieved October 23, 2011 from http://nepc.colorado.edu/publication/discipline-policies.

Louisiana Council on the Social Status of Black Boys and Men (2010). *Restoring and renewing our most vital assets: The Black boys and men of Louisiana.* March. Baton Rouge, LA: Author.

Lucas, S. R. (1999). *Tracking inequality: Stratification and mobility in American high schools.* New York: Teachers College Press.

Lucas, S. R. (2001). Effectively maintained inequality: Education transitions, track mobility, and social background effects. *American Journal of Sociology, 106*(6), 1642–1690.

Lucas, S. R., & Berends, M. (2007). Race and track location in U.S. public schools. *Research in Social Stratification and Mobility, 25,* 169–87.

Macedo, S., Assensoh, Berry, J., Brintnall, M., Cambell, D., Fraga, L., Galston, W., Karpowitz, C., Levi, M., Levinson, M., Lipsitz, K., Niemi, R., Putnam, R., Rahn, W., Reich, B., Rodgers, R., Swanstrom, T., & Walsh, K. (2005). *Democracy at risk: How political choices undermine political participation and what we can do about it.* Washington, DC: Brookings Institution Press.

Magnuson, K., & Duncan, G. (2011). The nature and impact of early achievement skills, attention and behavior problems. In *Whither Opportunity?: Rising Inequality, Schools, and Children's Life Chances,* ed. G. Duncan & R. Murnane, 47–70. New York: Russell Sage Foundation.

Mann, H. (1848). Twelfth annual report of Horace Mann as Secretary of Massachusetts State Board of Education. Retrieved from http://www.tncrimlaw.com/civil_bible/horace_mann.htm.

Margolin, L. (1994). *Goodness personified: The emergence of gifted children*. New York: Aldine DeGruyter.

Marsh, J., Springer, M. G., McCaffrey, D. F., Yuan, K., Epstein, S., Koppich, J., Kalra, N., DiMartino, C., & Peng X. (2011). *A big apple for educators: New York City's experiment with schoolwide performance bonuses*. Santa Monica, CA: RAND Corporation.

Martin, C. J. (1999). *Stuck in neutral: Business and the politics of human capital investment policy*. Princeton, NJ: Princeton University Press.

Maslow, A. H. (1954). *Motivation and personality*. New York: Harper and Row.

Massey, D. S., & Denton, N. A. (1993). *American apartheid: Segregation and the making of the underclass*. Cambridge, MA: Harvard University Press.

Massey, D., Rothwell, J., & Domina, T. (2009). The changing bases of segregation in the United States. *Annals of the American Academy of Political and Social Science, 626*, 74–90.

Matusow, A. (1984). *The unraveling of America: A history of liberalism in the 1960s*. New York: Harper and Row.

Mayer, B., & Watson, J. (2011). Investigators in Atlanta cheating scandal discuss culture of corruption. *USA Today*, July 25, 2011. Retrieved from http://www.usatoday.com/news/nation/2011-07-25-atlanta-school-cheating_n.htm.

Mays, V. M., Cochran, S. D., & Barnes, N. W. (2007). Race, race-based discrimination, and health outcomes among African Americans. *Annual Review of Psychology, 58*, 201–225.

McArdle, N., et al. (2011). *Segregation falls for Black children in most metro areas but remains high; fewer metros experience declines for Latinos*. Diversity Data Issue Brief. July. Retrieved from http://diversitydata.sph.harvard.edu/Publications/Child_Segregation_Issue_Brief_July_2011.pdf.

McCaffrey, D. G., Lockwood, J. R., Koretz, D. M., & Hamilton, L. S. (2003). *Evaluating value-added models for teacher accountability*. Santa Monica, CA: RAND Corporation

McCombs, J., Augustine, C. H., Bodilly, S. J., Cross, A. B., Lichter, D. S., McInnis, B. & Schwartz, H. L. (2011). *Making summer count: How summer programs can boost children's learning*. Santa Monica, CA: RAND Corporation.

McGirr, L. (2001). *Suburban warriors: The origins of the new American Right*. Princeton, NJ: Princeton University Press.

McGuinn, P. (2006). *No Child Left Behind and the transformation of federal education policy, 1965–2001*. Lawrence: University Press of Kansas.

McKee, G. (2011). "This government is with us": Lyndon Johnson and the grassroots war on poverty. In*The war on poverty: The war on poverty: A new grassroots history, 1964–1980*, ed. Annelise Orleck and Lisa Gayle Hazirjian, 31–62. Athens: University of Georgia Press.

McLaren, P. (1988). *Life in Schools: An introduction to critical pedagogy in the foundations of education*, 4th ed. New York: Longman.

McLoyd, V. C. (1990). The impact of economic hardship on Black families and children: Psychological distress, parenting and socioemotional development. *Child Development, 61*, 311–346.

McLoyd, V.C., Jayaratne, T. E., Ceballio, R., & Borquez, J. (1994). Unemployment and work interruption among African American single mothers: Effects on parenting and adolescent socioemotional functioning. *Child Development, 65*, 562–589.

McMahon, W.W. 2006. Education finance policy: Financing the non-market and social benefits. *Journal of Education Finance, 32*, 264–284.

McMurrer, J. (2007). *Choices, changes, and challenges: Curriculum and instruction in the NCLB era*. Washington, DC: Center on Education Policy.

McNeil, L. (2000). *Contradictions of school reform: Educational costs of standardized testing*. New York: Routledge.

Mehan, H., Hubbard, L., & Villanueva, I. (1994). Forming academic identities: Accommodation without assimilation among involuntary minorities. *Anthropology & Education Quarterly,* 25(2), 91–117.

Meier, D. & Woods, G., eds. (2004). *Many children left behind: How the No Child Left Behind Act is damaging our children.* Boston: Beacon Press.

Meier, K. J., Stewart, J. Jr., & England, R. E. (1989). *Race, class and education: The politics of second-generation discrimination.* Madison: University of Wisconsin Press.

Mencken, H. L. (1949). The divine afflatus. In *A Mencken Chrestomathy,* 443. New York: Knopf.

Metcalf, K. K., West, S. D., Legan, N. A., Kelli, M. P., & Boone, W. J. (2003). *Evaluation of the Cleveland Scholarship and Tutoring Program Summary Report 1998–2002.* November. Bloomington: Indiana University School of Education.

Mettler, S. (2005). *Soldiers to citizens: The GI Bill and the making of the greatest generation.* New York: Oxford University Press.

Metz, M. H. (1978). *Classrooms and corridors: The crisis of authority in desegregated secondary schools.* Berkeley: University of California Press.

Michael, D. (2008). *Jimmy Carter as educational policy maker: Equal opportunity and efficiency.* Albany: State University of New York Press.

Mickelson, R. A. (2001). Subverting Swann: First- and second-generation segregation in Charlotte, North Carolina. *American Educational Research Journal, 38,* 215–252.

Mickelson, R. A. (2005). The incomplete desegregation of the Charlotte-Mecklenburg schools and its consequences, 1971–2004. In *School resegregation: Must the South turn back?* ed. John Boger & Gary Orfield, 87–110. Chapel Hill: University of North Carolina Press.

Mickelson, R. A. (2008). Twenty-first century social science on school racial diversity and educational outcomes. *Ohio State Law Journal, 69,* 1173–1228.

Mickelson, R. A., & Bottia, M. (2010). Integrated education and mathematics outcomes. A synthesis of social science research. *North Carolina Law Review, 88,* 993–1090.

Mickelson, R. A., Bottia, M. & Southworth, S. (2012). "School choice and segregation by race, class, and achievement." In *Exploring the school choice universe: Evidence and recommendations,* ed. G. Miron, K. G. Welner, P. Hinchey, & W. Mathis, 167–192. Charlotte, NC: Information Age Publishing.

Mickelson, R., & Heath, D. (1999). The effects of segregation on African American high school seniors' academic achievement. *Journal of Negro Education, 68*(4), 566–586.

Migration Policy Institute (MPI) (2011). *ELL Facts.* Retrieved from http://www.migrationin-formation.org/integration/ellcenter.cfm.

Mileur, J. (2005). The Great Society and the demise of New Deal liberalism. *In The Great Society and the high tide of liberalism,* ed. Sidney M. Milkis and Jerome M. Mileur, 411–55. Amherst: University of Massachusetts Press.

Miller, G. (1989). *Giving children a chance: The case for more effective national policies.* Washington, DC: Center For National Policy Press.

Miller, T. R., Cohen, M. A., & Wiersema, B. (1996). *Victim costs and consequences: A new look.* National Institute of Justice Research Report, NCJ-155282. Washington, DC.

Ministry of Education. (2005). *Nurturing every child: Flexibility and diversity in Singapore schools.* Singapore: Ministry of Education.

Miron, G., & Urschel, J. L. (2010). *Equal or fair? A study of revenues and expenditure in American charter schools.* Boulder, CO: National Education Policy Center. Retrieved from http://nepc.colorado.edu/publication/charter-school-finance.

Miron, G., Urschel, J. L., Mathis, W. J., & Tornquist, E. (2010). *Schools without diversity: Education management organizations, charter schools and the demographic stratification of the American school system*. Boulder, CO: National Education Policy Center. Retrieved from http://nepc.colorado.edu/publication/schools-without-diversity.

Miron, G., Urschel, J. & Saxton, N. (2011). *What makes KIPP work? A study of student characteristics, attrition, and school finance*. National Center for the Study of Privatization in Education. New York: Teachers College, Columbia University, and Study Group on Educational Management Organizations, and Kalamazoo: Western Michigan University, 1–69.

Moe, T. M., & Hill, P. T. (2011). Government, markets, and the mixed model of American education reform. *Education Week*, April 20. Retrieved from http://www.edweek.org/ew/articles/2011/04/20/28moe_ep.h30.html.

Monk, D. H. (1994). Subject matter preparation of secondary mathematics and science teachers and student achievement. *Economics of Education Review*, 13(2), 125–145.

Moody, J. (2001). Race, school integration, and friendship segregation in America. *American Journal of Sociology*, 107(3), 679–716.

Moore, M. A., Boardman, A. E., Vining, A. R., Weimer, D. L., & Greenberg, D. H. (2004). Just give me a number! Practical values for the social discount rate. *Journal of Policy Analysis and Management*, 23, 789–812.

Morello, C., & Keating, D. (2011). Number of black D.C. residents plummets as majority status slips away. *Washington Post*, March 24. Retrieved from http://www.washingtonpost.com/local/black-dc-residents-plummet-barely-a-majority/2011/03/24/ABtIgJQB_story.html.

Moretti, E. (2004). Estimating the social return to higher education: Evidence from longitudinal and repeated cross-sectional data. *Journal of Econometrics*, 121, 175–212.

Morrison, K. A., Robbins, H. H., & Rose, D. G. (2008). Operationalizing culturally relevant pedagogy: A synthesis of classroom-based research. *Equity & Excellence in Education, 41*(4), 433–452.

Morgan, K. (2001). A child of the sixties: The Great Society, the New Right, and the politics of federal child care. *Journal of Policy History*, 13(2), 215–249.

Moses, M. S. (2002). *Embracing race: Why we need race-conscious education policy*. New York: Teachers College Press.

Moss, P. & Tilly, C. (1996). "Soft" skills and race: An investigation of Black men's employment problems. *Work and Occupations*, 23(3), 252–276.

Mosteller, F. (1995). The Tennessee Study of Class Size in the Early School Grades, *Future of Children*, 5(2), 113–127.

Mosteller, F., Light, R. J., & Sachs, J. A. (1996). Sustained inquiry in education: Lessons from skill grouping and class size. *Harvard Educational Review*, 66, 797–828.

Moynihan, D. P. (1965). *The Negro family: The case for national action*. Washington, DC: US Department of Labor.

Muennig, P. (2007). Consequences in health status and costs. In *The price we pay: The social and economic costs to the nation of inadequate education*, ed. C. R. Belfield & H. M. Levin, 125–141. Washington, DC: Brookings Institution Press.

Muennig, P., Fiscella, K., Tancredi, D. &Franks, P. (2010). The relative health burden of selected social and behavioral risk factors in the United States: Implications for policy. *American Journal of Public Health*, 100, 1758–1764.

Muennig, P., Robertson, D., Johnson, G., Campbell, F., Pungello, E., & Neidell, M. (2011). The effect of an early education program on adult health: The Carolina Abecedarian Project randomized controlled trial. *American Journal of Public Health*, 101(3), 512–516.

Muennig, P., Schweinhart, L., Montie, J., & Neidell, M. (2009). Effects of a prekindergarten educational intervention on adult health: 37-year follow-up results of a randomized controlled trial. *American Journal of Public Health*, 99(8), 1431–1437.

Mullen, A. L., Goyette, K. A., & Stuart, K. (2011, August 21). *Race and Ethnic Differences in College Applications*. Paper presented at the annual meeting of the American Sociological Association. Las Vegas, Nevada.

Murnane, R. J. & Steele, J. L. (2007). What is the problem? The challenge of providing effective teachers for all children. *Future of Children*, 17(1), 15–43.

Murray, C., & Herrnstein, R. J. (1994). *The bell curve: Intelligence and class structure in american life*. New York: Free Press.

NAACP Legal Defense and Educational Fund. (2006). *Dismantling the school-to-prison pipeline*. Retrieved from http://naacpldf.org/files/case_issue/Dismantling_the_School_to_Prison_Pipeline.pdf.

Nagaoka, J., & Roderick, M. (2004). *Ending social promotion: The effects of retention*. Chicago: Consortium on Chicago School Research.

Nasir, N., & Hand, V. M. (2006). Exploring sociocultural perspectives on race, culture and learning. *Review of Educational Research*, 76(4), 449–475.

National Advisory Commission on Civil Disorders. (1968). *Report of the National Advisory Commission on Civil Disorders*. Washington. DC: US Government Printing Office.

National Center for Education Statistics (NCES) (1997). *America's teachers: Profile of a profession, 1993–94*. Washington, DC: US Department of Education.

National Center for Education Statistics (NCES) (2000). *The digest of education statistics*. Washington, DC: US Department of Education.

National Center for Education Statistics (NCES). (2009). *Condition of education. Table A-6-2*. Washington DC: US Department of Education. Retrieved from http://nces.ed.gov/programs/coe/tables/table-lsm-2.asp.

National Center for Education Statistics (NCES). (2013). T*Public school graduates and dropouts from the common core of data*:School year 2009–10 (NCES 2013-309). Washington DC: US Department of Education. Retrieved from http://nces.ed.gov/pubs2013/2013309.pdf

National Commission on Excellence in Education. (1983). *A nation at risk: The imperative for educational reform*. Washington, DC: US Government Printing Office.

National Commission on Fair Housing and Equal Opportunity. (2009). *The future of fair housing*. Washington, DC: National Fair Housing Alliance.

National Commission on Teaching and America's Future (NCTAF). (1996). *What matters most: teaching for America's future*. New York: Author.

National Commission on Urban Problems. (1968b). *President's Message to Congress, "The Crisis of the Cities."* February 22. Washington, DC: US Government Printing Office.

National Council for the Accreditation of Teacher Education (2010). *Transforming teacher education through clinical practice: A national strategy to prepare effective teachers*. Washington DC: Author.

National Education Policy Center. (2010). *New KIPP study underestimates attrition effects*. Boulder, CO: Author. Retrieved from http://nepc.colorado.edu/newsletter/2010/06/new-kipp-study-underestimates-attrition-effects-0.

National Fair Housing Alliance. (2007). *The crisis of housing segregation*. Washington, DC: National Fair Housing Alliance. April.

National Mathematics Advisory Panel. (2008). *Foundations for success: The final report of the National Mathematics Advisory Panel*. Washington, DC: US Department of Education, Office of Planning, Evaluation and Policy Development.

Natriello, G., McDill, E. L., & Pallas, A. M. (1990). *Schooling disadvantaged children: Racing against catastrophe*. New York: Teachers College Press.

Neidell, M., & Waldfogel, J. (2010). Cognitive and noncognitive peer effects in early education. *Review of Economics and Statistics, 92*(3), 562–576.

Newport, F. (2009). *Little "Obama effect" on views about race relations: Attitudes toward race not significantly improved from previous years*. Gallup Poll, October 29. Retrieved from http://www.gallup.com/poll/123944/little-obama-effect-views-race-relations.aspx.

Newton, X. A., Rivero, R., Fuller, B. & Dauter, L. (2011). *Los Angeles: The influence of teacher and school characteristics*. Palo Alto, CA: Policy Analysis for California Education. Retrieved from http://www.stanford.edu/group/pace/PUBLICATIONS/WORKINGPAPERS/2011_PACE_WP_NEWTON.pdf.

Ngo, B., & Lee, S. (2007). Complicating the image of model minority success: A review of Southeast Asian American education. *Review of Educational Research, 77*, 415–453.

Nichols, S. L., & Berliner, D. C. (2007). *Collateral damage: How high-stakes testing corrupts America's schools*. Cambridge, MA: Harvard Education Press.

Nie, N., Junn, J., & Stehlik-Barry, K. (1996). *Education and democratic citizenship in America*. Chicago: University of Chicago Press.

No Child Left Behind (NCLB) Act of 2001, Pub. L. No. 107–110, § 115, Stat. 1425 (2002).

Noddings, N. (2006). *Philosophy of education*. Boulder, CO: Westview Press.

Noguera, P. A. (2008). *The trouble with Black boys...And other reflections on race, equity and the future of public education*. San Francisco, CA: Jossey Bass.

O'Connor, A. (1998). The false dawn of poor-law reform: Nixon, Carter, and the quest for a guaranteed income. *Journal of Policy History, 10*(1), 99–129.

O'Connor, A., Tilly, C. & Bobo, L. D., eds. (2003). *Urban inequality: Evidence from four cities*. New York: Russell Sage.

O'Connor, C., Lewis, A., & Mueller, J. (2007). Researching "Black" educational experiences and outcomes: Theoretical and methodological considerations. *Educational Researcher, 36*(9), 541–552.

Oakes, J. (1993). *Ability grouping, tracking, and within-school segregation in the San Jose Unified School District*. Los Angeles: University of California, Los Angeles.

Oakes, J. (2005) *Keeping track: How schools structure inequality*, 2nd ed. New Haven, CT: Yale University Press.

Oakes, J., & Guiton, G. (1995). Matchmaking: The dynamics of high school tracking decisions. *American Educational Research Journal, 32*(1), 3–33.

Oakes, J., Rogers, J., Silver, D., Valladares, S., Terriquez, V., McDonough, P., Renée, M., & Lipton, M. (2006). *Removing the roadblocks: Fair college opportunities for all California students*. Los Angeles: University of California/All Campus Consortium for Research Diversity and UCLA Institute for Democracy, Education, and Access.

Oakes, J., Wells, A. S., Jones, M., & Datnow, A. (1997). Detracking: The social construction of ability, cultural politics, and resistance in reform. *Teachers College Record, 98*, 482–510.

Oakes, J., Welner, K., Yonezawa, S., & Allen, R. (1998). Norms and politics of equity-minded change: Researching the zone of mediation. In *International Handbook on Educational Change*, ed. M. Fullan, 282–305. Norwell, MA: Kluwer Academic Publishers.

Obama '08. (2008). *Changing the odds for urban America*. Retrieved from http://www.barackobama.com/pdf/UrbanPovertyOverview.pdf.

Obama, B. (2010a). *State of the Union Address*. January 27, 2010. Retrieved from the American Presidency Project: http://www.presidency.usb.edu.

Obama, B. (2010b). *Speech to U.S. Chamber of Commerce on March 1, 2010*. Retrieved from http://projects.washingtonpost.com/obama-speeches/speech/190/.

Ogbu, J. (1978). *Minority education and caste*. New York: Academic Press.

Ogbu, J. (1987). Variability in minority school performance: A problem in search of an explanation. *Anthropology and Education Quarterly, 18*(4), 312–334.

Ogbu, J. (1988). Class stratification, racial stratification and schooling. In *Class, race & gender in American education*, ed. L. Weis, 163–182. Albany: State University of New York Press.

Ogbu, J. (2003). *Black American students in an affluent suburb. A study of academic disengagement*. Mahweh, NJ: Lawrence Erlbaum Associates.

Ogbu, J. & Simons, H. D. (1998). Voluntary and involuntary minorities: A cultural-ecological theory of school performance with some implications for education. *Anthropology and Education Quarterly, 29*(2), 155–188.

Olds, D. (2010). The nurse-family partnership. In *Investing in young children: New directions in federal preschool and early childhood policy*, ed. R. Haskins & W. S. Barnett, 69–78. Washington, DC: Center on Children and Families at Brookings and the National Institute for Early Education Research.

Oliver, M., & Shapiro, T. (2006). *Black wealth/white wealth: A new perspective on racial equality*. New York: Routledge.

Oreopoulos, P., & Salvanes, K. G. (2011). Priceless: The nonpecuniary benefits of schooling. *Journal of Economic Perspectives, 25*, 159–184.

Orfield, A. (2007). *Eyes for learning*. Lanham, MD: Rowman & Littlefield.

Orfield, A., Basa, F., & Yuan, J. (2001). Vision problems of children in poverty in an urban school clinic: Their epidemic numbers, impact on learning, and approaches to remediation. *Journal of Optometric Vision Development, 32*(Fall), 114–41.

Orfield, G. (1969). *The reconstruction of Southern education: The schools and the 1964 Civil Rights Act*. New York: John Wiley.

Orfield, G. (1975). Federal policy, local power, and metropolitan segregation. *Political Science Quarterly, 89*(Winter), 777–802.

Orfield, G. (1978). *Must we bus? Segregated schools and national policy*. Washington, DC: Brookings Institution Press.

Orfield, G. (1985). Ghettoization and its alternatives. In *The new urban reality*, ed. Paul Peterson, 161–96. Washington, DC: Brookings Institution Press.

Orfield, G. (1981). "Why it worked in Dixie: Southern school desegregation and its implications for the North." In *Race and schooling in the city*, ed. Adam Yarmolinsky, Lance Liebman, & Corinne Saposs Schelling, 24–44. Cambridge, MA: Harvard University Press.

Orfield, G. (1988). Race and the liberal agenda: The loss of the integrationist dream. In *The politics of social policy in the United States*, ed. Margaret Weir, Ann Shola Orloff, & Theda Skocpol, 313–56. Princeton, NJ: Princeton University Press.

Orfield, G. (2001). *Schools more separate: Consequences of a decade of resegregation*, Cambridge, MA: Civil Rights Project, Harvard University.

Orfield, G. (2009). *Reviving the goal of an integrated society: A 21st century challenge*. Los Angeles, Civil Rights Project/ Proyecto Derechos Civiles. January.

Orfield, G., & Eaton, S. (1996). *Dismantling desegregation*. New York: New Press.

Orfield, G., & Fischer, P., (1981). Housing and school integration in three metropolitan areas: A policy analysis of Denver, Columbus and Phoenix. Report to US Deptartment of Housing and Urban Development.

Orfield, G., & Lee, C. (2007). *Why segregation matters: Poverty and educational inequality.* Cambridge, MA: Civil Rights Project, Harvard University.

Orfield, G., & Lee, C. (2007). Historic reversals, accelerating resegregation, and the need for new integration strategies. Los Angeles. A report of the Civil Rights Project/Proyecto Derechos Civiles, UCLA.

Orfield, G., & McArdle, N. (2006). *The vicious cycle: Segregated housing, schools and inter-generational inequality.* W06–4. Joint Center of Housing Studies, Harvard University. August.

Orfield, G., Seigel-Hawley, G., & Kucsera, J. (2012). *E Plurbus Segregation.* Los Angeles: Civil Rights Project/Proyecto Derechos Civiles, UCLA.

Orfield, M., (2006). *Minority suburbanization, stable integration, and economic opportunity in fifteen metropolitan regions. A report by the institute on race and poverty.* Minneapolis, MN: Institute on Race and Poverty.

Orfield, M., & Luce Jr., T. F. (2009). *Region: Planning the future of the Twin Cities.* Minneapolis, MN: University of Minnesota Press.

Organization for Economic Co-operation and Development. (2011). *Building a high quality teaching profession: Lessons from around the world.* Retrieved from http://www2.ed.gov/about/inits/ed/internationaled/background.pdf.

Organization for Economic Co-operation and Development. (2010). *Economic Policy Reforms: Going for Growth 2010* (chapter 5). OECD Publishing. Retrieved from http://www.oecd.org/dataoecd/2/7/45002641.pdf.

Orr, A. (2003). Black-white differences in achievement: The importance of wealth. *Sociology of Education*, 76(4), 281–304.

Orr, M. (1999). *Black social capital: The politics of school reform in Baltimore, 1986–1998.* Lawrence: University Press of Kansas.

Osafehinti, I. O. (1987). Opportunity-to-learn and achievement in secondary school mathematics. *Studies in Educational Evaluation*, 13, 193–197.

Ost, B. (2009). *How do teachers improve? The relative importance of specific and general human capital.* Ithaca, NY: Cornell University. Retrieved from http://www.ilr.cornell.edu/cheri/workingPapers/upload/cheri_wp125.pdf.

Pacheco, M. (2010). English-language learners' reading achievement: Dialectical relationships between policy and practices in meaning-making opportunities. *Reading Research Quarterly*, 45(3), 292–317.

Parrish, T. B., Merickel, A., Perez, M., Linquanti, R., Socias, M., Spain, A., Speroni, C., Esra, P., Brock, L., & Delancey, D. (2006). *Effects of the implementation of Proposition 227 on the education of English learners, k-12: Findings from a five- year evaluation.* Palo Alto, CA: American Institutes for Research and West Ed. Retrieved from http://www.air.org/news/documents/227Report.pdf.

Passel, J. & Cohn, D. (2008). *U.S. Population Projections, 2005–2050.* Washington, DC. Report published by the Pew Research Center. Retrieved from http://www.pewhispanic.org/files/reports/85.pdf.

Patillo-McCoy, M. (1999). *Black picket fences: Privilege and peril among the black middle class.* Chicago: University of Chicago Press.

Patterson, J. (1998). Jimmy Carter and welfare reform. In *The Carter presidency: Policy choices in the post-New Deal era*, ed. Gary Fink & Hugh Davis Graham, 117–135. Lawrence: University Press of Kansas.

Patterson, J. (2001). *Brown v. Board of Education: A civil rights milestone and its troubled legacy*. New York: Oxford University Press.

Payne, R. (2005). *A framework for understanding poverty*, 4th ed. Highlands, TX: aha! Process, Inc.

Pearce, D. M. (1979). Gatekeepers and homeseekers: Institutional patterns in racial steering. *Social Problems, 26*(3), 235–342.

Pelavin, S. H., & Kane, M. (1990). *Changing the odds: Factors increasing access to college*. New York: College Entrance Examination Board.

Perlstein, L. (2008). *Tested: One American school struggles to make the grade*. New York: Holt.

Perry, P. (2002). *Shades of white: White kids and racial identities in high school*. Durham, NC: Duke University Press.

Peter D. Hart Research Associates (2008). *Teaching as a second career*. Princeton, NJ: Woodrow Wilson Institute. Retrieved from http://www.woodrow.org/images/pdf/policy/Teaching2ndCareer_0908.pdf.

Peter D. Hart Research Associates and Harris Interactive. (2005). *Americans' commitment to quality teaching in public schools*. New York: Teaching Commission.

Peterson, W., & Rothstein, R. (2010). *Let's do the numbers*. Briefing Paper 263, Economic Policy Institute, April 20. Retrieved from http://www.epi.org/page/-/BriefingPaper263.pdf?nocdn=1.

Petrilli, M. J. (2005). The Dems go back to school. Education Gadfly Weekly website, 5(30) (September). Retrieved from http://www.edexcellence.net/publications-issues/gadfly/national/gadfly090105.html.

Pettigrew, T. (1997). Generalized intergroup contact effects on prejudice. *Personality and Social Psychology Bulletin, 23*, 173–185.

Pettigrew, T., & Tropp, L. R., (2011). *When groups meet: The dynamics of intergroup contact*. New York: Psychology Press.

Pew Hispanic (2004). *Bilingualism. Survey Brief*. Washington, DC: Pew Hispanic. Retrieved from http://pewhispanic.org/files/reports/15.9.pdf.

Pew Research Center for the People and the Press. (2011). *Beyond red vs. blue political typology*, May 4. Washington, DC. Retrieved from http://www.people-press.org/files/legacy-pdf/Beyond-Red-vs-Blue-The-Political-Typology.pdf.

Pfeiffer, D. (2009). *The opportunity illusion: Subsidized housing and failing schools in California*. December. Los Angeles: Civil Rights Project.

Phillips, M., Brooks-Gunn, J., Duncan, G. J., Klebanov, P., & Crane, J. (1998). Family background, parenting practices, and the Black-White tests score gap. In *The Black-White test score gap*, ed. Christopher Jencks & Meredith Phillips, 103–145. Washington, DC: Brookings Institution Press.

Piaget, J. (1963). *The origins of intelligence in children*. New York: Norton.

Plotke, D. (1992). The political mobilization of business. In *The politics of interests: Interest groups transformed*, ed. Mark Petacca, 175–198. Boulder, CO: Westview Press.

Plucker, J., Muller, P., Hansen, J., Ravert, R., & Makel, M. (2006). *Evaluation of the Cleveland Scholarship and Tutoring Program: Summary report 1998–2004*. Center for Evaluation and Education Policy, Indiana University, Bloomington. Retrieved from http://www.ceep.indiana.edu.

Polikoff, A. (2006). *Waiting for Gautreaux: A story of segregation, housing, and the black ghetto*. Evanston, IL: Northwestern University Press.

Pollock, M. (2004). *Colormute: Race talk dilemmas in an American school*. Princeton, NJ: Princeton University Press.

Public Education Network (2004). *Demanding quality public education in tough economic times: What voters want from elected leaders*. Washington, DC: Public Education Network.

Putnam, R. (2000). *Bowling alone: The collapse and revival of American community*. New York: Simon & Schuster.

Quadagno, J. (1999). Creating a capital investment welfare state: The new American exceptionalism. *American Sociological Review, 64*, 1–10.

Ransdell, S. (2011). There's still no free lunch: Poverty as a composite of SES predicts school-level reading comprehension. *American Behavioral Scientist, 56*(7), 908–925.

Ravitch, D. (2010). *The death and life of the great American school system: How testing and choice are undermining education*. New York: Basic Books.

Ravitch, D. (2011). Waiting for a school miracle. *New York Times*, May 31. Retrieved from http://www.nytimes.com/2011/06/01/opinion/01ravitch.html?_r=2.

Ready, D. D., & Silander, M. R. (2011). School racial and ethnic composition and young children's cognitive development. In *Integrating Schools in a Changing Society*, ed. Erica Frankenberg & Elizabeth DeBray, 91–113. Chapel Hill: University of North Carolina Press.

Reardon, S. F. (2011). The widening academic achievement gap between the rich and the poor: new evidence and possible explanations. In *Whither opportunity? Rising inequality, schools, and children's life chances*, ed. Greg J. Duncan and Richard J. Murnane, 91–116. New York and Chicago: Russell Sage Foundation and Spencer Foundation.

Reardon, S. F., & Bischoff, K. (2011). Income inequality and income segregation. *American Journal of Sociology, 116*(4), 1092–1153.

Reardon, S. F., & Yun, J. T. (2003). Integrating neighborhoods, segregating schools: The retreat from school desegregation in the South, 1990–2000. *North Carolina Law Review, 81*(4), 1563–1596.

Reardon, S. F., Yun, J., & Chmielewski, A. K. (2012). Suburbanization and school segregation. In *Research on schools, neighborhoods, and communities: Toward civic responsibility*, AERA Presidential Volume, ed. William F. Tate IV, 85–102. Lanham, MD: Rowman & Littlefield Publishers.

Reardon, S., Yun, J., & Kurlaender, M. (2006). The limits of income desegregation policies for achieving racial desegregation. *Educational Evaluation and Policy Analysis, 28*(1), 49–75.

Rebell, M. A. (2007). Poverty, "meaningful" educational opportunity, and the necessary role of the courts, *North Carolina Law Review, 85*, 1467–1480.

Reckdahl, K. (2011). Homelessness in New Orleans rises 70 percent since Hurricane Katrina. *Times Picayune*, June 2. Retrieved from http://www.nola.com/politics/index.ssf/2011/06/homeless_population_in_new_orl.html.

Reider, J. (1987). *Canarsie: The Jews and Italians of Brooklyn against liberalism*. Cambridge, MA: Harvard University Press.

Resnick, L. (1995). From aptitude to effort: A new foundation for our schools. *Daedalus, 124*(4), 55–62.

Reynolds, A., & Temple, J. (2006). Economic returns of investments in preschool education. In *A vision for universal preschool education*, ed. E. Zigler, W. S. Gilliam, & S. M. Jones, 37–68. New York: Cambridge University Press.

Reynolds, A. J., Temple, J. A., & Ou, S. (2010). Impacts and implications of the Child-Parent Center preschool program. In *Childhood programs and practices in the first decade of life: A human capital integration*, ed. A. J. Reynolds, A. J. Rolnick, M. M. Englund, & J. A. Temple, 168–187. New York: Cambridge University Press.

Reynolds, A. J., Temple, J. A., Robertson, D. L., & Mann, E. A. (2002). Age 21 cost-benefit analysis of the Title I Chicago Child-Parent Centers. *Educational Evaluation and Policy Analysis*, 24(4), 267–303.

Reynolds, A. J., Temple, J. A., White, B. A. B., Ou, S., & Robertson, D. L. (2011). Age 26 cost-benefit analysis of the Child-Parent Center Early Education Program. *Child Development*, 82(1), 379–404.

Riehl, C., Pallas, A., & Natriello, G. (1999). Rites and wrongs: Institutional explanations for the student course-scheduling process in urban high schools. *American Journal of Education*, 107, 116–154.

Rist, R. (1973). *The urban school: Factory for failure*. Boston, MA: MIT Press.

Rivkin, S. G., Hanushek, E. A., & Kain, J. F. (2005). Teachers, schools, and academic achievement. *Econometrica*, 73(2), 417–458.

Robertson, E. (1992). Is Dewey's educational vision still viable? *Review of Research in Education*, 18, 335–381.

Rockoff, J. E. (2004). The impact of individual teachers on student achievement: Evidence from panel data. *American Economic Review*, 94(2), 247–252.

Robinson, R. (2000). *The debt: What America owes blacks*. New York: Dutton.

Rose, E. (2010). *The promise of pre-school: From head start to universal pre-kindergarten*. New York: Oxford University Press.

Rosenbaum, J. E. (1976). *Making inequality: The hidden curriculum of high school tracking*. New York: John Wiley.

Rosenholtz, S. (1989). *Teacher's workplace: The social organization of schools*. New York: Longman.

Rossell, C. H. (2003). The desegregation efficiency of magnet schools. *Urban Affairs Review*, 38(5), 697–725.

Rossell, C. H. (2005). No longer famous but still intact. *Education Next*, 5(2), 44–49.

Rothstein, J. (2010). Teacher quality in educational production: Tracking, decay, and student achievement. *Quarterly Journal of Economics*, 125(1), 175–214.

Rothstein, R. (2001). Poverty and achievement, and great misconceptions. *New York Times*, January 3. Retrieved from http://www.nytimes.com/2001/01/03/nyregion/lessons-poverty-and-achievement-and-great-misconceptions.html.

Rothstein, R. (2004). *Class and schools: Using social, economic, and educational reform to close the Black-White achievement gap*. New York: Teachers College, Columbia University, and Washington, DC: Economic Policy Institute.

Rothstein, R. (2010). *How to Fix Our Schools*. Washington, DC: Economic Policy Institute. October 14. Retrieved from http://www.epi.org/publications/entry/ib286/.

Rothstein, R. (2011). "Fact-Challenged Policy." *Policy Memorandum #182*, March 8. Washington, DC: The Economic Policy Institute. Retrieved from http://www.epi.org/page/-/EPI_PolicyMemorandum_182.pdf.

Rothstein, R., Wilder, T., & Jacobsen, R. (2007). Balance in the balance. *Educational Leadership*, 64(8), 8–14.

Rouse, C. (2007). The earnings benefits from education. In *The price we pay: The social and economic costs to the nation of inadequate education*, ed. C. R. Belfield & H. M. Levin, 99–124. Washington, DC: Brookings Institution Press.

Rouse, C., & Barrow, L. (2009). School vouchers and student achievement: Recent evidence and remaining questions. *Annual Review of Economics*, 1(1), 17–42.

Roza, M., & Hill, P. T. (2004). How within-district spending inequities help some schools to fail. In *Brookings Papers on Education Policy*. Washington DC: Brookings Institution.

Rubin, B. (2006). Tracking and detracking: Debates, evidence and best practices for a heterogeneous world. *Theory into Practice, 45*(1), 4–14.

Rui, N. (2010). *A meta-analysis of research on the effects of detracking reforms (1976–2002)*. Paper presented at annual meetings of the American Educational Research Association, Denver, CO.

Ruiz, R. (1984). Orientations in language planning. *Journal for the National Association for Bilingual Education, 8*(2), 15–34.

Rumbaut, R., Massey, D., & Bean, F. (2006). Linguistic life expectancies: Immigrant language retention in Southern California. *Population and Development Review, 32*, 447–460.

Rumberger, R. W., & Palardy, G. J. (2005). Does resegregation matter? The impact of social composition on academic achievement in Southern high schools. In *School resegregation: Must the South turn back?* ed. John Charles Boger & Gary Orfield, 127–147. Chapel Hill: University of North Carolina Press.

Ryan, J. (2010). *Five miles away, a world apart: One city, two schools, and the story of educational opportunity in modern America*. New York: Oxford University Press.

Ryan, R. M., & Deci, E. L. (2000). Self-determination theory and the facilitation of intrinsic motivation, social development, and well-being. *American Psychologist, 55*, 68–78.

Saez, E. (2009). Striking it richer: The evolution of top incomes in the United States. Retrieved from http://elsa.berkeley.edu/~saez/saez-UStopincomes-2007.pdf.

Sahlberg, P. (2011). *Finnish lessons: What can the world learn from educational change in Finland?* New York: Teachers College Press.

Saltman, J. (1990). *A fragile movement: The struggle for neighborhood stabilization*. New York: Greenwood Press.

Sampson, R., Sharkey, P., & Raudenbush, S. (2008). Durable effects of concentrated disadvantage on verbal ability among African-American children. *Proceedings of the National Academy of Sciences, 105*(3), 845–852.

Sanbonmatsu, L., Kling, J. R., Duncan, G. J., & Brooks-Gunn, J. (2006). Neighborhoods and academic achievement: Results from the Moving to Opportunity experiment. *Journal of Human Resources, 41*, 649–691.

Sanders, W. L., & Rivers, J. C. (1996). *Cumulative and residual effects of teachers on future student academic achievement*. Knoxville: University of Tennessee Value-Added Research and Assessment Center.

Saporito, S. (2003). Private choices and public consequences: Magnet school choice and segregation by race and poverty. *Social Problems, 50*(2), 181–203.

Sass, T. R. (2008). *The stability of value-added measures of teacher quality and implications for teacher compensation policy*. November. Retrieved from http://www.caldercenter.org/partners/florida.cfm.

Sawchuck, S. (2011). U.S. reforms out of synch with high-performing nations, report finds, *Education Week*, May 27. Retrieved from http://www.edweek.org/ew/articles/2011/05/27/33international.h30.html?tkn=ZYRFN03T3%2BKtySUg7b2qqeU78lyyp39Xv3%2FK&cmp=clp-edweek.

Schechter, C., & Bye, B. (2007). Preliminary evidence for the impact of mixed-income preschools on low-income children's language growth. *Early Childhood Research Quarterly, 22*, 137–146.

Schmidt, R. (2000). *Language policy and identity politics in the United States*. Philadelphia: Temple University Press.

Schoeni, R. F., Dow, W. H., Miller, W. D., & Pamuk, E. R. (2011). The economic value of improving the health of disadvantaged Americans. *American Journal of Preventive Medicine, 40,* S67–872.

Schofield, J. (1989). *Black and white in school: Trust, tension, or tolerance.* New York: Teachers College Press.

Schofield, J. (1995). Review of research on school desegregation's impact on elementary and secondary school students. In *Handbook of research on multicultural education,* ed. J. A. Banks & C. A. M. Banks, 799–812. New York: Simon & Schuster/Macmillan.

Schulman, B. (1998). Slouching towards the supply side: Jimmy Carter and the new American political economy. In*The Carter presidency: Policy choices in the post-New Deal era,* ed. Gary M. Fink and Hugh Davis Graham, 50–71. Lawrence: University Press of Kansas.

Schulman, B. (2001). *The seventies: The great shift in American culture, society, and politics.* Cambridge, MA: Da Capo Press.

Schultz, B. D. (2008). *Spectacular things happen along the way: Lessons from an urban classroom.* New York: Teachers College Press.

Schwartz, G. T. (1976). Urban freeways and the interstate system. *Southern California Law Review, 49*(March), 406–513.

Schwartz, H. (2010). *Housing policy is school policy. Economically integrative housing promotes academic success in Montgomery County, Maryland.* Century Foundation. Retrieved from http://tcf.org/assets/downloads/tcf-Schwartz.pdf.

Schweinhart, L., Monti, J., Xiang, Z., Barnett, W. S., Belfield, C., & Nores, M. (2005). *Lifetime effects: The High/Scope Perry Preschool study through age 40.* Monographs of the High/Scope Educational Research Foundation, Number 14. Ypsilanti, MI: High/Scope Press.

Scommegna, P. (2011). *Least segregated US metros concentrated in fast-growing South and West.* Population Reference Bureau. Washington, DC. Retrieved from www.prb.org/Articles/2011/us-residential-segregation.aspxShare.

Scott, J., ed. (2005). *School choice and diversity: What the evidence says.* New York: Teachers College Press.

Scott, J. (2009). The politics of venture philanthropy in school choice policy and advocacy. *Educational Policy, 23*(1), 106–136.

Scott, J. (2011). School choice as a civil right. The political construction of a claim and implications for school desegregation. In *Integrating schools in a changing society: New policies and legal options for a multiracial generation,* ed. E. Frankenberg & E. DeBray-Pelot, 32–51. Chapel Hill: University of North Carolina Press.

Scott, J., & Holme, J. (2002). Public schools, private resources: The role of social networks in California charter school reform. In *Where charter school policy fails: The problems of accountability and equity,* ed. A. S. Wells, 102–128. New York: Teachers College Press.

Sethi, R., & Somanathan, R. (2004). Inequality and segregation. *Journal of Political Economy, 112*(6), 1296–1322.

Severson, K. (2011). Systematic cheating is found in Atlanta's school system. *New York Times,* July 5. Retrieved from http://www.nytimes.com/2011/07/06/education/06atlanta.html?ref=Sunday.

Shanker, A. (1985). *The dangers of not having any new ideas: Remarks of Albert Shanker to the AFT QUEST Conference,* July 11. Retrieved from www.reuther.wayne.edu/files/64.3.pdf.

Shields, P. M., Humphrey, D. C., Wechsler, M. E., Riel, L. M., Tiffany-Morales, J., Woodworth, K., Youg, V. M., & Price, T. (2001). *The status of the teaching profession 2001.* Santa Cruz, CA: Center for the Future of Teaching and Learning.

Shonkoff, J. (2011). Protecting brains, not simply stimulating minds. *Science, 333*, 982–983.

Shujaa, M. (1993). *Too much schooling, too little education: The paradox of Black life in White societies*. Trenton, NJ: Africa World Press.

Shulman, L. (1987). Knowledge and teaching: Foundations of the new reform, *Harvard Educational Review, 57*(1), 1–22.

Siddle-Walker, V. (1996). *Their highest potential: An African American school community in the segregated south*. Chapel Hill: University of North Carolina Press.

Siegel-Hawley, G. (2011). City lines, county lines, color lines: An analysis of school and housing segregation in four southern metropolitan areas, 1990–2010. Unpublished doctoral diss., University of California, Los Angeles.

Silberman, T. (2002). Wake County schools: A question of balance. In *Divided we fail: Coming together through public school choice. A report of the Century Foundation Taskforce*. New York: Century Foundation Press, 141–166.

Silver, D., Saunders, M., & Zárate, E. (2008). *What factors predict high school graduation in the Los Angeles Unified School District?* California Dropout Research Policy Report #14. Santa Barbara, CA: California Dropout Research Project.

Silverman, A. (2011). Teaching Spanish to white kids is all the rage, even in Spanish-bashing Arizona. *Phoenix New Times News*, August 4. Retrieved from http://www.phoenixnewtimes.com/2011–08–04/news/teaching-spanish-to-white-kids-is-all-the-rage-even-in-mexican-bashing-arizona/3/.

Sinkkink, D., & Emerson, M. O. (2007). School choice and racial segregation in US schools: The role of parents' education. *Ethnic and Racial Studies, 31*(2), 267–293.

Sitkoff, H. (1978). *A New Deal for Blacks: The emergence of civil rights as a national issue in the Depression decade*. New York: Oxford University Press.

Skocpol, T. (2003). *Diminished democracy: From membership to management in American civic life*. Norman: University of Oklahoma Press.

Skrentny, J. (2002). *The minority rights revolution. Cambridge*, MA: Belknap Press.

Slaughter-Defoe, D. T., Nakagawa, K., Takanishi, R., & Johnson, D. J. (1990). Toward cultural/ecological perspectives on schooling and achievement in African- and Asian-American children. *Child Development, 61*(2), 363–383.

Sleeter, C. E. (2011). *The academic and social value of ethnic studies: A research review*. Report Prepared for the National Education Association. Retrieved from http://www.eric.ed.gov/PDFS/ED521869.pdf on July 27, 2012.

Sleeter, C. (2001). Preparing teachers for culturally diverse schools: Research and the overwhelming presence of whiteness. *Journal of Teacher Education, 52*(2), 94–106.

Small, M., Harding, D., & Lamont, M. (2010). Reconsidering culture and poverty. *The Annals of the American Academy of Political and Social Science, 629*, 6–29.

Smrekar, C., & Goldring, E. (1999). *School choice in urban America: Magnet schools and the pursuit of equity*. New York: Teachers College Press.

Smith, J. S. (2006). *Building New Deal liberalism: The political economy of public works, 1933–1956*. Cambridge: Cambridge University Press.

Smith, P. H., Arnot-Hopffer, E., Carmichael, C. M., Murphy, E., & Davis, A. V. (2002). Raise a child, not a test score: Perspectives on bilingual education at Davis Bilingual Magnet School. *Bilingual Research Journal, 26*(1), 103–21.

Snowden, J. (2009). *Fixing tenure: A proposal for assuring teacher effectiveness and due process*. Washington, DC: Center for American Progress. Retrieved from http://www.americanprogress.org/issues/2009/06/teacher_tenure.html.

Solorzano, D. (1992). An exploratory analysis of the effects of race, class, and gender on student and parent mobility aspirations. *Journal of Negro Education, 61*(1), 30–44.

Sorenson, A., & Hallinan, M. (1997). A reconceptualization of school effects. *Sociology of Education, 50*(4), 273–289.

Soss, J., Hacker, J., & Mettler, S., eds. (2007). *Remaking America: Democracy and public policy in an age of inequality.* New York: Russell Sage Foundation.

Sowell, T. (1981). *Ethnic America: A history.* New York: Basic Books.

Spencer, M. B., Swanson, D. P., & Cunningham, M. (1991). Ethnicity, ethnic identity, and competence formation: Adolescent transition and cultural transformation. *Journal of Negro Education, 60*(3), 366–387.

Springer, M. G. (2009). *Performance incentives: Their growing impact on American K-12 education.* Washington, DC: Brookings Institution.

Springer, M. G., Ballou, D., Hamilton, L., Le, V., Lockwood, J.R., McCaffrey, D., Pepper, M., & Stecher, B. (2010). *Teacher pay for performance: Experimental evidence from the project on incentives in teaching.* Nashville, TN: National Center on Performance Incentives at Vanderbilt University. Retrieved from http://www.performanceincentives.org/data/files/gallery/ContentGallery/POINT_REPORT_9.21.10.pdf.

Srikantaiah, D., & Kober, N. (2009). *How state and federal accountability policies have influenced curriculum and instruction in three states: Common findings from Rhode Island, Illinois, and Washington.* Washington, DC: Center on Education Policy.

Staiger, A. (2004). Whiteness as giftedness: Racial formation at an urban high school. *Social Problems, 51*(2), 161–81.

Staiger, A. (2006). *Learning difference: Race and schooling in the multiracial metropolis.* Palo Alto, CA: Stanford University Press.

Starfield, B. (1982). Child health and socioeconomic status. *American Journal of Public Health, 72*(June), 532–534.

Stearns, E. (2004). Interracial friendliness and the social organization of schools. *Youth and Society, 35*(4), 395–419.

Stedman, L. (1985). A new look at the effective schools literature. *Urban Education, 20,* 295–326.

Steele, C. (1992). Race and the schooling of black Americans. *Atlantic Monthly, 269*(4), 68–78.

Steele, C. (1997). Threat in the air: How stereotypes shape intellectual identity and performance. *American Psychologist, 52,* 613–628.

Steele, C. (2010). In the air between us: Stereotypes, identity, and achievement. In *Doing race: 21 essays for the 21st century,* ed. Hazel Markus & Paula Moya, 390–414. New York: W. W. Norton.

Steele, C., & Aronson, J. (1995). Stereotype threat and the intellectual test performance of African Americans. *Journal of Personality and Social Psychology, 69,* 797–811.

Steensland, B. (2008). *The failed welfare revolution: America's struggle over guaranteed income policy.* Princeton, NJ: Princeton University Press.

Sternberg, R. J. (1996). *Successful intelligence: How practical and creative intelligence determine success in life.* New York: Simon & Schuster.

Sternberg, R. J., & Horvath, J. A. (1995). A prototype view of expert teaching. *Educational Researcher, 24*(6), 9–17.

Stevens, B. (1990). Labor unions, employee benefits, and the privatization of the American welfare state. *Journal of Policy History, 2,* 23–60.

St. John, E. P., & Asker, E. H. (2003). *Refinancing the college dream: Access, equal opportunity, and justice for taxpayers.* Baltimore, MD: Johns Hopkins University Press.

Stockman, D. (1986). *The triumph of politics: How the Reagan revolution failed*. New York: Harper and Row.

Stone, D. (2002). *Policy paradox: The art of political decision making*. New York: W. W. Norton.

Strauss, R. P., & Sawyer, E. A. (1986). Some new evidence on teacher and student competencies. *Economics of Education Review*, 5(1), 41–48.

Street, P. (2005). *Segregated schools: Educational apartheid in post-civil rights America*. New York: Routledge.

Sturgis, S. (2011). NC voters reject pope-backed candidates in local school board battle over resegregation. *Facing South*, October 12. Institute for Southern Studies. Retrieved from http://southernstudies.org/2011/10/nc-voters-reject-pope-backed-candidates-in-local-school-board-battle-over-resegregation.html.

Sullivan, P. (1996). *Days of hope: Race and democracy in the New Deal*. Chapel Hill: University of North Carolina Press.

Sullivan, P. (2009). *Lift every voice: The NAACP and the making of the civil rights movement*. New York: New Press.

Sum, A., Khatiwade, I., McLaughlin, J., with S. Palma. (2009). *Key social, income, housing, civic, health and incarcerations consequences of dropping out of high school: Findings for Connecticut adults in the 21st century*. Monograph. Center for Labor Market Studies, Northeastern University. Retrieved from www.opp.org/docs/SocialImpacts.pdf.

Sunderman, G., ed. (2008). *Holding NCLB Accountable*. Thousand Oaks, CA: Corwin.

Sussman, N. (2000). The dynamic nature of cultural identity throughout cultural transitions: Why is home not so sweet. *Personality and Social Psychology Review*, 4(4), 355–373.

Swanson, C. B. (2009). *Cities in crisis 2009: Closing the graduation gap*. Bethesda, MD: Editorial Projects in Education.

Swanson, C. B. (2010). U.S. graduation rate continues decline. *Education Week*. Retrieved from http://www.edweek.org/ew/articles/2010/06/10/34swanson.h29.html.

Swanson, C. B. (2011a). Analysis finds graduation rates moving up. *Education Week*, May 31. Retrieved from http://www.edweek.org/ew/articles/2011/06/09/34analysis.h30.html.

Swanson, C. B. (2011b). Nation turns a corner: Strong signs of improvement on graduation. *Diplomas Count, Education Week*, June 9, 24–30.

Takaki, R. (1998). *A larger memory: A history of our diversity, with voices*. New York: Little Brown.

Tan, J., & Gopinathan, S. (2000). Education reform in Singapore: Towards greater creativity and innovation? *NIRA Review*, 7(3), 5–10.

Tan, S. (2010). Singapore's educational reforms. The case for un-standardizing curriculum and reducing testing. *AASA Journal of Scholarship and Practice*, 6(4), 50–58.

Tanner, L., & Tanner, D. (2007). *Curriculum development: Theory into practice*, 4th ed. Upper Saddle River, NJ: Pearson.

Taub, R., Taylor, G., & Dunham, J. D. (1984). *Paths of neighborhood change: Race and crime in urban America*. Chicago: University of Chicago Press.

Tavernise, S. (2011). A population changes, uneasily. *New York Times*, July 17.

Taylor, C. (1997). Does money matter? An empirical study introducing resource costs and student needs to educational production function analysis. In *Developments in School Finance*, ed. W. J. Fowler, 75–98. Washington, DC: US Department of Education.

Taylor, P., Kochhar, R., Fry, R., Velasco, G., & Motel, S. (2009). *Wealth gaps rise to record highs between Whites, Blacks and Hispanics*. July. Washington, DC. Pew Research Center.

Taylor, W. (2003). Title I as an instrument for achieving desegregation and equal educational opportunity. *University of North Carolina Law Review*, 81, 1751–1769.

The Teaching Commission. (2004). *Teaching at risk: A call to action*. Retrieved from http://www. nctq.org/nctq/images/ttc_teachingatrisk.pdf.

The Teaching Commission (2005). *America's commitment to quality teaching in the public schools: A national survey conducted by Hart-Harris*. New York: Teaching Commission.

Thevenot, B. (2010). Charter schools battle high teacher turnover. *Texas Tribune*, January 27. Retrieved from http://www.texastribune.org/texas-education/public-education/charter-sc hools-battle-high-teacher-turnover/.

Thorndike, E. L. (1924). Mental discipline in high school studies. *Journal of Educational Psychology*, 15, 1–22, 98.

Tienda, M., & Alon, S. (2007). Diversity and the demographic dividend. In *The price we pay: Economic and social consequences of inadequate education*, ed. Clive Belfield & Henry Levin, 48–73 Washington, DC: Brookings Institution.

Tienken, C. H. (2011). Structured inequity: The intersection of socio-economic status and the standard error of measurement of state mandated high school test results. In *NCPEA Yearbook*, 257–271. Lancaster, PA: Proactive Publications.

Timpane, M., & McNeill, L. M. (1991). *Business impact on education and child development reform*. Washington, DC: Committee for Economic Development.

Towles-Schwen, T., & Fazio, R. H. (2001) On the origins of racial attitudes: Correlates of child-hood experiences. *Personality and Social Psychology Bulletin*, 27(2), 162–175.

Tramaglini, T. W. (2010). Student achievement in lower SES high schools. Doctoral diss., Rutgers. Retrieved from http: // rucore.libraries.rutgers.edu/search/results.php?format= &key=ETD-°©-RU&query=tramaglini.

Tucker, M. (2011). *Standing on the shoulders of giants: An American agenda for education reform*. Washington DC: National Council on Education and the Economy. Retrieved from http:// www.ncee.org/wp-content/uploads/2011/05/Standing-on-the-Shoulders-of-Giants-An-A merican-Agenda-for-Education Reform.pdf.

Turner, M. A., & Garcia, D. A. (2006). Why housing mobility? The research evidence today. In *Poverty and race in America: The emerging agendas*, ed. Chester Hartman, 121–139. Lanham, MD: Lexington Books.

Tushnet, M. (1987). *The NAACP's legal strategy against segregated education, 1925–1950*. Chapel Hill. University of North Carolina.

Tyack, D. (1974). *The one best system: A history of American urban education*. Cambridge, MA: Harvard University Press.

Tyack, D., Lowe, R., & Hansot, E. (1984). *Public schools in hard times: The Great Depression and recent years*. Cambridge, MA: Harvard University Press.

Tyler, R. W. (1949). *Basic principles of curriculum and instruction*. Chicago: University of Chicago Press.

Tyson, K. (2002). Weighing in: Elementary-age students and the debate on attitudes toward school among Black students. *Social Forces*, 80(4), 1157–1189.

Tyson, K. (2008). Providing equal access to "gifted" education. In *Everyday antiracism: Getting real about race in school*, ed. Mica Pollock, 126–131. New York: New Press.

Tyson, K. (2011). *Integration interrupted: Tracking, black students and acting white after* Brown. New York: Oxford University Press.

Tyson, K., Darity, W. Jr., & Castellino, D. (2005). "It's not a black thing": Understanding the burden of acting white and other dilemmas of high achievement. *American Sociological Review*, 70(4), 582–605.

UNICEF (2001). *A league table of child deaths by injury in rich nations: Innocenti report card 2*. Florence: UNICEF, Innocenti Research Centre.

Urban Institute. (2006). *Children of immigrants. Facts and figures*. May. Washington, DC: Urban Institute. Retrieved from http://www.urban.org/uploadedpdf/900955_children_of_immigrants.pdf.

U. S. Bureau of the Census (2006). Poverty status of people, by age, race, and Hispanic origin: 1959–2006. Washington, DC: US Department of Commerce.

U. S. Bureau of Census. (2008). *An older and more diverse nation by midcentury*. Retrieved December 27, 2011 from http://www.census.gov/newsroom/releases/archives/population/cb08–123.html

U. S. Commission on Civil Rights (1967). *Racial isolation in the public schools*. Washington, DC: US Government Printing Office.

U. S. Department of Education. (2002). *Meeting the highly qualified teachers challenge: The Secretary's annual report on teacher quality*. Washington, DC: US Department of Education, Office of Postsecondary Education, Office of Policy Planning and Innovation.

U. S. Department of Education (2009). *American Recovery and Reinvestment Act of 2009: Education jobs and reform fact sheet*. Retrieved from http://www.ed.gov/policy/gen/leg/recovery/factsheet/overview.html.

U. S. Departments of Justice and Education. (2011). *Guidance on the Voluntary Use of Race to Achieve Diversity in Postsecondary Education*. December. 2.

Valenzuela, A. (1999). *Subtractive schooling: U.S. Mexican youth and the politics of caring*. Albany: State University of New York Press.

Ventry, D. (2000). The collision of tax and welfare politics: The political history of the earned income tax credit, 1966–1999. *National Tax Journal*. 53(4), part 2, 1–44.

Verba, S., Schlozman, K., & Brady, H. (1995). *Voice and equality: Civic voluntarism in American politics*. Cambridge, MA: Harvard University Press.

Verhoeven, L., van Leeuwe, J., & Vermeer, A. (2011). Vocabulary growth and reading development across the elementary school years. *Scientific Studies of Reading*, 15, 8–25.

Viadero, D. (2008). Working conditions trump pay. *Education Week*. Retrieved from http://www.edweek.org/ew/articles/2008/01/10/18conditions.h27.html.

Vigdor, J. L., & Ludwig, J. (2008). Segregation and the test score gap. In *Steady gains and stalled progress. Inequality and the Black-White test score gap*, ed. Katherine Magnuson & Jane Waldfogel, 181–212. New York: Russell Sage Foundation.

Vinovskis, M. (2009). *From a nation at risk to No Child Left Behind: National education goals and the creation of federal education policy*. New York: Teachers College Press.

Vogel, D. (1989). *Fluctuating fortunes: The political power of business in America*. Washington, DC: Beard Books.

Vogell, H. (2011). Investigation into APS cheating finds unethical behavior at every level. *Atlanta Journal Constitution*, July 6. Retrieved from http://www.ajc.com/news/investigation-into-aps-cheating-1001375.html.

Vygotsky, L. (1978). *Mind in society: The development of higher psychological processes*. Cambridge, MA: Harvard University Press.

Walberg, H. (1982). What makes schooling effective. *Contemporary Education: A Journal of Review*, 1, 22–34.

Waldfogel, J., Garfinkel, I., & Kelly, B. (2007). Public assistance programs: How much could be saved with improved education? In *The price we pay: The social and economic costs to the nation of inadequate education*, ed. C. R. Belfield & H. M. Levin, 160–176. Washington, DC: Brookings Institution Press.

Wang, M. C., Haertel, G. D., & Walberg, H. J. (1993). Toward a knowledge base for school learning. *Review of Educational Research, 63*(3), 249–294.

Wang, M. C., Haertel, G. D., & Walberg, H. J. (1994). Educational resilience in inner cities. In *Educational resilience in inner-city America: Challenges and prospects*, ed. M. C. Wang & E. W. Gordon, 45–72. Hillsdale, NJ: Lawrence Erlbaum Associates.

Warikoo, N. (2011). *Balancing acts: Youth culture in the global city*. Berkeley: University of California Press.

Warikoo, N., & Carter, P. (2009). Cultural explanations for racial and ethnic stratification in academic achievement: A call for a new and improved theory. *Review of Educational Research, 79*(1), 366–394.

Watanabe, T. (2011). Dual-language immersion programs growing in popularity. *Los Angeles Times*, May 8. Retrieved from http://articles.latimes.com/2011/may/08/local/la-me-bilingual-20110508.

Weiher, G. R. (1991). *The fractured metropolis: Political fragmentation and metropolitan segregation*. Albany: State University of New York Press.

Weiner, D. A., Lutz, B. F., & Ludwig, J. (2010). *The effects of school desegregation on crime*. August 16, revision of September 2009. National Bureau of Economic Research Working Paper NBER 15380.

Weir, M. (2005). States, race, and the decline of New Deal liberalism. *Studies in American Political Development, 19*, 157–172.

Weisberg, D., Sexton, S., Mulhern, J., & Keeling, D. (2009). *The widget effect: Our national failure to acknowledge and act on differences in teacher effectiveness*. New York: New Teacher Project.

Wells, A. S. (1993). *A time to choose: America at the crossroads of school choice policy*. New York: Hill and Wang.

Wells, A. S. (2009). *Both sides now: The story of school desegregation's graduates*. Berkeley: University of California Press.

Wells, A. S., & Crain, R. L. (1994). Perpetuation theory and the long-term effects of school desegregation. *Review of Educational Research, 64*(4), 531–555.

Wells, A. S., & Crain, R. L. (1999). *Stepping over the color line: African-American students in white suburban schools*. New Haven, CT: Yale University Press.

Wells, A. S., Duran, J. & White, T. (2008). Refusing to leave desegregation behind: From graduates of racially diverse schools to the Supreme Court. *Teachers College Record, 110*(12), 2532–2570.

Wells, A. S., & Frankenberg, E. (2007). The public schools and the challenge of the Supreme Court's integration decision. *Phi Delta Kappan, 89*(3), 178–188.

Wells, A. S., & Holme, J. J. (2005). No accountability for diversity: Standardized tests and the demise of racially mixed schools. In *School resegregation: Must the South turn back?* ed. J. Boger & G. Orfield, 187–211. Chapel Hill: University of North Carolina Press.

Wells, A. S., Holme, J. J., Lopez, A., & Cooper, C. W. (2000). Charter schools and racial and social class segregation: Yet another sorting machine? In *A Notion at Risk: Preserving Public Education as an Engine for Social Mobility*, ed. Richard D. Kahlenberg, 169–222. New York: Century Foundation Press.

Wells, A. S., Holme, J. J., Revilla, A. T., & Atanda, A. K. (2009). *Both sides now: The story of school desegregation's graduates*. Berkeley: University of California Press.

Wells, A. S., & Holme, J. J. (2004). How society failed school desegregation policy. In *Review of Research in Education*, ed. Robert Floden, 28, 47–100. Washington, DC: American Educational Research Association.

Wells, A. S., Lopez, A., Scott, J., & Holme, J. J. (1999). Charter schools as postmodern paradox: Rethinking social stratification in an age of deregulated school choice. *Harvard Educational Review*, 69(2), 172–204.

Wells, A. S., & Roda, A. (2008). Colorblindness and school choice: The central paradox of the Supreme Court's ruling in the *Parents Involved* cases. March. Paper presented at the American Educational Research Association Annual Meeting. New York, NY.

Wells, A. S., & Roda, A. (2009). *White parents, diversity and school choice policies: Where good intentions, anxiety and privilege collide.* Paper presented at the Vanderbilt School Choice Conference. Nashville, TN.

Wells, A. S., Roda, A., Warner, M., Hill, K., & Fox, L. (in press). Racial segregation in a multicultural suburban county: Where housing markets and school district boundary lines lide. In *The handbook of research on multicultural education,* 3rd ed., ed. James Banks. San Francisco: Jossey-Bass.

Wells, A. S., & Serna, I. (1996). The politics of culture: Understanding local political resistance to detracking in racially mixed schools. *Harvard Educational Review, 66,* 93–118.

Wells, A. S., Warner, M., & Grzesikowski, C. (2013). The story of meaningful school choice: Lessons from interdistrict transfer plans. In *Educational delusions? Why choice can deepen inequality and how to make schools fair,* ed. G. Orfield & E. Frankenberg. Berkeley: University of California Press.

Welner, K. G. (2001). *Legal rights, local wrongs: When community control collides with educational equity*. Albany, New York: State University of New York Press.

Welner, K. G. (2002). Ability tracking: What role for the courts? *Education Law Reporter, 163*(2), 565–571.

Welner, K. G. (2008). *Neovouchers: The emergence of tuition tax credits for private schooling.* Lanham, MD: Rowman & Littlefield.

Westheimer, J. (2011). Confronting power: Success isn't everything—but it's not nothing either. *Democracy & Education, 19*(1), 1–4.

Wheelock, A. (1992). *Crossing the tracks: How "untracking" can save America's schools*. New York: New Press.

Whitman, D. (2008). *Sweating the small stuff: Inner-city schools and the new paternalism.* Washington, DC: Thomas B. Fordham Institute Press.

Whitman, S., Williams, C., & Shah, A. (2004). *Improving community health survey: Report 1.* Chicago: Sinai Health System.

Wilentz, Sean. (2008). *The age of Reagan: A history, 1974–2008*. New York: Harper.

Wilkerson, Doxey. (1965). School integration, compensatory education, and the Civil Rights Movement in the North. *Journal of Negro Education, 34,* 307–308.

Wilkins, A. (2005). No surrender. *Education Gadfly,* September 22, 5. Retrieved from http://www.edexcellence.net/publications-issues/gadfly/national/gadfly092205.html.

Willie, C., Edwards, R., & Alves, M. (2002). *Student diversity, choice, and school improvement.* Westport: Bergin and Garvey.

Wilson, W. J. (1987). *The truly disadvantaged: The inner city, the underclass, and public policy.* Chicago: University of Chicago Press

Wilson-Cooper, C. (2005). School choice and the standpoint of African American mothers: Considering the power of positionality. *Journal of Negro Education, 74*(2), 174–189.

Winerip, M. (2011a). Message from a charter school: Thrive or transfer. *New York Times*, July 11. Retrieved from http://www.nytimes.com/2011/07/11/nyregion/charter-school-sends-message-thrive-or-transfer.html.

Winerip, M. (2011b). As best schools compete for best performers, students may be left behind. *New York Times*, July 24. Retrieved from http://www.nytimes.com/2011/07/25/nyregion/at-best-schools-competi...may-be-left-behind.html?_r=2&partner=rss&emc=rss&pagewanted=print.

Winerip, Michael (2011c). In college, working hard to learn high school material. *New York Times*, October 24, A17.

Wolman, H., & Thomas, N. (1970). Black interests, Black groups, and Black influence in the federal policy process: The cases of housing and education. *Journal of Politics, 32*, 875–897.

World Public Opinion.org (2008). *Publics around the world say governments should act to prevent racial discrimination. Most countries see progress in racial equality; some do not.* March 20. Retrieved from http://www.worldpublicopinion.org/pipa/articles/btjusticehuman_rightsra/460.php.

Wright, W. (2007). Heritage language programs in the era of English-only and No Child Left Behind, *Heritage Language Journal, 5*, 1–26.

Wrightstone, J. W. (1936). Appraisal of experimental high school practices. *Teachers College Record, 38*(3), 242–243.

Wrightstone, J. W., Rechetnick, J., McCall, W. A., & Loftus, J. J. (1939). Measuring social performance factors in activity and control schools of New York City. *Teachers College Record, 40*(5), 423–432.

Xu, Z., Hannaway, J., & Taylor, C. (2011). Making a difference? The effects of Teach for America in high school. *Journal of Policy Analysis and Management, 30*(3), 447–469.

Yinger, J. (1998). Housing discrimination is still worth worrying about. *Housing Policy Debate, 9*(4), 893–927.

Yun, J., & Reardon, S. (2005). Patterns of multiracial private school segregation. In *School choice and diversity: What the evidence says*, ed. J. Scott, 42–58. New York: Teachers College Press.

Zastrow, C. V., & Janc, H. (2004). *Academic atrophy: The condition of the liberal arts in America's public schools*. Washington, DC: Council for Basic Education.

Zehler, A., Fleischman, H., Hopstock, P., Stephenson, T., Pendzick, M., & Sapru, S. (2002). *Descriptive study of services to LEP students and LEP students with disabilities, vol. 1.* Washington, DC: US Department of Education, Office of English Language Acquisition, Language Enhancement, and Academic Achievement of Limited English Proficient Students.

Zhao, Y. (2009). *Catching up or leading the way: American education in the age of globalization*. Alexandria, VA: ASCD.

Zigler, E. (2011). A model preschool program. In *The pre-k debates: current controversies and issues*, ed. E. Zigler, W. Gilliam, & W. S. Barnett, 136–140. Baltimore, MD: Brookes Publishing.

Zill, N. (2010). Ten ideas for improving Early Head Start. In *Investing in young children—New directions in federal preschool and early childhood policy*, ed. R. Haskins & W. S. Barnett, 39–48. Washington, DC: Center on Children and Families at Brookings and the National Institute for Early Education Research.

Page numbers in bold indicate figures or tables.